THE SPRINGS OF MORALITY

CONTRIBUTORS

HILARY ARMSTRONG

FRANCES BRICE

E. F. CALDIN

COLIN CLARK

JOHN COULSON

JOSEPH G. DAWSON

HUGH DINWIDDY

FRANZ B. ELKISCH

ANTHONY HOWARD

DAVID H. N. JOHNSON

CLAUDE R. LEETHAM, INST. CH.

IRENE MARINOFF

JOHN MARSHALL

DOM SEBASTIAN MOORE

NANA KOBINA NKETSIA IV

DOM RALPH RUSSELL

DAVID SNELLGROVE

DOM ILLTYD TRETHOWAN

REGINALD F. TREVETT

GERALD VANN, O.P.

DOM AELRED WATKIN

MICHAEL J. WALSH, S.M.A.

ROBERT P. WALSH

THE SPRINGS OF MORALITY

A Catholic Symposium

Edited by
JOHN M. TODD

LONDON
BURNS & OATES

NIHIL OBSTAT: JOANNES M. T. BARTON, S.T.D., L.S.S.
CENSOR DEPVTATVS
IMPRIMATVR: E. MORROGH BERNARD
VICARIVS GENERALIS
WESTMONASTERII: DIE XXXI DECEMBRIS MCMLV

MADE AND PRINTED IN GREAT BRITAIN BY
THE BROADWATER PRESS LIMITED, WELWYN GARDEN CITY, HERTS, FOR
BURNS OATES & WASHBOURNE LIMITED
28 ASHLEY PLACE, LONDON, S.W.1
First published 1956

CONTENTS

v

CONCRETE MORAL PROBLEMS

MORALITIES OUTSIDE THE CHURCH

EDITOR'S INTRODUCTION

THE chapters of this book were read as papers at a symposium held at Downside Abbey, in Low Week, 1955. The fruits of the discussions which followed each paper have been embodied, so far as possible, in the text. In two cases it seemed best to add a separate note about the discussion, and this I have done. The authors of Chapters VI and X were invited too late to be able to be present at the symposium, although their subjects were both in the original plans of the sponsoring commitee.

I have to record our deep gratitude to the Abbot and community at Downside for welcoming us and our meetings. I thank all the contributors for co-operating with their editor so punctiliously. And here I should add a special word of thanks to Nana Nketsia IV, paramount chief of the English Sekondi State; the only member of the symposium who was not a Catholic, he came to give us first-hand factual material on primitive moralities, being specially qualified by his anthropological studies at Oxford as well as by his own status and beliefs.

The committee for which I act as secretary and for whom I have edited this book is composed as follows: R. F. Trevett (*chairman*), John Coulson, Hugh Dinwiddy, Dom Sebastian Moore, Dom Ralph Russell, Lancelot Sheppard, and myself. Whilst I have consulted them on all matters of principle, I alone am responsible for the editorial work. As will be clear from Chapter I, our intention is that *The Springs of Morality* should not be an isolated endeavour, but the first of a series of communications.

I

THE SYMPOSIUM

by

Reginald F. Trevett

THIS book is not merely a collection of essays by different hands. It is the result of a process of growth, and the record of a meeting at which the discussion of each paper developed in the context of a community at prayer. The book is addressed to the reader in the same spirit; he too is asked to join in the discussion and to seek a way or, if he has found it already, to continue therein with a greater awareness and a deeper humility.

Some three years ago a few priests and laymen in the west country formed themselves into a group which meets regularly for the purpose of 'communication'. Communication is a problem which has received startling and effective solutions in technical fields but which seems to have become increasingly serious and urgent at the personal level. Even the common-rooms of our Universities, so we are told, present a spectacle of disintegration, as the men of each discipline delve deeper and deeper into their own specialities and thereby find themselves isolated from those whose study lies elsewhere. In one of the papers of this collection, the writer compares the great world religions to high and isolated mountain peaks. The present-day divisions of knowledge may be similarly described. The analogy holds good in the sphere of vocabulary and meaning, for the very words we use signify one reality for one group of men and others for a second and a third. To those of us who are Catholics, such a state of affairs in the field of human knowledge is intolerable. We cannot accept, particularly in view of the urgency and tragedy of the contemporary situation, a more or less permanent division amongst those whose vocation it is to seek and to contemplate the intricacies of reality at all its various levels. We of all men have no excuse for cultural isolationism.

At all periods, there are certain temptations which beset the Catholic. His belief in a divinely guaranteed revelation concerning

A*   I

the relations of God and man, and the modalities in which such truth is mediated, may be debased into a mere defence of means, a safe apologetic for the *status quo* in his own time. As this *status quo* is historical, he may well find himself refusing to the Church, whom he purports to defend, all that vital living thought and action which makes the present the matrix of the future. On the other hand he may fall into the relativism of 'historicity', to use an expression of Marcel's, which holds that reality is always situational and that truth is in a kind of Heraclitean flux. Not that he will consciously abandon the solidities of his faith; but he may attempt to carry his legitimate concern for the problems of his time to such a pitch that instead of identifying himself, in the name of Christ, with his contemporaries and their problems—and this is not only legitimate but essential—he will tend to shift the very grounds of his faith from revealed absolutes to the relative enlargement of the field of merely human knowledge.

At the meetings of our group, we have tried to go forward on a positive and middle course, bearing in mind that great passage in the *Mystical Element of Religion* of Baron von Hügel in which he teaches that Christ's character and teaching 'require for an ever fuller and yet never complete understanding, the varying study and different experiments and applications, embodiments and unrolling of all races and civilizations, of all life individual and corporate, the simultaneous and successive experiences of the human race to the end of time'.

The key words here are 'experiences', 'simultaneous' and 'successive'. In all our discussions, we have tried both to deepen our knowledge of the meaning of divine realities and at the same time to live and think with our contemporaries. In practice this has simply meant that we have taken at each of our periodic meetings a single word, such as Love, Power, Inspiration, Order, and we have attempted to deepen our knowledge of the reality of which the word is the sign by sharing our own experiences and the truth we have each individually found in meditation and in study. Then we immediately follow this communication by a concerted effort to appreciate what the word we have considered means to our contemporaries; what are the points of contact between our concept of the meaning of the word and that held by those who do not share or only partly share our faith.

In this way, it seems to us that we are, however inadequately, bringing theology to bear upon experience and at the same time making it possible to develop theology itself. It is essential to remember that when *Fides* seeks *Intellectum*, it does not itself change, but extends its implications over an ever-widening field and thereby reveals riches in itself that were not hitherto obvious. The great medieval synthesis was evolved in this manner, but inevitably and rightly in terms of the medieval situation. Clearly, the fundamental principles of such a synthesis remain valid, but more is asked of the Catholic thinker today than a kind of intellectual Gothic revival.

One factor at the origin of the group's formation was a concern to see established in England an Institute of Theology at which it would be possible to study the inter-relation between doctrine and the concrete experiences of the life of the ordinary layman. There is no immediate practical prospect of such an Institute, but the point is that the group had no wish to be isolated and introverted. From our first meeting we felt that our attempt to deepen and enlarge our own 'communication' should be extended to a wider circle, some time in the future. So it came about that the symposium of which this book is the record was held at Downside Abbey during Low Week, in April 1955. This extension of our activities we hope to repeat from time to time in the future. By living together for this short period, by discussing the papers we read to one another, both formally and in private conversation, we were able to discover important points of contact between our different professional disciplines and between the contemporary world and the great traditions of morality.

We chose this matter of the rightness or the wrongness of conduct because it seemed to impinge more tragically, perhaps, than ever before upon the life of man in the contemporary world. We could not hope to provide an exhaustive treatment of every aspect of our subject; but we could ask as many as possible of the right questions and provide pointers to some of the right answers. Many moral problems are not even mentioned in our symposium. It is not that we are unaware of their existence and importance; but a line had to be drawn somewhere. The reader may well wish it had been drawn differently. Circumstances of one kind and another gradually moulded our programme into the form it has eventually taken and in which, with all its faults, we offer it to the public.

We were soon struck by the fact that all of us seemed to be approaching the whole subject from a similar angle and it was not the angle we had expected. Men are accustomed, in the ordinary run of things, to consider the rules of morality as an accepted code which they either follow as well as they can or revolt against in the name of individual freedom. It might then have been expected that those who joined in our symposium would have confined themselves to justifying or criticizing this the common attitude to morality. In a sense they did, but by a method of approach which all seemed unanimously—and that is the interesting point—to accept as a matter of course. When, after the symposium was over, the group who had organized it met to assess the work that had been done, a number of facts stood out as of primary importance. They are mentioned here because they arose as the products of the symposium itself, particularly of the discussions in which each man brought the contribution of his own personal and professional experience. It is essential to remember this. Nothing is so rightly distasteful to the reader as to be told in the introductory chapter what he is expected to get from a book such as this. Nothing is more fatal to the vitality of such a communication as this book is intended to be than a list of principles at its beginning, from which all the teaching in the body of the work is a series of deductions. The 'communications' of our final session are not of this character. They were and are the discoveries, however briefly and inadequately formulated here, which we ourselves had made *together* during the week that had just passed. As such they are offered to the reader. In this printed form they are a poor substitute perhaps for the vital communication between man and man in the personal relationship of the spoken word; but before the reader sets out upon the task of studying the different papers, it may be useful for him to know of the thread which linked them all together.

Man is *homo viator*, man on the road; but the road has no end here. Any experience may give rise to moral questioning, to the realization of the mystery of right and wrong; but this experience can be the starting point of a moral judgement only if it is first recognized as a pointer to man's relative, contingent being, his dependence on an absolute.

It is when man loves that the reality of this absolute reference is experienced in its most vivid form. Unless the moral law is seen as the law of love, as the art of self-giving, we find that men either hold the moral law to be non-existent or see and follow (or reject) it as an imposition from without, a mere technique of social living, an external pressure, a super-ego irreconcilable with liberty. In its ultimate reference, love unites man to God, and eternally, abidingly—

'Charity shall not pass away.' The Communist shows profound insight when he calls upon man to hate God, for it is love which denies his premiss that movement alone is real and all else an idealist construction.

If this is so, all forms of 'categorical' morality, whether religious or philosophical, are either tyrannical or powerless, according to circumstances, corrupting those who impose them and stultifying the souls of those who accept them. All codes of morality are valid only in so far as they allow and encourage men to love with utter self-giving. A moral code is not therefore truly a way of life until it is accepted, and accepted freely, as making it possible for love to liberate us from imprisonment in the closed world of the individual or social self. There are immediate consequences both in the field of the exercise of any authority whatsoever, and in the whole sphere of personal relations. There is no abstract morality. This man or that woman are the subjects who make moral judgements and act upon them. Morality has not as object man, whom it manipulates like a puppet; the importance of this in the education of children or in the delicate tasks of the confessor or the psychologist is abundantly clear.

God is not an abstraction, he is reality. All moralities based on abstraction—and situational morality is one of them—lack precision, do not bite into reality. *Homo viator* can only be delivered once and for all from abstraction in the body of Christ. In Christ law and love are one. In Christ, *homo viator* and *homo sapiens* are one, for Christ the Man is God the Son. From this primal, central, ontological, existential fact, all morality derives; the Church, which is man at one with God through Christ, is the society of divine love.

But abstraction always lies in wait at man's heels. The basic commandments of the Old Law are still valid; they are caught up into the love of Christ. But they can be and often are taught as negative threats. As the paper on the medieval period points out, the decline of the Middle Ages was marked by a morbid preoccupation with the Seven Deadly Sins. If, in the paper dealing with the moral problems of the present economic situation, there is an analysis of modern practice in the terms of these same sins, it is because it is only by recognizing our conduct for what it is, that we are likely to make the effort to square it with the law of love. What was at one time a sign of decadence can at another be the symbol of reality, a negative way of return. Yet however salutary a diagnosis of disease may be when the man is sick, it cannot be used as a cure, nor often as a threat when he is well. He will instance the multitude of cases where the wicked prosper and the good decline. Once again the categorical moral code without love is sheer power, corrupting, and corrupting absolutely in the end.

But this is not to say that love has not the precision that goes with close attention to detail and with observance of moral principles in the smallest matters. Only it is always applied within the context of the body of Christ. Love then guides the irresponsible back to responsibility, to detailed moral life; it guides the young onwards, the sick back to responsibility; it guides the impersonal structure of industry downwards and inwards to respect for persons and for material, and it guides the embryonic international society through to a full code of justice and the rule of law. Complete self-giving implies complete self-fulfilment; it is impossible to give oneself totally in love unless one has first fulfilled oneself totally. One must be oneself to be able to give oneself. Valid moral laws are consonant with the last end of man, his total fulfilment in Christ. The Church's detailed code of law is a law ordained by love to enable man to love.

All through the discussions of the symposium, the primacy of experience was constantly expressed. Not that we found experience to be the source of morality, but rather that it was the *door* to reality, the way to the source. It was by an analysis of experience that metaphysical and moral implications in our situation became evident. The moralist, like the analyst of words, runs the perpetual risk of mistaking the outward test for the inward reality. To live the experience at all its levels was to communicate not only with oneself, but with others and with God; it was to pass through and in law to love; or rather to see law as issuing from love, as the living structure of the organism of love.

Our study of Communist morality showed us that the contemplation of experience is not separate from the experience itself, that it is in the actual and everyday situations that the eternal stands secure. It is in the concrete situations that God is hated and attacked by the Communist in the name of success; it is an attack based on a rejection of European idealist moral philosophy, a rejection of the idea of an arbitrary categorical moral imperative, a rejection in fact of a pure abstraction which in practice has proved a complete failure. If this is the Communist's approach, who are we to throw the stones? For he has learned of the abstract God from the loveless code of the categorical Christian.

It is only by living every experience, every situation, to its innermost being that we find it opening out on to the heart of all reality, whose name is love; the love that sent his Son who died for love of man, and ascended that the Spirit of love might descend upon man and abide with him for ever.

II

THE PHILOSOPHICAL CONCEPT
OF MORALITY

by

Dom Illtyd Trethowan

SUMMARY

DOES natural ethics provide us with a science which is useful for apologetical purposes in the same sort of way as natural theology? Some Christian philosophers have thought that it provides us with the principle 'the good is to be pursued and the evil avoided,' and have tried to erect a science on this basis. The principle proves to be a tautology unless we introduce into it the notion of 'ought' and even the notion of God, and our opponents are not going to stand for this. Mr Nowell Smith's Penguin on *Ethics* shows that the notion of 'ought' can be evacuated of any traditional meaning without a logical contradiction and without falling foul of the meanings in which moral words are used by modern sceptics. We can hope to break into this iron ring only by persuading people to accept a theistic metaphysic. This acceptance is at the same time the recognition of moral obligation, and thus there is no natural ethics distinct and separate from natural theology or metaphysics. The acceptance of God's existence (which is not operated by syllogisms) leads to certain very general conclusions about human conduct, but does not imply with strict logical necessity the prescriptions of the moral law as made known to us by the Christian Revelation; moral theologians try to prove too much by the appeal to natural reason. Nevertheless the philosophy of ethics which flows from metaphysics does show us that the Christian scheme of morals must be looked at not as a matter of abstract principles or of arbitrary commands but as God's blueprint for the building of his city.

A PAPER entitled *The Philosophical Concept of Morality*, when it is to be followed by a paper on Christian morality (at the end of the

8

book), will be concerned to show the limits which philosophical thinking seems unable to pass, in the field of ethics, without the aid of Christian revelation. To put it in a less negative way, how much help can the Christian moral theologian receive from the moral philosopher? To what extent can he appeal, in justification of the conclusions which he reaches, to principles of reason and processes of thought which Christians and non-Christians alike may be expected to approve? Are there any rules of thought which are proper to the study of ethics and which are binding on theologians and philosophers, Christian and non-Christian, in the way in which the rules of logic are binding on them?

If we took that last formulation of the question as the correct one, we should have to say, I think, that the answer is simply 'no'. Christian philosophers have sometimes tried to make out that there is a fundamental principle of morality which is on all fours with the principle of non-contradiction in the sense that we can develop an argument on the basis of it and, on occasion, refute the statements of adversaries by reference to it. With the implications of the principle of non-contradiction I am not here concerned. What I am concerned to propose is that the moral principle which is thought to be a sort of counterpart to it in ethics—the principle that good is to be pursued and evil avoided—is a mere tautology. Of itself it will not lead us anywhere. Everybody uses the words 'good' and 'evil' to express what are called by contemporary moral philosophers 'pro-attitudes' and the reverse; what is meant by the words depends on the 'pro-attitudes' which the speaker happens to have. All we can get out of this is that everybody has certain likes and dislikes. We may go on to say that certain likes and dislikes are common to all persons who would be commonly accounted sane, but this will not help us to settle any question which would be commonly accounted to belong to moral philosophy. We have simply pointed out certain very obvious facts about human nature; we have not discovered anything which deserves to be called a principle of thought.

The Christian philosophers to whom I have referred are not so simple-minded as to suppose that their principle does lead anywhere without further explanation. But what they offer as a further explanation turns out to import into it notions which are very far from being inescapable. For they go on to tell us that the good which is to be pursued is not just any kind of good which we may happen to fancy but the good which belongs to a rational will. And, if this is not just a way of pointing to the obvious fact that we do not pursue things irrationally, that we expect to get something out of them (at least in the long run), it must be making some claim about human nature of a metaphysical kind, suggesting that man's rational powers commit him to a development along lines which we may call 'spiritual' rather than along others which may seem open to him. Such a suggestion is certainly not likely to be accepted as implied by any self-evident principle of thought. It may be something which *ought* to become self-evident as the result of a little reflection of a metaphysical kind, but that is quite another story.

Fundamentally it is the idea of *ought* which these philosophers are surreptitiously introducing. It is involved, they say, with the principle that good is to be pursued and evil avoided, because the principle presents itself to us as something which is true, whether we choose to obey it or not; the good which is to be pursued belongs to the rational will as such, and it is independent of any particular operations of will, which may not be in conformity with the ideal of rationality. Clearly we are being asked to consider as a self-evident principle not a harmless tautology but the idea of *ought* in the full traditional sense according to which we have a *duty* to settle a conflict of desires in accordance with certain definite views about man's purpose and destiny. But precisely in so far as this notion of obligation is slipped into the meaning of 'the good is to be pursued,' the principle ceases to be one to which we can appeal as one which must be accepted by anyone who philosophizes. Once again this notion of obligation *ought* to become self-evident. But we cannot claim it outright as we can claim the principle of non-contradiction.

There is no need to suppose that the philosophers who make this appeal to a principle are guilty of any deliberate legerdemain. What they are saying is that everything has a good which it pursues, and that to pursue this good and to fulfil its nature is one and the same; man has a rational nature; the good for him is therefore to behave in a fully rational manner and thus to attain the full development of such a nature, even though he may feel inclined to act otherwise. Once it is allowed that man's nature is rational in the required sense, that his rationality provides him with a programme and a criterion of values, it is fair enough to argue that he will be a fool to act against his nature. But it will not be altogether convincing, for a man may say that in his difficult circumstances he prefers to do without the advantages which are offered him—as things stand with him, it will be less troublesome, on the whole more advantageous, to vegetate.

Our philosophers, however, were perfectly aware that *ought* must mean something more than a recommendation to take a line of far-sighted self-seeking rather than a near-sighted one, or to take a more adventurous line rather than a pusillanimous one. Moral obligation, they realized, being of an absolute character and not being simply reducible to self-seeking, must imply the existence of a supreme law-giver. So their first principle proves eventually to contain or involve in some way not only a metaphysical claim about the nature of man and an assertion of an absolute obligation to fulfil his nature (or at least to aim at fulfilling it) but also an assertion of God's existence. But they were able to put forward their apparently disingenuous argument because all its stages seemed to them to be only different and more distinct ways of saying the same thing.

I shall suggest eventually that they were right in thinking along these lines, although their air of producing an apodeictic conclusion from a commonsense basis, acceptable to all parties in philosophical discussion, was certainly unfortunate. Perhaps we need not take very seriously the appearance of logical demonstration or even the appeal to principles of thought rather than to facts of experience. When these theses were excogitated it was fashionable to use that sort of framework. What makes the theses unsatisfactory for our purposes today is that they take for granted so much that we need to establish if we are to win the agreement of non-Christian philosophers.

What, then, are the issues which the Christian moral philosopher has to face at the present time? Let us first consider the question of rationality in human behaviour, taken in the broadest and least controversial sense. I have already claimed it as obvious that we do not pursue things irrationally, that we expect to get something out of them (at least in the long run) and this might be considered another instance of taking something for granted. But I do not regard this as a live issue in the debates which are engaging our contemporaries in the English-speaking world. It would be commonly agreed that our actions are motivated, and that the pursuit of ends is the context in which moral discourse arises. Nevertheless something should be said about those who follow the Kantian tradition (to use a convenient, but rather misleading, description of them). The late Professor Prichard is the standard representative. Prichard approved of Kant's 'categorical imperative' as strongly as he disapproved of his phenomenalism. It is a very curious thing that the man who had perhaps done most in his generation to overthrow the barriers which Kant had erected against any attempt at meta-physical thinking should be also the man who followed Kant most closely in his insistence on the autonomy of ethics. Kant, indeed, did try to bring in by the back door, as postulated by his ethics, con-clusions which he had rejected in the *Critique of Pure Reason*, notably on the immortality of the soul. But Prichard did not succeed in reaching metaphysical conclusions by any route. Thus we find him saying that we must obey the moral law simply because it presents itself to us as an absolute, although we can see no reason why it should do so and although it has no necessary connexion with the eventual fulfilment of our natures, with our happiness. Prichard's recognition of the absoluteness of the moral law was a genuine in-sight, but he could not relate it with anything else. 'Good' and 'right' were dissociated, and that they should be dissociated is unintelli-gible. 'You ought because you ought' is not likely to convince many people in our society; 'public-school religion' has been on the de-cline for several generations. Prichard's position, although fre-quently mentioned in philosophical discussions, is not influential. Its chief importance, for our purposes, is that it is grist for the posi-tivist's mill. That point will become clear very shortly.

If we want to know what we are really up against, we can hardly do better than turn to Mr P. H. Nowell-Smith's recently published *Ethics* (Penguin Books). Mr Nowell-Smith begins by criticizing 'in-tuitionism' in ethics, and in this connexion he criticizes both Sir David Ross and Professor G. E. Moore for assuming that 'moral words denote characteristics and that truth in ethics is discovered by observation.' The most famous instance of this assumption is Professor Moore's comparison between perceiving the morally good and seeing yellow. These thinkers line up with Prichard in that they, like him, regard moral judgements as self-sufficient, and it is no surprise when Mr Nowell-Smith proceeds to criticize Prichard for maintaining that 'our obligation to perform a duty is immediate and direct, neither requiring nor capable of supporting reasons.' I have already suggested that this criticism will be general-ly accepted by the public which Mr Nowell-Smith addresses: Prichard's claim is not made out. The point to notice here is that Mr Nowell-Smith feels himself justified in turning his back on 'in-tuitionism' altogether at this point, but there is another sort of 'intuitionism', for which I shall argue later, and which he seems never to have met, which does not claim to 'read off' moral charac-teristics but to provide a basis for the rational evaluation of such characteristics. But for the moment we must continue to follow Mr Nowell-Smith.

A large part of his book is taken up with an analysis of moral language; he dissipates many confusions, and it would have been a pleasure to quote from these passages if space permitted. I would venture upon the summary conclusion that he succeeds in account-ing for the moral language used by the great mass of educated Englishmen by referring to the conventions of society and to con-siderations of worldly advantage without feeling the need to envi-sage any metaphysical issues, thus by-passing traditional views of morality altogether. We may feel that certain facts of human ex-perience, which to us seem very obvious, are ignored or travestied in this account. But the fact remains that this analysis of language will commend itself, in principle, to the strongest current of thought in England at this time as doing justice to the sense in which the words 'good', 'ought', etc., are actually used. That, in a nutshell, is the position with which we are faced. How can we break into this iron ring?

Some illustrations will now be given. Let us begin with Mr Nowell-Smith's admirable treatment of hedonism:

> If I want to relieve the distress of a beggar, I want to relieve the distress of a beggar; I do not want my own happiness, pleasure or satisfaction. Likewise if I like giving pleasure to my sick aunt, what I like is giving pleasure to my sick aunt, not my own liking nor even the glow of satisfaction that I might get from being benevolent. Indeed, if the latter was what I really liked, I should be doomed to eternal disappointment, because I could never get just that glow unless I had acted for the sake of giving pleasure and not for the sake of the glow [p. 142].

We may feel that this must be leading to conclusions about human nature which will usefully approximate to the Christian view of the matter. But Mr Nowell-Smith is only concerned to show that it is 'quite unnecessary to invoke the Sense of Duty to account for the occurrence of altruistic action' (p. 143); human nature happens to include a tendency to altruistic action, on occasion, and it is also true that some people act on a sense of duty, but that too is just a fact (and an over-rated one, Mr Nowell-Smith thinks) which has no interesting or far-reaching implications. 'Ought-sentences', he goes on, 'are addressed to a rational agent as solutions to his prob-lems of choice and in consequence, they imply a pro-attitude on the part of the recipient.' Therefore they cannot be 'identified with commandments', since these (logically) need not be concerned with 'pro-attitudes'. This leads to the conclusion that 'the mere fact that a command has been issued by a competent authority, even by God, is not a logically good ground for obeying it.' The logical ground would be that we have 'a general pro-attitude for doing whatever God commands' (p. 192). Mr Nowell-Smith is not really expecting his readers to be interested in God's commands. For he writes off any attempt to introduce the subject of a last end for man; the conclusions of teleologists, he says, 'turn out to be disguised logical truisms, or to be false or at least questionable' (p. 220). That God's will might turn out to be at the same time our sanctification, our fulfilment, is never considered.

Mr Nowell-Smith may give us the impression of being uneasy about the sense of duty; we may think that he does not know what to make of it. Perhaps he (and most of his readers) feel that it had better be kept in cold storage until the psycho-analysts have finished with it. So we are unable to cash in on this uneasiness with any profit to the interests which we have at heart. There is one passage in Mr Nowell-Smith's book which might raise our hopes again; he is speaking of the lives of saints: 'they act on good moral principles but not for the sake of duty; for they do what they do for its own sake and not for the sake of duty' (p. 259). I shall have occasion to return to this passage at a later stage. Here it is sufficient to observe that whatever hopes it might raise are rudely destroyed, towards the end of the book, by our discovery that Mr Nowell-Smith does not believe in moral freedom, at any rate in the traditional sense. He criticizes Professor Campbell's defence of it as follows:

> That I know introspectively what it is like to choose may be true; but I cannot be said to know introspectively that my choice was contra-causal or unpredictable; and this is the point at issue . . . this is surely an issue which is to be settled not by self-observation, but by logical analysis.

Certainly a mere logical analysis of our use of moral words ('I could have . . .') will not reveal the fact of sin. Mr Nowell-Smith continues interestingly:

> And phrases such as 'determined', 'contra-causal', and even 'desiring nature' take us beyond psychology into metaphysics. To say this is not to condemn the phrases; perhaps metaphysics is just what is needed here. But a metaphysician is not a reporter; he is an interpreter of what he 'sees'; and it is over the interpretation that the disputes arise [p. 281].

This is interesting not only because the possibility of metaphysics is recognized, but because it leads us to ask whether the chief reason for the prevailing repugnance to metaphysics is not an unwillingness to acknowledge facts of a non-scientific character. It *is* the metaphysician's business to report such facts. Those who reject metaphysics commonly point to the extravagant variety of the metaphysical systems of the past—but this does not justify them in overlooking the fact that some metaphysicians at any rate do make reports. It is a prejudice to suppose that these reports do not deserve attention because they cannot be *scientifically* tested.

Mr Nowell-Smith goes on to make the same sort of analysis of responsibility as that which he made in an article in *Mind* some years ago. He seems to suppose that the traditional view necessarily involves a regress: as he puts it, to say that a man did not try hard enough to use his 'will-energy' involves answering the question: 'Had he sufficient second-order will-energy to enable him to make use of his first-order will-energy?' (p. 287). But this is simply to reject the unique fact of moral *failure*. Professor Campbell's very proper insistence on the case of the man who 'knows what he ought to do but is tempted to do something else' is dismissed ('this, so far from being the only case, is not even the commonest or most important,' p. 288). And when Mr Nowell-Smith turns to the question of exculpation and asks himself what is our reason for differentiating between two boys whose characters and actions are the same but who come respectively from bad and good homes, he replies that 'in the first case we have not had a chance to see what kindness and a good education could do, while in the second we know that they have failed' (p. 299). In other words, to exculpate is merely to say that punishment is not called for here. And to say 'he could have acted otherwise if . . .' means only 'he would have acted otherwise if . . .' (p. 300).

I have taken so long about illustrating the philosophical concept of morality, as regarded by our most influential contemporaries, because otherwise the full extent of our problem might not be appreciated. And it is necessary to add a few more remarks about the difficulties to which the traditional notion of responsibility gives rise. The difficulty which is uppermost, I think, in people's minds is the objection that sin is so irrational a business as to be really inconceivable. It is easy enough to understand that man's immoderate desires may lead him to disregard what is rational, but sin does not lie in having immoderate desires (although they are, no doubt, the result of sin somehow or other) but in deliberately fostering them or, more exactly, I should say, in deliberately neglecting those desires, velleities, interests (call them what you will) which we know to be our true guides—as a result we fall inevitably into irrational, immoral courses. We ought to admit frankly that sin is the surd in our system. The only convincing evidence of it—self-observation—is ruled out, as we have seen, by Mr Nowell-Smith. It looks like an absolute *impasse*. I cannot stop to discuss the philosophical prejudices which combine to create it or the other difficulties which we should have to face even if we managed to get through it (in fine, the reconciliation of God's omnipotence and goodness with a datum which, though it requires negative terms for its description, is certainly not nothing, but is yet not caused by God—and which leads to the most appalling consequences).[1] All I am concerned to point out here is that the iron ring of positivism cannot be opened from the inside (this was strikingly demonstrated recently by a broadcast debate between Fr Copleston and Mr Maurice Cranston on the subject of freedom). There must be an irruption from outside.

That, in my view, is precisely what we should expect when we discover the proper basis of the Christian ethic. The suggestion that it needs discovering may sound startling. But it will be remembered that the Christian philosophers with whom we began tried to locate it in a self-evident principle which proved to involve, somehow, the existence of God. And other Christian philosophers—Cardinal Billot, for example—have said that responsible moral action is impossible until the existence of a supreme legislator has been explicitly recognized; they also hold that this recognition requires a reasoning process, that God's existence is not, as they put it, 'naturally known'. It is obvious, then, that one can say nothing to the purpose on this subject without engaging in controversy, although it would be generally accepted by Christian philosophers that the basis of traditional ethics cannot be satisfactorily established unless we bring in the existence of God in some way or other. And it follows that the positivist *impasse* can be overcome only by the acknowledgement that ethics depends upon metaphysics.

The view which I wish to recommend differs from the views of the Christian philosophers just mentioned. It differs from the view of the first group in seeing the existence of God unambiguously as

---

[1] On these and other subjects touched on in this paper I have written (briefly) in *An Essay in Christian Philosophy* (Longmans, 1954).

THE PHILOSOPHICAL CONCEPT OF MORALITY 17

the keystone of the arch; it requires a definite apprehension of God as *constituting* the recognition of moral obligation. It therefore differs from the view of the second group in rejecting a process of argument which works up to the existence of God and then down to the establishment of moral obligation; that is to say, it is the view that the existence of God is apprehended *in* the recognition of moral obligation or that the recognition of moral obligation occurs *in* the apprehension of God. The apprehension of God *is* the recognition of moral obligation and vice versa. It is obviously impossible for me to present the case for this conclusion as part of a paper; I have tried to do so elsewhere.[1] But the more obvious objections to it will be briefly considered.

The most obvious retort is that this is either arguing in a circle or falling back on an appeal to self-evidence. It is not arguing in a circle because it is not arguing, at any rate in the ordinary sense of the word, at all. It is not trying to prove the existence of God from the sense of duty and at the same time to validate the sense of duty by calling in God. It is asking for recognition of the fact that the experience to which people refer when they speak of being *obliged* to live up to a moral standard and the experience to which people refer when they speak of discovering God in his action upon them are the same experience; whether or not it arises in the context of an explicit conflict of desires makes no difference to its fundamental character, which is the awareness of our dependence on God, apprehended obscurely but genuinely as actuating everything that we experience, starting with ourselves. If we can know ourselves through our actions, obscurely but genuinely, there is no reason why we should not know God in the same sort of way, and thus it becomes a matter of moment to persuade the positivist that there is a 'self'; that is why Dr Austin Farrer devoted most of his great book *Finite and Infinite* to that subject. It should now be clear that there is no appeal to self-evidence in the sense in which we appeal to the principle of non-contradiction as self-evident. Some awareness of God arises, we may suppose, in everyone's history, as the recognition that some *standard* imposes itself on him, although he may not realize that this is what the theists are talking about. But if the awareness is to 'take', he must be willing to be interested in it, and he may use his freedom to reject the standard; he can avoid the im-

---

[1] In *Certainty* (Dacre Press, 1948), in *The Meaning of Existence* by Dom Mark Pontifex and myself (Longmans, 1953), and in various articles, as well as in *An Essay in Christian Philosophy*.

position. He may move so far away from this experience of absolute value that he may need a complete re-education if he is to recover it. That is the position in which so many of our contemporaries seem to be; for them God's existence is certainly not self-evident.

The objection that a direct apprehension of God is being claimed has been answered, in effect, by what has just been said. It is true that we must speak, on this showing, of an 'experience' of God, but it is (if I may be allowed the phrase) a 'mediate experience'. Our answer to Kant must surely be that God does enter into the field of our experience, that experience is not only of sensible things but extends to the intellectual, the spiritual. This is not the usual appeal to 'religious experience', which tends to emphasize the emotional element to the neglect of the intellectual. It is rather the *undercurrent* of experience to which the appeal is made, and the word 'experience' is used in the widest sense. The awareness of God is involved in the awareness of ourselves in conjunction with our everyday objects. I have been in the habit of using a spatial metaphor and calling it a 'background' knowledge; since it is obviously of a unique kind, it can be indicated only by a metaphor, and I must be content to leave it there.

If this were accepted as the basis of an ethic, what could we build on it? Clearly the fulfilment of our natures becomes a programme with a definite meaning when our dependence on God is recognized. Apart from this recognition, it remains very vague and ambiguous. But will this natural ethic give us any clear information about God's purpose in our regard? It may be clear that our happiness lies in the knowledge and love of God, but what exactly have we to do about it and what is God going to do about it? We may suppose that we shall survive the death of the body and be rewarded for our efforts on earth by a fuller knowledge, but this is not clear. Natural theology has never flourished for long in the absence of organized religion and without some belief in a revelation. Nevertheless natural theology and the theistic ethic which goes with it are not to be disregarded. For the Christian thinker, the theologian, must always remember how our contact with God has been originally established and what it tells us. Otherwise we may easily talk nonsense about God and about the relation in which we stand to him.

It is not easy to say just how much this original contact can tell us, for we are not acquainted with it in a pure state. Our natural powers are impaired, and when they are healed by grace it is difficult to distinguish the effects of this healing from the effects of reve-

lation and of our supernatural elevation. But it seems pretty clear
that any genuine apprehension of God must carry with it the reconciliation of the 'good' with the 'right'. It must show us that God's
attitude to us is one of unchanging beneficence, and that our attitude to him must be one of love. Historically this attitude has been
overlaid with superstitions, but it must have persisted somehow in
so far as there has been any worship of *God*. Thus the answer to the
objection that the traditional ethic reduces to a long-sighted selfishness is that it proves to be the nature of man to give himself to God,
to return to God; his good lies outside himself, and therefore presents itself as duty. Dr Hawkins puts it admirably at the end of his
Aquinas paper *Nature as the Ethical Norm*:

> Love is in one sense an enlargement of the self and in a more
> appropriate sense a transcendence of the self. In the measure that
> love exists, no problem arises from the difference between self
> and other. An action done through love is necessarily both com-
> pletely unselfish and completely satisfactory to the agent. On this
> plane the difficulties of mere morality are solved, or perhaps it is
> truer to say that morality does not reach its full stature until it
> reaches this plane.

This is the point at which to look back at Mr Nowell-Smith's
reference to the saints: 'they do what they do for its own sake and
not for the sake of duty.' This is true enough if we suppose that duty
requires an actual conflict of desires. The saint has identified his
desires with the will of God. But the acknowledgement of God's
sovereignty, which is bound up with the apprehension of God, is
the final meaning of duty. Our duty is still our duty even when it is
identified with our happiness in the vision of God.

In conclusion I should like to suggest that in one way Christian
moralists have been inclined in the past to rely unduly on natural
ethics and in another way have not made so much use as they might
have done of the lessons which in fact it has to teach us. The recur-
rent appeal to nature in our moral theology is notorious. We are
always being told that forbidden classes of action are contrary to
nature. So they are, but you cannot expect people to see it unless
they have at least discovered the true purpose of human nature. The
moral theologians are not writing for the same public as Mr
Nowell-Smith, and they are not concerned with apologetics; even
so, they claim confirmation of their findings from moral philosophy
in a way which one must characterize as naïve. It is not sufficient
to say that lying is wrong because speech is naturally ordered to the

diffusion of truth; doubtless it is, but this does not settle Kant's question about the murderer who asks you where his victim is—it looks as though we must allow that in some circumstances a man may lose the right to be told the truth. The most difficult cases, of course, arise in the sphere of sexual morality. In fact the position, as I see it, in the most general way, is that we can *recommend* the Christian prescriptions about sexual morality on grounds of pure reason, but that we cannot *demonstrate their necessity*. That is to say, we can show that these prescriptions of the moral law are compatible with what we can discover by our natural powers about the purpose and destiny of man: we may make out a very plausible case for these prescriptions, provided that we appeal not only to the purpose of the sexual functions themselves but also to the psychological and social factors involved. But we cannot prove that they are required, absolutely, by the facts, unless we include the fact of Revelation. It may sound rather queer to say that the natural law cannot be fully known apart from Revelation. But this is not to say that certain things would not be wrong unless they had been declared to be wrong by Revelation. The view which I am putting forward has been misunderstood in that sense. What I am saying is that God knows how the destiny of the human race is to be best achieved and that this programme is therefore the law of our nature. It involves certain absolute prohibitions which natural reason may find understandable, indeed, but not evidently necessary.

The lessons which natural ethics have to teach us are disregarded by people who see no reason for explaining God's commands by reference to the fulfilment of human nature. Moral theologians generally prefer to appeal to nature in the abstract when they seek confirmation of their results from philosophy, and they are concerned only to show that this sin or that is contrary to nature. They are not so much interested in the purpose which we must suppose to lie behind prohibitions, the purpose of developing human nature on its true lines. It is difficult to attach any meaning to an offence against nature unless it can be shown to damage some nature in some way, that is, to impair its potentialities for development. But these theologians are unwilling to say that something is wrong because it has certain consequences; they want to say that it is wrong in itself, and this leads them to treat nature as if it were a mere rule or principle. To offend against nature and to offend against 'the rule of reason' is one and the same thing. But to offend against the rule of reason, on analysis, itself proves to mean producing consequences which impair the development of natures. What these theologians are trying to safeguard is the truth that we cannot judge whether our action is right or wrong by its consequences. But I think they should allow that when God declares certain classes of action wrong it is because he knows them to be contrary to human nature in the sense of being fraught with disastrous consequences for the human race, considered, as only God can consider it, in its entire historical reality. That sexual activity is wrong without exception outside of marriage would thus be due to the fact that God's plan for human society as a whole is attacked by it. But we cannot be sure of this apart from Revelation, for the good consequences in particular cases might seem to us to outweigh the bad ones.

Natural ethics does remind us, then, that the morally good is always the fulfilment of nature. Things are not right just because they are not wrong. They are right only in so far as they promote in some way the purpose of our existence, which is the worship of God. The fact that we are mostly occupied with providing the material conditions for fulfilling that purpose makes it especially important that we should remember what the purpose is.

HISTORICAL INFLUENCES

III

THE BIBLE

by

Dom Ralph Russell

AN attempt to assess the historical influence of the Bible on morality must be based on an appreciation, however inadequate, of the teaching which the Bible contains. Christ's moral teaching, though fresh with new life—new wine needing new wineskins (Mt. 9: 17)—does not destroy that of the Old Law, but brings it to perfection (5: 17). The foundations of morality are already laid in Genesis. There is only one God, who is holy and good and made all things good. Here at once is the answer to Dualism, fatal then, as now, to morals. Evil comes, not from an Evil First Principle, but from an evil will which rebels against God's command and incurs just retribution. The supreme moral evil is defiance of God: pride. The doctrine of an initial Fall shows that the human will is weakened and prone to evil. But there is morally good action amongst men, and the great human institutions, such as marriage and the family, are God-given and good. These principles provide a moral framework which excludes both pessimism and the notion of a self-sufficient progress.

Thus the Hebrews started with the immense advantage of knowing the One God. Not for them the problems which faced the loftiest spirits among the Greeks, puzzled by the immoralities of the Olympians. This holy God was no abstraction, but revealed himself in the history of his Chosen People as living, just and ready to save. Next, they possessed a clear, divinely sanctioned moral law. Other contemporary legal codes contain moral provisions, but the superiority of the Ten Commandments stands out in the monotheism of the first commandment, and the prohibition of sins of desire in the last two. These moral concepts were upheld, deepened and further purified by generation after generation of prophets. But since for centuries there was no clear notion of the lot of the soul after death, the sanctions expressed were rewards and punishments in this life only. The Book of Job and the Psalms reflect the troubles of mind engendered by this outlook. For definite solution they had to await the Sapiential Literature: 'The just will live for ever, and the Lord is their reward, and the care of them is with the Most High' (Wis. 3: 1–4; 5: 16f; cf. Dan. 12: 2; 2 Macc. 7).

This may serve to illustrate the vital principle that 'the Law brought nothing to perfection.' Not only was there moral progress within the Old Testament itself, but its final purpose was to introduce 'a better hope through which we draw near to God' (Heb. 7: 19). Attempts to assess its moral values without reference to the progressive realization of God's designs result in hopeless confusion.[1] Religious wars of extermination could thus seek their justification. Some early Protestants tried to defend polygamy from the example of the patriarchs. The Afrikanders interpreted the Great Trek as the Exodus and themselves as the Chosen People having divine authority to dominate the black nations around them. There is always a more subtle tendency to exalt the Law of the Commandments above the Law of Love and many a father or employer seeks to excuse his quite unchristian sternness from the Old Law. In fact, of course, it is a gross misrepresentation of the Old Law to speak of it as always stern. Not only does it stress the wrong of abusing the weakness of the stranger, the orphan and the widow, but it inculcates positive kindness, which extends to animals and even to personal enemies among fellow Israelites. The Sabbath was originally intended to be a day of gladness (Os. 2: 11) and, to take one more example, the Jubilee Year was eminently humanitarian.

For the modern conscience, formed by centuries of Christianity, probably the most perplexing problems are raised by the commands to destroy whole populations, by the Comminatory Psalms and by the *lex talionis* (a tooth for a tooth). Again, one must recall the total context of God's ways with man. A primitive people had to have precepts they could grasp. For the Semites, war was waged on behalf of one's god, and all captives could be destroyed if he so wished. Deuteronomy at least regulates this by exempting distant cities, though not the neighbouring ones which would corrupt Israel's faith (Deut. 20: 10–16). Our own times have seen demands to punish a whole nation, but how far this is removed from the Christian spirit may be gauged by Christ's rebuke to the impetuous young Apostles who wanted to copy Elias, and call down fire from

[1] Thierry Maertens, *Jerusalem, Cité de Dieu*, pp. 40, 41.

heaven upon a Samaritan city which had not received them (Lk.
9: 54, 55). The reaction to the imprecations in some of the psalms is
another index of the change. For even when we have said that these
express with oriental vividness the emotions of a poet intent upon
God's justice being vindicated, they do stand for a stage of morality,
and it is only when the Psalter is understood from the term to which
it is directed 'that it can become Christian prayer without the denial
of one of its verses'.[1] 'Sevenfold vengeance shall be taken for Cain,
but for Lamech seventy times sevenfold' shows that 'an eye for an
eye'—and no more—was progress. Later, sacrifices of expiation and
money fines were substituted in the case of offences hitherto punished by the *lex talionis* (Gen. 4: 15, 24; Ex. 21: 23–7). But God had
yet to bring the old text to contrast with the spirit of Christ: 'Lord,
how often must I see my brother do me wrong, and I forgive him;
as much as seven times? Jesus said to him: I tell thee to forgive, not
seven wrongs, but seventy times seven' (Mt. 18: 21).

Man's moral life requires worship, and feeds on its symbols.
Morality and liturgy cannot be separated without ruin to both. For
if man's senses and imagination are not given their proper religious
nourishment and exercise, they will be fed from sources either irreligious or at least dissociated from religion. A dryly intellectual
and legalistic form of instruction leads to widespread apostasy, just
as attention to nothing but the beauties of worship leads to formalism and corruption. Morality in the Bible is illustrated and exemplified by the finest human stories in the world, on which Christian
generations have been, and should still be brought up. Again, the
Israelites' morality is always to be seen as part of a life of worship
in which the whole people participated in sacrifice and Sabbath,
in Temple services and sacred song—the *introibo ad altare Dei* of the
Gradual Psalms. Religious rites (such as the Paschal supper) were
also part of home life. In all this worship Christ shared, and the
Epistle to the Hebrews is there to remind us that it, like the Commandments, was not destroyed but fulfilled when the earthly
Jerusalem passed into the abiding City of God.

As the summit of his religious and moral life, the Israelite possessed the command to love God 'with his whole heart and with his
whole soul and with his whole strength' (Deut. 6: 5). That raised him
far above the generality of surrounding peoples and brought the personal religion of prophets and psalms and the reverent cleanness
of heart required to approach the All-holy. This high religious mor-

[1] *Ibid.*

ality was now to receive its divine and transcendent consummation.

It was inaugurated by the preaching of the coming of the Kingdom of God. What is required to receive this divine gift (cf. Mt. 21:
43; Lk. 12: 32) is 'repentance', a change of heart from sin to God,
which in its positive aspect is 'conversion', a fresh orientation from
self to God. The endless rhythm of the relations of Israel to their
God is awakened again: infidelity, punishment, conversion, par-
don, the help of Yahweh. Jesus desired to transform the heart, the
inner centre of man's dispositions. Like the Baptist—whose requirements were embodied in a rite of baptism and included the observance of the most ordinary moral precepts (Lk. 3: 10–14)—he
started his preaching by this call to repentance. He sent his Apostles
to preach it (Mk. 6: 12), and it was always a first part of their
message, as has been the case with Christian preachers ever since
(Acts 2: 38; 17: 30; Heb. 6: 1). Beautiful examples come from St
Luke's Gospel: the sinful woman, the publican, the prodigal son,
Zachaeus, the good thief.[1]

The ethics of the New Testament cannot be separated from the
person, claims, actions and merciful miracles of their Giver. Nineteenth-century critics tried to divide Christian ethics from Christ.
But long ago the querulous demand: 'Why was not all this sold and
given to the poor?' received an answer which championed the
dignity and courtesy of personal love: 'Let her alone. Why should
you vex her? She did well to treat me so. You have the poor among
you always, so that you can do good to them when you will; I am
not always among you. She has done what she could; she has
anointed my body beforehand to prepare it for burial. I promise
you, in whatever part of the world this gospel is preached, the story
of what she has done shall be told to preserve her memory' (Mt. 26:
6–9 [Knox]). The fulfilment of the little prophecy might serve as a
warning to the ethical rationalist: the story and its lesson remain;
the attempt to live on Christian ethical capital without Christ has
been disastrous; another generation has squandered what rationalism had no power to keep.

The most powerful moral motive is love of a Person. The New
Testament tells of that Person 'whom you love without seeing him'
(1 Pet. 1: 7). The most lovable of the sons of men is at the same time
the Divine Son, in whom we see the Father and through whom we
go to the Father (Jn. 14: 9). This is the fundamental meaning of the

---

[1] Cf. the article 'Christianity in Apostolic Times', §643, in *A Catholic Commentary on
Holy Scripture*, on which I am drawing.

'faith' which Christ requires, that self-giving to his Person and message which describes the normal Christian attitude.[1]

There is no true Christian morality which is not Trinitarian. The Jews knew the Fatherhood of God as Creator, but not the Father who begets a Son. That within the One God there are three Divine Persons, a whole society of love, and that men could be called to share in the life of the Divine Persons, are mysteries to which human reason left to itself could not attain. But once revealed, they effect an immense moral change. The 'living God' is living above anything we could conceive, and calls us to share his life. Conformed to the Son by a sonship which raises our nature to share the Divine, we are brought by the Son to the Father and taught his will. In the Son made man, we contemplate God, seeing in a man like ourselves what God is like: 'He who sees me, sees the Father also' (Jn. 12: 45; 14: 9). The Spirit of Love, 'sent' by the Son as a consequence of his work of Redemption, will make us like the Son, and teach us the intimacy of approach to the Father (Jn. 14: 16–20; 15: 26; Gal. 4: 4–6).

The Sermon on the Mount is the Son's introduction of men to his Father, and is his own manifesto, the Moral Charter of the New Law.[2] It sets a new spiritual ideal which knows no bounds: 'Be you perfect as your heavenly Father is perfect' (Mt. 5: 48). The prayer he taught shows in its opening words, 'Our Father', that we are all brothers who share one heavenly Father (cf. Mt. 23: 9, 10). The first moral duty, paid in tender trust and expressed in three petitions, is to praise and thank our Father, begging that his will be done. When God is loved and honoured, human relations will be right. So the prayer passes to three personal petitions: for day-to-day needs, 'our daily bread', for forgiveness of sins on condition that we forgive others and for freedom from temptation and all moral evil.

The moral spirit and attitudes which follow are developed in the Sermon, and no commentary can take the place of reading and meditating it. The new outlook is expressed in the Beatitudes. Their standard is frighteningly high. This Christ knew very well:

[1] *Ibid.* Similarly 'to believe' is to accept the Gospel, and since this normally involves conforming oneself to the grace of salvation, Christ often says 'thy faith has saved thee' (e.g. Mt. 9: 22), and faith is equated with charity (Lk. 7: 47, 50), though not quite always (1 Cor. 13: 2, 8).

[2] The New Law, like the Old, is given on a mountain. The comparison is certainly intended: 'It was said . . . but I say to you. . . .'

'enter in through the narrow gate . . . for narrow is the gate and strait the way that leads to life, and few there are who find it' (Mt. 7 : 13, 14).[1] But this is the standard which he deliberately set at the opening of his public life, and to this he invites us. It attracts many a generous soul who might pay little attention to a religion preached in terms of seemingly watered down commandments.[2] The clash between the spirit of the world and the spirit of Jesus comes out most clearly in the contrast in St Luke's Gospel between the Beatitudes and the Woes (Lk. 6 : 20ff). Men ordinarily seek riches, comforts, pleasures, honours; the disciples of Christ are to look for happiness in poverty, privation, tears, persecution, and they must meet this last by charity alone.

The rest of the Sermon is equally categoric: 'unless your justice abound more than that of the scribes and pharisees, you cannot enter into the Kingdom of Heaven' (Lk. 5: 20). So this is something of vital import and the explanation which follows cannot be dismissed as unpractical because it is sometimes couched in the vigorous imagery of oriental parable.[3] The law of the Commandments, not a particle of which is abrogated, is to be absorbed and transcended by the Law of universal charity in ways which Jesus indicates: no anger, no divorce, no unlawful oaths at all, no showing off in good deeds, no resisting evil,[4] but love for all, even enemies. As for this being practical, the genuine Christians, the saints who take their life-programme from the Sermon, are just those who have the most practical effect on the world.

Those who will see their heavenly Father are the clean of heart. The great obstacle to fixing the heart upon him is the indulgence of disorderly desires. So, together with the shunning of impurity in thought, must go a trust in God which abolishes anxiety. It is that anxiety, characteristic of the scramble for riches and 'security', which, together with the love of pleasure, chokes the good seed of the Gospel (cf. Lk. 13: 22; 1 Cor. 7: 29–34). Again, Christ's outlook is the practical one. 'You cannot serve God and Mammon. . . Be-

---

[1] He did not say that all those who took the broad, downward path would perish, but that they were on the way to perdition.

[2] Our existing English catechism has sixty-six questions on the Commandments, and one towards the end enumerating the Beatitudes. Yet Christ set these first in his own teaching.

[3] E.g. 'if thine eye offend thee, cut it out and cast it from thee'; 'let not thy right hand know what thy left hand doth'; but the meaning is clear.

[4] Christ is here speaking to individuals, not of the authority of governments, cf. Jn. 19: 11; Rom. 13: 4–7.

hold the lilies of the field. . . Do not *worry* about tomorrow' (Mt. 6; 26–34). There is a morality for business and economic life! It does not exclude setting our needs before God (cf. 7: 11), nor that prudent provision for the future which may be today's duty. But it excludes the disordered covetousness, the lack of trust and the worry which produce nervous breakdowns and family limitation, make the economic régime 'hard, cruel and relentless'[1] and lead to wars. Again the injunction not to judge others nor trouble about their faults (7: 1–6) shows that Christ knew all about the psychologists' 'projection', whereby we magnify in others the faults we fail to face in ourselves, and the beam in our own eye is a magnifying glass for their mote.

Christ's ethics cannot be understood without reference to the eternal values in the next life. He has no truck with a Kantian purism which refuses to consider rewards. He sets heaven and hell squarely before men. But he is so far from neglecting this world that he describes the Judgement in positive terms according to the doing or omission of good actions to others (25: 31–46). Modern research is bringing out the eschatological element in the Sermon on the Mount. As St John's Gospel insists, eternal life and the judgement are operating here and now. But unless men keep the next world clearly in mind, they are not likely to seek the Kingdom of God first. They set their limitless desires upon material things, and then, of course, there will not be enough to go round. Here again, Jesus's teaching is practical economics.

Morality may be seen as a series of precepts, or as summed up in love. To the young man's question 'What must I do to obtain eternal life?' Jesus replied 'keep the commandments.' When he asked 'Which?' he was given a list, ranging from the obvious prohibitions and duty to parents to the Golden Rule (19: 16–19). But to the doctor of the Law who asked what is the great commandment, Jesus replied, 'Thou shalt love the Lord thy God . . . and the second is like to this: thou shalt love thy neighbour as thyself. On these two commandments hang the whole Law and the prophets' (22: 35–40). Jesus was the first to set these two commandments together, showing

---

[1] Pius XI in *Quadragesimo Anno*. The historical influence of the Sermon on the Mount is marked in the Social Encyclicals of the Popes. But naturally the whole Gospel has its part; thus Pius XII (Discourse to Italian Jurists, December 6th, 1953) deduces from Christ's advice to let the cockle grow with the good seed until the harvest that 'the duty of repressing moral and religious error cannot be an ultimate norm of action' (cf. Mt. 13: 24–30). He was criticizing and reproving a Spanish view.

that to keep the one is to keep the other, and in the parable which compared the priest and Levite unfavourably with the Samaritan, he added that one's 'neighbour' is everyone in need (Lk. 10: 30–7).

But he did not demand this love without providing in his own person the motive and the example. 'Follow me'; 'he that loves father or mother . . . more than me, is not worthy of me' (Mt. 10: 37; 16: 34). It is the unknown motive in practical kindness to others: 'As long as you did it to one of my least brethren, you did it unto me' (25: 40). To his Apostles he bears witness that it is because they have loved him that the Father has loved them (Jn. 16: 27). The immense love he inspires, which shines through the New Testament, was drawn out by the love he gave: 'The Son of man did not come to have service done him; he came to serve others and to give his life as a ransom for the lives of many' (Mt. 20: 28). 'If I am lifted up, I will draw all men to myself' (Jn. 12: 32); 'greater love no man has than this, that he lay down his life for his friends; you are my friends if you do what I command you' (15: 13, 14). This love, with the example of one meek and lowly of heart, makes easy the keeping of his commandments, which 'are not heavy' (Mt. 11: 29; 1 Jn. 5: 3). To share his love even to its ultimate consequences is a challenge of honour which he throws down to his friends: 'He that does not take up his cross and follow me, is not worthy of me' (Mt. 10: 38; 16: 24).

Christian morals are God-given, that is to say they flow from grace, which is a gift of God. God's 'giving' and man's 'receiving' are constituents of the order of grace proclaimed in the New Testament. God's love is not a sentiment but a 'giving'. He 'so loved the world as to give his own Son' (Jn. 3: 16). Indeed 'a man cannot receive anything unless it be given him from heaven' (3: 27). The Kingdom of God is 'given' (e.g. Mt. 21: 43); Christ's own love is expressed by the gift of himself, of his life, of his body in the Eucharist (Gal. 1: 4; Mt. 20: 28; 26: 26; Lk. 22: 19; Jn. 6: 51). The humility which is a necessary part of the Christian spirit is the expression of the truth that Christ has done all, and that we have nothing that we have not received (1 Cor. 4: 7). The Kingdom of God must be received as by a little child, we must become little children if we are to enter it, and the greatest in it is he who is a little child; the openness, simplicity, affectionate candour of a little child is the sum of this Gospel teaching on morality (Mt. 18: 3, 4; Mk. 10: 15). This is not of course the 'childishness' rebuked by St Paul (cf. 1 Cor. 3; 1ff; cf. 14: 20; and doves and serpents, Mt. 10: 16). The supreme moral tragedy of the perverse will lies in rejecting

instead of receiving—'and thou wouldst not' (Mt. 23: 37). But
there is also the lazy, ungenerous will, like that of the man who hid
his talent (25: 24–30). For grace is meant to issue in meritorious
action, and God crowns his own gifts by crowning man's merits.
Although he does so freely, and may reward a hundredfold, there
is correspondence between merit and reward: the merciful will
obtain mercy, those who acknowledge Christ before men will be
acknowledged, and those who lose their lives for him will save
them.

Christ did not leave his morality as an abstract system. He en-
acted it himself on Calvary, and he set it in a concrete rite. Christ
crucified and risen is the centre and source of salvation. He gave
himself to his Father and to his own in a sacrifice which is the sacramental enactment of Calvary, and he consummated his union with
them in the gift of his Body to be eaten and his Blood to be drunk.
The Last Supper gathers into itself all Christian morality. Christ
chose a supper—a love feast which men well understand—for this
'uttermost proof of his love' (Jn. 13: 1 [Knox]). 'Greater love no
man hath than that he lay down his life for his friends. . . Take and
eat; this is my body which is given for you.' Thus the sacramental
and the moral life are essentially linked. To teach his morality,
Christ chose the great human symbols: a meal uniting friends in
love, bread that nourishes life, wine that delights the heart. But in
a way truly divine he set reality beneath the Symbol, and Reality
is himself: 'The bread which I will give is my flesh for the life of the
world' (Jn. 6: 51). When he offerred himself to his Father in the most
perfect act of religion, he offered himself for his brethren in the
most perfect act of fraternal love. Finally, he ordered his followers
to 'do' what he had done—to offer the same sacrifice with the same
mind and heart. That is why the Mass is the source and centre of
the spirit of Christian morality (cf. 1 Cor. 10: 17).

Hence Christian morality has never been lived fully unless it
came, and was seen to come, from the Mass. This is only to say
what Pope St Pius X has said: 'The primary and indispensable
source of the true Christian spirit is the active participation by the
faithful in the Holy Mysteries. . .' Thus a corporate, liturgical spirit
is a pre-requisite to moral reform within the Church. Happily, our
moral teaching is beginning to start from our share in the Mass. It
is not with the Commandments that it should start, or at least not
rest in them, but state clearly that they are only an introduction. It
was in the warm, intimate setting of a Supper which was also a

B*

sacrifice that Christ gave his own, new commandment. The Law of the New Covenant is not 'graven in letters upon stone', but, as had been promised, 'set in thy heart' (2 Cor. 3: 3–11; Jer. 31: 31–3). Unless this is grasped, morality will seem cold, and souls be repelled. At the same time the essence of the Sacrifice of the New Covenant (Lk. 22: 20; 1 Cor. 11: 25), which Christ was offering and in which he invites our participation, is surrender of our will to the Father (Jn. 15: 10). Thus it comes from a heart given in love to God and to others. 'Active participation' should normally help this, but—lest the letter again kill the spirit—it should not be forgotten that what is essential may be given equally well or better by the deaf and dumb or ignorant. To sum up, then: while the Commandments are a necessary substratum, we now see that Christian morality comes from Christ and the sharing in the Christian Mysteries. These will be primarily Baptism, the Mass, and their fruit, the Mystical Body. Perhaps the greatest influence of the Bible on morality has been exercised by inspiring the Liturgy.

Christ's moral teaching can no more be separated from the Resurrection than it can from the Crucifixion and the Last Supper. It is quite unchristian to think of his heroic sacrifice apart from its triumph. Trust in our heavenly Father assures us that he will accept and crown the sacrifice and say 'My turn now'. 'Ought not Christ to have suffered these things and entered into his glory?' (Lk. 24: 26). But the Resurrection is no isolated event. Christ did not only die for our sakes, but also rose, to bring his brethren into glory (Rom. 4: 25; Heb. 2: 10; 2 Tim. 1: 8–12). The whole spiritual cosmos is altered: 'Behold, I make all things new' (Apoc. 21: 5). The Resurrection brings the Messianic Last Days when the redeemed are incorporated into Christ's sacrifice and triumph. Christ's first greeting to them is 'Peace', and he will send his Holy Spirit to gather God's sin-scattered children into one, and give them peace in himself, without barrier of sex or class or race (Jn. 20: 20; 10: 11–16; 11: 52; cf. Eph. 2: 15; Gal. 3: 28; Col. 3: 11). For the ancient temple of God's worship is substituted the sanctuary of Christ's Body (Mt. 26: 61; Jn. 2: 19–22); and Christians themselves will become 'sanctuaries of the Holy Spirit', and face onwards towards the Day when Christ himself will come again to consummate all things, and God be all in all (1 Cor. 6: 19; 15: 28).

And now we may turn to the morality of St Paul. That great Pharisee, brought up in the strictest sect to blameless observance of the Law, had persecuted the Church out of zeal for the Law (Acts

26: 5; Phil. 3: 4–6). Yet he had known also the agony of finding another 'law' in his members which kept him sin's captive, and the Law of the Commandments, holy as it was, could not help him but only multiplied transgressions by increasing knowledge (Rom. 7: 7–25; Gal. 5: 17). Then Christ and Christ's grace had burst upon him to free him from 'this nature doomed to death' (Rom. 7: 24f; 1 Cor. 15: 55–7). Whereas the other Apostles had learned gradually to know Christ during his earthly life, it was the glorious, risen Lord who had shone upon Paul's consciousness on the road to Damascus, the Lord against whom he was kicking by setting observance of the Law above the Redeemer, the Christ who continued to live in the least of his brethren: 'Saul, Saul, why dost thou persecute me?' (Acts 9: 3–5). This revelation that the death and resurrection of God's own Son are the decisive event for all mankind was what Paul was sent to make known to all nations (Gal. 1: 12–16; Acts 22: 21).

He brought the good tidings that Christ had died and risen not for the Jews alone but for all men because all were sinners and needed redemption (Rom. 5: 8, 10; 1 Tim. 1: 15). The practical experience of sin on a vast scale in great towns like Corinth and Ephesus gave him materials for the terrible picture of vice in the Epistle to the Romans. But he saw far deeper. He saw the universality of sin, which, coming from its ultimate source in the first Adam, has taken possession of the whole human race, since all are sinners through his fall and subject to disordered desire. This state the Law only aggravated by making sins into transgression of an ordinance clearly known. By force of his own will alone man could not extricate himself (Rom. 5: 12–21; 1 Cor. 15: 22). Modern depth psychology is rediscovering this universal character of sin.

But the grace of Christ, the Second Adam, is far more abundant and more profoundly efficacious than the sin which came by Adam (Rom. 5: 15–20). In the blood of the Son of God we find the Redemption that sets us free from all sins (Col. 1: 13). While the struggle between the spirit and the flesh continues in man (as Paul knew very well, e.g. 1 Cor. 5: 1–6, 20), our guilt is entirely washed away in baptism. We are now clean and sanctified (6: 11), a 'new creation' (Gal. 6: 15), 'no longer darkness but light in the Lord' (Eph. 5: 8). Hence St Paul's outlook on the Redemption—which on God's side is all love and union—is far more positive than negative. Indeed, five times out of seven, the word stands for the wide process by which God gives us in Christ graces destined to expand in the glory of heaven.[1] He insists, too, that the grace of Christ heals our nature and enables us to keep the Law (Rom. 8: 4). He has none of the pessimism of those forms of Protestant thought which consider human nature still radically corrupt, oppose Christian humanism, and are obsessed by an individualist pre-occupation with salvation. No! Such is the efficacy of being 'in Christ Jesus' that we are able to have in us 'that mind which Christ Jesus had in him', and to think on all that is true and good and lovely (Phil. 2: 5ff; 4: 8). St Paul is very human because he is the Apostle of grace!

So Christian morality, for St Paul, arises from our union with Christ who died and rose for us, and this union is brought about when we are born again by baptism. Baptism, and no longer the Commandments, is the source of our morality. We cannot go back to the slavery of sin and its deadly consequences simply because we have been baptized 'into Christ', and have really, though sacramentally, died and risen with him (Rom. 6: 3–12). Sinners cannot possess the Kingdom of God, but we do possess it, for we have been washed, sanctified, justified in Christ and the Holy Spirit (1 Cor. 6: 9–11). The theme of the Epistle to the Galatians is that now we are not under the Law, but under grace.

This new moral life, springing from baptismal grace, is a life shared, concorporate with Christ: 'With Christ I hang upon the Cross, and yet I am alive; or rather, not I; it is Christ who lives in me' (Gal. 2: 20). Thus baptism gives the Christian his life-programme: the development of the dying and rising of Christ within himself. He is to suffer with Christ, and gradually be transformed into Christ's image from glory to glory (2 Cor. 3: 18; Rom. 6: 3–12). So 'when Christ appears, who is your life, you too will appear with him in glory,' and finally the risen Christ will bring our bodies to triumphant resurrection (Col. 3: 1–4; 1 Cor. 15). On this the Fathers based their baptismal homilies. It was easily grasped when the baptized were largely adult converts, baptized by immersion, 'rising again' from the waters, proceeding after Confirmation (which usually followed immediately) to their first Mass and Communion, and continuing consciously their baptismal life. The renewal of the Easter Vigil offers Christian educators a great opportunity.

The vivifying and directing principle of the new life is the Holy

[1] I have developed this in *A Catholic Commentary*, § 645, art. 'Christianity in Apostolic Times'.

Spirit whom we have received. If we walk under the influence of the Spirit, we shall not fall back into the ways of that 'flesh' which those who are Christ's have crucified (Gal. 5: 16–24). Acting so, there is no Law against us. Born of the Spirit, we share the morality of freedom for 'where the Spirit of the Lord is, there is liberty' (2 Cor. 3: 17; Gal. 4: 21–31). St Paul lays great stress on conscience, and a properly instructed conscience under the Holy Spirit's influence will be our guide. This does not mean that liberty can be made an excuse for licence (Gal. 5: 13), or for breaking the Law of Charity by using freedom to lead into sin those less well instructed (1 Cor. 8, 9; Rom. 14, 15). It does not mean exemption from obedience to the Gospel, to the moral code, or to apostolic authority —and St Paul uses this last to lay down very precise instructions and to control the use of special spiritual gifts (Rom. 1: 5; 1 Cor. *passim*; 2 Cor. 10: 5, 6; 2 Thess. 3: 14). Moreover civil rulers, whose power also comes from God, must be obeyed, and taxes paid where they are due (Rom. 13: 4–7).

But then, obedience to God-given authority goes with liberty properly understood. The point is that this liberty comes from within, indeed it *is* the Christian life.[1] It is animated by the charity which is poured into our hearts by the Holy Spirit (Rom. 5: 5). 'Love is the fulfilling of the Law', and so involves all the Commandments regarding God and other people (Rom. 13: 10). And this is a love which is to grow continually in understanding until we are 'filled with all the fullness of God' (Eph. 3: 14–19). Far too much emphasis has been placed upon St Paul's doctrine of faith. Vital and initial as faith is, St Paul's 'faith' is the 'faith which works through charity' (Gal. 5: 6). Hope too is necessary, for we have to hold on to what we do not yet possess in fullness (Rom. 8: 24). But of all the virtues, charity is the greatest, and that alone will abide eternally (1 Cor. 13). To grasp what charity means to St Paul one must read his great hymn upon it, and that will show that this love of God and man is a humble love, which is not puffed up nor self-seeking even in spiritual gifts, but kindly, cheerful, hopeful, long-enduring.

The great passages about charity in St Paul's epistles follow upon descriptions of the Mystical Body of Christ. We are not baptized in spiritual isolation; we are baptized into an existing spiritual reality: the Body of Christ, the Church. Membership of the Body provides the manner and sphere of our action which is based on sharing the

[1] Cf. C. Spicq, *Morale Chrétienne et Requêtes Contemporaines*, art. 'La Morale Paulinienne', to which this section on St Paul is much indebted.

life of Christ with all the other members of the Body (cf. Rom. 12; 1 Cor. 12; Eph. 4: 5; Col. 1: 24). We are, as St Paul constantly says, 'in Christ'. This must be carefully understood. The Body is not an amorphous mass. The Son of God made man retains his own divine Personality. Each of us keeps his own personality and liberty. Yet we are united in a unity far more than moral. There is identification with Christ, though not identity. And as Christ's life flows through the whole Body and is diversified in the different members, we are 'members one of another', dependent on each other, necessary to each other like the limbs of a body.

So each is to use the graces given to him in order to 'build up the Body of Christ'. Doing the truth in love, we are to grow up into Christ through whom the whole body is to grow, built up in love. And here we find the place of authority in the Body, for all functions within it are given by Christ to build up the Body, and there are shepherds and teachers to serve those other members who all have their own function and their own grace. So again it is on our membership in the Body that St Paul bases motives for moral action. Because we are members one of another, we are to tell each other the truth and not lie, nor be puffed up and ambitious, nor steal, but work in order to be able to help others; honour, and sympathize with one another, and keep unity by a charity that is kindly, merciful and forgiving (Eph. 4: 11-32; 1 Cor. 12: 31). The motives he gives for chastity—and the thing is to be noted by Christian educators—are not expressed in terms of the holiness of the Law, but in those of the holiness of the body, which is a sanctuary of the Holy Spirit and a member of Christ, belonging to him and not to us (1 Cor. 6: 13-20). It is when he speaks of the Jews and the pagans that he cites the Law which they should obey—either the Law of Moses or that which their conscience finds within them (Rom. 2: 12-16).

Here, then, is the strong, positive, glad morality of St Paul. Its structure is Trinitarian. The Father's love took the initiative in our salvation and willed that we should be like his Son, incorporated in him who died and rose for us (Rom. 5: 8-11), and this assimilation is the work of the Holy Spirit: 'May the grace of our Lord Jesus Christ and the love of God and the communion of the Holy Spirit be with you all' (2 Cor. 13: 13). That imparting of the Spirit (not genuine if it leads to breaking the commandments or opposing the teaching of Jesus, Gal. 5: 16ff; 1 Cor. 12: 3), is constitutive of Christian life. It is essential in the life of prayer, for only the Spirit who is from the Father can sound the depths of God and teach us to pray as we ought (1 Cor. 2: 10–16), so here contemplation joins with morality. The Christian life is to be lived in the fear and reverence of God (Phil. 2: 12), but in great confidence, boldness and power; for God makes all things work together for good for those who love him (Rom. 8: 28), and is able to do infinitely more than we ask for or can conceive (Eph. 3: 20); so that being 'filled with all the fullness of God', we can do all things in him who gives us strength (Eph. 3: 19; Phil. 4: 13). Since he gave us his own Son when we were sinners, how can he fail to give us all other graces too (Rom. 8: 32)? So while it is salutary to realize that we must all appear before Christ's tribunal (Rom. 14: 10), the prospect of death should be a reason for joy to those who love Christ, since it means union of all of us together with him (1 Thess. 4: 18). For his friends, to live is Christ, and to die and be with him is much the better (Phil. 1: 21–4).[1]

The purpose and essential character of the relations between the sexes had already been shown in Genesis: God blessed man and woman and said: 'increase and multiply . . . a man is to leave his father and mother and cleave to his wife, and they will become two in one flesh' (Gen. 1: 28; 2: 24). Christ recalled marriage to this God-given dignity and uniqueness, explaining that the Mosaic permission for divorce had been a concession to 'hardness of heart' (Mt. 5: 31f; 19: 3–12). The shocked surprise of the disciples, and the fact that the other Synoptists and St Paul (Rom. 7: 3; 1 Cor. 7: 39) make no exceptions, suggest that the phrase 'except for unchastity' in Matthew must bear some other meaning understandable to contemporary Jews, and it is highly probable that the word here translated 'unchastity' meant, as also in Acts 15: 20, and 1 Cor. 5: 1, an invalid marriage within degrees of kin forbidden by the Mosaic Law.[2] Teaching in a society with a healthy moral code, Christ did not need to say much on sex. But he marked the wrongfulness of unlawful desire (Mt. 5: 27, 28), honoured marriage by his presence (Jn. 2), used the marriage-feast as a symbol for his Kingdom, invited those to whom it was given to virginity for the sake

[1] Terrible wreckage has been made in morality by errors about St Paul's doctrine of Predestination. With him, it is a doctrine of hope: God, who has begun a good work in us, will not for his part give it over. We can fail (e.g. 1 Cor. 9: 27), but that is our own fault, and so far from decreeing anyone's damnation, God shows much patience (Rom. 9: 19ff). What St Paul says of the 'rejection' of collectivities or 'types' is not simply to be applied to the lot of individuals, and the Semitic expression 'hate' means to prefer someone else to that person. Cf. *A Catholic Commentary*, art. cit.

[2] J. Bonsirven, S. J., *Le Divorce dans le N.T.* (1948).

of the Kingdom (Mt. 19: 11, 12; 22: 2ff) and showed kindly and sympathetic forgiveness to repentant sinners (Lk. 7: 37; Jn. 8: 3ff).

St Paul was dealing with pagan converts living in an immoral society, and had often to speak of the rights and duties of marriage, upon which 1 Cor. 7 is a little treatise. It is quite untrue that he depressed the condition of women; on the contrary he initiated a revolution in contemporary morals by insisting that the wife had equal rights with her husband, and the man equal duties of fidelity. It is equally wrong to think that he regarded marriage as no more than a *remedium concupiscentiae*, a remedy for sexual desire. Writing to a congregation in a corrupt city, he gives advice full of common sense, but he calls the married state a 'grace', a 'charisma', one of those God-given states in the Mystical Body whereby that Body is built up in Christ (1 Cor. 7: 7). And to the Ephesians he describes the union of husband and wife in terms of the mystical union of Christ and the Church, a wonderful passage from which is rightly inferred that Christian marriage is a sacrament by whose grace husband and wife are enabled to love each other even to death with a share in Christ's own love (Eph. 5: 22–33).[1] He defends marriage against heretics, and makes clear that its pleasures are God's gift, to be received with thanksgiving and sanctified by prayer (1 Tim. 3: 35), and the Epistle to the Hebrews speaks of the dignity and holiness of the marriage relations (Heb. 13: 4).

At the same time St Paul firmly upholds the hierarchy in the family. The wife is to reverence and be subject to her husband, while he is to love and cherish her with tender respect. She wins her salvation by her Christian motherhood. Children are to obey their parents in all things 'in the Lord'—which shows the right motive and limits; the father is not to be unkind to the children, lest they lose heart (Eph. 5: 21–6: 4; Col. 3: 18–21; 1 Tim. 2: 15).

Those who reject celibacy have been hard put to it to explain St Paul's teaching that a state of virginity dedicated to Christ's service (this is the crucial point) is even better than marriage. To this, and the undivided attention which it makes possible, he invites those to whom it is given (1 Cor. 7).

Where this great synthesis on the use and sanctification of sex has been put into practice, men and women have risen to heights of holiness and society has been healthy. St Paul may be thought to have known what he was doing when he set the ideal of virginity

---

[1] Marriage is a 'second best' only for those who turn down a call to consecrated virginity.

before the pleasure-loving Corinthians, and the ideal of Christian marriage before the Manichaeist Ephesians.[1] The magnificence of God's creation, fearlessly accepted, is filled by the spirit of Christ and the sacrificial love of the Cross.

Of the social morality of St Paul there is only space to say that his remedy for evils is not a revolution—to have abolished slavery would have meant economic disaster and been anyhow impossible —but the penetration of the spirit of the Gospel. 'There is neither bond nor free, for you are all one in Christ' (Gal. 3: 28). Slaves were to have the dignity of serving Christ in their master, and masters to remember the rights of the slave and that the Lord who would judge was no respecter of persons (Eph. 6: 5–9). The eventual result has been the abolition of slavery.

St John's moral teaching is summed up in his first Epistle. 'God is love; he who dwells in love, dwells in God and God in him. . . If we love one another, then we have God dwelling in us, and the love of God has reached its full growth in our lives . . . love has no room for fear . . . love drives out fear when it is perfect . . . we love God because he gave us his love first' (1 Jn. 4: 9–21). St John's moral teaching goes straight to the Word Incarnate and flows back upon men. What a warning to systematizers not to separate Christian morals from contemplation! With sin the 'son of thunder' tolerates no compromise: 'Let no one deceive you . . . he who sins is of the devil . . . he who does not love abides in death' (1 Jn. 3: 7–15). If we say we have no sin, we deceive ourselves, but if we confess our sin, God is merciful to forgive, and the blood of Christ cleanses us from all sin (1 Jn. 1: 7–10). But how positive it all is! We must love, and we must come to the Light, the worst tragedy of sin being that it stops men coming to the Light because their works are evil (Jn. 3: 19). For men remain in darkness unless they come to the saving Light (1 Jn. 1: 4, 5).

This matter of the Light illustrates the way in which St John's contemplation sees all morality in Christ. The early Christians, St Paul included, followed the Jewish moralists in speaking of the ways of light and darkness according as men lived virtuously or sinfully, (e.g. 2 Cor. 6: 14), and fashioned their precepts and lists of sins accordingly. But for St John the 'way' is not a series of precepts, but Christ, and the 'children of the light' are not just those who keep commandments, but those who walk by him who is the True Light which enlightens every man (Jn. 1: 9; 8: 12; 12: 46). Again, life

---

[1] Knox, *A New Testament Commentary*, II, p. 144.

has been promised to those who kept the Commandments (Lev. 18: 5), but now it is Christ who is the Life and gives eternal life to those who eat his flesh and drink his blood (Jn. 14: 6; ch. 6). The Gospel Prologue marks the opposition between the Jewish exaltation of the Law given by Moses and the grace and truth brought by the Divine Word Incarnate (Jn. 1: 2, 17).

The Paschal Supper commemorated the 'passing' from Egypt's slavery into God's Land of Promise, the commandments being given on the way. When Jesus, who so loved his own, was about to pass from this world to the Father, he started the Supper with the washing of the feet—a practical lesson in love and humility. During it, he poured out his heart to his disciples for whom he was dying, and gave the new commandment which bade them love as he was doing: 'I am the vine, you the branches; abide in me, and I in you. . . As the Father has loved me I also have loved you. Abide in my love. If you keep my commandments, you will abide in my love . . . a new commandment I give you . . . this is my commandment: that you love one another, as I have loved you' (Jn. 13: 34; 15: 1–12). Love of God and man cannot be separated: 'He who loves not his brother whom he sees, cannot love God whom he does not see' (1 Jn. 4: 20). This love is to be Christ's. Morality can go no higher.

'Everything in the Scriptures has been divinely inspired and has its uses: to instruct us, to expose our errors, to correct our faults, to educate us in holy living' (2 Tim. 3: 16). Indeed, as St Jerome said, to be ignorant of the Scriptures is to be ignorant of Christ—and so of Christian morality. The Fathers, who knew their Bible so well, used its great stories, as they were meant to be used, to instruct on the moral life, seeing the Old Law fulfilled in the New. Christendom came from men who knew their Bible, and, very soon, as the Christian spirit unfolded, there became apparent the moral riches contained in the Biblical account of all that concerns the Virgin Mother of God.

Throughout Christian history heresy has distorted this or that Biblical datum with terrible effect; indeed much of the contemporary revolt from morals is the result. Yet, even within heresy, knowledge of the Scriptures and personal love of Christ helped to counteract the particular tendency. The Catholic Church kept the whole Bible and all its teaching, but Catholics, from ignorance or misinterpretation, allowed much of the charity which should have been theirs to grow cold. In fact, every age has fallen far short of Biblical morality, and needs to be brought back to the source. In our own time, we see dreams of material Messianism superseding the vision of the Kingdom of God. It is essential, therefore, that we should show that the coming of Christ is no *dies irae*, day of wrath, for his lovers, but a trysting, and amid the terrors of the atom bomb we can repeat: 'When you see these things come to pass, lift up your hearts, because your redemption is at hand' (Lk. 21: 28).

We cannot oppose an earthly paradise by a negative morality of prohibitions and threats. Christianity is a returning to paradise, and it is the vision of the reign of Christ and the paradise of God that draws the hearts of men. 'I am now sending thee to the gentiles. Thou shalt open their eyes and turn them from darkness to light, from the power of Satan to God, so that they may receive, through faith in me, remission of their sins and an inheritance among the saints' (Acts 26: 18; Apoc. 2: 7).

IV

THE HISTORICAL INFLUENCE OF
THE GREEKS AND ROMANS ON
CHRISTIAN MORALITY

by

Hilary Armstrong

INTRODUCTORY NOTE

THE study of Greek morality is obviously necessary for a full understanding of the European Christian tradition. It may however seem of less importance to those who hold most strongly that Catholic Christianity is not only European but universal and that one of the great tasks imposed on Catholicism in our times is to disentangle Catholicism from its European setting and to express it in terms of other traditions of thought and culture. This concern with adaptation is entirely legitimate: but it should not lead us to think that we can neglect any living part of our existing tradition. The adaptation of Catholicism cannot mean its disincarnation. We cannot just take the 'spirit of Catholicism' out of its European body and put it into an Asiatic or African one. The life of the Body of Christ will go on, and may well pass from a purely or predominantly European to a predominantly Asiatic or African stage of development. But, because it is the continuous life of one body, it will inevitably bring a great deal of its past with it. Just as we English Catholics are and ought to be not just purely English but Jewish and Greek, Syrian and Roman and much else besides in our religious life and thought, so the Asiatic or African Catholic will have to be all this and more, as well as Indian, Chinese or African. And if his attitude to all this complex past is neither merely servile nor merely hostile but one of live, intelligent and discriminating affection, his own culture will benefit from it without any danger to its own vitality and individuality. A 'pure' culture is as unreal and unattractive a conception as a 'pure' race. All the great peoples and all the great cultures (most of all our own) are magnificent mongrels.

ONE of the main contributions of the Greeks to moral theory, as to philosophy in general, is the extraordinary variety of questions they raised and discussed, clearly, in simple terms, though with no lack of real subtlety and sensitiveness, and often in very memorable language. We find in Greek thought moral relativism, extreme and in various more moderate forms; we find the attempt to deduce the laws which ought to govern human behaviour from scientific observation of the way in which men, or at least certain carefully selected men, actually behave; and we find the assertion of the existence of a divine, universal and absolute moral law discoverable by the human reason because of its kinship with the divine. It is this last line of thought, which became the central and dominant one in Greek philosophy after Aristotle, which, so it seems to me, provided the main positive contribution of Greek and Roman thought to Christian morality. I therefore propose to concentrate in this paper on its great idea of natural or divine moral law, and also to say something about its ideal of human goodness, the perfect philosopher; for to the men of this central tradition, from Plato and Aristotle onwards, philosophy was a love of and pursuit of wisdom in a sense which both presupposed and included moral goodness. You could not be a wise man, a *sophos*, without also being a nobly good one, a *spoudaios*. We all know how important the idea of natural law has been in Christian morality; and the ideal of the perfect philosopher appealed so strongly to Christians, at least to educated Christians, from the time when they first came really to know it, and seemed to them so in tune with their own ideals,[1] that it was quite natural to them to represent Christ on sarcophagi in the dress of a philosopher;[2] the early development of monasticism was strongly influenced by the asceticism of late Greek philosophers—St Gregory of Nyssa even speaks of the monastic life as 'the philosophic life': and this asceticism, and the whole ideal of the *spoudaios*, has left its mark on later Christian moral theory and practice. This concentration means that I shall, unavoidably, in a paper of this sort, have to leave out a very great deal that is worth talking about. My few generalizations about main tendencies do not at all represent adequately the richness and variety of Greek moral discussion. I shall

---

[1] Except in the extremely important matter of humility. I shall say more about this later.

[2] Admittedly this was an adaptation of a pagan art-convention, but even so, Christians would hardly have tolerated it if they had not felt there was some real harmony between the philosophic ideal and the perfection of Christ.

be able to say very little about the attempts of the great fifth-century Sophists to develop a purely humanist morality. I shall have to leave out many of the most interesting and important moral discussions in Plato and Aristotle—those, for instance, on pleasure and self-love. We shall not be able to explore the ethical byway which leads to the garden of Epicurus, that passionate prophet of a fugitive and cloistered virtue, who only comes into the history of natural law in a negative way, because he protested so strongly against the idea and its whole metaphysical background as one of the deadliest causes of fear and anxiety in the minds of men. The worst omission, from the point of view of this paper, is that I shall say nothing about the great contribution of Aristotle to what may be called technical scholastic ethics. To do so would take us very far from the main subject of the paper and, if I tried to deal with the subject at all adequately, would involve a great deal of detailed discussion, of interest only to specialists, which I do not really feel competent to undertake. Also, I believe myself that the decisive influence, here as elsewhere, of Greek thought on Christianity was the influence of Platonists and Stoics (who had learnt a great deal from Aristotle) on the Fathers rather than the much later, relatively restricted and secondary, influence of Aristotle on the Scholastics.

Originally there was only unwritten law in Greece; there as in other societies the rules regulating societies and human behaviour were an affair of custom and tradition, considered as having some sort of divine sanction. When written codes of laws came into existence in the different states there continued to be recognized 'unwritten laws', customs and traditions which were not incorporated in state laws and some of which, like those dealing with the right of burial and the protection of suppliants, were regarded as having a very special divine sanction. But there is not in these beliefs any idea of a divine universal law superior to the positive law of states, though it was easy for such an idea to develop out of them: and we must not forget that positive state law was very often regarded as itself sacred and divinely sanctioned; for the Greek city was church as well as state, a religious society united by the common worship of the city gods and heroes which was its chief duty. The idea of a divine universal law did however appear early in Greek thought. In the Ionian philosophers we find the idea of a cosmic law which maintains justice among the contending elements of the universe; and one of them at least, Heraclitus, makes this law a living law, a divine intelligence, and the source of human law.

All human laws are nourished by one, the divine: for it governs as far as it will, and suffices for all, and overcomes all.[1]

And in the great Athenian religious dramatists of the fifth century, Aeschylus and Sophocles, the idea of a universal divine moral law appears clearly. In the *Antigone*, above all, Sophocles has expressed with unsurpassed force and clearness the reality of the divine law and its absolute superiority to all human laws. Antigone is one of the great symbolic figures of the doctrine of natural law. She dies for obeying the gods rather than men, for the divine law which she apprehends in an inseparable unity with her love for her dead brother; and her opponent, Creon, who maintains against her the law and order of the state in inseparable unity with his own self-importance, is left at the end by the bodies of his wife and son, who have died by their own hands, hating him, as the result of his action and for his punishment. Here is a rough translation of Antigone's answer to Creon when he asks why she has not obeyed his regulations.[2]

It was not Zeus who made me this proclamation, nor did Justice, who keeps house with the gods below, lay down laws like these for men. I did not think that your proclamation had such strength that you, a mortal, could over-run the sure, unwritten customs of the gods; for these are not of today or yesterday, but live for ever, and no one knows from where they came to light. I was not going to pay for breaking these in the gods' court through fear of any man's intentions. I knew quite well that I was going to die—how should I not?—even if you had not announced it. But if I am to die before my time, then I myself regard it as a gain. If anyone lives as I do in much trouble how can it not be a gain to die? There is no pain for me in finding this fate, but if I had left the body of my mother's son unburied, that would have made me suffer; there is no suffering in *this*. And if you think I am behaving foolishly, perhaps it is a fool who condemns my folly.

But in the fifth century there also appeared the first criticism of the idea of natural and divinely sanctioned morality in the great *nomos-phusis* controversy, the argument about whether religion and morality were in some way rooted in the nature of things, or were just matters of human custom and convention, of which the first signs appear in Herodotus. The argument had started before the appearance of the Sophists, those dignified wandering professors, teaching the art of success in life for extremely high fees, who were

[1] Diels, *Vorsokratiker*, 1. 22.B.114.   [2] ll. 450–70.

the first professional educators: and they should not be made entirely responsible for the great and pernicious influence which the idea of morality as only a human convention had in the later fifth and early fourth century. Their professional concerns did however lead them to a man-centred humanism, agnostic in religion, and relativist in morality. Protagoras seems to have tried very hard to find some sort of satisfactory purely humanist basis for morality; but some Sophists, and, still more, some of their aristocratic pupils, like the atheist tyrant Critias, went pretty well as far as possible in the direction of pure immoralism. It was against this exclusively man-centred relativism that Socrates, and Plato, following him and vastly developing his teaching, reacted. In speaking about Plato, I must be very short and excessively overdogmatic. The alternative would be to go on for hours and hours, and pages and pages—finally reaching with triumphant assurance conclusions which probably no other student of Plato would accept. As I see it, the essentials of Plato's moral teaching are these. There exist eternal, divine, unchanging moral standards which are objective, transcendent realities, the moral Forms or Ideas, with their mysterious first principle the Form of the Good, which is 'beyond being', 'cause of being and intelligence', 'the sun of the intelligible world'. These are natural in the profoundest sense because the world of Forms or Ideas is true being, the real nature of things, and because it is man's natural end and purpose to know them and live by them, and because according to them the whole universe is directed. For there are also gods, and one supreme God, who have formed and rule the universe with perfect wisdom and goodness. I do not think that Plato himself makes the relationship between Forms and God sufficiently clear for us to be sure what he thought, though the Middle and Neo-Platonists develop from his writings the doctrine of the Ideas as 'thoughts of God' which has passed into Christian philosophy. In any case it does seem to me clear that Plato thought that the end and purpose of man was simply to be as good a man as possible and that he could attain the end by the right use of his god-like intelligence to know the Forms, know, worship and obey the gods, and rule his lower emotions and desires; and that success or failure in this would be rewarded or punished with inexorable justice in the next world.

We should note that in Plato's philosophy 'natural' has acquired the sense which it kept for ever after in Greek and Christian moral thinking; it refers, that is, not to the way in which people actually behave but the way they ought to behave. Its use implies that moral goodness is in the nature of things and that our nature has an end or purpose which it must accomplish and a standard which it must reach if we are really to be our true selves. It is most important that we should explain to our contemporaries that this is what we mean when we talk about 'natural law' or in general use 'natural' in a moral context. The infidels will very easily get the better of us if we let them involve us in argument on the assumption that 'natural' refers to the way in which people, or animals, in fact behave—as when we say that it is 'natural' for a cat to be sick occasionally, and 'natural' for the poor beast's master to lose his temper on the occasion.

Aristotle abandoned Plato's transcendent moral standards. This was part of the general movement of his mind away from Platonic metaphysics and religion, which continued in his school and led the early Peripatetics to something much more like modern scientific atheism and materialism than anything else in Greek thought, and, possibly, to the attempt to produce a purely empirical morality based on scientific observation of biological facts (we really do not *know* very much about the early Peripatetics; there is a great deal of intensive research into, and vigorous debate about, their ethics, going on at the moment, and it would be most unsafe to be too positive). But Aristotle's own mature and fully-developed moral philosophy is not of the scientific-empirical type. (In describing it I shall have again, as with Plato, to be much too short and over-dogmatic.) Aristotle is, in his own way, as thoroughgoing a teleologist as Plato. He believes that man has a natural end which it is the whole purpose of human life to fulfil as completely as possible. There is for him no divine moral standard for man, transcending human nature; so he thinks that the way to arrive at a knowledge of the good which is man's end is by a philosophical inspection, clarification and logical development of the moral presuppositions of good men—and in practice this means, of good, intelligent, upper-class Greeks. The good man becomes the source of moral standards; and Aristotle insists that the process of moral philosophizing can only be carried out by men of mature and settled moral goodness. The foundation of morality in Aristotle's thought may seem to us very shaky. But, given that the men whose moral presuppositions are being inspected are really good men and that the study is carried on with a good deal of practical wisdom, moral sensitiveness and insight, the method is obviously capable of throwing a great deal of light on particular moral problems, and providing a good deal of stimulation to living well: and in fact no one can read Aristotle's ethical treatises with any degree of genuine understanding without being aware that he is dealing with a really great moralist whose conclusions on particular points usually deserve to be treated with much respect. And his insistence that man is essentially a moral being and that his attainment of his end is first and foremost a matter of moral and intellectual virtue has no doubt had a great influence in many times and places in making men see that the moral law is not arbitrary or conventional, but profoundly natural. There are many worse moral philosophies than an Aristotelianism which has not lost touch with Platonism; when it does, the history of the early Peripatetic school may show us what happens; it leads straight into a scientific humanism which is the most profoundly irreligious of all humanisms, because it not only denies God, but blocks all the roads of thought which might lead men's minds back to him.

With the Stoics, the idea of a universal, divine moral law, rooted in the nature of things, binding on all men, found its full expression. Plato's moral law was in principle universal; but he did not attempt, in theory or practice, to apply it to public affairs except in terms of individual Greek city-states. But the Stoics put forward with admirable clearness and force the idea of the whole universe as one great city-state, the 'city of God', governed by the universal law which was the divine reason, superior to all local human laws, naturally known to and binding on all men, and under which, ideally at least, all men were brothers and equal except for their difference in virtue. The practical effects of this doctrine were by no means as revolutionary as a simple statement of it might suggest; but, after all, the same might be said of Christianity; and the Stoic ideal did often make a very considerable difference to the practice of the many Greek and Roman statesmen and rulers whom it influenced. Unfortunately the doctrine of natural law in Stoicism is bound up with a crude pantheism which represents God as material and wholly immanent in the universe, a sort of perfectly good and wise gas pervading all things. But this made less practical difference than might be supposed, for in their personal religion and morality, the Stoics were most inconsistent and paradoxical pantheists, and would think of, and pray to the God of whom they claimed to be actual physical parts in a way only appropriate to a transcendent spiritual being. And their doctrine of natural law was easily detachable from strict Stoic pantheism and became part of the common stock of ideas connected with a vaguely uplifting cosmic theism which attracted many people, round about the beginning of our era, who were not adherents of any precise philosophical school. Here, for instance, is perhaps the finest statement of it, which does not necessarily imply any sort of pantheism; it comes from the *De Republica* of Cicero, who, whatever exactly he was, was certainly not a Stoic.

> The true law is right reason in accordance with nature, spread abroad among all men, stable and eternal. . . This law may not be amended, nor are we allowed to restrict its application, nor can it be altogether repealed; nor can senate or people free us from this law, nor must we look for anyone else to explain or interpret it. There is not one law at Rome and another at Athens, nor one now and another hereafter, but for all time one eternal, unchangeable law will bind all peoples, and there will be one common master and commander of all, God, who drew up, spoke for, and put forward this law. He who does not obey it, is running away from himself, and by the very fact that he despises the nature of man, will suffer the worst of punishments, even if he escapes the other torments which people believe in. [1]

In the teaching of the Neoplatonist Plotinus, who is the last of the really great pagan moralists, attention is concentrated on the individual rather than society. Philosophers in the Hellenistic and Roman periods were often spiritual directors as well as teachers; and of all those directors of whose activity we know anything, the greatest and most attractive was Plotinus. He was a man who devoted his life to giving help to other people—spiritual help first and foremost, but also if they needed it, help of an extremely material and practical kind. [2] So it is primarily with individual perfection that he is concerned. But in his teaching, the doctrine of the eternal divine law which is the divine thought is provided with a more satisfying metaphysical foundation than it had yet had, one which was taken over by Christian philosophers with few, though important, modifications. In his system, the moral Ideas or Forms, with all the others, exist eternally in inseparable unity with a Divine Intellect which is pure spirit. Stoic materialism and pantheism are explicitly rejected, and so is the theoretically absolute determinism that went with them. And man's moral life is given a new depth

---

[1] *De Republica*, III. 22. 33. Cicero throughout the passage is using the language of Roman constitutional procedure.

[2] Cf. Porphyry's *Life*, Chapters 9 and 11 (pp. 49–50 in my *Plotinus*).

and a new significance because for Plotinus it is not only the way of serving God, but the way to union with God, and God is the only good for man, and nothing in life is really important except to find the way to him.

It was this insistence that man's whole life ought to be a journey to God, and that nothing matters except finding him, and the radical demand that went with it for the separation of the mind from all earthly desires and ambitions (and the giving up, if possible, of all earthly possessions) which the Christian fathers admired in the pagan philosophers. They recognized them as true seekers after God, and they thought that the Platonists in particular knew a good deal about him. They also saw in them a great fault of pride, in that they believed that they could reach God by their own strength, and despised the only true way by Christ and his Cross; and in this the Fathers were on the whole right. It would not be true to say that there is *no* room for anything corresponding to the grace of God in Plotinus's system; it would be true to say that there is very little room for it. He has very little sense of the contingency and precariousness of creaturely existence, and of man's absolute dependence for his goodness on the generosity of God. It is this that makes the greatest difference in the atmosphere when one turns from Plotinus to St Augustine. And it is this which makes Plotinus, and all other pagan philosophers, so unsympathetic towards the wicked, and even the weak. If you regard goodness as your own conquest and achievement, you will naturally be proud of it, and feel little sympathy for those who have failed to attain it. But though the Fathers criticized the pride of the pagan philosophers, they admired, adopted and practised their austerity. One of their strongest reasons for allowing, and even recommending, the reading of Greek philosophy, was that it taught men to despise earthly things and to look for human well-being to the life of virtue alone which leads to God. In the controversy between Stoics and Platonists on the one side, and Aristotelians on the other, about whether virtue alone was sufficient for well-being, or whether 'external goods' were necessary also, the early Christians were solidly on the side of the Stoics and Platonists. We should not, by the way, misrepresent Aristotle's position. The 'external goods' in whose necessity he believed were not precisely material comforts and amenities. They were good birth, good looks, good children and good friends, a position enabling one to do noble service to the community, and enough material goods to enable one to practise the virtue of generosity.

Aristotle would have regarded anyone who thought it moral and civilized to devote one's life to money-making, or to keep on increasing one's material needs and exploiting the universe to satisfy them, with nearly as much moral indignation and quite as much intellectual contempt as the Stoics or Plotinus. The question (a much more difficult one to answer than some people appear to think) about the precise difference between the Platonic and the Christian attitudes towards the body and the senses is not really relevant to an attempt to determine the value of this austerity of the pagan philosophers and the Christian Fathers, because the demand for complete detachment and the insistence that virtue alone is enough for human well-being are common to both Stoics and Neoplatonists. Nobody could have accepted the physical world more thoroughly, in theory at least, than the Stoics, for whom it was the only possible, and the best possible, world, because it was God, or, in the most dualistic possible way of putting it, God's body. But on this point of morality, their teaching is the same as that of the most other-worldly of Neoplatonists, Plotinus. (There are of course other important differences between the moral teaching of Plotinus and that of the Stoics; on free-will and on the lawfulness of suicide he, and the Platonists in general, are much nearer to the Christian position than to that of Stoicism.) The Stoics' concentration on this world did not lead them to hold that anything in it was worth while except the life of virtue and service of God and men. (One might say of the ancient moralists, with few exceptions, that for them man's success and happiness in this world lay not in experiencing or having, but in being, and so making his proper and distinct contribution to the universal order by the perfection of his own nature; he is a performer in the Great Dance, not a member of the audience, and it doesn't matter how much he sees of it, or how much he enjoys it, as long as he does his part well.) And the Neoplatonists' vision of a destiny for man far transcending this world did not lead them to deny their duty to their fellow men here and now, or to disbelieve in the goodness of the visible world. There is nothing in the writings of Plotinus like the terrible disgust and weariness with the world which breaks through sometimes in the diary of the Stoic Marcus Aurelius. The *Enneads* are full of imagery which shows an intense delight in the beauty of this world, as they are full of the clearest affirmations that it is a good and holy world, though not the best and holiest. And in fact, Neoplatonic philosophy has generally appealed to poets and artists, and has more than once been a powerful stimulus to science as well as art. Nor is there in genuine Platonic morality any neurotic horror of sex or exaggeration of the importance of sexual sin. For both Plato and Plotinus the sensualist, the lover of beautiful bodies, is on the road to God, though with a very long way to go—Dom Illtyd Trethowan has spoken of a great passage in Plato's *Symposium* as 'the first *Itinerarium mentis ad Deum* in our Western records'[1] —and Plotinus shows the same road in his treatise *On Dialectic*.[2] For Plato, the man who is certainly on the way to be hung up for ever in hell as an awful example is not the lover, even in the most superficial and carnal sense of that word, but the tyrannical man, the ambitious, utterly unscrupulous careerist whose unmeasured passion for wealth and power leads him into injustice and cruelty to others.

To sum up, then. It seems to me that the greatest positive contributions to Christian morality which came from the Graeco-Roman tradition were, first, the clearly formulated conception of an absolute and universal moral law rooted in the nature of God and naturally knowable to man by that in him which is at once most fully human and most Godlike, his intellect; and second, the highest ideal, perhaps, of human goodness that man without the help of revelation and grace has ever reached. The Christian saint, certainly, transcends the pagan sage: but that does not give very commonplace, imperfect, worldly Christians like ourselves the right to patronize Socrates, Epictetus or Plotinus, still less the great saints and doctors of the Church who admired them, and in many ways shared their ideal.

---

[1] *The Meaning of Existence*, p. 176.   [2] *Enn.* i. 3.

V

THE HISTORICAL INFLUENCE OF THE EARLIER AND LATER MIDDLE AGES ON MORALITY

by

Dom Aelred Watkin

IN one sense there is something singularly unsatisfactory in dealing with periods or epochs. In the first place, the tendencies of any particular age cannot neatly be pigeon-holed into divisions of time so largely artificial. If we analyse the temper of mind prevailing in a given period we shall find that not only were there many, even in that age, who were not typical of it but also that there were many, living perhaps centuries beforehand or afterwards, whose whole viewpoint is typical of the age of which we speak. That is one reason why it is so often dangerous to speak of any period or periods in isolation.

But there is also another difficulty. We may perhaps with some accuracy diagnose a prevailing temper of mind, but we soon discover that the translation of a fresh mental outlook into terms of concrete behaviour does not take place immediately, nor in every branch of thought or culture. As a general rule, I think, we may regard painting, for instance, as a progressive art and one that reflects the spirit of the age almost immediately; but music, on the other hand, seems usually to be a conservative one. We can notice this tendency in almost all fields. Theological thought, as reflected in the outlook of the ordinary man, is never a consistent expression of changes in the climate of opinion. There will be progressive and conservative elements, some of which will achieve victory in some fields, others in others. Thus any general statement we may choose to make about the moral teaching and practical behaviour of any age must always be modified by these considerations. There will always be exceptions, always incongruities, always facts which would seem to contradict the generalizations we have made.

Armed then with these preliminary considerations and warnings we may now—for our purpose—divide the Middle Ages into two halves: the Age of Growth and the Age of Decline.

It is then to the first of these two periods—the age between the coronation of Charlemagne and the twelfth and thirteenth centuries —that we may first turn. On the material level it was, in the main, an epoch when barbarism and invasion were giving place to organized institutions of Christian government. At a deeper level it was a time when men attempted, though fitfully and uncertainly, to translate the Kingdom and rule of Christ into terms of human institutions and modes of behaviour. We have then these two elements at work: the material forms and institutions, a syncretism of Greco-Roman and barbarian elements, and below these the consciousness of Christ reigning in and through the hearts of the baptized, informing and moulding these material forms and institutions and prompting standards of conduct.

In considering the springs of moral behaviour during this time we must, I feel, keep before our minds certain presuppositions which were latent, if not always formulated.

First, there was a profound consciousness that by grace man is so united with Christ that Christ lives in him and he in Christ. With and in Christ man can do all things, without him he can do nothing. We can see at once that if we are made so one with Christ that St Paul can say 'I live, now not I, but Christ lives in me' certain consequences follow immediately. In the first place, the life of Christ is an eternal one, and therefore if we live by it we are already in the depths of our being living in eternity. It is true that we can die to this eternal life by choosing something less, but that life can never die to us, nor can human events take it from us unless we will them to do so. Hope is then based upon a certainty not only that victory will be ours unless we deliberately and consciously throw it away, but that victory is in a sense already ours. Hope does not therefore convey the suggestion that its consummation is a precarious one, but rather it is a trust and confidence that all is well, and is well now. The keynote of the life of the Christian is a confidence which strikes at the roots of fear.

Another result of this sense of oneness with the living Christ is that the world of human experience acquires a new validity. Our thoughts, our actions, our efforts, are actions of the Christ within us; all that we say or do, save for sin and selfishness, is an action of Christ. This means that every action, save for sin, is a sacramental one. In itself the material world is dying—we are dying, all is dying.

We die by words, by breaths, by days, by hours. All round us are the marks of death. The trees wither, houses fall, rocks erode, empires vanish—all is fugitive and evanescent. Apart from Christ everything is phenomenal, all is a symbol of death. With Christ, on the other hand, everything changes its character: material things as seen, heard and handled by Christ become not symbols of death but sacraments of life. The life of Christ in men is gradually transmuting the material world from its old insubstantiality. Time and place become sacramental expressions of eternal life, and in that life all human experience finds its fulfilment and its meaning. Because our actions are the actions of Christ the effects of them stretch out beyond time and place, because they are the actions of Christ they become a real participation in the redemption of the world. In fact the Christian does not merely receive the merits of the redemption of Christ but actually shares in that redemption itself. Thus it is that every human action, thought and impulse which is not sin has a real and abiding value. Everything is worth while and our actions are charged with a content of reality which we cannot even begin to conceive.

Finally, oneness of the individual with Christ supposes a oneness between all Christians. One with him they are one with each other. Therefore the Catholic Church is not merely a body of men subscribing to the same doctrinal formulae and obeying the same visible head, but a real living unity, a unity that stretches out beyond time and place, though incarnate in time and place. Indeed, all corporate institutions of human society are no chance aggregations of individuals, but corporate bodies in which each member is as necessary for the others as the others are necessary for him.

Put very roughly and briefly, these are some of the consequences that follow from the Christian doctrine of oneness with Christ; a doctrine which consciously underlay both the institutions and the moral teaching of the period of which we are speaking. Moral teaching was therefore conceived of as the guide to growth, the law of love as the law of nature. If all things were created by God through Christ—*omnia per ipsum facta sunt*—to use them according to his will in grace is *instaurare omnia in Christo*, to wrest them from the effects of evil and refashion them into what they originally were and at root are—because made through 'the Image of the invisible God', the revelation in time and place of uncreated beauty.

Moral behaviour, then, to this way of thinking is not something that is made, its principles are not constructive (in the legal sense),

c

it is but the expression in the world of action of what is; it is but treating facts as facts. All positive law, whether of Church or state, is seen but as an adaptation and expression in particular circumstances of those divine and natural laws which are but the intrinsic laws of reality.

But another factor must also be taken into consideration. If Christ becomes incarnate in the heart of every Christian, he does so uniquely in each individual. Each individual—because possessing a unique personality—expresses Christ uniquely in this world of time and place. Each man in Christ can do what no one else has ever done or can ever do again. And by so doing he consecrates his material environment uniquely. It is from this angle that we should approach the so-called feudal system. Indeed, as St Anselm said, 'and is not he who is called a serf in the Lord, the Lord's freeman?' and the Popes now began to call themselves *servi servorum Dei*, a title which would among contemporaries inevitably be translated as 'serfs of the serfs of God'. Thus John, the villein, ploughing the West Field of Stratton-on-the-Fosse on Monday, March 27, 1150 is (because it is he—John—tilling that piece of earth, then) spreading the Kingdom of God uniquely: he is carving his stone in that temple not made with hands, his action is of unique and eternal importance, he has a function in society, he has a justification for his existence not only in the world to come, but here now.[1] The whole social structure of society is based upon this concept of uniqueness of function; it is the attempt to reproduce on earth the society of the blessed in heaven.

Again, it was this awareness of the living presence of Christ in the heart and its uniquely multiplied and sacramental expression in the world of men that gives a positive tone to early medieval moral thinking. It was for a later age to develop a preoccupation with material causality, here it was the final cause which alone was considered, not only as the end of action but as the very interpretation of the material factors through which action works. Moral behaviour then, did not consist in avoiding sin but in doing good. It consisted positively in the carrying out of the divine and natural laws and it was certain that those laws could be discovered and could be obeyed and it was certain that in such obedience alone was freedom and fulfilment to be found. To give but one example: 'Husbands love your wives', says the Apostle. To the early medieval mind such love was therefore possible—but it was not love resting

---

[1] I am not of course claiming that John thought consciously in this way.

merely upon the intoxicating insecurity of romance, it was not something that 'happened', but it was something to be made, something to be done, something to be given. To love or not to love was in the power of man in Christ and love being the very love of Christ, Christ loving, cannot of itself know 'change or shadow of alteration'. Adultery was not wrong because forbidden, but forbidden because it was a flight from reality, the denial of a total handing over of oneself in love, the denial of the divine and therefore permanent character of human love in the hearts of the baptized.

Let us take another example. It was wrong to make more than the accustomed profit in commercial dealings: first, because any object of sale is—literally objectively—worth so much and no more and to pretend anything else is to fly from reality and therefore to sin; second, because money unjustly acquired is not what money should be—the material means sufficient to carry out a divinely ordained function in human society—therefore such money is unjustified, a material lie, something unreal in its context. Finally, because by depriving our neighbour we are attacking his function in society and are defrauding Christ. Behind and beyond all is that ultimate truth, pronounced by divine lips and consecrated by human experience, 'it is more blessed to give than to receive.' It was this truth that was seen—not as a special vocation for the unusually pious—but as a fact, as an expression of reality, a statement of the actual working of things.

We may take two other signs of the real nature of the underlying moral assumptions which I have described. It might well be said that the Vatican at the time of the reformation was a pattern of Victorian respectability compared with the Lateran during part of the tenth century. But there was never the slightest chance that the reform which followed from the tenth-century degradation should degenerate into an attack on traditional doctrine in the name either of humanism or of an individualistic Christianity. The second sign is that of the Benedictine monks of Cluny, and the long survival of their widespread foundations. No other medieval monastic reform maintained its fervour for three hundred years. The sheer substance of this achievement would have been impossible in an age whose underlying motives were not those we have described.

One could multiply examples indefinitely, but I hope enough has been said to show in very general terms the pre-suppositions which underlay the moral teaching of the early Middle Ages, of the period which we have termed the period of growth. Before moving

on to the next period, it may be as well, in passing, to mention the
Holy Roman Empire, perhaps the greatest achievement in the
sphere of organization of the early Middle Ages. It is mentioned
here, because, at a first and superficial glance, the strife between
pope and emperor might seem to contradict what has just been said
about the concepts that underlay early medieval society. Nevertheless if we look more closely we shall see that the Holy Roman Empire
was conceived of as the material expression in the sphere of politics
and administration of the rule of Christ; and if, as we frequently find
at the period, there is acute conflict between pope and emperor, it
was not in these earlier days that the secular was at war with the
ecclesiastical; rather it was precisely because no such distinction
existed that the trouble came. Both swords were thought to be held
in the hands of one person alone, Christ. Both pope and emperor
were considered to be Christ's vicars or representatives on earth. But
this concept of a double expression of a single power soon failed in
practice, for though not diarchic in theory (and to conceive it as
such is to misconceive the words of Pope Gelasius) it soon became
so in practice, for in practice it was seen that the functions of the
pope and emperor were to interpret Christ to the world in different
and distinct ways. The imperial rôle of ruler and lawgiver is not the
same as the papal prerogative of preserving truth and effectively
binding and loosing souls. Thus there is a deep gulf between Nicaea
and Canossa, between the capitularies of Aachen and the bull *Unam
Sanctam*. Nevertheless it was on account of this fundamental belief
in the unity of earthly administration, *omnis potestas data est mihi in
coelo et in terra* (all power is given to me in heaven, *and on earth*),
rather than in a frank recognition of diversity of function that disputes between pope and emperor raged.

The motto of Mary, Queen of Scots, was 'in my end is my beginning', but Peter Pan regarded his sixth birthday as 'the beginning of the end', and if I fix the thirteenth century as my dividing line
between an Age of Growth and one of Decline it is merely because
it is in that century that we can most clearly see both the culmination of growth and the onset of decay. It is clear that from this
century onward the outlook of earlier times was becoming greatly
modified. In practice the notion of a substantial union with Christ
was fading and as an inevitable result a profound disintegration of
human experience followed. This disintegration denied in practice
any real connexion between the material and the spiritual; there
were now two sets of laws, two categories of experience, the spiritual

and the material, the natural and the supernatural. Though it was admitted that the material and the natural could be fused with the spiritual and the supernatural, such a fusion was an accidental one, dependent not upon some substantial connexion between the two, but upon the purely subjective element of the purity of the intention of the individual. Instead of material things being used by Christ dwelling in men, they could only be used for Christ. This division once made, the chasm deepened as time went by. We can perhaps see this better if we look first at the one side and then at the other.

The spiritual, the eternal, was now—in practice—conceived of as something apart from the world of time and place, of experience and emotion. Existing thus apart, the spiritual inevitably began to be regarded in a different light. Among the devout two distinct classes of person appeared. There were the mystics and the contemplatives. But these were few in number and inevitably restricted in influence; the devout for the most part fell into our second category. For these more ordinary, perhaps less adventurous souls, the spiritual life cut out for itself fresh channels. Having lost in practice the conviction of complete oneness with a Christ living in them now, most of the devout tended to regard Christ merely as a historical figure to be imitated across the distance of centuries. This was by no means all loss: those ages are the period of a simple devotion to the humanity of Christ which yet gives us some scent of its fragrance; but it was by no means all gain.

We can see this clearly if we look at another trend with which this new outlook was closely allied. A loss of awareness of the presence of the life of the victorious and risen Christ in the human heart is bound to result in a feeling of precariousness. Hope has no longer that sense of profound assurance which should characterize it; if material things are bound up accidentally only with the life of the spirit, they must always be regarded with a certain fear, a certain suspicion. There is at this time a tendency to regard the created world as a huge ambush in which opportunities for sin, for selfishness, lurk behind every natural impulse. Suspended uneasily between a Christ who went from earth many centuries before, and a Last Judgement whose frowning advent might be expected at any moment, the devout naturally were filled with misgivings about the world around them. How easily may human love turn to sin, may human endeavour resolve itself into worldly ambition, how useless are the objects for which men strive! And behind all strides the grim figure of death, no longer seen as the culminating moment of human life when man in perfect confidence and trust hands himself over totally in utter sacrifice to the Father: death is now the spectre at the feast, the pursuer who is slowly gaining.

It was all these considerations that tended to invest later medieval religion with an autumnal sadness. *Les Trois Vifs et les trois Morts*, the horrific majesty of the Last Judgement, the Seven Deadly Sins with their appropriate punishments, appeared more and more upon the walls of the churches. Tombs now showed beneath the recumbent effigy of prince or bishop, in all the pomp of what was now regarded as purely human pride, a grisly corpse decaying in its marble shroud, and consumed by worms and reptiles. The Sorrows of our Lady, the physical sufferings of Christ, were more and more the objects of popular devotion. *Timor mortis conturbat me* was more and more upon the lips of the pious.

And in particular how tedious are so many of the moral treatises of the time! Contrary to usual belief the pious of the later Middle Ages indulged in a puritanism which went far beyond that seen in later times. How frequently marriage was denigrated as very much a 'second-best', how vividly were portrayed the dangers of human love, with what futility was all human endeavour depicted! No longer did men think in terms of wresting material things from death and frustration by the life of the Christ that was within them; rather they took a severely negative view which saw the pathway to heaven as one merely of avoiding sin and the occasions of it and of limiting human experience as far as possible.

Moreover this loss of a certainty based upon the evidences of things not seen led to an earnest desire for material assurance that all was well. The element in the sacraments of the Church that works almost irrespective of the state of mind of the minister, the *opus operatum* as the theologians call it, was the mainstay of the devout. There was little notion of really offering with the priest the Sacrifice of the Mass; instead the congregation were passive spectators of something that was automatically being wrought for them. The sacraments were tending to turn into the magical. Other assurances were eagerly sought for, indulgences tended to become more and more extensive, more and more eagerly sought for by the pious. To such a state did things come that pardons, relics, trentals and pilgrimages became in the eyes of many simple believers something not unlike a spiritual insurance policy.

'When religion becomes divorced from imagination', says Burckhardt, 'it leads to magic in the many and to rationalism in the few.' The elements of rationalism were far from lacking. Divorced from their counterpart in human experience, the dogmas of the Church tended, at the hands of theologians, to become arid matters of reasoning: subtleties increased, the expression of a dogma with theological precision came to be regarded as a total expression of fact. The dogmas of the Church may well be compared with the address of someone we know and love, the accuracy of the person's address is essential if we are to find the person; nevertheless the address of a person cannot be a substitute for that person himself. Thus it is with the theological expression of religious dogma—it is necessary, it is true, but it is not all. To rest in it is to become rationalistic, to mistake the expression of a truth for the truth itself, to divorce the truth from the totality of human experience. The very elements which gave precision to scholastic theology in its golden age were now but too frequently transposed into mere rationalistic formulae. Theology grew apart from spirituality, dogma grew away from the life of prayer and from a liturgy which was everywhere becoming more and more an automatic hieratic formula.

Thus we can see that the divorce of religion and life tended to create a subjective individualism in the devout and an arid rationalism among the learned. What effect did this divorce have upon the material and therefore the moral side of life? It is at once obvious that if things of time and place are considered to have an only accidental connexion with the things of the spirit, the material will take on a completely fresh character. No longer existing as a sacramental expression of Christ in the visible world, the material will begin to take on an independent life of its own. The pious will fear the natural and the material precisely because of this quality of independence; the less pious will exploit to the full all the possibilities of a material world unfettered by any considerations save those of expediency.

This resulted in both loss and gain. Both were very considerable. What was gained? The chief gain—though of its nature it could not be a lasting one—was a vivid consciousness of the value of artistic, intellectual or emotional experience as it is in itself. Instead of being a symbol or sacrament of something higher, human creation, human love, human knowledge were pursued for their own sake. It is true that if we look deeper we shall see that it is only because these things are symbols and sacraments of something higher that they have a validity in themselves—but this knowledge is not

one that leaps to the eye. At first sight the symbolic or the sacramental seems to take away from the value of things as they are in
themselves, and the first pursuit of things—of life, of living—as an
end in itself is a new experience which hides the inevitable frustration which must eventually follow when it is realized that 'what is
of flesh is flesh' and that flesh in which the life of the Word has
not become incarnate is something essentially phenomenal and
evanescent.

Thus the supposed emancipation of the natural and the material
—an emancipation only completed in the Italian Renaissance of the
fifteenth century—brought with it much to deplore. It is reflected
in the moral order in an entirely new outlook which grew up with
regard to the relationship of the State and the Church. The new
attitude brought about a complete cleavage between the ecclesiastical and the royal power. Disputes about spheres of action there are
always bound to be, but once it became accepted as a fact of human
society that the two powers of State and Church existed each as co-
equal and co-ordinate, existed each in its own right, inevitably
they became opposed. Any attempt by the Church to interfere in
the life of the State was regarded either as the intervention of a
sacerdotal class out for its own ends, or else as the attempt of the
family or race represented by the papacy to control domestic
politics. Conversely the papacy and the Church tended to see in
every action of the State a threat to its own security. No longer
living in the conviction of an ultimate reconciliation—however
hardly gained—by which all human power whether of Church
or State was an expression of Christ drawing all men and institutions together into himself, Church and State lived each in fear of
the other.

This conflict had of course begun long before our period—it
formed indeed the most difficult meeting ground for nature and
grace—but our period marks both the height of this conflict and
also the winning of the initiative by the State. At the opening of our
period both Boniface VIII and Philip the Fair and their apologists
had in the action and reaction of conflict taken up positions neither
of which was wholly tenable. As is the way of conflict, expression
declined from being a statement of truth into a catalogue of an
opponent's errors. Nowhere was there anything constructive, there
was no bridge which led to real reconciliation. Fear held both
aloof.

The growth of the national State, the concept of a State which lived by laws emanating either from itself or from the position of its sovereign, quickly became transmuted into the concept of the secular State. The divorce of the material and the spiritual was here complete. The notions of a Marsiglio of Padua would have seemed incomprehensible to most minds of a couple of centuries earlier. And the more the secular character of the State was emphasized, the more the Church either reacted from it or became its captive. The captivity was disastrous, the reaction almost as much a calamity, for little or no attempt was made to harmonize the elements of matter and spirit: a harsh assertion, although a true one, of the primacy of the spiritual was all that was forthcoming. Conflict ended in stalemate and stalemate in compromise, and towards the end of our period we begin to reach the age of Concordats and Golden Bulls.

If fear underlay the unconstructive nature of the conflict between the national State and the Church, a similar fear, following like the first from the loss of the victorious conviction of Christian Hope, underlay so many of the democratic or constitutional movements of the time. Ceasing to be regarded by their subjects as representatives of Christ, but thought of simply as men, ceasing to regard themselves as representatives of Christ, secular rulers tended more and more to an authoritarianism which moved ever closer to autocracy. Richard II of England with his latter-day concept of the law as reposing and reposing alone in the breast of the king—*in scrinio pectoris*—is a not untypical example. Such assumptions of arbitrary authority naturally aroused fear and suspicion in men's minds, and it is now that constitutions, systems of checks and balances, democratic movements come ever more to the fore. Basically products of fear rather than of principle, they soon found numerous and brilliant apologists and it is not long before we find these apologists arguing that all power exercised in the State is a power delegated to the ruler or rulers by the people at large. Each conflict but deepened the general feeling of insecurity, divisions between group and group widened and sectional interests quickly crystallized into esoteric and restrictive organizations.

Nowhere is this seen more clearly than in the later medieval gilds. Many of these craft-gilds were merely rings of wealthy capitalists endeavouring to restrict production in a time of declining trade by raising the standard of their products in order to keep up prices. It is true that there was a benevolent side to these institutions and that corporate religious duties played a considerable part in them;

c*

nevertheless the fact remains that they were closely identified with new economic concepts, concepts based on the emancipation of commercial practice from the direct control of religion. The most that was conceded to religion was the power to condemn open stealing or fraud; for the rest, trade and merchandise must exist unhampered by any other claims or considerations than their own.

All the main external events of this period reflect this growing disintegration of human experience, accompanied as it inevitably was by an ever-growing feeling of insecurity. The Babylonian Captivity was but the attempt of the national State to bind the Church to its will, the Great Schism with its counterpart in the Conciliar Movement was but a repetition in the realm of Church government of the contemporary constitutionalism resulting from fear of tyranny or arbitrary government. As always, the more frightened people became the more violently did they behave. The laws against heresy were everywhere becoming more drastic and we may think more cruel. Yet it was not cruelty that lit the fires of Smithfield but rather fear resulting from the conviction that everything which remained that was true and valid in a decaying world was being threatened.

Put in a nutshell, what had happened? A new and disturbing element had appeared—a new concept—that of the 'secular', a kind of 'No-man's land' lying between grace and sin and liable to be occupied by either. Inevitably, once a unity has become split up, the elements of truth in all its divisions tend to strive one against another. This *tertium quid*—the secular—provided the background for an even more thorough disintegration. If the secular or 'natural' can only be made holy accidentally by the devout, the new notion provided a happy hunting-ground for the indevout. The secular, the latter began to consider, can only work by secular laws: the precepts of the State, the principles of art, the laws of commerce were, it was now thought, laws which existed in their own right apart from, though not necessarily in contradiction to, those of religion. It is a different thing to buy and sell within the limits of the Ten Commandments and to buy and sell to support Christ incarnate in ourselves and in our neighbour.

It was little wonder that holy souls became more and more fearful of this growing 'secularization' of outlook; it is not surprising that in view of this segregation of human impulse from the sphere of religion moralists should tend to swing too far in the opposite direction and to view all actions not directly 'religious' with misgiving. But once accepted, how impossible to recover the confidence which went with the earlier integration of human experience: the 'devout' and the 'ordinary-man' grew ever further and further apart from each other and in place of the harmony of a functional society there was present an ever-increasing sense of fear and mistrust.

Morality had now to deal with two distinct categories of human experience. There was the secular sphere which worked by material laws and the religious sphere which was concerned with the secular only—as it were—at second-hand. In the past the only ground of conflict had been between sin and grace; now we have yet another, that between the sacred and secular. Removed from the main stream of human experience—now largely regarded as purely 'secular'—the moral teaching of Christianity began to take on what appeared to many to be an almost arbitrary character, to teach standards, laid down by God it is true, but having little relation to the natural urges of the human heart which are the stuff of daily life. Indeed a large and influential school of theologians taught quite openly that the moral law was an expression of God's will for men but that for any mere human to attempt to discover any objective principles in its decrees was not only impossible but almost blasphemous.

And from all this, of course, so much more followed. Men began to consider material sin of little account provided no formal sin was committed and hesitated to enlighten the sinner who sinned in good faith. Others regarded obedience to the moral law as a submission to God's will—as indeed it is—but the apparent capriciousness of that will was thought to be a sure sign that faith and human understanding were not merely remote from each other but even opposed. The devout, therefore, tended to look upon all human endeavours with an infinity of cynicism; the indevout regarded moral laws in a purely negative fashion—secular affairs followed secular laws and moral teachings were either purely utilitarian (for example, if stealing be allowed no one's property is secure) or a purchase price necessary for eternal bliss but frustrating human experience rather than freeing it.

All that I have said may appear to paint too gloomy a picture of the age with which we are dealing. It may seem ungenerous thus to portray the age of a Dante, of a Petrarch, the age of the great Italian painters, the age of a Catherine of Siena, a Bridget of Sweden, a Julian of Norwich or of a Nicholas of Cusa, the age of

Flamboyant architecture in France, of Perpendicular in England. But we are trying to make a broad generalization. It is not therefore towards a few great heroic figures, whose qualities of mind and heart raised them above the age in which they lived, to whom we must turn if we are to give a genuine picture of this period; it is rather the ordinary behaviour and outlook of the ordinary person— whether seen in public or private life, whether cleric or layman— that we must consider.

Nevertheless in spite of all that we have said there is in the human heart a great desire to re-integrate the whole of human experience in terms of itself. This living by turns of numerous different lives— an emotional life, an intellectual life, a religious life—this sense of having constantly to alternate between the claims of various depart- ments of human experience, is ultimately at variance with the basic impulses of the human personality. Deep down there is the wish to live but a single life in which every department of human experience has its part to play as the reflection and the expression of the whole unified personality. It was here that the great Renaissance of the fifteenth century stepped in. As an outburst of new discovery, new thought, new interests and new knowledge, it seemed at long last to give human experience something for which it could live and by which it could live. It gave a freshness and vitality to the jaded human spirit, it seemed to open up fresh fields in which the creative and exploring mind could find the fulfilment for which it craved.

Of course this was an illusion. The cult of humanism, apart from the God who became Man and in whose life alone are we men, was doomed to an early frustration. Left to itself all purely human ex- perience ceases eventually to satisfy; the human spirit yearns for the eternal and unlimited, it can never be satisfied completely by what is, apart from Christ, something transient and fugitive. Yet at the end of the period of which we speak, this was hardly apparent. The vitality of the new humanism seemed a dynamic force beside the dead rationalism of so many theologians, beside the rather gloomy pieties of the devout. It was no wonder that the Renaissance swept all before it. It is true that the papacy did try to welcome the move- ment, but at that time it was attempting too much. What was achieved in the twelfth century with nothing but gain to the Church was now in the fifteenth like offering strong drink to weak heads. Instead of the Church triumphantly interpreting the real values of the new humanism in terms of Christian doctrine, humanism tended to swallow up the Church. In fact it was clear that a crisis was imminent.

The Age of Decline was followed by an Age of Revolution, and this in turn was followed by the Age of Indifference; it seems likely that it is left to our own age—an age wearied of effete individualism, an age that looks to reintegrate human values into a single unit of experience, even if it be under the unpleasing form of National Socialism, an age in which the doctrine of the Mystical Body of Christ has been revived so notably in the Church—once again to reject the myth of the secular and return to a sounder morality based upon a hope which like St Augustine's *gratia victrix* is triumphant, invulnerable and compelling.

VI

THE ENGLISH PROTESTANTS

by
Frances Brice

THE distinctive features of Protestant morality in this country could be summed up, for many people, in the phrase 'the Nonconformist conscience'. In its popular usage, this is often taken to have a somewhat negative content, comprising total abstinence, censorship of literature, the Victorian Sunday; in other words to be in a Puritan strain alien to a healthy Catholic tradition. But this is an inadequate appreciation of a vigorous force which, in its hey-day, had a profound influence on all branches of our national life. One of the greatest nineteenth-century spokesmen of the Nonconformist conscience, Hugh Price Hughes, indicated its comprehensive scope in a rallying cry, 'We Christians, when we unite our forces, are simply irresistible. Let us then combine heartily to abolish slavery, drunkenness, lust, gambling, ignorance, pauperism, mammonism and war. After that is done, we shall not have much difficulty in settling all our theological and ecclesiastical differences.' This indicates much of the strength and weakness of Protestant morality in its dominant period, the later nineteenth century.

Such ringing optimism was not characteristic of the early years of the Victorian era. At that time, a common political position among Christians was Toryism, typified in the remark of the Rev. Jabez Bunting who ruled autocratically over the Methodist Conference: 'Methodism hates democracy as much as it hates sin.' As E. G. Rupp has pointed out, Bunting, in opposing the growing liberalism of his day, anticipated the Oxford Movement and the Syllabus of Errors. Evangelical preaching, which had once revolutionized formal religion, developed its own limited conventions. The Congregationalist Dr R. W. Dale, one of the great Nonconformist preachers of the late nineteenth century, denounced the complacent and circumscribed pietism that had become characteristic of much of Free Church life. Speaking of the impact of Non-conformity on morals, he inveighed against ministers who 'think there is something like profanation in attempting to show from the pulpit by what political measures our legislation might be made more righteous'.

Dale himself put forward a view of the State as an institution which, under God, the Christian conscience could shape until it served the ends of political and social justice; this is seen particularly in his sermon at Westbourne Park chapel in April 1893, in which he spoke of the chapel attitude of Nonconformists toward the State. His vision was of a state made completely Christian:

> Let all ranks in the State discharge their secular duties under the influence of the Spirit and the law of Christ; let commerce, let social habits, let those mutual relations of the different classes of the community which civil legislators cannot regulate, all be moulded and penetrated by the principles of Divine law enthroned in individual consciences and the Spirit of the Gospel diffused through individual hearts; let statesmen come from the sanctity of private communion with God to the great tasks of legislation and of diplomacy, and without any formal profession of a national faith, the national acts will be harmonious with the will of God.

(This links up, incidentally, with his strong arguments against the principle of an Established Church.)

During Dale's lifetime, the massive support given by Nonconformists to the Liberal Party (led by the Anglican Gladstone) made them a mighty political power in the land. This power was shown in 1890 when Hugh Price Hughes demanded Parnell's resignation because of his part in the O'Shea divorce case. At a great meeting in St James's Hall, in which converted toughs were 'chuckers-out' of Irish hecklers, he made one of his most famous utterances: 'We stand immovably on this eternal rock: what is morally wrong can never be politically right.' In the same vein, the *Methodist Times* in 1896 boasted: 'Sir Charles Dilke defied the Nonconformist conscience and he destroyed himself and his party. Lord Rosebery ignored the Nonconformist conscience for a racehorse, and the world sees the result.' This was perilously near to intoxication with the prospect of political power, and to the imposition of moral standards on unwilling and unconvinced subjects. One is reminded of Baron von Hügel's discerning words about the proper autonomy of the secular: 'Religion will have to come to see that it cannot attain to its own depth, it cannot become the *chief thing*, if it does

not continually renounce to aspiring after being *everything*.' It is, in
fact, arguable that the most impressive aspects of the influence of
Protestant morality are in other than these political directions.

These other aspects were, to a large extent, the result of the juxta-
position in time of the Evangelical Revival of the eighteenth century
and the Industrial Revolution; for the latter intensified many acute
social problems that were a challenge to the moral conscience of
Christians. The response came from both the Established and the
Free Churches, for the religious revival of the eighteenth century
infused new life into both; we should remember that the founder
of Methodism remained to the last a member of the Church of
England. The moral laxity and corruption prevalent in much of
eighteenth-century England are too well known to need description
here. The religious atmosphere of the time was, in many ways, a
counterpart of this; latitudinarian tendencies meant that Christianity often slipped into Arianism, Deism or the preaching simply of a
moral code—a morals without religion—which John Wesley regarded as most dangerous of all. Ministers of the Established Church
were often more interested in sport than in religion, and lax in the
performance of their duties. Conscientious parsons, like John
Wesley's father, had to contend with lethargy and indifference, not
to say outright hostility among parishioners. The old dissenting
bodies were not in much better state. Their energies seemed to have
been exhausted by the struggle for religious liberty, their numbers
were dwindling, their influence small, and they had in some cases
become affected by Unitarian influences. Some retained their
Calvinist traditions, often in an extreme form, with an emphasis on
faith at the expense of works. Wesley recounts in his *Journal* many
meetings with such: 'Finding a general temptation prevail of leaving off good works in order to an increase of faith, I began to expound the Epistle of St James, the great antidote to this poison.'

Wesley's Arminianism was an attempt to maintain a knife-edge
balance between Pelagianism and Calvinism. In his sermon on
Free Grace, in 1740, he attacked 'the horrible doctrine of predestination'—which was later lampooned by Burns in 'Holy
Willie's Prayer':

> O Thou, wha in the heavens dost dwell,
> Wha, as it pleases best Thysel',
> Sends ane to heaven, and ten to hell,
>   A' for Thy glory,
> And no' for ony guid or ill
>   They've done afore Thee!

Wesley put forward much the same arguments against the Calvinist view as those of St Ignatius Loyola in the *Spiritual Exercises*. He did, in fact, often take up a position where he was accused of being a Catholic. For instance, he records 'The report now current was that I was a Papist, if not a Jesuit' and the rumour that he 'kept two Popish priests in his house'. Best, perhaps, among many such incidents is one in Yorkshire where he was described as a 'Presbyterian Papist'.

Wesley was no systematic theologian, though it is striking how much of his theology approximates to a Catholic view. Rather, he cared supremely for saving men's souls and had a burning faith in the infinite worth of every individual person. This led him to carry the gospel to the poorest and most degraded, the uncouth, ignorant and despised, many of whom were beyond the reach of the ministrations of the ordinary clergy. It has been said that the open-air preaching of Wesley and Whitefield and their followers was the first organized preaching among the working classes since the days of the friars. Like the *Mission de France* today, it was an attempt to win the industrial population back to Christianity.

Wesley's preaching had something in common with the general tradition of evangelical preaching—developed later by Spurgeon and Moody, and in our own time by Billy Graham—in its appeal for a personal response to Christ, and a sense of personal responsibility in the implications of that decision. This emphasis does not mean that Wesley believed in the necessity of catastrophic conversion, after which all would be light and peace. Much has been written about his own conversion, but he himself rarely referred to it, and it played a very modest rôle in the life of Wesley and his companions. As he said in 1768, 'I have not, for many years, thought a consciousness of acceptance to be essential to justifying faith.' This attitude is at one with his care and respect for the individual person; he had a striking capacity for seeing the spirit of God in all men. He saw it in pagans like Socrates, in Catholics like St Francis de Sales, St Ignatius Loyola, and members of the Trappist Order, and in Jews he met, 'some of whom seem nearer the mind that was in Christ than many that call him Lord'. His approach to people is summed up in his greeting: 'Dost thou love and fear God? It is enough! I give thee the right hand of fellowship.'

For Wesley, 'Love to God and to all mankind is the centre of religion,' and this had clear social and moral implications. As he wrote in his preface to the *Methodist Hymn Book*, 'The Gospel of Christ knows of no religion but social, no holiness but social holiness.' As with his theology, his attitude to social problems was not a consciously wrought theory, and a unified whole, but a response to a particular set of circumstances. One could list Wesley's attacks on war ('a horrid reproach to the Christian name... When wars break out, God is forgotten'), on the liquor traffic ('All who sell . . . are poisoners general'), on the abuse of money (he instilled the notion of stewardship), his interest in education (his disciple Hannah Ball preceded Raikes in starting Sunday schools), in public health (in 1746 he founded the first really free medical dispensary in England), in systems of co-operative industry among the poor.

More significant, however, was Welsey's influence in stimulating a moral awareness of problems that were tackled with evangelistic zeal by men and women sharing his values. An instance of this is Wesley's interest in prisons, which dated from his undergraduate days. In one period of nine months he preached sixty-seven times in various prisons, but he was for long, as he says in his Journal, 'forbidden to go to Newgate for fear of making them wicked, and to Bedlam for fear of driving them mad!' One of Wesley's disciples was John Howard, who was greatly influenced by hearing him peach on 'Whatsoever thy hand finds to do, do it with thy might.' This test might well apply to Howard's lifetime, spent in labouring to make prisons more humane places, for he regarded the criminal as a man with a soul of infinite worth who might be reclaimed to a better life. Howard's work was taken up by Elizabeth Fry, though she was more concerned with women and children in prisons. In her service she applied the Quaker vision of the presence of the Divine 'Seed' in all men, however apparently degraded, and she is an outstanding example of the Society of Friends' impressive record of 'concern' for the needy and afflicted. Yet it is significant that at this time Elizabeth Fry met with some opposition within the Society, where there was a strong streak of quietism and withdrawal. As Janet Whitney says: 'They regarded religion as a state of mind manifested in certain peculiar habits of dress and speech and in avoidance of frivolous and wordly things.' They did not find in it an irresistible impulse towards activity. This tension between quietism and activism is found throughout the history of Christianity, and was probably particularly acute at this time. Those with a sharp awareness of the need for Christians to apply their morality to social evils often had to contend with the view that the Christian's business was to concern himself with his private morality and keep himself unsullied by the world—a view exemplified especially in the Plymouth Brethren. Quakers were also concerned in the agitation against slavery, and here again there is a direct link between Wesley and Wilberforce, who was the prime mover in this field. Wesley, in his *Thoughts upon Slavery*, had said, 'I absolutely deny all slave-holding to be consistent with any degree of even natural justice' and he taught his followers to look on the negro slave as a brother in Christ. The last letter he wrote was to Wilberforce, urging him to 'be not weary in well-doing' in his struggle for the emancipation of the slaves. Wilberforce was a prominent member of the Clapham sect, which did so much to instil a Christian spirit and an attitude of trusteeship into our relations with the colonies. This group included many influential public men—a Governor-General of India, a chairman of the East India Company, several members of parliament and Sir James Stephen, Under Secretary at the Colonial Office. Whatever their political or ecclesiastical allegiance, all were bound together by their evangelical Christianity which owed much to Wesley's inspiration. In many ways they show the influence of Protestant morality at its best—not tied up with any particular party or Church, but the achievement of devoted laymen infusing Christianity into their work, as man's reasonable service to his Redeemer.

The greatest single example of the influence of evangelical morality in nineteenth-century England is in the person of Lord Shaftesbury, a member of the Church of England, who described himself as 'an Evangelical of Evangelicals'. He made a clear avowal of the mainspring of his work when speaking against the employment of women and children in mines. 'I have been bold enough to undertake this task because I must regard the objects of it as being created, like ourselves, by the same Master, redeemed by the same Saviour and destined to the same immortality.' He applied this principle to his onslaught on the main social evils of his day—the exploitation of child labour in factories, mines and chimney sweeping, the harsh treatment of lunatics (a pioneer here in the eighteenth century was the Quaker Tuke) the neglect of abandoned and destitute children (this links up with his interest in the Ragged Schools and with Dr Barnado's work), bad housing conditions and the evils of liquor and opium. Emphasizing and himself living by the paramount importance of the spiritual life, he nevertheless laboured unceasingly throughout his life to remedy the material conditions in which people lived.

Despite Shaftesbury's quarrel with the Salvation Army, many

aspects of his work were continued by that body. Though considerable improvements had taken place in living and working conditions, nevertheless there remained at the end of the nineteenth century large numbers of destitute and uncared for people living in slum conditions of appalling squalor. To reach these, William Booth, a Methodist minister, in 1864 created the East London Revival Society which was organized in 1878 as the Salvation Army. In his book *In Darkest England and the Way Out*, he described the situation of the 'submerged tenth' in London. 'What a satire it is upon our Christianity and our civilization that the existence of these colonies of heathens and savages in the heart of our capital should attract so little attention... Why all the apparatus of temples and meeting houses to save men from perdition in a world which is to come, while never a helping hand is stretched out to save them from the inferno of their present life?' He appealed for help from Christians 'to rescue some, at least of those for whom they profess to believe their Founder came to die'. Again, we see the emphasis on the infinite worth of every human person made manifest by Christ's sacrifice on the Cross.

In vivid first-hand sketches, General Booth drew a picture of life among criminals, drunkards, prostitutes, the starving and the homeless, abandoned and neglected children and workers in the sweated industries. He described the slums 'in which huddle together in festering and verminous filth, men, women and children. They correspond to the lepers who thronged the lazar houses of the Middle Ages. As in those days St Francis of Assisi and the heroic band of saints who gathered under his orders were wont to go and lodge with the lepers at the city gate, so the devoted souls who have enlisted in the Salvation Army took up their quarters in the heart of the worst slums.' Such work was not just a matter of doling out assistance from above, but a going down and sharing in the life of others and transforming it. 'The Salvation officer... goes down into the street, and from door to door, and from room to room' seeking out the needy in the highways and byways. Their organization built up a whole system to show forth the love of God to all men, not only by religious services but in concrete practical terms—cheap food depots, doss houses, night shelters, city industrial workshops, rescue homes for prostitutes, preventive homes for girls in danger, the prison gate brigade, the slum brigade, 'preaching the Gospel with the mop and scrubbing brush'. The slum sisters went to live among the people they were trying to help. 'Here they live, all the year round, visiting the sick, looking after the children, showing the women how to make themselves and their homes decent, often discharging the sick mother's duties themselves, cultivating peace, advocating temperance, counselling and ceaselessly preaching the religion of Jesus Christ to the Outcasts of Society.' Admirable as their practical work is (their Mayflower training home for neglectful mothers springs to mind) we should remember that it is geared firmly to their preaching of the Gospel, which they undertake in truly missionary fashion at the street corner and in the public house. Pre-eminently among Nonconformists they carry on the tradition of taking religion out to the people.

How far was the impulse to social activity the work of a few dedicated individuals? What of the influence of morality on the rank and file member of the church and chapel? The Evangelical Revival had infused a passion for moral righteousness among its followers. Wesley in his *Character of a Methodist* (1742) insisted: 'By salvation he means holiness of heart and life. . . It is nonsense for a woman to consider herself virtuous because she is not a prostitute, or a man honest because he does not steal. May the Lord God preserve me from such a poor, starved religion as this.' In his *Rules for the Society of the people called Methodists* he outlined the principles of Christian morality in private life, work and business. The influence of the movement undoubtedly helped to raise many working-class people from a life of ignorance and brutality to one of responsibility and intelligence, inculcating the virtues of hard work, honesty, thrift, sobriety and sound family life. Religion was very much an affair of the home, with an emphasis on family prayer and the reading of the Bible. This was not necessarily the dreary experience it has been painted. As one writer has said, 'When we, their grandchildren, think of them as miserable, it is because we imagine that people can only be happy in our way.' Outside the home, religious life centred in the chapel—'It might be some little Bethel along the village street with coloured texts upon the distempered walls, with gallery and rostrum, and varnished pews and the inevitable aspidistra, often very ugly,' but it was an alive centre, not only of worship and fellowship, but of culture, if of a limited kind, and education. Jack Lawson, in his autobiography *A Man's Life*, maintained that the chapel was the social centre of the workers: 'They drew together, found strength in their weakness and expressed to each other their hidden thoughts and needs. Here men first found the language and the art to express their antagonism to grim conditions and injustice. . . The most powerful force for the mental and moral elevation of the workers during the industrial era has been this contemptuously called "Little Bethel".'

The influence of the chapel recalls the part played by Protestantism in democratic movements. One stream of the Dissenting tradition of the sixteenth and seventeenth centuries had moved in a markedly democratic direction. The Quakers, especially, with their emphasis on the 'inner light' in every man, and their rejection of any priesthood except the priesthood of all believers, show this tendency in a highly developed form. Wesley himself rejected any democratic elements in church government ('We are not republicans') and insisted on a rule of 'No politics' among his preachers. Yet certain features of Methodist teaching and organization provided admirable training in self-government. The Methodist system of bands and classes gave full scope for active lay participation in the life of the church. Class meetings assembled weekly, under leaders who acted as lay pastors, and developed a strong spirit of fellowship and co-operation. A wealthy manufacturer might have as his class leader one of his own workmen. Wesley's use of lay preachers also had widespread results. It was, for one thing, a great educating force, as Wesley encouraged his preachers to do at least five hours' reading a day, and to carry round books to distribute to others. The fifty volumes of the Christian Library, which Wesley selected from a wide field, were designed as guidance in this and did much to create a taste for good reading, and to supply books at reasonable prices. Men who began by learning to read the Bible and religious books applied their literacy to wider fields and did not fail to read the newspapers. Those who preached or led class meetings acquired a facility for self-expression that could be turned in other directions and the links of Methodism with the Trade Union and political movements have often been explored.

In its early years, Methodism tended to be conservative or aloof from politics, but there is an early connexion with Trade Unionism in the famous case of the six 'Tolpuddle Martyrs' in 1834. Three of these agricultural labourers were local preachers and two were active members of the Methodist chapel. From that time, there has been a tradition of interest in the Trade Union movement. Nonconformist homes nurtured such leaders as Arthur Henderson and Ernest Bevin. Sidney Webb said of the Primitive Methodists of Durham: 'They did great work from village to village: families were transformed, and these men stood out as men of character, gaining the respect of their fellows. . . Trade Unionism was itself largely the result of the elevation of character brought about by religious conversion on individual leaders.' Lloyd George believed that this link had had tremendous influence: 'The movement which improved the conditions of the working classes, in wages, in hours of labour and otherwise, found most of its best officers in men trained in institutions which were the result of Methodism. I never realize the effect which Methodism has had upon the national character so much as when I attend international congresses. It has given a different outlook to the British and Americans from the outlook of the Continentals—John Wesley inaugurated a movement that gripped the soul of England, that deepened its spiritual instincts, trained them and uplifted them. . .' More tendentiously Mr Morgan Philips, addressing an International Socialist Conference in 1950, said 'Socialism in England is Methodist, not Marxist.' Sweeping though this may be, there is something in the analysis that accounts for the peculiar genius of Socialism in this country. The extent to which the Welfare state has been accepted by all parties is perhaps an indication of that concern for social justice that is, in so many ways, a heritage of Protestantism in this country.

English Protestantism, especially in its Victorian manifestations, had serious limitations, which have often been caricatured and which provoked Matthew Arnold's distaste for 'the hideous and grotesque illusions of middle-class Protestantism'. We are perhaps too apt to colour our picture of Victorian Protestantism with memories of Edmund Gosse's very moving *Father and Son* and too easily embarrassed by the moral earnestness which characterized even agnostic Victorians. G. W. E. Russell, speaking of his evangelical upbringing, said: 'I recall an abiding sense of religious responsibility, a self-sacrificing energy in works of mercy, an evangelical zeal, an aloofness from the world and a level of saintliness in daily life.' Their virtues of integrity and compassion sprang from that fervent love for God and for one's fellow men which John Wesley preached in an age which needed it, as does our own.

SECONDARY SCIENCES CONTRIBUTING TO
THE CONCEPT AND PRACTICE
OF MORALITY

VII

MORALITY AND PSYCHOLOGY
by
Franz B. Elkisch

THEOLOGIANS are concerned about the development of modern psychology lest this new science should undermine the moral structure of Catholic teaching. This apprehension is understandable when we consider the extent to which psychology has already penetrated our culture and is still influencing modern thought. In addition there exists a strong anti-Christian attitude in the Western hemisphere for which psychology, by and large, provides a foundation. Anti-Christian psychology is forceful in its attack on what are considered to be the fetters and chains of Christian morality, but it acts under a misconception, for actually it is not morality as such against which psychology protests, but the false moralistic superstructure which is the cause of many neurotic tensions and breakdowns and which is wrongly identified with Christian morality by many psychologists. Certain psychological theorists claim that feelings of sin or guilt can be reduced to the resultant effects of experiences in early childhood which recapitulate ancient, ingrained mechanisms in the Oedipus situation. Advancing this statement further they say that the earliest discernible moral attitudes and their subsequent development are dependent upon the child's nursery training. Were this theory held to be the whole truth then the system of Christian morality, with its alleged divine origin, must collapse indeed and the mature personality would find the objective reasons for his morality in the social structure alone to which he has to become attuned as a final goal. Because psychology has a strong and wide appeal in this twentieth century, a serious responsibility, in propounding theories of this nature, cannot be denied. It is in this context that the true value of the Catholic psychotherapist can be found. He has access to all the psychological theories and practices but it is his vocation to use them not as an end in themselves but as a means within the frame-

83

work of Catholic teaching. This process of assimilation is in full swing at the present time.

Many difficulties arise because modern psychology began outside the Church in the doctor's consulting room as an offspring of natural science. After many discoveries and conquests of the external world had been made by all the various sciences, medical psychology turned its attention to exploration of the inner world, of the unconscious mind, which proved to be as fascinating a process as the discoveries made in biology or any other of the modern sciences. Almost intoxicated by its successes and the speed at which this new science gained ground, optimistic and enthusiastic psychologists regarded their work as a remedy, not only for individual ills but also for those of our whole society. These views are shared even by people holding high position and office in world affairs; for instance, Dr Brock Chisholm, [1] Director in 1947 of the World Health Organization under UNO, declared 'That it is the task of psychiatry to devise the right environment; for the art of living is something that psychology, and psychology alone, can teach. Psychiatrists, in fact, must become specialists in living.' And then again, 'Psychologists are the people to whom we must look for the improvement of human nature.' For such people psychology has a missionary appeal; it is for them the religion of the future since it gives the appearance and promise of a working religion in which the individual will be adapted to the current cultural pattern but which will make no demands beyond a humanitarian ideal.

To Catholics these ideas are fantastic but the knowledge of their existence is relevant to the problems of this paper since they show the danger to which inflated psychology is subject. The moral problems, present in psychology, are linked with the clash between humanitarian and Christian moralities.

In moral matters psychology had a bad start. Christians were shocked when Freud's method was known and even now, after more than fifty years, the original misgivings and suspicions are not fully dispelled. The method gave an impression of profound immorality because the main theme in the analytical procedure was catharsis, the release of repressed forces which has an effect similar to the opening of Pandora's Box. There were revealed many undesirable qualities such as, amongst others, sexual thoughts and desires, hatred and aggression against those for whom on the conscious level was felt love and gratitude. In fact, the whole gamut of repressed

[1] Joad, *Recovery of Belief*, pp. 62–3.

emotional life was released. It was asked, 'Is man really such a beast as the Freudian theories showed?' Also, 'Is it right to submit to this process? Was it not sinful to let those things come up at the risk, perhaps, of enjoying bad thoughts and fantasies?' The analytical concept seemed to be in complete opposition to the idea of goodness and virtue in man. If those emotions really were harboured in the unconscious mind, surely the greater wisdom would lie in locking up those horrors safely and turning away from psychology.

However, these objections belong to the past and it is now firmly established that, as well as creative and positive forces, the instinctual life presents negative and hostile aspects. To the credit of psychology it is now recognized that by controlled release of the repressed emotions their destructive character takes on a positive tone. On the other hand by imprisoning the undesirable elements of psychic life man usually makes it impossible for himself to achieve a mature personality and to follow the precept of the Gospel by giving himself to God with the whole of his being.

In some cases, it is true, unconscious instinctive forces are so powerful in relationship to the ego that their release constitutes a grave danger to the personality, to the extent even of insanity. I remember a young man of twenty-eight who, although intellectually sound, was, as it were, emotionally crippled. A terrifying experience of being in hell, occasioned during an illness in adolescence, had changed him from a lively normal boy to a dutiful automaton. The duration of this experience was brief but a priest had to be called in to calm him. He survived the shock as a rational and moral being only at the cost of sacrificing the whole of his emotional life. A thick callous scar formed and prevented the chaotic as well as the creative potentialities rising to consciousness. Apart from such serious pathological cases there are similar ones of a milder nature where ruthless repression is the safe procedure. Nevertheless, in the majority of cases, rather than shrink back from the dangerous zones of the psyche it is wiser for men to undertake missionary work on the dark continent within himself and to convert the inner savage, be it the inner Jew or the inner Big Brother. When the necessity of assimilating the hidden shadow is acknowledged then it is clear that the immoral method of which Freud was accused becomes a moral duty.

It is now recognized that the unrealized, unconscious forces project their contents into the outside world, causing the individual to see the existing Jew as bad, the neighbour as nasty, the friend as mean and, in fact, everything and everybody but himself as loaded with vice and immoral behaviour. However, the objective examination of man's own inner life will convince him that in the unconscious half of his nature the moral laws are far from being observed. This investigation in itself can have a very beneficial effect provided it is accompanied by the experience of the fact, and the acceptance of the existence of the projected qualities in the individual himself. Man's acceptance of his nature has to be preceded by its knowledge. The process of facing hidden and repressed elements of the unconscious is very painful but, at the same time, it is a necessary condition for becoming mature and whole.

The switch-over from the traditional teaching of repression and victory by will power to an attitude of facing facts frankly and observation of the transformation of undesired qualities in himself is not easy for man to achieve.

In the Church we often see fine young men and women who, through virtuous resistance to temptation and repression of their undesirable qualities, have become spiritually ethical types of being, ultra-supernaturalists in the sense of the word as used by Mgr Ronald Knox. Unfortunately, however, they have run away from themselves and for their own sakes it can only be hoped that a crisis or breakdown will ensue to help them in the assimilation of the other side of their being. Usually a long time elapses before such people realize that the sinful nature of man is not an intellectual concept to be argued and discussed but a reality and fact within themselves to be experienced in the concrete actuality of their existence.

So far I have dealt with the necessity of releasing repressed instinctive forces despite their immoral content and now I want to describe the psychological structure in which the individual has to find his balance. At this point a factor of utmost importance is the realization of an inner psychic system in which the ego is a battleground of two opposing powers; one being the Id which is 'the primary force of instinctive energy'[1] and the other the Super-Ego which 'designates a structure in the unconscious mind built up by early experiences'[2] and is formed according to the moral pattern authoritatively imposed by parents or their deputies. In an overstrung system the tension between the demands of the Id and the censorship of the Super-Ego is the source of many neurotic conflicts. It is clear that, viewed from this standpoint alone, moral conflicts

[1] Flugel, *Man, Morals and Society*, p. 34.   [2] Drever, *Dictionary of Psychology*.

are seen only in the light of the violation of the Super-Ego which, in the psyche, is the representative of the cultural pattern. The logic of the following step that moral conflicts are of a social order must be admitted and therefore in view of this the aim of the analysis seems rightly directed towards fitting the patient into the existing moral pattern. If the analyst himself is not a Christian, faithful to his belief, there is a danger that the analysis will have an anti-Christian effect. No matter how much the analyst may argue that he is not taking sides, that he is not interested in moral problems at all, that he is only concerned with the person who is sick and, furthermore, that religion and morality enter into the analytical situation as little as in that of treating a fractured leg, the analyst's basic attitude, his own *Weltanschauung*, will form an essential part of directing the treatment. Even in general medicine it is an axiom that the patient as a whole should be treated and not his appendix alone. To a far greater extent does this principle apply in psychology. In a neurosis the whole of the personality is involved and therefore moral and spiritual problems cannot be excluded. As Jung says:[1] 'The problem of neurosis extends from the disturbed sphere of the instincts to the ultimate questions and decisions of our whole *Weltanschauung*' and the therapy along biological lines does not suffice but requires a spiritual completion. When, therefore, analyst and analysand do not speak the same spiritual or religious language it is not surprising that an analysis often comes to an abrupt end at the moment when the sphere of guilt and sin is approached. Anyhow a Catholic will not be able to accept a moral order of which the Super-Ego is the supreme judge. When the attempt has been made to explain away guilt and sin by such rationalistic terms as self-inflicted punishment or offence to the Super-Ego, a Catholic, far from being freed from conflicts, will find himself subject to a new conflict: that between the moralities of psychology and his religion. One particular patient I have in mind knew that she had guilt feelings of the morbid type which she realized would respond to rational explanations and reduction to early childhood experience, but while she agreed with the analyst on the question of the false guilt, she was unable to obtain from him a clear definition, in analytical language, of the true guilt nor of the differentation between the true and the false. Therefore the whole situation came to an *impasse*.

While this type of psychology has built a rational structure to

[1] Introduction to *God and the Unconscious*, by Victor White, O.P., p. xiii.

explain the workings of the psyche there is another system of psycho-therapeutical thought centred around Jung. His influence is noticeable, and the validity of his ideas is recognized and accepted, in many psychological movements. In my opinion the chief differ-ence between these and the former groups lies in the fact that Jung's approach does not follow the line of effective causality but has a final end in view. Jung sees the psychic life as a self-regulating sys-tem with a goal towards which the flow of energy is definitely directed. Jung argues that the neglect of the irrational side of the psyche has resulted in the over-development of the conscious and rational side, thus leading men into an unbalanced state. On the developed side we have the intellectual, rational function, on the other, the irrational functions of an intuitive and instinctive character equally important to the whole of men's being. In con-sequence of this lack of equilibrium, nervous disorders of a whole-sale magnitude are the order of the day. Jung gives full recognition to the tendency in human nature to swing back to an innate state of harmony and the whole aim of the process of the Jungian analysis is to give the *vis mediatrix naturae* an opportunity to function. Whilst the rational faculty of the individual is respected in Jungian analysis great emphasis is placed on the value of the emergence of spon-taneous powers, which correspond to what the theologian describes as *gratia naturalis*. The moral issue here is transferred from the social sphere to the inner psychic realm and the integration of the per-sonality in the process of individuation is a goal for which the in-dividual strives as his moral task. Self-fulfilment as against and beyond social adaptation designates definitely a higher standard of moral order.

This rough division into two main groups of psychologists still obtains generally though it would have been more clear ten years ago; since then modifications, dissensions and heresies have de-veloped within the groups. At the present time there are, even amongst Freudians, less orthodox sects who resent a too materialis-tic outlook; also the number of eclectic psychiatrists is increasing. Even non-Christian psychiatrists have been known to wish for more religion as they see it as a preventive or even cure of the many nervous diseases which fill the hospitals. All this change does not fundamentally affect the Catholic psychologist who has always felt secure within the steady life of Catholic faith. He is free to use any method or technique developed in modern psychology and he is not tied to any of the philosophical, metaphysical, pseudo-religious, or pseudo-spiritual ideas which bind the psychological creed of many of his colleagues to a particular *Weltanschauung*. As a matter of fact amongst Catholic psychologists there are Freudians, Adlerians, Jungians, all of whom are working successfully according to the method best fitting their own individual temperament and that of their patients.

As with all other professions and activities, psychiatry encounters the conflict between current ethics and Christian morality. The Catholic psychologist respects the divine origin of the moral laws and is in complete opposition to his non-Christian colleagues who have tried to build a morality based on the psychology of neurotics. In the treatment of cases a very interesting and important fact has come to light in relation to morals—it has been clearly shown that nervous breakdowns are not the result of Christian moral laws but of the manner in which neurotic patients over a number of years force their natures to comply with moral standards. The neurotic lives in a psychic world in which his system is shaped according to a legalistic, moralistic, autocratic form which he must follow without deviation and in this process the moral laws become twisted into the neurotic system and lose their essence. It would seem that psychologists, crying down Christian morality, arrived at their conclusions from the travesty of Christian morality presented to them by neurotic patients.

The neurotic conflict, as recognized by many psychologists, is fundamentally a moral conflict; the conflict aroused in a man by what he should do but does not want to do. The neurotic is imprisoned in a fixed tyrannical system which is formed partly by the inherited dictates of his own nature, constitutionally deeply ingrained in his psychic system, and partly by his educators through the formation of the Super-Ego. This particular reaction pattern is not easy to change because it is anchored in the collective as well as in the personal unconscious and if success is to be attained, depth psychology is demanded. Berdyaev[1] states the fact of this problem precisely when he says 'Victory over the subconscious instinct of tyranny is one of the most fundamental moral tasks.'

The devastating effect of this inner system can be illustrated in many cases. I have selected a few showing both the presence of the conflict and its results. I shall not deal with specific moral problems but attempt to indicate the underlying false moralistic mechanism which is a fundamental matrix out of which develops the diversity

[1] *The Destiny of Man.*

of neurotic disorders, classified in modern times so often as entities in themselves. However, it is only in the surface emergence that the differences are striking and seem to call for different approaches. The root cause of the various problems is one and the same, the inner tyrant, and has to be dealt with at that level.

The first case is that of a young man of twenty-two who was masturbating to an exceptional degree. He was finally sent to me by his priest who realized that he was acting under compulsion. The excessive uncontrollable masturbation was only one facet, although the most striking, of a whole neurotic syndrome. He was lazy, aggressive, utterly discontented and regarded as a failure by his parents. He was also the cause of constant quarrels at home. It would be wrong to look upon these further symptoms as the effect of masturbation and to think that health would be restored were the bad sexual habit alone overcome. The correct attitude would see masturbation as one of, and equal to, the other symptoms. This young man could not cope with his extremely strong instinctual life which erupted at a number of weak points in his character, and, in spite of almost heroic efforts, the situation had become worse over a period of years. The trouble began when as a boy at a Catholic boarding school one of the masters wrongly accused him of indecent behaviour with another boy. At the time he had no actual knowledge of the crime of which he was accused. He had merely a vague sense that certain things should not be done but what these certain things were he did not know. The headmaster then gave him a good talking to about this sin of which again he had no understanding. This incident, coupled with a rather cruelly delayed caning, affected his attitude towards his instinctive sexual nature at puberty which at that time was just beginning. He avoided any thought or action which he felt might be wrong and began to develop an extremely strict tyrannical attitude towards himself as the result of which he became very scrupulous. Supported by the boy's own respect and love for the headmaster, this method seemed to be very effective for some years. No bad thoughts or even feelings passed the threshold of his consciousness. He had himself under perfect control and was regarded at home and in school as a model boy who never caused his parents or teachers any trouble. But this period of exemplary behaviour was comparatively short. The strain and stress under which he lived, constantly watching himself and scrutinizing his actions, was too great. Finally the brain became tired and the overfatigue of the repressing function of the mind plus the dynamic pressure of the repressed instinctual life resulted in the breakdown of the barrier and the flooding of the personality with undesired compulsive thoughts, feelings and actions. These took the form of masturbation, sexual fantasies and all the other rebellious symptoms with which we had to deal in the analysis. Adding to this boy's difficulties was an extremely strong mother-fixation plus a tense home atmosphere which created in him the constant dread that something terrible might happen. Thus he was attacked on two sides: by unmanageable inner forces and by unfriendly external circumstances. This caused him to be always on the defensive. These attacks, however, would not have affected him in so devastating a manner had his conscience been less delicate. It registered the fine oscillations of the psychic climate in which he lived and constantly presented him with the problem of good and evil.

This boy's story is typical of innumerable neurotic people. A dictatorial principle seizes tyrannically upon them from the conscious side in the form of scrupulosity and from the unconscious as compulsion. It will be clear that the answer to both is to deprive the tyrant of its power by changing an attitude to life that is fundamentally wrong. Before discussing this point further I shall present the effect of moralistic attitudes in one particular form of married life peculiar to the Catholic religion. I refer to the observance of living as brother and sister which occasionally has to be adopted by married couples. As with any sacred institution, marriage demands the fulfilment of certain obligations before its proper spiritual character can be attained; it must not be assumed that the moral laws governing married life are arbitrarily imposed to serve mere moralism. They are the logical outcome of conditions inherent in the sanctity of married life.

However this particular relation in married life presents great problems; three couples who sought my advice experienced difficulties which could not be dealt with on spiritual and moral levels alone. The common factor uniting these people was that they were all converts from one form or another of Protestantism. They had all grown up in a puritan atmosphere and their natures had developed accordingly. One of the couples shared the same bedroom and the wife told me that sex no longer bothered them and that they could easily keep to the rules of the Church. However, they lived in self-deception. The wife, who was my patient, had neurotic symptoms before she was received into the Church but these had increased considerably afterwards, a fact which was most disturbing because she had naturally expected that, apart from the promises connected with the faith, a great improvement in her personal difficulties would take place. In point of fact, matters grew considerably worse. She became scrupulous and tense and, after a while, was sent to me but unfortunately proved to be unsuited to the psychological approach. She has now left the Church but in the few times that she saw me she realized that she had not fully grasped the moral significance entailed by the promise she had made. It dawned on her that it is not possible by a sheer act of will-power and some psychological gymnastics to subdue a passionate nature. The second couple for certain reasons had to practise sexual abstinence for a year. In this time the wife developed a state of great tension marked by emotional explosions, depressions and general restlessness. The dominating thought occupying her mind all day and every day was 'I wonder if we shall be good tonight or not!' The third couple had three children and had lived as brother and sister after their reception into the Church for eight years before I saw them. They adhered to the rules strictly and in great faith, but the atmosphere in the house was terrible, filled with quarrels and outbursts of temper. It might be said that only in the letter of the law was the commandment of chastity kept. Now I do not mention these cases to prove that sexual abstinence in married life is an impossibility. It can be, and often is, a shining example of personal sanctity and can enhance spiritual powers. A generalization built upon a few cases alone can give false conclusions and it is not suggested that these cases should have been handled differently. These couples were received into the Church by conscientious priests; they were of mature age at the time, and their sincerity had been tested beforehand. However, when it is asked wherein lay the failure of these people the answer again is to be found in the inner tyrannical attitude. They were sure that they could meet any difficulty that might arise but, although unaware of it, they were very egotistic and convinced that by the power of the ego alone they could master their instincts. Their motto might have been: 'Where there is a will there is a way.' The unhappy result was that they did not see God or the essential truth of the Church but only the sixth commandment. This had become their idol. It is hardly to be expected that a system trained and educated for centuries in puritanism can suddenly switch over into the climate of grace which, as St Paul tells us, alone can set man free from a nature thus doomed to death. Only a few are ready for it. When a young novice enters religious life he is tested for years before making his final vows. Converts from tribal religions remain as catechumens for considerable periods of training before they are given the responsibilities involved in baptism. But all my patients were expecting and expected to make the change from one attitude of life to another almost in a single day. The fact was overlooked that they had in their very blood the tyrannical attitude inherited from their puritanic forefathers.

It is, of course, not suggested that puritanism has to be regarded as the cause of neurotic conditions, but where an over-strict attitude to life prevails, innate mechanisms, latent in human nature, will come to the fore in certain people who have a delicately conditioned conscience and will give rise to psychological difficulties. To mention just two more of the many existing moralistic systems, Jansenism and the strict Rabbinical laws, which in the long ghetto period of Judaism regulated Jewish life, have a like effect. *Apropos* of this, it may be interesting to note that in the far east psychological disorders appear to be almost unknown.

Examples of cases could be multiplied at will. Although the symptomatology of the problems may occur in such differing forms as masturbation, chaste marriage, homosexuality, birth control, also aggression, depression, compulsion . . . the basic origin of the disturbance is identical and can be traced back to the same source which holds the individual fast in the immature atmosphere of fear created by a dictatorial psychic system. When the Holy Father, in his address to psychologists in Rome in 1953, mentioned material sin and said that 'it [psychotherapy] can for the moment tolerate what remains inevitable,' he may have had similar cases of compulsive action in mind. Perhaps we are confronted with those situations far more frequently than is generally assumed. Usually a weakness of the will is held responsible for any violation of the moral order and little or no account is taken of the compulsive force with which instinctive powers are so frequently asserted. Great changes have taken place, e.g. in the treatment of masturbation over the last twenty years, and a far more tolerant attitude has arisen because the compulsive character of sexual powers in adolescence has been recognized. The boy whose story I recounted was reassured by his priest that no mortal sin was involved, that his habit was a disease and not a moral question. In view of this it is perhaps legitimate to assume that these three couples might have been led gradually, but more securely, into the new life had their own tyrannical natures been better understood. The extent of our conditioning by the attitude of our forebears is, perhaps, not sufficiently recognized. The past three hundred years of puritanic training must have greatly affected the racial collective unconscious of this country, a fact which should be very much in the thoughts of Catholics of long heredity since with the increasing number of converts there will be many in whose unconscious mind the puritanic attitude still acts with compulsive power. A sympathetic understanding of these psychological conditions will not lead to weakness or laxity. But the strict attitude which is a helpful and necessary discipline for the average personality would only reinforce and strengthen the psychic pattern of a puritanical structure. The unconscious is not just a concept or an idea which can be either recognized or rejected; it exists as a fact and manifests itself in attitudes often so strong that they are beyond the control of the individual, in fact are what we call compulsive. Where a whole nation is concerned and the racial unconscious is affected many generations must pass before the power of this puritanical attitude is lessened. For the individual however the situation is different. Psychology gives him the singular opportunity of gaining an insight into his overstrung system to an extent which, e.g., examination of conscience would be unable to provide. It is a process which in ordinary language is called maturity and which, like all growing up, is painful. It puts the individual under new obligations. The widened-out and enlarged consciousness requires the individual to leave greatly cherished ways of childhood and to live as a new man, according to the standard of Christian morality. No wonder that the majority of people shy away from this task and prefer to remain immature and undeveloped even if this means to go on suffering; anyhow it is suffering in the old fashion, in the accustomed way of childhood, it is suffering one knows, and as we have to admit, it is not easy to break the law of inertia which holds us static in the traditional way and to move towards the unknown. However, those who have the courage to grow up will find that by doing so the way is paved for grace to work even in the hidden depth of the unconscious. Dostoievski must have realized this when in his *Brothers Karamazov* he said: 'What seems to be bad in you will grow purer from the very fact of observing it in yourself.' This process is greatly supported by what is commonly called relaxation but it is far more than a physical exercise. It is a process which, when understood correctly, becomes a basic attitude to life; it reduces the tension on all levels—physical, psychological and mental—to a normal scale, deprives the despotic moralistic system of its power and establishes a condition of well-balanced freedom. Provided it is in its intention directed to the supreme end, it is nothing other than relaxation into love, relaxation *in manus tuas* (into thy hands).

I hope I have been able to show that there is no conflict between morality and psychology for the simple reason that morals as such are intrinsically no part of psychology. Although, as I have shown, moral problems must enter the analytical situation, any school that claims a specific moral code should be treated as highly suspect because it is overstepping its territory. The relationship of psychology to morals lies in the treatment of the neurotic effects produced in the psyche by legalistic, tyrannical, in other words false or superficial moral standards. The part psychology plays within the Church is therefore of great value, for by lessening the ties of false superficial morality the psyche is open to the influence of the true and divine moral law.

VIII

MEDICINE AND MORALITY

by

John Marshall

FROM our early years we are taught that the enemies of our salvation which we must fight against all the days of our life are the devil, the world and the flesh. Among these three, the devil tends to assume pride of place in our minds. The reasons for this are that, from an early age, we learn of his fall from grace, for the story of Lucifer is usually one of the first we are told in our formal religious instruction, and is, therefore, long remembered. The idea of him 'as a roaring lion going about seeking whom he may devour' (1 Pet. 5: 8) impresses itself upon us by the vividness of its imagery. Moreover, the devil, for all that he is a spirit, is to the childish mind a more concrete entity than the world or the flesh. The various pictorial forms in which he is portrayed encourage a lively appreciation of his existence, and engrave themselves indelibly upon the imagination.

Satan may assume so great a stature in the mind that the size of the other enemies of the soul is, by comparison, diminished, and the dangers which threaten us from them are obscured. The catechism does indeed state that the flesh is the greatest enemy of our salvation, but, nevertheless, a great deal of our early religious instruction is concerned with the devil. Christ himself referred to the activity of Satan in the parable of the cockle and the wheat, where he is depicted as the enemy over-sowing cockle among the wheat (Mt. 13: 24). It is well to remember, however, that in the parable of the sower (Mt. 13: 4) Christ described the other enemies of the soul besides him who was represented by the birds of the air.

Medicine is concerned with the third of these enemies, the flesh. It is the purpose of this paper to describe some of the recent advances in knowledge of the anatomical and physiological basis of the forces which are comprised under the term, the flesh. This is not intended to be a comprehensive review of current knowledge, nor can all the facts be considered as being equally well established. Observation and experience in the field of the anatomical and physiological basis of the human personality and emotions have a relatively short history, and new facts are coming to light every day. Much is still uncertain, more is still unknown; but such discoveries as have been made pose interesting questions about the relationship between the tendency to evil and the will to good in man.

In primitive animal forms such as the lizard, almost the whole of the cortex or outer layer of the brain is concerned with the receipt of impulses which serve the sense of smell. This cortex is constructed in three layers, and is known as the archicortex, because of its old development. There is another form of cortex, the neocortex, which is a six-layered structure, and is a prominent feature of the brain in higher animal forms. The lizard has only a minute area of the six-layered cortex but, as we observe progressively more complex animals, we find that the neocortex develops gradually at the expense of the archicortex. Thus, through the rat, dog, monkey and man, the archicortex becomes less and less, while the neocortex grows at a tremendous rate, folding over and burying the archicortex from surface view.

In addition to this anatomical fact, there is the observation that man is much less dependent on his sense of smell than are lower animal forms. Animals such as the lizard and the rat are guided largely by their sense of smell. For man, sight, hearing and touch are the main sensory channels by which he learns about the world around; the presence or absence of his sense of smell, apart from depriving him of certain pleasures, such as the scent of the rose, is largely a matter of indifference. For this reason and others, the study of the part of the brain concerned with smell, or the rhinencephalon as it is called, and its connexions, was greatly neglected. Because in lower animals the rhinencephalon is associated with the sense of smell, it was tacitly assumed that it served the same function in higher forms; and because in higher forms the sense of smell is not so important, the actual function of the rhinencephalon in such species was not subjected to investigation by observation and experiment until very recently.

In the latter part of the last century it had been observed that excision of parts of the cortex in monkeys was followed by changes in behaviour, but it was probably Papez (1937) who first suggested that the rhinencephalon in higher forms has a new function, and is concerned with behaviour and emotional life. Since that time,

D*

much experimental work has been done in animals, and a great deal of knowledge acquired. In addition, since Moniz introduced leucotomy in 1936 for the treatment of mental disorders, much has been learnt about the effects of extirpation of different parts of the brain, including portions of the rhinencephalon, in man. It is now recognized that, though the sense of smell may have declined in value in man, the rhinencephalon has not thereby lost its importance, for it is the organ of emotional expression, and subserves much of the behavioural aspects of man's existence. The most striking effect which can be produced by interference with part of the rhinencephalon is the development in cats and monkeys of what is called 'sham rage'. This occurs when a portion of the rhinencephalon known as the amygdaloid nucleus is removed, or its connexions cut. In this state a previously docile animal becomes ferocious; it attacks to kill without any regard for its own safety or for the odds against it. This behaviour comes in sudden episodes, and is accompanied by all the signs of anger such as dilatation of the pupils and bristling of the hairs. Such a condition has been described by Fulton (1951) in man, following inadvertent damage to part of the brain during an operation. The patient was a young Irish boy whose demeanour before the operation was polite and considerate to all. After the operation, he showed sudden outbursts of extreme irritability, accompanied by a stream of foul, obscene language. His behaviour was threatening, his pupils were widely dilated and he sweated profusely. These outbursts settled over a period of three days, but for a couple of months he was bad-tempered and unreasonable, and liable to outbursts of great irritability. Here then we see temptation in its organic form, not the work of the devil, but the direct effect of anatomical and physiological change in the organism itself. We see, as it were, the anatomical substrate of the capital sin of anger. How far, if at all, such a one is culpable we shall consider at a later stage in the discussion.

An equally, if not more striking example of the effect of physical disturbance on emotional life is from the sphere of sexual temptation, as shown by Erickson's (1945) famous case. This patient was a woman of fifty-five years, who for some thirteen years had experienced tremendous waves of sexual feeling and desire for intercourse. These feelings beset her at least once every day, and sometimes more frequently. She resisted them to the best of her ability, and with great perseverance, but they nevertheless continued and, not infrequently, culminated in an orgasm. She was considered to be an example of nymphomania, and discharged from hospital. Some time later, she developed signs indicative of brain disease; further investigation revealed that she had a tumour growing in that part of the brain in which sensation from the genital organs is represented, and involving also the area of the cortex which I have described as being concerned with emotional response. This tumour was successfully removed, and she made a good recovery. She never again experienced the excess of sexual desire, and was to all intents and purposes normal. In this patient we have a most startling example of an excess of sexual feeling being provoked by brain disease. It was not that her moral sense was depressed or perverted, as sometimes happens in patients with brain damage. She was, in fact, much distressed by the feelings which swept over her with irresistible force, and took great steps to avoid and control them, without any apparent success. I am not, of course, suggesting that all people who are beset with sudden sexual feelings are harbouring within their skulls a brain tumour. Such a concept is manifestly absurd. But I am endeavouring to show that the passions have an anatomical substrate and a physiological mechanism beneath them, which can be aroused or provoked by specific material conditions.

A further example in this sphere may be quoted. This was a patient of Foerster and Gagel (1933), who was having a tumour removed from the base of the brain under local anaesthesia. Whenever the tumour was manipulated, the patient became talkative, and told ribald jokes to the nurses present. When the tumour was not being disturbed, he conducted himself with seriousness and decorum. The urge to tell ribald stories was clearly associated with the disturbance of the base of the brain which occurred when the tumour was manipulated.

But it is not brain lesions alone that can produce abnormal emotional behaviour. Disturbances in the level of calcium in the blood, and of the blood sugar level are two examples of biochemical changes which may cause emotional reactions. Aub (1945) described the case of a woman who received an excessive dose of insulin, so that her blood sugar fell to an extremely low level. She rapidly became suspicious, believing that the nurses were opposed to her, and were trying to kill her. She refused treatment from them that would restore her blood sugar, because she believed they were trying to poison her. When the level of sugar in the blood was restored to normal, her suspicions rapidly subsided, and she became her normal self. Thus, a change in the biochemical constitution of the blood was able, within minutes, to convert a quiet, friendly woman into a hostile, suspicious person.

Another disturbance which may produce changes in the emotional response of the individual, and subject him or her to what appear to be severe temptations, is in the secretion of the endocrine glands. The secretions of these glands are called hormones, the most strikingly effective of these being testosterone, which is produced by the male sex glands. The development in a boy before the age of puberty of a tumour which elaborates testosterone will produce precocious sexual development on the physical plane, accompanied by sexual drives and interests equal to or even in excess of those of a grown man. Removal of the tumour is accompanied by a regression of these feelings and urges which children are, of course, ill-equipped to resist. More dramatic, however, is the observation of the effect of injecting testosterone into an individual. In those who, by reason of some congenital defect, are lacking in full sexual development on the physical plane, and show a parallel absence of interest in the opposite sex, such injections may produce the typical sexual feelings and impulses of normal adults. Equally, testosterone given to a normal person will heighten his sexual appetite, fire his imagination and increase the frequency of his spontaneous sexual activity. He may think that he has the devil within him, but it is not the devil but testosterone that is at work.

The effects of endocrine disturbance in the female are not so clear cut. Tumours of the endocrine glands developing in childhood may well precipitate a premature puberty, and give rise to the sexual feelings and desires of the mature adult which, in turn, will subside with the removal of the tumour. And I think it is not only the premature appearance of these phenomena with the development of the tumour, but their subsidence when it is removed, which so clearly establishes the connexion between its presence and the feelings or temptations of the patient. The effect of the injection of female hormones is not, however, so well established. Opinions differ as to their efficacy, though cases have been described of heightened sexual desire following their administration.

These examples show, therefore, that many of the feelings, urges and desires which beset humanity are not the direct mysterious instillations of the demon, but depend on anatomical connexions, which can be studied, divided and stimulated. These anatomical connexions subserve physiological mechanisms, which could not function without an intact anatomical substrate. We need not look to Satan for the source of our troubles, but can find within a disturbed bodily state the seeds of our destruction.

Now in endeavouring to illustrate my theme I have chosen the most arresting examples from the medical literature, but I think one meets, in everyday medical practice, many examples, less striking in their effects, but, nevertheless, posing real problems to those interested in the relationship between mind and body, and between temptation and the will. For an example I may take the after-effects of a head injury. When a person sustains a severe concussion, there is caused a *commotio cerebri*, which may have far-reaching consequences. A man may have been a good husband, a conscientious father and a hard worker until he sustained his head injury. He then becomes irritable and bad-tempered at home, and is the cause of many quarrels and even of blows. At work he cannot or does not apply himself, and may show a reluctance to work despite his family responsibilities. His tolerance for alcohol is reduced, and hence his previously harmless Saturday night drink is now sufficient to intoxicate him, with further harmful consequences to himself and his family. All these difficulties, though striking in the aggregate, are, taken singly, in the minor key. Occasionally indeed the effects of a head injury are so devastating as to make it clear to all that the sufferer is mentally deranged; but I am referring to the large number of patients whose behaviour would never suggest mental deterioration to the layman. There is little to distinguish such a one from the person who was always bad-tempered, irritable and feckless by nature except the fact that the changes followed the head injury. So it is that the family find it hard to accept the head injury as causing the change in personality, and experience difficulty in meeting the behaviour with sympathy and tolerance. The person is judged to be giving way without cause to temptations to anger, quarrelling and drunkenness.

Consider also the sexual troubles and urges, which sometimes beset elderly men as a result of the enlargement of the prostate gland, or as a result of premature ageing (arteriosclerosis) in the arteries of the brain. A man, previously without blemish, finds himself indulging in practices which are reprehensible to his moral sense, and which not infrequently involve him in trouble with the police. Such patients are often greatly distressed, not only by the public consequences of their acts, but also by their moral implications. They feel that after a lifetime of persevering struggle against the enemies of their salvation, they have been overcome and defeated. They may despair. They do not sense within themselves an organic change, but feel that they must have failed, though they cannot see how or why.

These are but a few examples of the way in which bodily change can give rise to moral problems. Many others could be quoted. The devastating effects of severe or continuous pain are well known. The victim may pray for death, or may take steps himself to secure his death, when he can no longer bear the suffering. The demoralizing effects of starvation were seen only too vividly in the concentration camps of the recent war. Lying, covetousness, theft were all motivated by the struggle for self-preservation in the face of starvation. It is probably not without significance that Satan sought to tempt Christ when he was hungry, having fasted for forty days and forty nights in the desert (Mt. 4: 1-11).

But these are all pathological states. Do physiological upheavals ever raise similar problems? I suggest they may do so. I have already shown that testosterone produced by pathological tumours, or given by injection, has potent effects on sexual life and imagery. At puberty, the sex glands begin to produce this substance in increasing amounts, and there is much evidence that the transition from childhood to maturity is not accomplished smoothly, even on the physiological plane. Physiological imbalance is a prominent feature of adolescence; the ready blush, the tendency to fainting, and the clumsy inco-ordination of arms and legs are all evidence of this. Imbalance in the production of the sex hormones is probably equally a feature of this period of life. The problems of adolescence, therefore, may not be simply those of learning to cope with a new, but well-adjusted, function, but may involve the integration into the personality of a function which is not only new, but is also itself for a time passing through a phase of maladjustment. The force and intensity of a pathological process may afflict the adolescent until the metamorphosis is complete. His problem may not be one of psychological adjustment only, but may demand endurance of a period of frank disequilibrium on the physiological plane also.

I have said enough, I hope, to make it clear that alteration in the physical state of a person can be the basis of temptation. May I now go a step further? Pathological states undoubtedly provide the material for temptation; times of physiological transition may equally well do so; may it be, therefore, that many of the daily temptations to lust, anger and sloth have their origin in the day-to-day fluctuations in the anatomical and physiological mechanisms I have described? May they be not mysterious interventions from without, but simply reflections of the tides of physiological, biochemical and endocrine activity, which surge to and fro within us? No doubt they are influenced and excited by sensory percepts from the world around us. The mechanism underlying anger will be attuned to the insults which may fall upon our ears; the sexual apparatus will be stimulated by the visual stimuli calculated to arouse it. But the effectiveness of the sights and sounds, in any particular instance, will depend to some degree on the state of the mechanism attuned to receive them. The threshold of responsiveness may be raised or lowered by habit, training and previous experience; it may be affected by disease as I have shown; but it may, even in the absence of outside stimulation, show spontaneous activity.

We have seen that the removal of parts of the brain, irritation of parts by pathological processes, disturbance of the biochemical content of the body and the circulation of excessive amounts of hormones in the blood stream can all give rise to emotional states and feelings which are indistinguishable from those arising in temptation. Anger and lust have both been produced by disease states. These two were chosen as offering the most outstanding examples, but similar examples of covetousness, gluttony and sloth could equally well have been described. It is not my purpose to indicate whether the disturbance of the brain operates through biochemical and hormonal changes in the body as a whole, or whether the biochemical changes are primary, and produce in turn secondary effects on the brain. Such considerations are indeed of interest, but are irrelevant to my present purpose. My aim has been to show that some people, by reason of their physical state, are predisposed to act in a certain way. This predisposition is greater than is found in normal people, and may also be more manifest at certain times of life. I have not been concerned so far to discuss the moral implications of such a tendency, when it leads a person to pursue a course of action which is immoral; I have merely tried to demonstrate by concrete examples the fact that such a predisposition can arise as a result of physical changes in the person.

Following upon these considerations, I would pose two questions. The first is, What is the relationship between the activity of Satan and the phenomena which I have described? Do the majority of temptations arise simply because of the physical disturbances that have been outlined? Are these outside the influence of the devil, or has he the means of direct intervention in these processes?

The second question has a more practical bearing, and concerns the question of responsibility, in the face of these phenomena. No matter whether temptation arises because of physical change within the body, or whether it is precipitated by forces from without, the question of responsibility must still be faced. That certain acts are intrinsically evil, and always constitute material sin cannot be doubted. Moralists have, however, always recognized that culpability may be reduced in particular instances by the circumstantial features of the individual case. How can one recognize such circumstances, and how does one deal with them? Many will say that this is the moralist's problem and not the doctor's, but such an evasion fails to meet the needs of either doctor or patient. Patients frequently seek out the Catholic doctor, because he is a Catholic, and their ears are keenly attuned to the tenor of his remarks. They do not expect from him a moral judgement, but they are undoubtedly influenced by him. Even though he refrains from any explicit or direct statement, his attitude towards their problem may encourage or discourage the belief that theirs is not in essence a moral but a physical failure. Even though he vouchsafes no opinion, his approach to their trouble orientates their own approach. And, not infrequently, he is brought more closely to grips with this issue of responsibility when the patient challenges him with a direct question. Supposing we are treating a patient who has fallen for the two hundredth time. He says, 'I do not want to fall; I go to confession as soon as possible after; I resolve with all sincerity never to fall again, and yet I know, as surely as the sun will rise tomorrow, that I shall fall again.' Is it the verse which says 'Not till seven times; but till seventy times seven times' (Mt. 18: 22) that should be quoted to him, or is it the concept of the irresistible impulse which is needed to sustain his despairing efforts? May one quote the story of the homosexual in the Cahiers Laennec who, having been to confession, cried out, 'If I die before seven o'clock tonight, I shall be saved'? Are the impulses engendered by some physical states irresistible? Could the woman with the thirteen years of sexual torment have always resisted the temptation? How must we interpret St Paul's phrase 'And God is faithful, who will not suffer you to be tempted above that which you are able: but will make also with temptation issue, that you may be able to bear it' (1 Cor. 10: 13)?

The conscientious physician often feels acutely the force of these

problems when faced with the individual case. He will look in vain
in his medical text-books for guidance. Do the moralists have an
answer?

References

Aub, J. (1945), 'Relation of Endocrine Secretions to Psychiatry'. *Digest of Neurol. and
    Psychiat. 132*, 31. Hartford: Institute for Living.
Erickson, T. C. (1945), 'Erotomania (Nymphomania) as an expression of Cortical
    Epileptiform Discharge,' *Arch. Neurol. Psychiat.*, Chicago, *53*, 226.
Foerster, O. and Gagel, O. (1933), 'Ein Fall von Ependymcyste des III Ventrikels. Ein
    Beitrag zur Frage der Beziehungen psychicscher Storungen zum Hirnstamm,'
    Ztschr. f. d. ges. Neurol. u. Psychiat., *149*, 312.
Fulton, J. F. (1951), *Frontal lobotomy and Affective Behaviour. A neurophysiological analysis*,
    Chapman and Hall, London, pp. 159.
Moniz, E. (1936), *Tentatives operatoires dans le traitement de certaines psychoses*, Paris,
    Masson et Cie, pp. 248.
Papex, J. W. (1937), 'A proposed mechanism of Emotion', *Arch. Neurol. Psychiat.*,
    Chicago, *38*, 725.

NOTE ON CHAPTER VIII

DISCUSSION which followed Dr Marshall's paper at the symposium supplied the following outline of a possible answer to the questions put at the
end of his paper.

There seems to be evidence that in special cases Satan may have the
means of direct intervention, but it would be unwise to assume this in any
particular case, since such cases are probably extremely rare. Generally
the activity of Satan appears to be indirect. His aim presumably is to
produce a state of disorganization and bewilderment. It should be clearly
understood that to produce such a state is not to produce a sin, bewilderment being precisely a factor diminishing guilt. It should also, however,
be clearly understood that there is a sin which may be committed in these
circumstances whose evil lies outside the particular sphere concerned,
and this is the sin of despair. It is surely this sin which the devil has in
view.

There can be no doubt of any sort that physical and mental states exist
in which responsible action is no longer possible in one or more spheres
of activity. In certain cases this is recognized quite clearly, for instance
madness. And there are clearly other pathological states, both mental
and physical, where some actions may be compulsive. It is the borderline
cases which present the real difficulties, the cases of adolescent physiological disturbance and the compulsive acts of neurotic married couples.
We may state the problem thus: an action cannot at the same time be
compulsive and sinful. It is never right for a doctor to say to a patient:
'Of course it is sinful, but you can't help it.' That is a contradiction in
terms. It is in such a context that the patient is easily tempted to despair
and the chances of bringing him back to a state where he can exercise
full moral responsibility are greatly impaired.

What then can the doctor do? First we may emphasize his position as a Christian, a member of the body of Christ, a mediator of the healing power of the incarnation and redemption. He has a specific charismatic position within that body. His task is to heal; and it will be well to confirm the impression given by Dr Marshall that the doctor cannot isolate his healing work in a purely departmental bodily context. When Jesus healed, it was a total healing.

What then is the doctor's task in our situation? Surely it is to provide, without any hesitation, knowledge of the facts. He must say clearly: 'So far as I can see—your condition is such that sometimes you have been unable to avoid such or such an action. It is my task to cure you, to bring you back to that normal physical condition within which you can exercise your free will, and undertake full moral responsibility for all your actions.'

In such circumstances it is clearly essential for the doctor to be in sufficiently close contact with a priest to be able to inform him of what he has said and what he is doing so that the priest may have the benefit of his diagnosis in guiding the patient back to responsibility on the specifically spiritual level, and so avoid the impasse already referred to, 'It is sin but you can't help it,' in which the patient's remaining sense of responsibility may well be sapped and his temptation to despair may lead him to avoid any further attempts to receive the sacraments.

It will be worth stating a further conclusion here. It would be a good thing if lectures were given in seminaries from such first-hand experience as that provided by Dr Marshall's paper. The essential material of typical cases of conscience can then be presented in the first-hand vivid language of the doctor's professional diagnosis. Many cases which eventually reach the psychiatrist's or neurologist's consulting room might be put right at an earlier stage if sufficient general knowledge on the physical and psychological side were available to the particular confessor concerned.

It is not suggested that difficult cases can be avoided. These there will always be. Human diagnosis, whether spiritual, psychological or medical, can never be perfect. But it is suggested that a great mass of only slightly abnormal cases could be more satisfactorily treated in the light of modern knowledge, particularly those of adolescence and of the compulsive acts of neurotic couples. It is clear also that if this is to happen, communications between priest, doctor and psychiatrist must be kept open; there must be scope for constant consultation between them as a matter of course, not as matter of exception.

Chapter XVI, 'The Confessor's Problem', by Fr Gerald Vann, O.P., is relevant to these matters and provides a more extensive discussion of some of the implications of this answer to the doctor's questions.—*Editor*.

IX

MORALS AND ECONOMICS

by

Colin Clark

MOST of the younger economists today, and also many not-so-young, take a positively prophylactic care lest their science be contaminated by *normative statements* or *value judgements*; or, to reduce the matter to its real essentials, deny that economists should have any *preferences* as between this order of society or that. Preferences between different orders of society, or between different codes of conduct, are indeed themselves to be treated as material for the economist to feed into his system, and to be regarded as carrying no more ultimate significance than the preferences which a man may have between different brands of toothpaste. Whatever Marshall or Professor Pigou may have regarded as the ultimate objectives of economics does not concern us now; quite probably indeed we have not even read what they had to say on this subject, knowing in advance how distasteful we would find it. The economist now undertakes to do nothing more than to describe what consequences will follow from what actions, meanwhile remaining strictly indifferent as to whether any action is ever worth taking or not. Some purists would not even be satisfied with this description, but would say that his object was no more than to give an orderly description of the events which actually occur.

If this be true, it inevitably follows that economics, *per se*, must be completely useless. The more intellectually honest holders of these beliefs demonstrate, somewhat reluctantly, this painful conclusion; others try to evade it. Those who admit the uselessness of economics *per se* can of course go on to point out how useful economics may be in the hands of anyone from outside who has supplied the necessary 'value judgements'. But these thoughts, on further reflexion, do not appear very consoling. Rather the reverse, when we think of some of the 'value judgements' which are floating around in the modern world, and contemplate the prospect of the resources of economic science being used in their service.

It is a paradox that prominent members of the Vienna and London Schools (as they used to be called), who so actively promulgated the doctrine that economics was a science dealing purely objectively with the flow of consequences to be expected from given causes, were also passionate, and sometimes quite convincing, upholders of a particular form of society. In such cases they have to explain their success, modestly, as being due to some kind of split personality. The economist in them, dispassionately and with no interest in the ultimate consequences, works out the chains of reasoning; then the other part of their personality, the part which makes value judgements, comes along with some statements which give value and purpose to their economic conclusions.

These points of view have now found wide acceptance, and indeed with many have become firmly held articles of belief, to be treated as axiomatic. Let no attack be made on their position. Let nothing be said which will disturb the most scrupulous conscience of the most devout amoralist. But let us ask him to consider, more pragmatically, whether his system works. If we have no idea of the order of society or the code of conduct which we want, or if different people have different preferences on this subject, which we take into account along with their preferences on more purely economic matters—we have, under such circumstances, long since given up any hope of getting any *useful* results. But are we now not finding—and indeed having it demonstrated to us by mathematical analysis—that under these conditions we cannot even get consistent or coherent results? Is not economic science rapidly relapsing into what is, quite literally, chaos?

To use still more modern terminology, it is indubitably true that the problems become more manageable if the rules of the game are less frequently altered. What is proposed here is that, while a broad fringe of the rules should be treated as alterable from time to time, certain basic rules should be treated as permanently unalterable. This accords fully with the tenets of moral philosophy, which teaches that there are certain basic rules unchangeable for all men, at all times, and in all places; but that there are also others whose applicability, or at any rate whose importance, will vary with circumstances; while further some moral problems remain unsolved, or at any rate, no general agreement can be reached on them. Moreover, laws, social institutions and customs (which constitute some of the most important 'rules' with which the economist has to deal) may vary very greatly under different circumstances, even when the underlying moral concepts remain entirely unchanged. Those who disbelieve in any form of moral philosophy are not therefore asked in any way to alter their disbeliefs, but merely to discuss, with all the indifference and scepticism which they are accustomed to employ, whether any such system of limitations makes it possible to obtain useful and coherent results, which our present set of rules does not.

The concept of pure science, of scientific results in themselves useless, or only useful in pursuit of some 'values' to be determined by someone outside the field of the science in question—these concepts, surely, only reached economics because of the example and prestige of other sciences much older and more distinguished than itself. But, after all, two of the oldest established and most important sciences were mechanics and agricultural science, and there was never any doubt that their object was to render direct assistance to mankind in its daily tasks. It was later that sciences more closely resembling what we now call pure physics and pure biology developed. Men pursued these, as they had pursued astronomy and pure mathematics from an earlier date, out of a pure love of knowledge, without knowing whether the results would ever be useful to anyone or not—and in fact premature attempts to make remunerative application of the results of science, in astrology and alchemy, did a good deal of harm.

But all the same, practitioners of pure science have always been, and are now, aware that they are dealing with a subject matter which is also dealt with by applied scientists, and that the conclusions of the pure scientist, even of the astronomer or mathematician, have a way of proving useful at a later date. Faraday, when Gladstone asked a highly materialistic question as to what use his electrical discoveries were, replied, with considerable prescience, that some future chancellor would be able to tax them. It is probably beyond the wit of the philosopher to unravel all the different elements which are present in scientific work—direct desire to promote the welfare of mankind, love of knowledge for its own sake, aesthetic satisfaction, and other elements still harder to analyse—but we know that they are all there.

The older sciences have had infinitely more effort devoted to them, and have worked to far higher standards of precision, than has ever been the case with economics. These considerations alone should make the economist hesitate before he claims the degree of abstraction from mundane ends which they sometimes claim. But, in any case, there is a more fundamental difference. While the natural sciences may have some metaphysical or aesthetic rôle to play, their 'application' lies entirely in the field of enabling mankind to produce and use material goods. If these goods include dangerous poisons and habit-forming drugs and indecent pictures and weapons of war, that is not (as he persistently points out to us, with some justification) the scientist's fault. Other people have organized society in such a way as to use his science to produce these goods, and the responsibility is on them. And this puts the economist on the spot—he cannot shift all the responsibility on to the politician and the philosopher.

It is surely significant that Cambridge began the teaching of economics as a branch of the Moral Sciences Tripos. Later, under Marshall, economics secured the right to be studied as a purely independent course—a right which Oxford and many other Universities have always denied it. But there is no need to point out how faithfully Marshall and others who have come after him preserved the point of view that economics, even when studied as an independent Tripos, remained essentially a special form of the science of morals, of framing the rules of human conduct. Somewhat more sophisticated, the European Universities, when they began to teach economics in the nineteenth century, treated it as a branch of law. Law is (or should be) in accordance with morals, so far as it goes; but it is clearly recognized that out of the whole field of moral obligations, law only deals with those which it is possible or expedient for civil authority to enforce; and there are also many provisions of law which, though necessary for purposes of administration, have no foundation in morals, and are therefore morally binding only in so far as obedience to lawfully constituted civil authority is a general moral obligation.

Economics thus studied as a branch of law has doubtless been useful in training many generations of European higher civil servants. It has not produced so many high flights of theory as has the economics of the English-speaking countries—but it may have avoided some of our errors too.

It is true that the morals taught by the older Cambridge school were Utilitarian; gradually becoming less rigid and dogmatic, as they passed from Bentham through James Mill, John Stuart Mill, Sidgwick and Marshall to Professor Pigou. It is also true that they sought to approach these problems mathematically—to unite morals and mathematics in one rigorous logical structure was the greatest dream of Victorian Cambridge. They did not see, however —their historical vision was short and uncritical—that Bentham had been guilty of the immense presumption of claiming that the entire system of morals, by which mankind had lived for so long, could be re-written by one philosopher in a short period of years— to say nothing of undertaking the job of rewriting the whole of law, public administration and economics as well. Nor did the Cambridge Victorians see (being somewhat inward-gazing) how short-lived Benthamite Utilitarianism was going to be, how quickly it would be rejected by all philosophers. In one of Disraeli's parliamentary wisecracks, at the expense of some pedant on the opposite bench—'Even Mormon', he said, 'now has more followers than Bentham.' This was as long ago as the 1870's.

Now, it is almost impossible to find an economist who will look at Utilitarianism seriously, let alone adopt it.

If we reject Utilitarianism, but still want a code of morals to bring into economics (for purposes of hypothetical discussion only, not to offend anybody's conscience), we must go back a bit further. We could start with the Ten Commandments, which have the advantage of being comprehensive and concise, but which also need considerable interpretation and illustration before we can understand their application to all issues of morals.

More applicable to our purpose are the highly sophisticated medieval studies of psychology which led to the categorizing of the Seven Deadly Sins. These do not constitute specific and comprehensive listing of moral rights and wrongs—they do not directly mention murder or theft, for example—so much as a listing of those states of mind which, if a man allows himself to indulge in them, will certainly lead him to perform immoral and anti-social acts. Conversely, there are a number of virtues listed, with less numerical precision, which lead to good acts.

The seven sins, as we all remember, are pride, anger, sloth, lust, gluttony, envy and avarice. There is probably, to this day, no better analytical account of them in the English language than the Parson's Tale in Chaucer. (Doubtless the holy man's ideas had been sharpened by listening to some of the stories told by the other pilgrims.)

Let us now be more specific. If economics has any object at all, other than to be an intellectual and mathematical exercise, this object is—we no longer dare say to promote men's welfare—but, perhaps we may say, to enable them to follow their preferences.

If so, we next have to face two basic questions, which, phrased in the old manner, ran thus. Can we assume some sort of Law of Diminishing Utility, whereby man finds increasing supplies of the same commodity gradually becoming less interesting, and that therefore there should be some rational way of apportioning goods between men; and secondly, does a man's economic welfare depend solely upon the goods he receives and the efforts he has to make, or does it depend also, and if so, does it depend positively or negatively, upon what other men are receiving? (Doubtless it is possible to re-write this sentence in the modern terms of indifference and scales of preference, but, on this occasion at any rate, the older language appears to be the simpler.)

It is at this point that we get straight into moral categories. The first and most important moral principle is that one man's attitude towards his neighbour's welfare should always be positive, never negative. We are not entitled to wish another man to be deprived of any of his goods, except in so far as we wish to see unjustly acquired goods restored to their rightful owner, or as a punishment inflicted by lawful authority for some offence committed. These terms must be carefully defined and observed, and the burden of proof is always on the would-be depriver.

The virtue of justice consists in scrupulously refraining from any action which will deprive any other men of their lawful possessions or rights, and of acting to restore them if they have been so deprived. It is, however, a somewhat negative virtue. The greater virtue of charity can be simply defined as a positive desire for other men's welfare, both material and spiritual.

We can all readily agree how desirable it is that some people, at any rate, should be possessed of this virtue. But a little further reflection will show us it is not merely desirable, but is also necessary. Without some measure of charity, as we have defined the word, there cannot be any social order.

The work of the world could not indeed be done without it. The ordinary man going about his ordinary daily routine—the cowman, the bus conductor, the shop assistant—is he all the time making careful calculation of advantage and disadvantage? These states of mind which the economist analyses may be more applicable to the case of a merchant, though not always even to him—for the ordinary man they are only likely to be applicable at a time when he is thinking of changing his job. What keeps him to his full routine is, at any rate for many men, the sense that he is performing an important duty to his fellow men, which, for the religious man, is to a large degree co-terminous with his duty to God.

Among those with more interesting vocations—scientists, artists, teachers—it is taken for granted that service to their fellow men is the principal motive of their lives and work.

Totalitarian states start off with great claims about service to one's fellow man (so long, that is, as he belongs to the right race or class). We should be grateful for having had the opportunity of learning from our own experience what we might otherwise have found difficulty in believing, how quickly the motives of love for one's fellow men are displaced by hatred of enemies and fear of punishment—and how cumbrous and unworkable their economies become.

We thus come by comparatively simple reasoning to the firm and important conclusion that there can be no ordered society (therefore, *a fortiori*, no economic order) unless it be founded on the practice of the virtues of justice and charity, and the discountenancing of the opposed sins.

There is more than one sinful state of mind which may lead men to commit offences against justice. But the first one which we should consider is envy. This state of mind should be defined as simply as possible as the hatred of another man's well-being (whether material or spiritual); it does not matter, in the first instance, whether we wish to see him deprived of his goods for our benefit, or just to see him deprived of his goods. Note that this definition by no means always coincides with the modern colloquial use of the word. If we say to a friend 'I envy you your house!' this may just be an emphatic way of saying that we think it a very beautiful house; but if we think that he ought to be deprived of it, then (unless we have proof that he obtained it by unjust means) we are committing the sin of envy, in the full sense of the word.

Now let us turn back to the other basic question, which, for convenience, we have described under the heading of whether or not a Law of Diminishing Utility prevails. Can men's desires be satisfied, or largely satisfied, by an increasing abundance of goods, or does abundance, in certain cases, leave desire as avid as ever, or even inflame it further? This state of mind—leaving aside questions of sex, which do not concern us directly now—when it appears in respect of material goods, is defined as gluttony or greed. Gluttonous desire, so defined, is inherently sinful, and we are guilty of condonation if we attempt to assist others to satisfy such desires. The law recognizes this principle, in respect of habit-forming drugs, and treats the selling of such drugs to an addict as a grave offence. In a milder manner, the law may punish a publican who continues to supply goods to an already intoxicated customer.

But the economist, also intoxicated—'by the exuberance of his own verbosity'—makes no attempt to distinguish between demands or 'preferences', but offers to satisfy them all, in order of their supposed urgency. Some indeed, coin the dreadful phrase 'consumer sovereignty'. 'The customer is always right' may be a convenient working rule for department store salesmen; but is it to be implicitly accepted by economists who claim the right to give advice on the most difficult affairs of State?

If we take morals into account, we conclude that the object of economics—and a thoroughly desirable object it is, seeking the welfare of others (which is true charity)—is to enable men to satisfy their *legitimate* desires (using the word in both its legal and moral sense). We are not responsible if normal legitimate goods are, without our knowledge, put to illegitimate uses. It is not the duty of the economist to suppress the manufacture and distribution of shotguns and rat-poison because men sometimes use them to murder their wives. But we are certainly responsible if we knowingly permit illegitimate uses.

Our refusal to enquire into the nature of desires, or to distinguish between them, has led us into the absurd position of tolerating those forms of business which seek, not to satisfy desire, but to inflame it by advertising—'those crafty men who do not hesitate to stimulate human desires, and when they have been aroused, satisfy them at their own profit' specifically condemned by Pope Pius XI in *Quadragesimo Anno*. Clearly this is morally illegitimate. Mankind has enough unsatisfied desires already, without advertising agents deliberately adding to them.

The translation of this principle into a practical code of conduct will be difficult but not impossible. Advertising which gives people information enabling them to satisfy desires which they possess already (the small advertisements in the local newspaper are the clearest example of such advertising) is not only legitimate, but clearly desirable. But advertisements which set out, directly or by implication, to evoke desire—all the most expensive and sophisticated types of advertising—are illegitimate. The principal weapons of the advertising agent, it is said, lie in his appeals to the emotions of fear, greed, lust and snobbery, every one of them harmful and wrong.

While gluttony is defined as inordinate desire for certain material goods—drink is now the most frequently mentioned, gluttonous eating having been more a fault in medieval and Victorian days—we are also familiar with the inordinate desire for money as such, which is avarice. The definition of both words turns on the word 'inordinate' and there are of course border-line cases. Even more than with other problems of conscience, individual circumstances must here be taken carefully into account. We can never hope to write down which categories of transactions are avaricious, and which are not. But we can easily detect flagrant cases of avarice, as with flagrant cases of drunkenness. Even if the economist or the legislator cannot find any just and practicable means of restraining avarice, it is certainly our duty to refrain from encouraging it to still further excesses. That it encourages avarice is the real gravamen of the charge against a free-enterprise society. Not for centuries has this charge been so trenchantly and effectively stated as it was in Keynes's pamphlet of 1924, *The End of Laissez-Faire*. Keynes may have been a secularist but he was a great believer in right and wrong.

At this stage, we can hardly do more than pose the issue of avarice. Some public action should be possible to reinforce the individual conscience in this matter, though we should not overrate its possibilities. Medieval authorities, civil as well as religious, condemned speculation and money-lending, transactions which were probably at that time predominantly avaricious. It is a more difficult problem for us, because we see that such transactions, while sometimes undoubtedly avaricious, are equally clearly, on many occasions, socially beneficial. Medieval doctrine taught that it was an offence against justice, motivated by avarice, to buy at less, or sell at more, than a just price. So, we must agree, it is. But many people in the modern world seem to have remarkably *simpliste* ideas of what medieval philosophers considered a just price. (This applies particularly to those considerable elements of public opinion whose ideas on economics were formed, directly or indirectly, by Douglas Credit advocates, who taught even worse nonsense than usual on this subject.) The idea has gained wide currency that medieval philosophers upheld a crude cost of production theory of value, and many people, particularly farmers, often ask why this admirable system of fixing prices on ascertained costs of production, which they erroneously believe to have existed in the past, could not be reinstated. The cost of production theory of the just price was discredited at a very early date in the Middle Ages. It was pointed out, quite truly, that this idea in itself offended against justice, by requiring the purchaser to pay for any indolence or inefficiency on the part of the producer. When the doctrine of the just price was put into its final form, in the later Middle Ages, it was agreed that a just price was that which was freely negotiated between buyer and seller, when neither party took any advantage of any *ignorance* or *weakness* on the part of the other. The practical conclusion from this seems fairly clear—a basically free-market economy, with intervention if you find any group of buyers or sellers in a weak bargaining position, or suffering from undue ignorance.

Progressive taxation can probably be defended, *inter alia*, on the grounds that it gives some discouragement to the man whose principal object in life is mere avaricious accumulation. This is true; but the reasoning must be handled with great care. While some such men are to be found at all income levels, and deserve to be discouraged, it is very probable that others are attempting to earn and accumulate for entirely desirable and unavaricious ends: a tax is bound, unfortunately, to discourage both classes equally. There is plenty of evidence that, in this country at any rate, progressive taxation of income has already been carried far beyond any reasonable limit.

There is also the danger, that while we may be successfully removing the opportunities for avarice in one group of men, we are fanning the flames of envy in another. When taxation becomes 'a political issue', we are in real danger on this score. When we impose taxation on any class of men, not because the just needs of the State require it, and not because we have evidence that they are showing a tendency for avaricious accumulation, but just because we think 'they have got too much money and they oughtn't to have it', then we have crossed the subtle dividing line which divides justice from envy. If we are genuine in our object of discouraging avarice, at the same time needing to defray the necessary expenses of the State, we would find it far more prudent in the long run to have much lighter and much less progressive taxation of income, but in its place some system of progressive taxation of capital (which scale of progression, however, should fully take family needs into account).

The present extremely high rates of progressive income taxation have weakened the forces of avarice, though they have damaged a great many beneficial social forces as well. But it is interesting, and rather sinister, to watch a certain type of man who no longer seeks money, but rather power. He may do this through building up the powers and resources of a company, or of a nationalized business, or of a government department, or of a newspaper, or any other of the powerful organizations in which the modern world abounds.

There is one thing upon which we all find it comparatively easy to agree; that the quest of power for its own sake is the most dangerous of all forces in the modern world. But what we now call the lust for power, and tend to regard as a fairly modern phenomenon, is in fact almost identical with what our ancestors called the sin of pride, the first of the Seven Deadly Sins. Pride is a great deal more than self-adulation, which may indeed be a comparatively harmless fault, if it does not result in action. Pride in its most dangerous form shows itself in action, when we make our will prevail *because it is our will* and for no other reason. In this matter, Hitler appears to have plumbed the lowest depths so far attained by mankind. What makes pride so much more terrible than the other sins is that while they are generally found in weaklings, it is often the best and strongest men who succumb to pride, They seek power—economic or political—for objects which are truly good, and strenuously exert their will in order to bring them about, until, by almost imperceptible stages, the original object is forgotten, and it becomes their object to impose their will on others, because it is their will. Rightly this is regarded as one of the most terrible of sins.

It may be that some reorganization of our social order will be possible which will mitigate this fearful evil. But is it not a purely political question? Not altogether. The economist has something to do with it, although the political scientist must play the major part here. We must reconstruct our society so as to disperse power, both political and economic, wherever possible, not concentrate it. At the moment we are cheerfully engaged in doing the exact opposite. Although we did not heed his advice Acton knew what he was talking about, and we shall soon be in for trouble. It was indeed Keynes who, in spite of his criticisms of free-enterprise society in *The End of Laissez-Faire*, also said (for he was a man of very balanced judgement) that the real cause *for* free enterprise lay in the fact that it made possible the utmost decentralization of economic decisions. (Unfortunately, he appears never to have printed this dictum, though he certainly made it.) Laski's teachings, now known throughout the world, to the effect that the ultimate wisdom of political science is to be ever building up the powers of the State, at the expense of smaller political authorities, and extending these powers into the economic sphere; the extraordinary tolerance with which the majority of modern economists regard the increasing monopolization and centralization of industrial organization; both of these errors spring from a naïve, perfectionist view of mankind. Has it required the shocking experiences of the last generation to remind us that man is prone to sin, and that while a prudent reconstruction of the social order may do something to mitigate this tendency, it will never entirely prevent it; and that the most dangerous and deadly sin is the sin of pride, or love of power?

Using therefore the convenient categorization, which our forefathers prepared for us, of the Seven Deadly Sins, we see that four of them have a direct bearing upon economics. Sloth, or neglect of ordinary duties, does not at present concern us very much. But it is a point still to be made that an economic system should not encourage or condone such neglect, as did the 'Old Poor Law' in this country, or as perhaps do some features of economic life in oriental countries today.

The two remaining sins, anger and lust, which may provoke murder and adultery, have little to do with economics. They keep the Sunday papers going instead.

Even those who do not accept the moral code, or who believe that morals are purely relative, or a matter for individual choice, or some similar pernicious doctrine, must nevertheless agree that an economic system bound by these (or similar) moral limitations becomes far easier to handle, and its problems much more capable of solution. After all, when it comes to the point, it turns out that we all in fact hold very similar views about the dangers of envy and avarice and the lust for power; and on gluttony there is very little divergence of opinion.

The application of these simple moral principles will bring us into conflict with three of the most powerful forces in the modern world—advertising, monopoly and centralization—which makes it more interesting.

X

INTERNATIONAL RELATIONS

by

David H. N. Johnson

RECENTLY there has appeared upon the scene a new academic discipline known as International Relations. What are the terms of reference of this discipline?

According to Dr Schwarzenberger, of the University of London, an acknowledged authority on the subject, 'The study of international relations is the branch of sociology which is concerned with international society.'[1] Professors Palmer and Perkins, of the University of Pennsylvania, who have recently written a book over twelve hundred pages long, simply entitled *International Relations*, introduce their study as follows.

> While the study of international relations [they say] has emerged from its earlier status as a poor relation of political science and history, it is still far from being a well-organized discipline. It is heavily dependent upon economics, geography, sociology, psychology, and anthropology, as well as upon political science and history. It also draws from agriculture, education, engineering, law, medicine, military science, religion, semantics, and many other fields. Moreover, it is still too subjective in character and content, too likely to be perverted from its real purpose— the analytical study of interstate relations—by proponents of a Utopian or of a power-political approach, to mention only the extreme 'schools'.[2]

In view of its dependence upon already established disciplines, it is not surprising that the new subject continues to meet with a certain scepticism in some halls of learning. University curricula are already notoriously overloaded. Nevertheless it is a safe prediction that International Relations has come not only to stay, but also to grow in significance.

[1] *Power Politics* (1951), p. 8.   [2] *International Relations* (1954), p. 5.

The experts quoted above gave it as their view that the real purpose of International Relations as a discipline is 'the analytical study of interstate relations'. Strictly speaking, of course, the word 'international' means 'between nations' rather than 'between states'. But, when we use the word today, we tend, it is true, to think of relations between states (e.g. the United Kingdom, the United States of America and the Soviet Union) rather than between nations (e.g. the English, the Welsh and the Scots). Therefore, we may accept the statement by the experts as to the purpose of their study.

The meaning of such words as 'nation' and 'state' is a matter upon which political scientists could argue indefinitely. But for our present purposes we must limit ourselves to a severely practical definition of each. We may regard a 'nation' as a group of people, with a cultural awareness of itself as distinct from other groups of people, with common traditions handed down from the past, and with common aspirations for the future. We may regard a state as a political or legal entity, consisting of a government ruling over a number of people within a certain territory. Rivers of blood have flowed in the attempt to realize the ideal of the so-called 'Nation-State.' But many states contain within themselves more than one nation; and not a few nations find themselves governed by more than one state.

Relations between states, therefore, are the subject matter of International Relations. This being so, the first question which has to be asked is whether this is a subject upon which a specifically Catholic view can, or should, be taken. There are some branches of learning (e.g. theology), upon which, *ex hypothesi*, a specifically Catholic view exists. There are others, however, upon which a distinctly Catholic point of view is more or less inconceivable. One can hardly speak, for instance, of a Catholic Mathematics, a Catholic Chemistry, or even, when viewed purely in the abstract, of Catholic Philosophy.[1]

The answer to the important preliminary question whether there can, or should, be a specifically Catholic view on International Relations depends upon whether this subject be regarded as a descriptive science or as a normative science: whether, that is, the purpose of the subject is to study the manner in which states actually *do* conduct their relations with each other, or whether it is to study

[1] See the review by Fr Hilary J. Carpenter, O.P., of *An Essay on Christian Philosophy* by Jacques Maritain in *The Tablet*, March 26th, 1955, p. 300.

the manner in which states *should* conduct those relations. We must, therefore, consider this question.

It is not possible to proceed far in the study of International Relations without coming across the expression 'Power Politics'. This is the very title of Dr Schwarzenberger's treatise. And, as we have seen, Professors Palmer and Perkins referred to the 'power-political' approach to the subject. What does this expression mean?

According to Dr Schwarzenberger, the essence of power politics is that 'groups within the international society tend to do what they can rather than what they ought.' Power politics, he continues,

> signify a type of relations between States in which certain patterns of behaviour are predominant: armaments, isolationism, power diplomacy, power economics, regional or universal imperialism, alliances, balance of power and war. . . Each group considers itself not merely as a means to a common end, but as an end in itself. At least for purposes of self-preservation, any measure which is required to achieve this object is deemed to be justified. Law and morality within this social environment are limited to a relatively subordinate position. The hierarchy between groups is measured by their weight in any potential or actual conflict.[1]

This is not a happy picture, and some may think it does not represent quite accurately even the present relations between states. But whether that be so or not, the point I wish to make is that the assessment of the part actually played in international affairs by power, and by other forms of pressure based upon might rather than upon right, is a matter of history and sociology rather than a matter upon which Catholic moral teaching can throw any particular light.

But when International Relations is regarded as a normative science, when it is a question of the standards which *should* mark the conduct of relations between states rather than of the patterns which do actually mark them, then there not only can be, but there must be, a Catholic point of view. For neither the impressive bureaucratic organization behind the modern state, nor the spurious philosophies and psychological apparatus upon which many governments rely to stimulate the loyalty of the governed, can conceal the fact that states are mere groups of human beings organized in a certain way, and that the rulers of states are themselves human beings, not supermen exempt from the ordinary canons of morality. International Relations, therefore, in the last resort concern the rela-

[1] *Op. cit.*, p. 13.

E

tions between man and man and, as such, they must come within
the purview of Catholic moral teaching. As Sir Desmond Morton
has well said:

> All Catholics recognize the moral principles of the Natural
> Law, of the ten commandments given to Moses and of the super-
> natural extension of these laws declared by our Lord, upon which
> the Church bases her teaching of man's moral duties and obliga-
> tions towards God, the family and himself, and towards others
> who are not of his immediate family. But all men are truly one
> family, whence similar principles apply to the relations of all men
> whatsoever; between man and man, family and family, between
> one group of families and another group, and thus, between
> nation and nation, sovereign state and sovereign state. It is no
> more justifiable for one state to rob another than it is for one man
> to steal; nor for one state to destroy another, than for one man to
> commit murder.[1]

Professors Palmer and Perkins, in the passage quoted above, referred to the tendency of writers on International Relations to belong to one or other of two extreme schools, namely, the 'Utopian'
and the 'power-politicial'. In so far as this statement implies that
experts on international relations, like other human beings, tend to
divide themselves into optimists and pessimists, idealists and realists,
it is no doubt correct. It is not, however, entirely correct to imply
that the 'power-political' approach is necessarily pessimistic. It is
true that Dr Schwarzenberger, after saying that 'Power politics
have been a constant feature of international relations,' proceeds to
remark that 'It appears therefore prima facie justifiable to work on
the assumption that *plus ça change, plus c'est la même chose*.' Nevertheless the same author adds the wise reservation that 'This is not
meant to imply that because international relations have been—
and are—conducted on this footing, they must always be continued
on the same basis.'[2] Men, he says, are free to organize their relations
on the basis that humanity constitutes a single community—if only
they have the will. Nevertheless, it must be admitted that the
'power-political' approach, in and by itself, tends to be a somewhat
pessimistic one.

If it be true that optimism and pessimism are opposite errors
which ought to be eschewed in the study of International Relations,

---

[1] From an article entitled 'Morality in International Relations' in *Blackfriars*, April
1955, p. 108.

[2] *Op. cit.*, p. 17.

then Catholics ought to be particularly well equipped to avoid both of them. Conscious of man's sinful inheritance, they are not likely to be deceived by panaceas for the abolition of war and strife and for the easy realization of paradise on earth. Equally their religion counsels them against the sin of despair. The Catholic approach is rather that, because of original sin, man's journey through life will never be an easy one; but nevertheless that, since nature may be perfected by supernatural grace, man can, if he will co-operate with grace, obtain even on this earth a fair measure of peace and harmony.

This brings us to a consideration of the standards which, in the Catholic view, should mark the conduct of groups of men towards each other. The first point which strikes one, as one proceeds to examine this question, is that, although International Relations may be a new academic discipline, there is nothing new about the problems which constitute its subject matter. These are virtually as old as the human race itself, although they present themselves to the moralist under different forms. The Roman Empire at the height of its power and glory; the same Empire in decline; the barbarian invasions; the period of medieval Christendom; the Reformation and nationalism; the French Revolution and liberalism; the Industrial Revolution, capitalism and socialism; the Russian and Nazi Revolutions and totalitarianism; the nuclear age; all these and countless other phenomena have formed the background against which the Church, as a divine society living in the world, has had to carry out her mandate of witnessing to the truth and preaching the gospel. A study of Catholic teaching on International Relations reveals, therefore, two main features: first, essential consistency of basic principles; secondly, remarkable variety of forms of application of these principles, depending upon the contemporary pattern of human organization. A vivid illustration of this truth is given by the fact that one of the first problems to tax the wisdom of the Fathers of the Church was whether it was lawful for a Christian to serve in the armies of the Roman Empire, whereas one of the most difficult of contemporary problems is, or may soon become, whether a Christian may serve in a hydrogen bomb unit.[1]

Whatever the political background, the Church has consistently preached the goal of a peaceful international order. As St Augustine said: 'And thus we may say of peace, as we have said of eternal life,

[1] See the article entitled 'A Conversation on the Hydrogen Bomb', by F. H. Drinkwater, in *Blackfriars*, April 1955, p. 114.

that it is the end of our good. . . For peace is a good so great, that even in this earthly and mortal life there is no word we hear with such pleasure, nothing we desire with such zest, or find to be more thoroughly gratifying.'[1] And again, 'Peace between man and God is the well-ordered obedience of faith to eternal law. Peace between man and man is well-ordered concord. Domestic peace is the well-ordered concord between those of the family who rule and those who obey. Civil peace is a similar concord among the citizens. The peace of the celestial city is the perfectly ordered and harmonious enjoyment of God, and of one another in God. The peace of all things is the tranquillity of order.'[2]

But peace is not only order. It is also justice and charity. Or rather it is the result of all these three. To quote St Thomas Aquinas:

> All the precepts and counsels of the Divine Law go to furnish man with aids for fixing his mind on God and removing obstacles to such attention. For these purposes man needs to live at peace and concord with his fellow-men. For man needs to be aided by man, as well to the preservation of life and limb, as also to the end that one man may inflame and incite and instruct another to yearn after God. In the absence of peace and concord, man's mind must be disquieted by contentions and fightings, and hindered from aspiring to God. And therefore the Divine Law has made provision for the preservation of peace and concord amongst men by the practice of justice. . . But it is not enough for peace and concord to be preserved among men by the precepts of justice, unless there be a further consolidation of mutual love.[3]

In our times the Popes have no less consistently stressed that the preservation of international peace is impossible without order, justice and charity. Pope Benedict XV, in his Encylical *Pacem Dei Munus* of May 23rd, 1920, written after the end of the First World War and at the time of the inauguration of the League of Nations, said: 'Things being thus restored, the order required by *justice* and *charity* re-established and the nations reconciled, it is much to be desired . . . that all States, putting aside mutual suspicion, should unite in one league, or rather a sort of family of peoples, calculated both to maintain their own independence and to safeguard the *order* of human society.'[4] As recently as 1954 Pope Pius XII, in his Easter Allocution, asked poignantly: 'When will the rulers of nations realize that peace cannot exist in an exasperating and costly rela-

---

[1] *City of God*, Book xix, Chapter xi.   [2] *Ibid.*, Book xix, Chapter xiii.
[3] *Summa Contra Gentiles*, Lib. iii, Cap. cxxx.   [4] Italics ours.

tionship of reciprocal terror, but only in the Christian rule of universal *charity*, and particularly in *justice*. . . ?'[1]

What distinguishes the writings of Christian spokesmen on international affairs from those of others is, more often than not, the constant reference, as common in the twentieth century as in the thirteenth, to the virtue of charity. This should not surprise Christians, brought up on the famous Pauline passage: 'And now there remain faith, hope, charity, these three: but the greatest of these is charity.'[2] Obviously, in Catholic eyes, the greatest hope for the peace of the world is that all peoples and their rulers should come to accept the truths of the Christian faith and live by them.

Nevertheless Catholic teaching does not insist that a peaceful international order is impossible between states which have not accepted the Christian ideal, although obviously its realization is more difficult. This point was well expressed by Cardinal Bourne, Archbishop of Westminster, in his Lenten Pastoral of 1934 when, referring to the weaknesses of the League of Nations, he said:

> Then again it has been impossible to build up the League on purely Christian principles. It has to embrace within its scope great nations which have never accepted the Christian ideal, and are governed by doctrines and traditions which, in many respects, contradict that ideal. Nevertheless, the solidarity of all mankind, which is the consequence of all being alike creatures of Almighty God, ought to form some kind of basis for bringing the nations closer together. Certainly it is the duty of Catholics, by word and action, to give all the support they can to the League of Nations and to endeavour so to improve it as to make it a real and permanent instrument for the preservation of the peace of the world.

It is immensely reassuring to the Catholic student of international affairs that he can turn to almost any authority, whether it be St Augustine in the fifth century, St Thomas Aquinas in the thirteenth century, the Spanish Dominican Francisco de Vitoria (1480–1546), the Spanish Jesuit Francisco Suarez (1548–1617), the Italian Jesuit Taparelli d' Azeglio (1793–1863), or any of the Popes of the present century—to mention only a few—and that he will find the same basic principles asserted, albeit against a different background. Catholic doctrine, however, has not confined itself to stating in the abstract the need for order, justice and charity. It has always been

---

[1] Again italics ours. Obviously, in the sense in which we have used these terms (p. 120 above) His Holiness is referring to the rulers of states.

[2] 1 Cor. 13: 13.

concerned, and still is concerned, with the practical application of these principles. For it is not enough for the Catholic apologist to go on satisfying himself with the validity of his principles, however valid they may be. The world, certainly the anxious world of today, expects, and is entitled to expect, from Catholicism pronouncements of the utmost clarity on the fundamental problems of international order.

The quotations from Pope Benedict XV and from Cardinal Bourne, which have been given above, are only two examples, among hundreds which could be mentioned, of the constant interest of the Church in the organization of international society and in the practical application of the doctrine that the human race consists essentially of a single family destined to a common end and that, as St Thomas said: 'man needs to be aided by man.' Possibly the clearest expression of this doctrine is that contained in the following famous passage from Suarez:

> The reason for the Law of Nations [he says] is, that the human race, though divided into no matter how many different peoples and nations, has for all that a certain unity, a unity not merely physical, but also in a sense political and moral. This is shown by the natural precept of mutual love and mercy, which extends to all men, including foreigners of every way of thinking. Wherefore, though any one state, republic or kingdom be in itself a perfect community and constant in its members, nevertheless each of the states is also a member, in a certain manner, of the world, so far as the human race is concerned. For none of these communities are ever sufficient unto themselves to such a degree that they do not require some mutual help, society or communication, either to their greater advantage or from moral necessity and need, as is evident from custom. For this reason therefore they need some law whereby they may be directed and rightly ruled in this kind of communication and society. And although this in great part comes from natural law, yet not sufficiently nor directly for all purposes. Therefore it has been found possible to introduce some special laws by the customs of the peoples themselves. For as in one state or province customs introduce law, so in the whole human race international laws could be introduced by custom.[1]

Over three hundred years later, at the very beginning of his pontificate, Pope Pius XII was to be found calling for 'a due recognition of the basic principles of international law and a determina-

---

[1] *De Legibus ac de Deo Legislatore*, Book II, Chapter XIX, paragraph 9.

tion to abide by them'. Among these principles the Pope mentioned 'that each nation shall be allowed to keep its own liberties intact, shall have the right to its own life and development'; and further that 'any pact which has been solemnly ratified in accordance with the rights of nations shall persist, unimpaired and inviolable.' While, however, treaties must be observed, situations may arise, owing to unforeseen circumstances, in which it would be unjust to hold one party to the letter of his engagements. In such cases the old pact should be altered, or a new one substituted for it. But this does not mean, warned the Pope, that each party is entitled to assume to itself the right of violating its engagements at its own discretion. 'Such behaviour', His Holiness continued, 'can only deprive nations of the spirit of confidence which ought to exist between them. It is utterly subversive of the natural order, and leaves nations and peoples severed from one another by deep rivers of distrust.'[1] Wherefore 'it is of the first importance to erect some juridical institution which shall guarantee the loyal and faithful fulfilment of the conditions agreed upon and which shall, in case of recognized need, revise and correct them.'[2]

Catholic doctrine, therefore, attaches the greatest importance to the observance of the principles of international law and to the elucidation and enforcement of these principles by international courts and tribunals. What then is the Catholic conception of international law?

It is not, as is sometimes thought, a conception which would base the rules of international law exclusively upon deductions from a philosophical premiss of Natural Law. Suarez, as we saw, stressed the importance of custom. Taparelli d'Azeglio no less emphasized that international authority 'resides, as of right, in the common accord of the associated nations and it is for the members of the association to determine under what form this authority is to be exercised'.[3] And, as we have just seen, treaties 'solemnly ratified in accordance with the rights of nations' have binding effect. The Catholic conception, therefore, is rather that, in the first place, the rules of international law depend for their validity upon treaty and custom, just as the laws of any single country may depend for their validity upon statute and custom: but that, ultimately, all human laws are referable to the eternal standards of Natural Law and

---

[1] Encyclical *Summi Pontificatus*, October 20th, 1939.
[2] Christmas Message of Pope Pius XII, 1939.
[3] *Essai Théorique de Droit Naturel*, Book VI, Chapter V, paragraph 1366.

Divine Law. Catholic doctrine, therefore, rejects in international affairs, no less than in national affairs, what Pope Pius XII has referred to as 'a juridical positivism which invests purely human laws with a majesty to which they have no title, opening the way to a fatal dissociation of law from morality'.[1]

Positivism in international law takes the form of the assertion that this legal system has no other basis than the consent of states. No less an authority than the Permanent Court of International Justice itself seems to have given expression to this fashion of thinking when in a famous passage—with which all international lawyers are familiar—it said:

> International law governs relations between independent States. The rules of law binding upon States therefore emanate from their own free will as expressed in conventions or by usages generally accepted as principles of law and established in order to regulate the relations between these co-existing independent communities with a view to the achievement of common aims. Restrictions upon the independence of States cannot therefore be presumed.[2]

It is, therefore, not surprising that international tribunals of lesser rank have given vent on occasions to opinions which would reduce to nothing the authority of Natural Law in international affairs. To give only one example, a tribunal once said:

> The law of nature may have been helpful, some three centuries ago, to build up a new law of nations, and the conception of inalienable rights of men and nations may have exercised a salutary influence, some one hundred and fifty years ago, on the development of modern democracy on both sides of the ocean; but they have failed as a durable foundation of either municipal or international law and cannot be used in the present day as substitutes for positive municipal law, on the one hand, and for positive international law, as recognized by nations and governments through their acts and statements, on the other hand.[3]

It is not fair to blame modern international lawyers for the dis-

---

[1] Christmas Message, 1942.

[2] The *Lotus* Case in 1927 (P.C.I.J., Series A, No. 10, p. 18).

[3] *North American Dredging Co. Claim*, 1927 (United States–Mexico General Claims Commission: Opinions of Commissioners, 1927, p. 21). It should be explained that lawyers use the expression 'municipal law' to distinguish the law of individual countries from international law. It has nothing to do with the word 'municipality': it means rather 'national law'.

repute into which the idea of the Natural Law has fallen. The reason lies rather in the corruptions which that idea has undergone since the days of the Schoolmen, and in particular in the eighteenth century. For Emerich de Vattel (1714–67) the Natural Law ceased to be regarded as a law laying down fundamental norms of conduct for men conceived of as rational, social beings dependent upon one another. It came instead to be treated as a system of law applicable to the so-called 'state of nature' so popular with eighteenth-century philosophers. Applied to the relations of man to man the 'state of nature' was always a somewhat unreal abstraction, although it gave rise to the revolutionary theory of 'natural rights'. But, applied to the relations of state to state, the philosopher's idea of the 'state of nature' was not too far removed from the reality of power politics. It was no coincidence that Vattel's treatise on international law[1] with its extended emphasis upon the 'natural right' of self-preservation, came to be relied upon by Foreign Offices. In such hands theories of international law, which purported to be based on Natural Law, were in fact indistinguishable from positivism.[2]

If an attempt be made to assess the present state of theories of international law, it may be said that traditional positivism is no longer in quite the commanding position that it once was, at any rate in the western world. Article 38 (1) of the Statute of the International Court of Justice directs the Court to apply, in addition to treaties and customary rules, 'the general principles of law recognized by civilized nations'. Although this phrase was present in the Statute of the former Permanent Court of International Justice, drawn up as early as 1920, there has been a growing realization of its constructive potentialities. The phrase is a somewhat ambiguous one, and the requirement that the principles concerned be 'recognized by civilized nations' is even positivist in tone. There is certainly no disposition to admit that the phrase authorizes the Court to apply the principles of Natural Law in the sense that Catholic philosophers understand those principles. Nevertheless it is generally agreed that, under this provision, the Court is entitled to apply what is sometimes called a 'modern law of nature'.[3]

---

[1] *Le droit des gens, ou principes de la loi naturelle appliqués à la conduite et aux affaires des nations et des souverains.*

[2] For a brilliant treatment of this question see J. Stone, *Legal Controls of International Conflict* (1954), pp. 14–17.

[3] See Bin Cheng, *General Principles of Law as applied by International Courts and Tribunals* (1953).

E*

The conclusion to be drawn is clear. No more important task confronts the Catholic philosophers of today than the statement of the idea of Natural Law in a form intelligible to lawyers and educated laymen. All lawyers, whatever their doctrinal persuasions, agree that the foundations of juridical science lie outside of, and beyond, juridical science itself. The proper presentation of the idea of Natural Law, which has been truly described as 'an indissoluble link between law and morals',[1] is therefore a matter for the philosopher, not the lawyer.

That this task is peculiarly urgent is clear from the fact that, though a certain suspicion of Natural Law remains, there is a greater readiness than for some time past to accept the principle that behind all positive law there stands an objective moral law.[2] In the international sphere the General Assembly of the United Nations has recognized this principle by declaring that 'genocide' —which it defined as 'a denial of the right of existence of entire human groups'—'shocks the conscience of mankind, results in great losses to humanity . . . and is contrary to moral law and to the spirit and aims of the United Nations.' Accordingly the General Assembly affirmed that 'genocide is a crime under international law which the civilized world condemns.'[3]

On the very same day the General Assembly gave instructions which envisaged the preparation of 'a general codification of offences against the peace and security of mankind, or of an International Criminal Code'.[4] The idea of an international criminal law, which would be permanently codified and therefore immune from charges of 'judicial legislation', such as have sometimes been levelled against the Nuremberg trials of 1946, is altogether a new departure. But Pope Pius XII has left no doubt of the sympathy with which he regards these developments.[5]

So far in this discussion we have considered those aspects of Catholic moral teaching which have as their object the preservation of international peace. Catholic doctrine, however, has always accepted the proposition that it may on occasions be lawful for a state to resort to war. The conditions of a 'just war' came to be elaborated with great care in the Middle Ages and were as follows: (1) a just cause; (2) the war must be necessary in the sense that there

---

[1] A. P. d'Entrèves, *Natural Law* (1951), p. 91.
[2] See A. L. Goodhart, *English Law and the Moral Law* (1953), p. 30.
[3] Resolution 96 (1) of December 11th, 1946.   [4] Resolutions 94 (1) and 95 (1).
[5] Address to the *Congrès International de Droit Penal*, October 3rd, 1953.

are no other available means of restoring justice or preventing the continued violation of justice; (3) there must be a formal warning to the offending state and the war must be formally declared; (4) the war must be declared and waged only by the sovereign authority; (5) the good to be attained by war must be reasonably supposed to be greater than the certain evils, material and spiritual, which are bound to result from the war; (6) the war must be declared and conducted with the right intentions; and (7) only so much violence may be used as is necessary.[1] Essentially, these conditions still apply, although naturally in view of the increasing destructiveness of war the Popes of modern times have urged the total abolition of war itself.

If, however, war should unhappily break out, Catholic teaching insists, as it has always done, that the principles of the moral law apply no less than in times of peace. Many rules of international law, some conventional, some customary, have been accepted by the states in a common effort to mitigate the inevitable harshness of war. Naturally the Church gives her blessing to such attempts. But, under modern conditions, it has become increasingly difficult not merely to observe these rules, but even to know what they are.

All else today pales in significance before the dreadful question whether it is or is not lawful to use the atomic or the hydrogen bomb. In terms of positive international law it is not possible to answer these questions with clarity.[2] What is Catholic teaching upon the subject?

On September 30th, 1954, whilst addressing the eighth Assembly of the World Medical Association, Pope Pius XII defined the attitude of the Church to the new weapons which science has placed at the disposal of belligerents, when he spoke as follows:

There can be no question, even in principle, of the lawfulness of atomic, chemical and bacteriological warfare, except when it must be judged indispensable to self-defence. Even then, however, every effort must be made to avoid it by international agreements, or to set precise and narrow limits to its use, in order that its effects may be limited to the strict requirements of defence. And should the evil consequences of adopting this method of warfare ever become so extensive as to pass utterly beyond the control of man, then indeed its use must be rejected as immoral.

[1] See J. Eppstein, *The Catholic Tradition of the Law of Nations* (1935), p. 93.

[2] J. Stone, *op. cit.*, pp. 342–8, and L. Oppenheim, *International Law*, Vol. II (7th ed., by H. Lauterpacht, 1952), pp. 347–52.

In that event, it would no longer be a question of defence against injustice and necessary protection of legitimate possessions, but of the annihilation, pure and simple, of all human life within the affected area. That is not lawful on any title.

Clearly this is a pronouncement of the greatest importance to which moralists and students of international relations, Catholic and non-Catholic alike, are certain to have increasing recourse for guidance. For Catholics of course it is especially significant since, as the Pope said in his letter of November 2nd, 1954, to some two hundred and fifty Cardinals, Archbishops and Bishops gathered in Rome for ceremonies in honour of our Lady, not only the Divine Law, but also 'the whole matter of the Natural Law, its foundation, its interpretation, its application, so far as their moral aspects extend, are within the Church's power.'

In a witty article in the edition of *Blackfriars* of April 1955, a conversation takes place between three imaginary priests (Philip, James and Jude). Philip is a pacifist, who takes the view that the hydrogen bomb has proved the fundamental rightness of the pacifist position. Jude believes that war in a just cause is lawful, but that it must never be fought with nuclear weapons, even in self-defence or retaliation against an unjust aggressor who uses them first. James thinks that it may be permissible to use nuclear weapons in certain circumstances. Although the conversation ends somewhat abruptly, the impression seems to be given that Jude's approach is the right one.

For our part, for what it is worth, we are inclined to agree with James. Even yet a position does not seem to have been reached in which it can be said of any weapon that its use is unlawful in all circumstances, at all times and in all places. This does not mean that such a position may never be reached. As Cardinal Griffin, Archbishop of Westminster, said in a sermon on March 13th, 1955,

> The problem, therefore, rests upon whether this bomb [i.e. the hydrogen bomb] can ever be brought sufficiently under control that, given a just war, it can be directed only against unjust and violent aggressors. The answer to this must lie with those who have access to the necessary scientific knowledge.

Unless and until a negative answer be given to this question, it would be rather rash to assume that the use of the hydrogen bomb, or any other weapon, would in all circumstances be unlawful. Rather the presumption would be that, provided the conditions governing the declaration and conduct of war referred to above were satisfied, the use of such weapons would be compatible with the moral law.[1]

[1] The problem of the atomic bomb could also come under the heading 'Concrete Moral Problems' in so far as it could raise a moral problem for the regular member of the armed forces and for the conscript. This leads on again to the moral problem raised by the conscription of men who believe war to be an absolute evil. This problem itself rises within the moral relationship of the citizen with the state. A further concrete moral problem arises for the Christian member of the anti-Christian state. This whole political sphere has been left aside for treatment at greater length another time.—Ed.

CONCRETE MORAL PROBLEMS

XI

THE SCHOOL TEACHER'S PROBLEM

by

Claude R. Leetham, Inst. Ch.

THIS is not a thesis; it is an attempt to offer considerations to students of morality by a member of the teaching profession, within the limits of a few pages. The matter is, therefore, disjointed, but the questions are those that occupy us most. Positive statements have been written with trembling hand.

It is not possible to separate the problem of the teacher and morality from that of education, for education has as its objective a man's perfection, the training, that is, of a child's sensitive and intellective perceptions to the service of the will. Every conscious human activity is a moral activity and every conscious human act is a moral act. Moreover, for the baptized Christian the moral acts are directed to a supernatural objective. The Christ principle within the child cannot be rejected or ignored in anything it does, for membership of the Mystical Body of Christ must make for an integral life in which there can be no selection of objectives.

The teacher's problem begins with himself; he must first be imbued with the ideals that he seeks to convey. He must, as well as being an expert in some branches of knowledge and a trained practitioner of certain techniques, have the same objectives as he hopes to instil into those committed to his charge. His problem is always with him, in that his own struggle for Christian perfection must be waged while he is trying to form a child to the highest ideals. He must be a person of the highest integrity, and must constantly watch lest his life become routine. He readily accepts the daily task, but he tends to concentrate on the things which give him confidence, such as his technical ability and his experience. It is not easy to preserve the humility and the reverence that he should have before a soul made after the image and likeness of God, committed to him by Providence. His experience is accompanied by a loss of enthusiasm; he tends to rely on formulae; he expects predicted reactions.

The problem, as I shall put it, is restricted. It will have to be my own problem based on many years of teaching and guiding a group of two hundred and fifty boys, boarders. They come from the most promising group of all, for their parents are professional men who have known no privileges, or executives who have made their own way and who, often enough, have sampled state education for their children in early life, but have found that it does not fulfil their ideals. The heavy incidence of taxation has made it a difficulty for them to find boarding-school fees. They are mostly good Catholics, pillars of their parish; and the children, before they come to us, have, as a rule, had a good formation. I find that the social changes and the new outlook have had many advantages for the children. We take boys at about twelve years of age, after what is really the most critical time of their lives, for their conscience has been formed and their relations with their parents settled. It appears to me that a boy is closer to his parents than ever before. He knows the struggle that his father has to make; there are no servants in the house. He knows that all the hopes of his parents are settled on him. For this reason I think boarding schools should open their doors wider to parents. They should be allowed to come as often as possible, for the danger of a boarding school is that it tends to break up a child's life, so that things that happen there bear too little relation to his home life. A boy's relations with a group in which he lives may be totally divorced from his relations with his brothers and sisters, with his parents. Group life and group loyalty have many dangers. The teacher should on no account attempt to take the parents' place, he should supplement their influence, and supply what they cannot give. He should above all watch carefully lest he seize the children's affections in the sense that he allows them to rest too much in his own personality; a suspect attitude for one who should give rather than take. Parents should be able to walk in and out of the school as though they shared in the experiences of the group.

The exemplar of the perfect teacher is Christ, and the teacher has to present to the child Christ as his ideal. Morality which aims at anything less than this is very defective. It has been well said that the first intelligent recognition by a child is the smile by which he recognizes his mother. Teaching must use this natural benevolence. It must be the background that inspires the child's confidence. Moral influence must in the same way have as a prerequisite mutual benevolence, which, like appetite, is nature's gift for a child's need. It is the natural way to inspire confidence, it gives serenity to the acquisition of knowledge, it encourages receptivity, it enables a child to accept a teacher, to follow an example. Without charity, there can be no integral teaching. I often think that when a mother tells us that we do not understand her child, she is merely using her instinct to convey to us that the mutual understanding that she as first teacher had with her infant is not present. The bridge then, between teacher and child, must be that of charity on the part of the teacher, benevolence on the part of the child, leading to obedience as his first conscious moral act.

A child, from understanding what is right, must learn to make it his own; and here we must get to the practical difficulty with which we greet a new boy; he has sometimes had some tainted moral experience. He has usually had the moral help of a good background, but it is sometimes the case that things have happened to the child of which the parents know nothing. Modern life is too full of adult spectacle for a child not to have some confusion even of conscience, with the influence of newspaper, wireless, strip cartoons, the cinema and television. Children's discussion of adult problems is a reflection of what they hear. Right and wrong are confused in a whirl of unsavoury facts. The law, state regulations, common practice, erode their naturally formed conscience through unspoken doubts: man-law, social behaviour, try to usurp the conviction of moral law. Talk on the part of adults about personal problems which they think the child does not understand is too free; the child is apt to discuss them, but never with the right people, and most frequently the child who poses as an expert is one who makes this his way to friendship with others, and he begins with anatomical knowledge and often ends in an experiment. You therefore take your boys without any real knowledge of their experience.

I think the first most valuable moral experience of a child in a boarding school is its Catholic atmosphere: it is a good ambient in which to grow. It is healthy, it is holy; the boy's religious instinct quickly reacts. He becomes, I think, more aware of the supernatural, but at the same time this very easily lapses into routine. He takes favourably to discipline. His numerous activities occupy him. He learns something about his relations with other people, for in his group he is not allowed that egoism which is his most spontaneous characteristic. I have noticed without cynicism that boys who are classed as unselfish and always want to give a hand nearly always want to help only adults, to get away from their companions.

School discipline is not a moral virtue. Discipline is necessary for the good order of an institution and we tend to suppose that it has durable effects on the life of a boy; we tend to over-emphasize it so as to have a tidy place. You can so easily use the boy for the sake of the school: whereas, of course, the school is for the boy. While the boy benefits from discipline, we must be careful lest the good order of the house becomes more than an element for the boy's upbringing. Discipline should have as its objective the training of the will at the earliest possible stage in a boy's schooling. This has its limitations, for the boy lives on spontaneity, but I think it should be at once applied to a child's religious life. For instance to his weekday Mass. Small boys are generous, they easily find the energy to get up for weekday Mass, but they should be allowed to ask to get up. They should be presumed to want to sleep. This, I think, has great value throughout a boy's school life. It is especially valuable when he reaches adolescence, when his will is weak. A small boy's will is strong; spontaneous if impulsive, but strong.

I think it is a great mistake to allow boys to think of morality as if it were sex. A child's instruction on moral questions should from the outset be integral. The law is one, 'Thou shalt love the Lord thy God with thy whole heart, with all thy strength; thou shalt love thy neighbour as thyself.' As Rosmini well said, and I am using the principles that I learnt from that great pioneer of education, 'You should always speak to children as if they were going to be heroes': 'Boys prefer to climb than to crawl.' If every Christian is called to perfection, if the ideal is the ideal of love, how can you offer them anything less? Are you going to save the souls of children by teaching them some minimum couched in negatives? Is our moral approach often not too naturalistic, so that a boy who leaves us may merely have learnt to be a 'decent chap'? Should not morality be more closely tied to life? and should not motive be a force from the very beginning? Is the morning offering sufficient? Too often you hear boys ask, 'If you do this, is it a sin?' They want to know how far they can go. When we teach the commandments and tell them that it is wrong to tell a lie, are we teaching them to love truth, the first object of the mind? Too often we find that a boy's conscience is defective in its love of truth. When he comes to that particular moment of adolescence there is nothing a child will face with such reluctance as a fact. Do we teach as part of our morality the love of God with all our hearts? I think we make too much of fear in youth and not enough of love. When we say 'Thou shalt not steal', are we teaching them to be honest? Do we teach the great law of justice? Ideals are easily received in the pre-adult stage; even though they are not seen as principles. It is the moment when so many say they 'want to be priests'. Morality should be placed on the highest plane, and at this stage I think more should be made of the dignity of baptism, the mark by which they are Christ's, and boys should be given a clearer idea of what is meant by supernatural living.

One or two examples may be given of the false conscience that we allow children to develop. Swearing, for instance. I remember during the war, when I was looking after troops, being invited by an English chaplain to translate a list of sins that he had written out into Italian, for the benefit of his Italian prisoners. They pointed to their sin and he saw the English, and one sin there was one we hear so regularly in confessions, 'I have sworn.' There is no Italian for it. Underneath it he had 'I have blasphemed,' and blasphemy is indeed a sin; but the strange words that are common expletives in English—to call them sins of swearing is, I think, ridiculous: worse than that, it prevents a boy from examining his conscience. Another sin that is over-taught is disobedience. It is morally wrong to teach a child that he commits a sin if he breaks a school rule. My own religious rules do not bind under sin, and yet boys will confess disobedience to the end of their lives when they mean breaking a regulation. You hear, however, too little about defamation of character, uncharitableness to companions, or even calumny which is so much more rife than is commonly thought. All forms of injustice occupy too little place in the formalistic moral teaching that is too common. A child's social justice can have full scope in his own playroom, as can his charity; he can be made aware of the need to give. I think too much is made of the word duty as a slogan, not enough made of charity as the complete virtue. To love God and to love your neighbour are the same thing. Is it not better to teach a child to see Christ in the boy he does not like than to tell him to be kind to him? Can anyone tell me what is servile work? What should boys be taught in this matter? We must be scrupulously honest with children.

As the child moves towards adolescence we often notice that he has over-identified himself with his group and this brings further problems. He is probably at his most irresponsible stage, happy in the spontaneous activities and friendships that he enjoys. He has very little sense of inner compulsion. He can be cruel and thoughtless. He does not know the meaning of gratitude and he tends to live for the hour. This is where he often takes on a lasting habit of making excuses. They are not his; they are made up for him by his social sense. If his team loses a game it is due to the fact that the other team were older or bigger than his, or that the referee was obviously biased. He finds solace in quoting other people. 'They all do it, everybody says so.' But group morality is the very curse of our modern society.

I think that we should be careful of punishments, at least a punishment should not be at the expense of justice: the child has the dignity of a person. I don't mean we should not use the stick, but it seems harsh to hit a child unless it is necessary. There are many other things that can be done. The cane should be a last resort. The argument of the stick-wielders is that the children don't mind: that it makes men: in fact it can make them exhibitionists, but at the end of it all what has been gained for the child? Some suffer more than others, some are beyond fear, some rather glory in their pain. Punishment should never exceed what is necessary, and I can think of nothing worse than an automatic schedule of punishments by which you play cat and mouse with the boy. The mouse gets away with a lot. I think punishments should be small when a small one will do, private when a private one will do, and that in any case they should not be merely the result of bad temper. I have never been impressed with a pre-adolescent's sense of justice. It always relates to himself; it is nearly always biased. Nor do we enlighten his mind by an injustice like a 'general penance', which is supposed to be just for youth; unjust for adults. On what ground can twenty boys be punished for the fault of one? It is also a confusion of conscience to walk out of a class and put the boys 'on their honour' (with no choice on their own part) to behave well in your absence. This is all part of using a boy and his conscience as a means not an end; sacrificing him to 'good order'. Why should a boy 'own up', when you cannot find a delinquent? An adult has no such obligation.

Adolescence varies considerably in the age at which it strikes a boy. Some are never aware of it, but mostly boys at some time lose their spontaneity. They lose their zest. They find they have nothing to do, although all kinds of clubs invite their membership. Their creative instinct seems to drop to a low level and may meet the problem of their own sex in an acute form. It is their most difficult moment. Their religious life, which tends to be less fervent, requires stimulus. It can be that boys tend to drift with a peculiar instinct towards a homosexual stage. They preserve the ideal of friendship, which is their better self, and keep close to those whom they admire, yet at the same time by some unerring instinct they will go with other boys either in the same condition or junior to themselves, yet as unresisting. They never make a mistake in their victims and therefore the consequent damage and misery is very difficult to put right. The thing may go on for months and then under the influence of a good director stop, and perhaps begin again. In my own experience I have never known such a boy to become a homosexual once he was sent home out of the human relationships that had made the deviation possible.

Self-abuse is at this time prevalent and its treatment is very difficult. The boy is at this time egocentric without appreciating the fact that he is self-obsessed. His bad temper, his lack of energy, the trouble that it brings upon himself in matters of discipline, are all attributed to other people. This is a generalization, and of course it is only true of the boys who have such problems. It is at this moment that parents whose relations with their boys are good and normal should be brought in to help, yet it is customary to keep them out of the problem. Here I would say how harsh I think some moralists are on the adolescent. If mortal sin must be deliberate, and have full consent of the will, I submit that struggling adolescents are not mortally guilty. One could argue about deliberation, but as a rule it is not present, but what I would like to stress is that a child's will at this stage is in its weakest moment. It is ineffective. This does not only apply to the matter of self-abuse, but to his every activity. He just cannot make up his mind. He wanders aimlessly. He is almost in an unhappy dream. In particular, therefore, I think a boy who acquires such a habit should not be treated with frightening warnings, much less with untrue prognostications about his future. What is often an unhappy moment in a boy's life is a crisis that we should do our best to solve for him by prayer, encouragement and the resources of self-denial and the sacraments. The point of weak will is one I submit to moralists the more readily in that there is evidence to show that modern life tends to bring on adolescence before it is naturally due. It is a strange phenomenon noted in recent years that boys lose their voices nearly a year earlier than was true twenty years ago. It is certainly a fact that cathedral choirs have thought of bringing in girls to sing because the treble voices were breaking so early! There is no moment of a man's life when his will is less capable of dealing with such an impulse, and yet its onset is very great when the will is at its feeblest.

The question so constantly discussed is when should boys be told about their sex life, and I should put the moment very early. I should say that before a boy leaves home he should have been told a great amount. I think he should be told all, if for no other reason than because he is living in a peculiar world, where nearly all the springs are tainted. If you wait until adolescence, it appears to me that the information is in nearly every case too late. It can only correct what has been wrongfully acquired. A child interested in cricket scores picks up much more than that from the papers. We could add that his very notions of right and wrong are tinged with modernity; even comics which are not classed as 'horror' show private investigators whose job it is to perform some feat of tracking, but they need not represent right or even law. It is not generally known that firms which advertise toys and practical jokes also specialize in indecent pictures. Need we mention the indecent art studios, as they call themselves? Moreover, even some of the strong man stuff is a trap for youth. A boy is invited to become a strong man. The price of the course is beyond him, but throughout his adolescence the correspondence still comes with reduced price until at length he is offered the course with 'two books on sex' (an actual quotation). In the days when boys used to read, a very different influence was brought to bear; apart from adventure stories, they had their comics, and the world there described was one in which people did not even do things for money but for honour and patriotism. The world of sex was absent. Now if a boy is given a book it may be of great interest, but the chances are that there will be lurid passages which he will not ignore, as you can see by the way the books are handled.

This brings up the question of censorship. It seems reasonable that boys should read newspapers, even at school, as soon as they are old enough to take an interest in world affairs; but surely all newspapers cannot be admitted. On the other hand, I think it dangerous to cut out pieces of newspapers. Illustrated papers are the most dangerous of all, throughout a boy's school life. I do not hesi-tate to proscribe all film magazines and a number of others. The wireless is difficult to control if you have scattered common-rooms. More dangerous than 'Variety' can be lengthy sessions of jazz which become a drug on a young man, and could do him harm in that they preclude him from musical culture, but worse still because the erotic nature of jazz influences him without his knowledge.

When the boy has passed the crisis of his adolescence he presents a new problem, which again calls for much patience. At this stage, having become aware of himself he has no conception of his personality, and he wants to cover up every effort that you make to induce him to examine his make-up. It is a period of great pessimism. A boy looks at his face and he wonders what sort of a man he is, and strangely the prospect does not appeal to him. All his vanities with his hair and his dress mark no corresponding appreciation of what he sees. His very conceit, if conceit takes him, is the uncertainty that makes him so pathetically positive. At this period it seems very important to awaken his sense of responsibility. The more mistakes he makes the better, provided it gives you an opportunity to enlighten him. I do not think the boy needs punishment at all, or very rarely, provided you can place firmly on his shoulders an appreciation that what he does emanates from his own will. I find it of value to ask some such delinquent a series of questions and then invite him to return in a week's time with his views. It is also very useful to push him into some responsibility, but it should be a group responsibility, something like a common-room committee in which his position is shown to be the result of the esteem of his fellows. I think we are too hard on conceit. It is a difficult matter because the boy in such a mood tends not to be receptive. It may be galling, but I do not think it is a sign of any moral fault; it is an erroneous judgement.

At this stage, when boys are fifteen or sixteen, they will have by their position a number of privileges, and a privilege can always be shown as having a corresponding duty, for in a school sense a privilege is a right. It is achieved by right of status or qualification and should never depend on the whim of a master. In fact, the loss of privilege should only be possible on the failure of the corresponding duty, and it is a good system to have the privileges restored by a public body or committee of his own fellows. A boy then learns that his acts are his own. Other responsibilities on committees or as house prefects or ultimately school prefects can be shown to the boys as a laudable ambition, if you can demonstrate that he gives something in the way of service.

It is a curious fact that so many boys on becoming aware of themselves, learning their gifts and their limitations—and these have mostly to be demonstrated to them—react with great candour and even humility. It is all so new to them and it is sometimes very amusing to find a boy—this is no uncommon feature—persuaded that he has missing just the one quality he would like to have. It is sometimes the quality that is writ large upon him. I remember a boy showing me what he had written in bed one night. 'I have no dignity,' and he gave an instance that I passed him in the cloister and called his attention to a visitor and he had half turned his head and walked on, not sure whether I had called him. This was the example he gave, which fortunately had come under my own observation. His real trouble was that he had too much dignity to be really sociable with others. Another boy said that he thought he had brains but he was sure he had no initiative, which was his most obvious quality. I hope this will not be seen as a digression, for a boy's morality depends very greatly on his having a clear idea of his own personality.

It is only then that he begins to have a clear view of his influence on others. Boys tend to think that they do not count or that they are so ordinary that what they say and do does not make any difference. In fact, a senior boy makes a difference in all his public activities to all those who are junior to him, and the experience can become convincing in a very short time. With a sense of responsibility he easily develops his spiritual life at a moment when he begins to understand the principles upon which he has been living. They come before him with a new force. He appreciates their value and accepts them, and you soon notice how quickly he becomes in, say, a debating society, a keen judge of moral principles. Things are not seen in their complexity, but a natural, or rather a supernatural, insight enables him to feel for the right solution. I have noticed that in meetings of the Social Guild social justice is seen more clearly by a boy than by a man. It is the young man's best moment for principle, although he too easily sees things in black and white.

Such a boy by now can integrate even his games into his religious life, provided a school has not allowed a good spirit to dominate moral principle: it is very easy. It can happen that the traditional school ethic and even the religious ambient may make a boy conform unreflectingly with the way things are normally done, but this can be even dangerous if he cannot view what he does as conforming to principle. Often this danger is shown in the way a boy behaves at home, where the change of atmosphere is enough to reveal how little he has really acquired, and therefore all through the boy's school life, his duties to his family and the relations that he should have with his parents need emphasis.

Into the life of a senior boy it is not difficult to bring a healthy relationship with girls. A senior boy can at school have the ideal of a Catholic partner. He can be encouraged to take dancing lessons, though his parents should not force him, for it often happens that the boy will not go out to a dance in the holidays and will profess to contemn girls, merely because he cannot dance. His sixth form common-room can be encouraged to organize dances with other schools where there are girls of the same age. Reverence for girls is one of the natural virtues of the boy and this is easily fostered, provided he is not too segregated. Standards of organization and behaviour are very high, for boys' committees are usually strong bodies. These dances and resulting friendships can be nearly the equivalent of what the boy could have at this age if he lived at home. One is not naïve enough to think that these policies can be anything but efforts to face a problem.

It is very difficult to find consistency among those who have charge of boys, where all should be imbued with the same spirit. Varying theories of education when they touch the matter of moral and spiritual integration are harmful in a single community, and to my mind the spiritual director should not be the segregated person he is in some schools. One of the great dangers of the Catholic school is the fragmentation of interest, study, games, and religion. It is easy for a boy, if brought up in such an atmosphere, to shed his piety, leaving him what appears to him a good education.

The work of the teacher cannot be complete unless the boy is directed into the best of all fields for the exercise of what he has been taught; and this is the society of the parish. It is the boy's proper place in the Church: it is his divinely ordained spiritual home. It is the natural sphere for his activity directed to an ultimate end, and the parish, which completes the spiritual life of the family and is its home, should be shown as a human group where a young man learns to guard against frustration, and find his place in the universal spiritual society. He should learn what the parish has to give and what he should give to the parish. It is the foundation for his Catholic action, which may indeed have to wait for fulfilment, but which he can accept as an activity ultimately required of him, and here again he should have impressed upon him before he leaves school the dignity of his baptism, by which he becomes a sharer in the Divine nature. It helps him towards the practice of the charity that has been impressed upon him. It makes him respect the dignity of a human person; it is a safe foundation for his exercise of social justice and gives serenity to his outlook.

These remarks leave out very much. Thus, what of the boy's critical sense? In fact all must be done to teach him to see through the slogans that clamour so rowdily. If guided, he is likely not to be receptive of everything that is said, but of course he cannot be given experience, and the onslaught made by the world must be endured. However, if Catholic boys' experience of national service is any indication of their reactions to the first impact, I feel that such an education gives them nothing but confidence and strengthens their principles. University life is a far greater test, but we can only form his ideals, give him a great love of truth, teach him to know himself, offer him as his ideals the love of God and of his neighbour as the fulfilment of the law. The supreme principle is the moral principle, by perfecting which man perfects his personality. Perfections of nature, whether of body or mind, are only partial perfections. Personality resides at its highest in the principle of will which is ordained to seek truth. There is no distinction between scientific and revealed truth. Boys can be made to understand this and religion enters into education by harmonizing every activity, social tendency, and all that is included in the desire for happiness. Throughout there must be unity. The mind guides the heart and the affections, and the will guides life. Illuminated by grace, the mind guides the will to universal charity. I do not think that the problem of morality for the teacher is any greater in this stage of society than at any other time, provided the teacher is fortunate enough to have children committed to his charge who have already in their most formative years had a sound Catholic foundation.

Since writing this paper I have read the 'Charity' edition of *Lumen Vitae*. I have preferred to leave the paper as it stands so that it may be the more easily criticized in the light of the interesting thesis of Père Gilleman, S.J.

XII

THE SEX PROBLEM

by

Reginald F. Trevett

SEXUALITY is fundamental in our being. We are all involved in its processes, and in the options it presents to us at various stages of our lives, and in particular, at certain critical moments. It is not possible for us to stand apart from our sexuality in order to look at it objectively. We are immediately aware only of its evolution in our individual self, and of its objective influence on the lives of others. In what sense then can we have any real knowledge of sexuality? How can we hope to find any ethic, any morality of sexual life? Is it not merely a datum, a mysterious force within us to which we are essentially passive? Should we attempt any metaphysic of sex, could we claim any validity for our conclusions, for our sexual code? Are we not forced to base such an ethic on mere custom, on a kind of 'agreed syllabus' of morality, on an unsuspected because unconscious projection on to our sexual life of emotional phenomena, the yearning for security for instance?

Such questions clearly derive from an acute sense of our involvement in processes from which we cannot divorce ourselves in fact, but only in imagination. They lead to the ultimate question—'Is not all metaphysics wishful thinking?' It is not my business here to argue for or against the possibility of metaphysics. But, on the other hand, I shall not ask assumptions to be accepted which would make the vital mysteries we are considering mere counters in a game that has no final meaning or value apart from the moves of which it is composed. I shall set out from the fact of involvement itself and, from within the real situation, contemplate the existential, here and now, choices with which our sexuality brings us face to face.[1] By an analysis of the results of our choice in one direction or another, we may hope to determine with some accuracy whether choice A leads

---

[1] I wish here to acknowledge my debt to Père Lestapis, S.J., and his book *Amour et Institution Familiale*, Edition Spes.

to an impoverishment of our being as we experience it, whilst choice B leads to an enrichment. For whatever may be our relations with being itself, we have real experience of being as experienced and therefore real knowledge of it. If therefore we say that a choice which clearly enriches our being by increasing its range and depth is a 'good' choice, whilst one which impoverishes our being by narrowing its range and diminishing its depth is a 'bad' choice, we are not thereby claiming to say more than that such goodness and badness are relative to, are in function of, our involvement and limited because involved experience.

Such an experimental criterion of ethics may seem at first sight a poor substitute for a highly differentiated and elaborated moral system based on a philosophy of essence or on a complete metaphysic of human personality and destiny. May I say at once that I am not adopting this perspective merely to be in the fashion of current existentialism or logical positivism. I am not competent to deal with these movements. But it does appear that, whatever their ultimate place in the history of philosophy may prove to be, they have here and now one obvious methodological advantage. They draw attention to aspects of the human condition which a more *a priori* metaphysic might well miss or neglect. I do not think that by taking note of these aspects we *ipso facto* cut ourselves off from all hope of judgements other than those relative to our condition and having no meaning apart from that condition. In the words of Louis Doucy, 'To look at things from the angle of situational being is to put oneself in the true condition of human thought.'[1] And later he writes, 'Truth is drawn from the depths of being by that hidden presence of the spirit which makes each being part of an order and called to proclaim order in every mode of its being; so that not only is a being in a situation, he situates *himself* by a fundamental orientation of his life, which is the bearer either of truth or of falsehood.'[2] In other words, an absolute judgement is implicit in the word *is*, however relative may be the situation of which and in which it is used. In the fact of my being there is implied a certain order both of being and of truth in so far as I am able to become more and more conscious of myself and of my involvement in the processes of which I am neither the author nor the complete fulfilment.

With this echo of the absolute in our ears, we may turn to questions strictly limited to the existential situation of our sexuality both before and in marriage, and in particular at the great moments of

[1] *Recherche de la Famille*, Editions familiales de France, p. 109.
[2] *Op. cit.*, p. 113.

choice. Here again, Doucy is to the point. He writes: 'Morality . . . reveals itself without ambiguity in the specific occasions when its demands are clear, but it escapes us when we wish to comprehend it as a separate essence.'[1] It is in these single occasions that we attempt here to distinguish the enriching from the impoverishing choices rather than in an effort to build an abstract ethic.

So far, we have proceeded philosophically. But as Christians we have a revealed moral code. What need have we to bother about the philosophical approach? Surely because our Lord came not to destroy but to fulfil. However, the Old Law, the natural experience and options, the natural notions of good and evil, are not annulled or superseded by revelation. Rather, as I hope we shall see in the final section of this paper, are they assumed and so transformed into the higher order of supernatural charity. In an inquiry such as this, it is essential to ask and seek to discover what are these natural, experienced facts which are to be assumed into the life of Christ and the Church. In our actual living of these mysteries of life, failure to appreciate the nature which grace perfects may lead to grave errors of judgement and even to defective conduct. Finally, the discovery of the ethic implicit in our existential situations and its series of options still leaves intact the mystery of success in the moral life. A glance, however cursory, at the sexual chaos of man's history and at the moral failures in our own individual lives reveals the tragic dichotomy of which St Paul speaks. The things I would not, I do, and the things I would, I do not. This hard, brute fact of disorder, of disease, of sin, brings us face to face with the fundamental existential problem of ethics. How can man, who lives in two realms, that of the spirit and that of the flesh, live in fact in both at the same time in perfect peace? How can man learn to *be* good? How can he learn to *do* good? In the complete answer to these questions lies the whole theology of grace.

We are faced with our first choice at the puberty stage. Till then, our sexuality has been not dormant indeed, but experienced at a level which cannot be called specifically genital. We have been born both through the operation of biological laws and, at a far deeper level, as the result of a profound relation between our parents which transcends the purely biological order, a relation of which biological sexuality is one expression, one of the most important, and without which there is no birth of new persons. This relation is all-inclusive. It issues into various acts, various attitudes which are both the sign of the fundamental relationship and, in so far as they are

[1] *Op. cit.*, p. 87.

genuinely expressive of that relation, signs which achieve what they signify. They both express and foster the relation.[1]

We cannot embark here upon an existential analysis of the family as we experience it. But we must note that the puberty struggles have to be undertaken in function of the preceding growth of our personality in its relations with others both in and outside of the family circle. Should there be faults, retardation, a failure to achieve genuine relations with others as they objectively are in themselves, then we face the puberty crisis with our emotions and will turned in on to self. To use a psychological term, we are in a state of narcissism.

At puberty, we experience our sexuality at two levels. There is an outward-looking tendency, an impulse to hetero-sexuality. Hitherto, we have lived with our parents, our brothers and sisters, but their sexual character has been present to our consciousness in a purely objective state. It has not been a stimulant for our genital sexuality. I use the word 'genital' for there is ample evidence to justify the Freudian doctrine of a non-genital, diffused infantile sexuality. But at puberty we become conscious of the other sex outside the family circle in a different and more subjective way. At the lowest level (and by 'lowest' I am not implying any judgement of value. I use the term to indicate an instinctive rather than a volitional attitude) we experience our awakening genital sexuality as an organic urge to pleasure in the function of the sex organs themselves, apart from any hetero-sexual attraction. At the highest, most personal level, we experience a desire for relationship with a member of the other sex, a relationship complete and including every region of our physical and spiritual being. In the language of experience, we fall in love.

This complex situation imposes an option. Sexuality for us faces in two directions. It may either become the sign of our own self-love, a symbol of narcissism, effecting what it signifies, driving us further and further into the isolation of the self and away from relations with others, or it may become the effective sign of our deliverance from self, of our relations with others. I have already pointed out the immense importance of pre-puberty growth for the happy issue of the crisis of adolescence. Time forbids me to say much of the tragic consequences of a childhood in which the problems of relationship have not been solved. A great deal of the misery

---

[1] It is true that some children are born as the result of lust or sordid calculation. Nevertheless sexual intercourse of itself involves us in a profound human relation whether we consciously accept or reject the consequences of that relation.

found in chronic masturbators and homosexuals is due to this cause. A consideration of family as distinct from specifically sexual morality would have much to say to, and about, parents and society in general and about the frequent failure of both to promote the true growth of the child. Here we can only insist that the question of responsibility in these tragic, though by no means hopeless, cases is extremely difficult and delicate. Diatribes against sexual abnormalities or interested defences of them are both equally unrealistic and immoral. The advance of medical knowledge has shown that the hormonal endocrinal development of the child at the puberty stage of itself gives rise, apart from any psychological considerations, to vigorous and almost uncontrollable sexual urges. It is obvious that any false notion of repression, any arousing by the child's educators of a false sense of guilt concerning sexuality itself, will aggravate the already critical situation. Here, if ever, there is urgent need for close co-operation between the moralist and the doctor; in the case of Catholics, between the confessor and the physician and psychologist. I would go so far as to suggest that one of the most important tasks ahead of us is to consider frankly the sexual problems of the adolescent from every point of view and to create a new social conscience and practice in this regard. The publication of *New Problems in Medical Ethics* edited by Dom Peter Flood (Mercier Press, Cork) may well prove a landmark. There is abundant evidence to show that the wholesale landslide of young people from religious practice is largely the result of sexual difficulties. It is important to note that the level of consciousness varies in individuals. A man whose consciousness is still orientated to the past, for instance, will experience his sexuality in a nostalgic form. This fact can only be mentioned here but is of great significance in the treatment of particular cases.

'A man shall leave father and mother and cleave to his wife.' This is a fundamental goal of the awakening genital instinct. If we choose to follow the profounder promptings of the instinct itself, we are open to a new relation, that of man and woman in the function of procreation. This new relation cannot but be an enrichment of the self. But we are immediately in the presence of a second option. We may divorce the intense pleasure of sexual intercourse from its biological end. We may seek this pleasure entirely for its own sake. This drags us back to narcissism, for to seek pleasure for its own sake can only mean to seek it for our own sakes. Our relation to persons of the other sex then becomes one of master to slave. The partner in

F

the sexual relation is not for us a subject in its own right with whom we enter into a real relation, but a mere object, to be used for the purposes of our own pleasure. The history of the world's Casanovas and Don Juans demonstrates that the pursuit of sexual orgasm divorced from personal relations and the biological end leads to an ever-increasing isolation of the self, and to an ever more exasperating inability to find the full pleasure that is sought. It may be objected that many engage in sexual intercourse outside marriage in order to give pleasure rather than to experience it. An increased awareness of the profound personal nature of the human sex act will reveal that such pleasure is only given or received at the cost of deep wounds to the personality of both parties.

We find in other periods of history, and at the present time in other civilizations, a tendency directly opposite to the one we have just been discussing, the tendency, that is, to consider sexuality as no more than a biological fact, and women as mere producers of children. The great Moslem sheik with his harem and multitude of children is an example of this attitude. Nearer home in time and space, we have the Victorian man of substance, who married in order to have an heir, and whose wife was the necessary apparatus for the production of this highly desirable commodity. In neither of these cases is there any question of love.

'Love' is the key word to the whole mystery of sex and marriage. It is a word with a long and distinguished history. No analysis of its meaning can ignore the fact that among the peoples of Christian culture, it has undergone a profound transformation. The 'Eros' of Plato, noble concept though it was, lags behind the 'Agape' of the New Testament. We in the west would be appalled were we to succeed in divesting the word of all Christian associations and then attempt to base our lives upon the poor remainder. In the words of Taine:

> In Italy during the Renaissance, in England under the Restoration, in France under the Convention and the Directoire, we see man becoming a pagan in the style of the first century A.D. By the same token he found he had become what he was in the days of Augustus and Tiberius—hard and voluptuous. He abused both himself and others. Brutal or calculating egoism had again achieved the ascendancy. Cruelty and sensuality flaunted themselves, and society became a cut throat's alley, an evil haunt.[1]

---

[1] *Les Origines de la France contemporaine. Le Régime moderne*, Volume 11, pp. 118–19, quoted in *Recherche de la Famille*, p. 236.

At this stage it would be dishonest to make apologetic use of this quotation. I intend merely to use it as showing what has always happened when Europeans have attempted to return to a pre-Christian concept of love. If such a pre-Christian concept is the true one, if it corresponds to man's true nature, and growth, then, putting aside all question of a revealed morality for the moment, we should have to adopt it ourselves, as most of our post-Christian contemporaries attempt to do. But is it a true concept? Is love, as our forefathers have known it, merely a Christian fantasy, or at best a divine revelation cutting across the whole natural sexuality of man? We must tread warily here. The question may perhaps be best put, in the context of the present enquiry, somewhat as follows: Is the experience of falling in love as we know it in the west entirely of religious derivation, or is it inherent in the structure of the human being, however difficult, if not impossible, it may be to have this experience without the conditioning of two thousand years of Christianity?

If the key word to a human ethic of sexuality is 'love' the key word to a human philosophy of love is 'relation'. If we discover that a pure human relationship can only be established on the basis of love as we understand it, then there is no truth in the view that Christianity has imposed a superhuman notion of love, having no roots in man's natural being as such. A detailed analysis of our developing being at every level reveals the fact that our being as such is relational. We come to say 'I' only through contact with the 'Thou'. The more complete the out-going of the 'I' to the 'Thou' the fuller is our being. On the other hand, the more we refuse or restrict our union with others, the less are we true selves, the narrower is the range, the shallower the depth of our own being. We are face to face with the option of enriching or impoverishing our being. If this opening of the 'I' to the 'Thou' is in fact what love is, then it is through love that we become ourselves, that we attain to the full stature of the relational being we potentially are.

The love of husband and wife is not the only form of union between the 'I' and the 'Thou', but for the majority of us it is the form involving the most complete giving of self. I am setting aside the still higher, still more complete self-giving of consecrated virginity, whereby sexuality is transformed into a still closer union with the 'Thou'! In and through Christ and the Church, the sacrifice of the normal sex function, far from destroying or suppressing the sexual character of a man or a woman, causes it to serve a deeper and more intimate union of man with God and with our fellow men.

Apart from this exceptional and specifically Christian state it is obvious that the gift of self in marriage is the most complete and therefore the most enriching in the whole scale of creaturely being. When those who are in love in this total sense face the options confronting them they see clearly the direction of the morals of marriage.[1] In the first place, there is the option of a temporary or a permanent union. Christian thinkers in the past have deduced the necessity of indissoluble marriage from the physical and psychological needs of children. Such arguments are clearly valid and of great weight. The more recent emphasis on the nature and structure of love may make them seem academic and incomplete. I believe it is necessary to accept the challenge of the philosophers of love in our time. By so doing, we shall not have to throw aside any of the earlier arguments. We shall confirm and enrich them by others of equal force and validity and, given the conditions of our present situation, of more immediate relevancy.

If we choose a temporary form of marriage, we at once condition our self-giving and so impoverish both our own being and that of the 'other'. Our relation is a narrow, half-hearted, self-withdrawing affair. The freedom of both partners to break off the union at some future time surely implies that the union is here and now based on an illusion, the illusion that the 'other' can only be united to me for so long as the feelings and joys of love and companionship are present. When these disappear, it is assumed that love itself is dead and union is no longer possible. This illusion, so common in our times, so great a temptation to those whose marriages have come to the pass where it seems easier to hate than to love, cannot be brushed aside with airy gusts of theology or pharisaical condemnations. For it arises from a profound sickness in the western soul. The Christian moralist must enter into the realities of this sickness, not to condone or compromise, but, by sharing the agony and suffering of those who are afflicted by the disease, to do what he can to cleanse their souls from the evil which afflicts them.[2]

---

[1] I purposely leave aside the question of the *moment* when the couple fall in love. At other times and in other civilizations it has been taken for granted (rightly or wrongly) that love follows marriage. At present, in England at least, it is considered essential that marriage should be based on a love already in existence. It remains true in either case that the fullness of that love can normally only be achieved in the married state itself.

[2] The case books of sexologists and psychologists reveal that a large proportion of unsuccessful marriages are due to sexual maladjustments. In so far as the latter are

Since de Rougemont published his *L'Amour et l'Occident,* no consideration of love in our time can neglect the philosophy underlying the myth of Tristan and Isolde, a permanent tincture in the love of western man. The essence of the myth lies in its concept of love as a spiritual union militating against the body's enslavement to biological necessity. Death alone really unites the lovers. The myth in its pure form is rarely seen working to its logical conclusion in two human lives, but it is ever with us in less absolute shapes, and in particular in the illusion that love is the equivalent of joy and happiness.[1] The fact of relation of our relational being, of the fundamental necessity of the I–Thou relation, makes it clear that love is involved at far deeper levels than those of euphoria and contentment. How many marriages go wrong because the true nature of love was not realized at the outset? For love is the mutual union in self-sacrifice of two persons. It may initially manifest itself, and usually does, at the superficial level of attraction and joy in each other's company, and in marriage in the joy of intercourse. But of its nature it transcends these levels though it does not cease to include them. Love involves a self-giving from which there is no return. The self, once given, is no longer recoverable. 'For better for worse, in sickness and in health.' This is not the statement of an ideal or the enunciation of a code of conduct imposed by a religious or social system. It is simply the statement of how love works. That the love of so many married couples does not in fact work like that, merely means that they have never been truly in love at all, and that is their tragedy. They have undertaken the obligations of a great physical and spiritual cosmic force, which is not present in their superficial mutual attraction. For self-giving is a real death to self, involving profound and often acute suffering. No matter how happy a marriage may be, no matter how united the partners are, their happiness and unity have been, and continue to be, bought at a great price, the price of constant renouncement. At times, the sacrifice is made by the wife, at others by the husband.

---

the consequences of ignorance or a false attitude to sex itself, a sound education is the ultimate remedy. In particular cases, the harassed doctor may well consider divorce to be the only solution. But divorce itself implies a failure to face the realities of the situation.

[1] There is much research to be done on the effect of industrial civilization on the relations of the sexes. See Gabriel Marcel's *Homo Viator,* p. 157. It is also obvious that the themes of illicit love as a great adventure, and of so-called 'romantic' love as the genuine thing, pervade literature and its modern derivatives, and give a very superficial account of the whole business.

At the deepest level, our need for others and our desire for self-independence are engaged in deadly struggle. In every successful marriage, the partners carry the wounds by which self-love is slain. And, by the paradox which is at the heart of our creaturely being, it is only by complete acceptance of what may seem to be abject submission to another person that we attain that full relationship in which alone we become truly ourselves. Even at the natural level, it appears impossible that such a sacrifice, whatever its ultimate result, can be made without the loss of a legitimate love of self. Indeed, this sacrifice could not be made unless it were the sign of the offering of ourselves through and in our human relations to the absolute source of all being.

We have said that the self once given is irrecoverable. This statement sums up the whole philosophy of relation, for a genuine relation with another produces a new existential reality—a community, 'I' and 'Thou' becoming 'We'. The deeper the We-relation is, the more integrated are those who form it. To break that relation (in so far as it can ever really be broken) is to break not only the relation itself, but to disintegrate, in part at least, the selves who form it. What we recover after such a divorce is not the self, but fragments of it. It is strictly inconceivable that a we-relation can be broken, for once love has established it and sealed it by the spiritual and biological signs of consent and consummation, it is on an existential plane analogous to that of the relation of parent and child. The contemporary problem is therefore not so much that of people falling out of love, as of the dubious character of much that passes for love itself. We may note that the universal custom of confirming marriage by religious rites and sanctions suggests that man senses that he must situate marriage in the infinite, unchangeable context of the divine, of the absolute OTHER, if human nature is to enter successfully into the realm of permanent relation.

Love in its purity, in its utter self-giving, involves a change of being, a new life (I speak still of the natural order). This does not imply that there are no temptations to descend to a lower, self-centred and therefore less human level. What is implied is that such temptations are an urge to inhumanity.

Our next option concerns contraception, one of the most crucial and complex issues of our time. Here again, I shall not argue against it in the traditional way, but content myself with suggesting that the root principle of any ethical judgement in the matter lies in the fact of the 'sign' in the existential reality of sexual intercourse as the visible sign of love, union and self-giving. To be fully human the sign must itself be integral. If tampered with, it is no longer the sign it should be. It can no longer effect what it signifies, mutual love. Paradoxically, it cannot be a fully human sign, if it is distorted by human ingenuity.

The essential fact to remember in dealing with this problem is that there is a deliberate attempt to prevent the spermatozoa from reaching or fertilizing the ovum. But love demands the whole movement of the self to the loved one. However apparently unselfish are the motives for contraception, the objective fact remains that contraceptive intercourse is not intercourse at all, but an act of self-love. It cannot be a sign of self-giving. By the law of the union of the soul and the body, the sign, since it is misdirected and defective, is bound to effect in some degree what it signifies in itself, i.e. a loosening of the I–Thou relation. Further, although the spirit is free and choice is real, yet the biological plane has its own laws, of which man is not the absolute master. He is involved in the working of these laws, which minister to his needs. To effect a radical change in their direction and significance is to assume that man is absolute master of the physical universe of which he is a part. But this is absurd, for his whole situational life demonstrates the essential relativity of his existence and his involvement in the great cosmic processes.

I am well aware that such statements of the simple truth concerning man's case will cut little ice with our contemporaries, and that the realist view of sexuality which we have outlined brings us face to face with serious problems in everyday life. But it is man's lot to face such problems. By attempting to avoid them, he raises others of graver import. But here again, it is necessary for the moralist to enter into the genuine anguish of mind which leads so many to adopt these practices. He stands no chance of success, if he remains apart from the real situations which drive people to these desperate remedies.[1]

A character in one of Marcel's plays says 'To love a person is to say—You will not die.' No reflexion on the mystery of marriage can

[1] Within the limits of this paper, it is impossible to deal with the delicate yet highly relevant question of the relations of man and wife in the actual practice of sexual intercourse. All we can say, in our present context, is that the art of love-making in marriage is one in which western man would appear to be sadly deficient. The moral implications of intercourse which is largely selfish are obviously of prime importance, as are also the inhibitions due to a puritanical or Manichean fear of sex as such. But these considerations would require a separate paper.

neglect the fact of death. If by death we mean the total annihilation of a loved one, it is obvious that our whole nature rebels against such a possibility. The metaphysical implications of this refusal, leading, as they do, to a radical criticism and rejection of the superficial identification of consciousness with bodily existence, are beyond the scope of the present enquiry. I can only refer the reader to the masterly treatment of the question in Marcel's *Homo Viator*. But the mystery of death and its effect on our sexual relationships is of the highest importance at this stage of our argument.

We have seen that a full acceptance of the sexual mystery reveals what we may rightly call an incarnation of love. But death suppresses the body, at least for an unknown period of time. Assuming that the normal relations between two conscious beings are only possible through the instrumentality of the body, assuming also that the primary function of sexuality is reproduction, death would seem to suppress not only the body, but all relations which exist through its instrumentality. Is our love then doomed to die with the bodies of those we love? The fact that, even amongst Christians, a second marriage after the death of one of the partners is tolerated, seems to indicate that this may be the case, since fidelity to the marriage bond, which we have seen to be of the essence of the married relationship, ceases to be considered as of obligation. Is married love then merely a temporal thing, and is the title of Père Carré's book *Companions for Eternity* a contradiction in terms? We know from our human experience that it is a metaphysical impossibility to consider the dead as absolutely absent, as having no further relation with us. And their continued presence is much more than a memory of them as they were in the past. But it is a relation in a dimension of which we are not conscious, the dimension of the absolute and the abiding. The question which thus faces us is whether this dimension is already present in our this-world relations with one another. In theological terms, do our human relationships, as is the case with contingent being in general, subsist ultimately in God? Is the foundation of our married relationship the presence of God himself at the centre of the We-community which we form? If that is so, and the marriage rites of all civilizations indicate the conviction of mankind that it is, then we enter the region of relation on the plane of the absolute and the eternal, whether or not we are conscious of it. As our sexuality becomes in marriage the sign of our love for one another as well as the means of reproduction, so in the realm of the absolute, our mutual love becomes the sign of the love of God for his creation, because it is itself based on and maintained by that love, when death has severed all the biological, this-world links that bind husband and wife together, love remains but as assumed wholly into its abiding centre. This is not incompatible with re-marriage in this life, for the former, this-world love is now in an absolutely virginal state. It is indeed this virginal love which is at the heart of marriage itself and is made absolute by death. Virginal love can be shared. That is its great power and glory. So the second marriage becomes itself another sign, destined to the ultimate virginal union in Christ and the Father and so compatible with fidelity to the essence of the first marriage. But we have reached the plane of the great themes of religion.

In *Recherche de la Famille* (p. 246) Canon Masure writes:

> The Catholic morality of marriage ... in its condemnation of polygamy and divorce which were tolerated on the Old Testament, is thus a dynamic morality, a morality of value and progress. It is not an external addition to a natural morality already established independently and to which it brings obligations foreign to the primal end of the institution itself, obligations which are therefore burdensome, additional and perhaps even intolerable. No! it leads a nature already adapted and called to the supernatural order along a road marked out for beings enjoying the gift of reason by their own deepest tendencies. At the same time, the latter if left to themselves, would never have been able to see clearly enough to perceive these laws, nor have had sufficient strength to obey them.

The supernatural morality of marriage is derived from the fact that Christian marriage is a sacrament. The theology of marriage is at present undergoing considerable development. The relation of sexuality to the sacramental life of the married may well be made clearer as the whole theology of the lay vocation is developed both in the theological writing and still more in the actual business of day-to-day living.

The plain fact, which is the traditional teaching of the Church, is that the sacrament of marriage is the sign of the union of Christ and the Church. In their married life at all levels husband and wife are signs to themselves, to their children and to their neighbours of this divine-human union. This simple reality, this august vocation, is the source of the supernatural morality and spirituality of the Christian family.

We have already noted that the biological processes of sexuality

F*

are destined to be the outward sign of the mutual love of man and woman. For the Christian couple this mutual love, which assumes the biological relations into itself, becomes the sign of the relation of the incarnate Son of God with the human race. The natural options now have to be considered in a new light. To the young Christian struggling with his awakening genital sexuality, the option of narcissist self-indulgence or the love of 'the other' is now not only a choice between self-integration and self-disintegration, but between sex as the sign of our denial of God and sex as a sign of our union with him in and through the Church. The natural sign with all its biological, psychological and social implications is thus to be assumed into the transcendent sphere of the union of God and man in the Incarnation.

The option of Don Juan is now the choice between the denial of 'the other' as a temple (at least potentially) of the Holy Spirit, and the acceptance of 'the other' as not only a Thou in his or her own right, but as (at least potentially) a member of the Body of Christ. The option between temporary and permanent union is now not only a choice between self-love and the true love of self-giving, but also the choice between the positive living out of the fact of marriage as a sign of Christ's eternal union with the Church, and a virtual denial of that union *de facto* if not *de jure*, a refusal to live out the consequences of that union by which Christ wedded our race and incorporates into himself those who time after time are unfaithful to him. The option between contraceptive and fruitful marriage is now not only the choice between sexual intercourse as the sign of mutual love or as a sign of that love's diminution, but also the choice between sexuality as a sign of the fruitfulness of Christ's love for mankind or as a sign of our *de facto* denial of that fruitfulness in our married lives. The marriage bed of the Christian lies in the shadow of the Cross and the font. To deny children to the font is to restrict the fruitfulness of the Church's womb. I am not of course advocating what we may call indiscriminate child-bearing, but true generosity and vitality. It must be said that to restrict the number of our children by legitimate means is not a course to be undertaken lightly. There are valid reasons for such restriction, and where they are present, it would be wrong to suggest that there is a lack of fruitfulness. On the other hand, to bring children into the world with no intention of assuming the full responsibilities of parenthood is a grave dereliction of duty in both the natural and the supernatural orders, for the primal end of marriage is not only the procreation but also the education of children. It now only remains for us to assemble the conclusions our brief inquiry has led us to. We must say that in the natural order the series of existential options offers the choice of a descent into a state of comparative personal indifferentiation and disintegration, or of an increasing self-integration through mutual spiritual and physical self-giving relations. In the supernatural order, our sexuality is assumed into the eternal relation of the incarnate God with the human race he has redeemed. If we accept the vocation of marriage as the sacrament, the efficacious sign in our lives of the union of Christ and the Church with all that this implies in our conduct, then we are able to achieve self-abandonment to God in our vocation, and thereby find ourselves again in the transcendent and eternal relations of the Father, the Son and the Holy Spirit. So our marriage becomes for us the means of our fuller incorporation into Christ, of our working out in daily life of the virtualities of our baptism and confirmation, of the showing forth of that unity of Christ and the Church which is the first fruit of the daily sacrifice-sacrament of the Holy Eucharist.

Finally, if it seems that this treatment of the morality of sexuality and marriage is far removed from the daily struggle throughout life against temptation to sexual sin, let me conclude by a reminder of the basic fact that man has to *choose*. At the root of every temptation lies the primal urge to consider ourselves as beyond choice, as absolute, as the centre and source of our own being. This temptation is present and in a particularly virulent form in the realms of sex, where it is so often disguised as an immediate desire for a strong type of pleasure. To refuse the call of 'the other', to refuse to die to self, is to refuse the truly human state. It is only by dying to myself in my love for others that I become myself as God intends me to be. In so far as we accept our vocation to share in the sufferings and death of Christ, the daily temptations, even the daily falls if repented of, are the very means whereby we choose and attempt to make our sexuality the sign of the love of man for woman and of the love of God for man.

XIII

THE EMPLOYEE'S PROBLEM

by

Robert P. Walsh

IT is not a simple task to discuss morality from the viewpoint of the employee. One reason is the difference that exists between the types of temptation presented to a mill worker, for example, and to the senior clerk in a local government office. This difference is a very real one and, while all employees are subjected to the same temptations against the Ten Commandments, it would be correct to suggest that some types of employees, or let us call them workers, are more subjected to certain temptations. For example the girl working in a chocolate factory has a peculiar temptation to steal chocolates. Fortunately the employers appreciate this and it is usual to allow the girls to eat all they will, and experience has shown that after a very short time the new girl will have had enough and that she will stop eating chocolates while making them. The man working in a brewery becomes accustomed to the smell and sight of beer and very easily falls prey to the temptation of drinking too much. The docker unloading a ship has far more frequent temptations to theft than most workers have. Some of these occupational temptations are fairly obvious and can be appreciated with little thought; others are unknown except to those who are close to them. Observation and second-hand information suggests, to give one example, that far more smutty and obscene cross-talk goes on between the sexes in a cotton mill than will be found in factories or offices.

If one tried to assess the degree of guilt in any given case many factors would have to be considered. As an interesting side-issue the theory must be mentioned that the peculiar difficulties of the cotton worker are partly due to the warm moist climate of the mill. In case this seems far-fetched it might be recorded that many regular soldiers of the pre-1939 days when the overseas tour of duty was taken in India have given evidence that the climate of India and the smell of some flowers of an exotic character combined to make it far more difficult to resist temptations to impurity than would be the case in a British garrison town. The evidence of these soldiers suggests that there may well be aphrodisiac climates as well as situations, pictures and drugs.

No one, to my knowledge, has made a serious study of occupational temptations. They are very real and the fact that they are taken for granted often makes it difficult to resist the general trend. In some industries the problem takes the form of initiation ceremonies and there are grossly obscene initiation customs.

Perhaps that indicates my first problem; there are so many occupational temptations that it is difficult in a short paper to list them. Some of these occupational temptations are extremely old; in some industries they are becoming a thing of the past. The result is to weaken the powers of resistance against the particular type of temptation, be it to theft, be it to immodesty or whatever form it takes.

A second difficulty in writing this paper is the differences that exist in upbringing and outlook. To use the term 'employee' as a generic term is misleading. Inside the ranks of employees there are a vast number of types. The man who works in a civil service office does not behave in the same way as the man working in a Birmingham factory. It is not that one is more likely to sin than another; rather it is what is traditional in the outward behaviour. The civil servant may be capable of swearing as badly as anyone else but he does not lace his every sentence with a frequent use of 'f—' and of other words that refer to sexual organs or to the act of copulation. In his circle it is not done whereas in other circles it is done and so frequently as to become boring.

A third difficulty in writing this paper is the danger of generalizing. It is so simple to take a few sets of circumstances and from them to draw a general theory. Indeed when one begins to appreciate the complexity of this problem the temptation to short-circuit it and to produce a general theory on the basis of a few instances or on the experiences of a limited type of employee is almost irresistible.

Perhaps the first question that might be asked when the title of this paper is seen is 'Why discuss the worker in a distinct category?' because surely the general temptations of the worker are those to be found among employers and teachers and doctors. That is of course true in that the moral problems of all the many grades that make up the 'worker' all relate to one or other of the Ten Commandments. Yet, as has been suggested, those temptations take different forms among different types and the particular type of temptation that might be met by, say, a historian, perhaps the temptation to intellectual dishonesty, will be very different from the temptation of a goods porter on the railway or young girl in a factory. These differences are sufficient to justify a separate examination.

One preliminary problem needs to be mentioned and that is the widespread ignorance of the rules of morality. There are, of course, a very great number of exceptions, yet, even as we pay tribute to these exceptions, it must be recognized that by and large the mass of the working class pay no attention in some circumstances to moral principles. There are limits beyond which behaviour will seldom go and there are communities which would not tolerate the attitude that is commonplace in other communities. Among the more educated groups, and that includes a vast number of employees, there is at least an intellectual understanding of the problem and though many will break many of the commandments it is possible to secure an intellectual agreement that it is wrong to break most of them. Among the general run of factory employees—and you will appreciate my difficulties in classifying the genus 'employee'—there is an incredible ignorance of the principles of right and wrong and a pronounced unwillingness to discuss such an idea.

Some of the moral problems that exist are easily seen as moral problems and in reality are outside our scope because they are just examples of straightforward sinning which goes on in this world without any regard being had to the social group or classification of the sinner. Other problems ought to be as readily recognized for what they are but tend in particular industries to be taken for granted. A third set of these moral problems is bound up with the general philosophy of life to be found among the various types of workers.

Far be it from me to attempt to suggest that all employees are of a kind and I hope that I will avoid the danger of ascribing the evil traits of some to all and that no one will forget that while I have to paint a black picture there are very many bright spots in life.

Before we actually discuss the problems, perhaps a few recollections will help to paint the backcloth and thus help the discussion to maintain contact with reality.

There is the widespread interest in sex which is not confined to the reading of modern novels and the seeing of the more popular films. In the working class areas of big cities the children grow up in an atmosphere of it. In my childhood in Kentish Town, in London, young children would normally chant after a couple who walked down the side-street in which the local youth played; the chant usually went in this style: 'Have a go, Joe, your mother won't know, we'll mind the baby.' Perhaps such a background explains many of the moral problems of factory life.

One of my early jobs was for a tramway company and I had to collect statistics to help the company to decide if more trams were needed over a certain route. The ideal position for this job was to find a snack bar and do the work through the window. This led to an acquaintance with the local 'lads of the village', the 'wide boys' and so on, because these cafés and snack bars were their meeting places. From their conversations one learnt a lot about the district and it served to confirm personal impressions of the casual manner in which sex is widely regarded.

Many years later I sat in at a meeting of a parish committee discussing the organization of a sports day for the parish. In deciding the details many things were needed, rope to mark off the running track, paper for duplicating the programme, posters and so on. One after another members of that committee were given the task of getting one specific item on the list. Bill was told off to get some rope because there was plenty in X-works where he was employed. John would get the duplicating done, including the paper, because he worked in an office. Eric worked in a drawing office and he was to get the posters done on the office reproduction machine.

Another job I had for a short time in my youth was helping to sell houses. They were 'jerry-built' houses without any doubt and so were all the others in that suburb of London where a score of firms were putting up houses as rapidly as possible in the housing boom of the 1930's. In every show house some unfortunate youths, helped by their seniors, day after day told a string of lies to persuade the prospective buyer that the house was well-built and that the houses of the competing firms were all of very inferior quality. In the house where I performed at least eight lies were told to every viewer.

I can remember meeting Joe, who was a local councillor in his spare time and who also received widespread praise for his annual donation to the local children's hospital of a large consignment of toys. Each toy was a work of art, each had moving parts which worked just as they should. Few knew that all the metal used in those toys was stolen from the factory in which Joe worked.

Mary was a part-time nurse who stocked the medicine cupboard at home with aspirins and other simple remedies brought home from the hospital.

It is worth giving some thought to these episodes which are very typical and could be repeated a thousandfold.

One interesting aspect is that, on the whole, these thefts are taken very much for granted. A large section of the ordinary people in this country do not see these acts as being immoral. The true story of the parish committee, quoted above, illustrates that this is so among Catholics who ought to be better instructed. Side by side with this fact must be placed another; that in most cases these people behave with the utmost rectitude under other circumstances. At home, in the day to day contacts with neighbours, shopkeepers and so on a very high standard is normal. This dualism is commonplace and is rather extraordinary. I have heard a father tell off his son for stealing a little article from a market without seeing any problem in the fact that he regularly stole from his place of employment.

Perhaps the explanation is that in personal relations the principles of morality are seen as good things whereas with an impersonal or anonymous body no principles seem pertinent. Perhaps it is along those lines that one must go to understand how general is the disregard for moral principles as applied to railway fares and to income tax.

In the industrial areas of Britain it is regarded as normal to take things from work. The building worker assumes that he has a right to take home odd lengths of wood and the ends cut off planks. In most cases there is nothing wrong with this because such wood is waste and it must be very rare indeed for an employer to organize the collection of such waste wood to sell to firewood merchants. Those building workers are at one end of the scale and at the other end are those workers who make lighters while working in aircraft factories or steal materials of use and of value in the productive processes of the works.

Of course straightforward theft exists. I think a distinction has to be drawn between the open theft and the taking home of odd pieces of material. The latter is not regarded as theft by the employee; he assumes that he is entitled to act in such a manner. This petty pilfering is commonplace and must represent a large addition to the overheads of a firm. But the man who picks up a length of rope because his wife needs a new clothesline, the man who takes some metal sheets to make toys for the children, the club secretary who takes notebooks, etc., from the office to keep his club records, such people seldom think of their actions as being immoral. Usually they take them so much for granted that they do not even take precautions against being found out. One widely accepted axiom is that what is waste or is lying around, or is unlikely to be used, belongs to the finder. ('Finding's keeping' is the common phrase.)

On the other hand straightforward theft is recognized as such. Every cotton mill in Lancashire loses a fair amount of cloth. The interesting point as regards such theft is that it is seldom condemned. The thief is often admired for his courage or condemned for his rashness and the other workers will often admit that they wouldn't have the nerve to steal. Far too often no moral judgement is passed and the whole question is judged on the basis of the laws of the land. It is fear of the magistrates' court and not an awareness of the moral law that prevents far more thieving. This merely reinforces the comments on the widespread ignorance of moral principles already mentioned.

At times one will find a worker who will attempt to justify his petty pilfering on the grounds that his employer does not pay him a just wage. Such a man is rare and it is seldom that he believes his own excuse. More often the reply to a question is that the firm has plenty and won't miss it. Other times the reply to a question will relate to the conduct of the firm. A firm that is careless about its materials or that allows what appears to the workers to be excessive waste will find that its workers help themselves to far more of the firm's property than would be the case in some neighbouring firm where stockkeeping is more rigid and where careful planning eliminates avoidable waste.

Petty pilfering is widespread. The commercial traveller who puts down fictitious expenses is guilty of it; and this is a very common practice. I even remember a traveller telling me that he was expected by his sales manager to keep his expenses up to a certain level because his sales manager overcharged on his expenses and did not want too wide a gap between his and the travellers'. The sales manager who looks for an excuse to take someone to lunch so that he can charge up his own lunch to expenses is guilty of it. During the 1951 general election I was a candidate and in my constituency a number of firms welcomed the candidate to address the workpeople and then entertained him to lunch. Nothing wrong in this at all, although I wondered about a firm that took me to a distant road-house for lunch and the party included every executive in the firm and the meal was almost a banquet.

At the other level of the social scale you will find the workman who fills up his time sheet to cover his day without giving any true indication of the time spent on a particular job. Sometimes his foreman will tell the workman to book up more hours. At times the idea is to convey the impression that the section is fully occupied; sometimes the foreman thinks it enhances his own importance; sometimes it is frankly to cover up hours of idleness.

At times such practices are based on an obscure sense of danger. The tendency for the manager is always to expect what the best man can do to be done by all. To the worker, who appreciates the wide differences of physique and of mental alertness and of natural skill that exist among any group of workers, this attitude of the manager is unreasonable and unjust. Therefore he takes a defensive attitude of seeing that the good worker does not do so much that the manager will feel bound to egg on the slow worker. Again, there is an ever-present fear of prolonged unemployment among many workers. The memories of the 1930's persist and have an effect on the current thinking of many workers. Basically this is a psychological problem but it often has this effect, that men will work slowly in case the management feels that some men can be discharged.

Let it be said at once that there are very many workers who work well and in a conscientious manner. Many of these are among the older age groups and they frequently complain that the workers today are not like they were in their youth. This is probably true because there has been a pronounced weakening of the moral code. It is general and one meets it when people complain of the lower level of workmanship in quality goods. The blame is also widespread because the lowering of moral standards is widespread.

Some more examples will help to illustrate the problems that exist. The first one is from 1939 and was only possible on the scale described because of the type of government contracts at that time which were on the basis of cost plus ten per cent. Thus it was to the employer's financial interest that costs should be as high as possible and, unfortunately, some employers fell to the temptation. I remember a wages clerk who used to bring home about four pounds over and above his wages each week. Every wage clerk in his firm did the same. The foremen and the senior staff took home far more than that. Every workman would have perhaps two hours a week fictitious overtime included in his pay. A vast amount of work that was not done was shown in the records and the money for this was shared out so that there should be no disgruntled workman willing to create a fuss. That was, of course, an extreme case. It is not unknown, to go down the scale to minor acts, for busmen to make enough money by taking fares and not issuing tickets to pay for the cups of tea he and his driver consume during the day.

Such acts are accepted as wrong, although not necessarily accepted as morally wrong, but as wrong because they are contrary to the rules of that employment and if discovered would lead to the sack.

There are other types of practices which would appear to be doubtful morally that are taken as legitimate by all concerned. It is not thought wrong for a man who has to place an order for his firm taking a commission on the side. He, usually speaking, is not being bribed to place the order to the disadvantage of the firm and the commission is to prevent him tossing a coin to see which of two equal offers should be accepted. It is not thought wrong for a firm hoping for an early decision on some point to send a present to the person who would make the decision. A vast amount of Christmas presents are sent out by businessmen, not in the sense of seasonal good cheer, but to influence future business.

Far more doubtful than this type of bribe is the idea that it is right to charge what the market will bear.

Some time ago (August 1954) the *Catholic Worker* carried an article describing the practices in one merchant's office. The article described the costing procedure in a firm and suggested that this was normal among that type of merchant. The costing led to excessive profit. Following that article I met a well-known Catholic, managing director of a firm in a similar line of business to the one described in the article. This gentleman repudiated the facts and as an alternative plea claimed that if true they were confined to one firm and were not general. Unfortunately I shortly afterwards received details of a transaction in which his firm was involved. For a particular job a certain figure was quoted. The firm of the gentleman mentioned above and some of his competitors all quoted about the same figure.

The customer assumed that as the quotations were all about the same the figure must be a just one. His agent advised negotiations and finally a figure was agreed on little more than one-third of the first quotation. Perhaps it is the modern version of the eastern bazaar and perhaps it is the modern theory that one charges for a service what the market will stand.

In the abstract a firm can work out its overheads and assess the costs involved in a job and when a margin for gross profits is added a firm price can be quoted. This can happen, and in theory does. In practice it does not always happen. It is not unknown for a local authority to receive tenders for a job and to find that the tenders are all within a few shillings of each other or so arranged as to make it obvious that the competing firms have decided that one of their number should have this job. Not long ago the local authority on which I sit decided to cancel a plan for building some small blocks of houses because it was obvious that the building firms were rigging the tenders.

Primarily such practices are the concern of employers. But what of the clerks who type out the tenders and do the costing work involved knowing full well what is happening? Can they in good conscience continue in such employment? If the firm's policy is, when costing up a job, to add a few pounds in case there are some extra telephone calls to be made, to add a few pounds for this or that, problems do arise. In the present state of society where no one believes in the just price (apparently not even Catholics) it cannot be said that such a procedure is wrong. But it has social implications that result in hardships for poor families. The tenders for the building of houses mentioned above would have resulted in some families paying about seven shillings a week more rent than would have been necessary if the tenders had been similar to the level of other building work done for the particular Council.

This social aspect of so many of our modern problems is often overlooked. In the days when the just price was the accepted basis one knew where one was. No doubt it was often got round and fraud and deceit and theft were not unknown. But today it is not accepted and groups of firms will work on some completely contrary principle, such as that prices must be such as to allow the most inefficient firm to survive. To what extent do the employees of such firms who co-operate in working out such a principle share in the guilt of the employers?

Clerical workers of one type or another have as many moral problems as have manual workers. There are progress clerks who are expected to record an alibi for any and every delay in the progress of a job through the works. The newspapers tell us of many instances in Soviet Russia where industry produces fictitious figures to cover up mistakes; this is a practice far from unknown in British industry.

Workers in shops also have their problems. There are many goods sold under a false description. Recent legislation has restricted the possibilities of this type of fraud and if shoppers would insist on seeing a B.S.I. symbol on everything they bought the opportunities would be even less. But there are articles sold under misleading descriptions and known to the trade as being misleading. Shop assistants will repeat manufacturers' claims that some articles are shrinkproof, or the colour is fast, well knowing from previous complaints that these claims are false. From time to time reports appear in the press of court cases in which a trader will blandly assure the court that such and such a description is normal in the trade even though obviously incorrect. Anyone who has access to annual reports of Inspectors of Weights and Measures will know how frequent misrepresentation is.

Two other problems need a mention because they are so common. The first one, which has already been touched on, is covered by the term 'restrictive practices'. There are understandable motives behind many such practices; fear of unemployment, fear of working oneself out of a job, fear of being worked too hard. But even when this is recognized it does not alter the immoral nature of some of them. There was a period when the *Scottish Daily Express* would not print a section in colour because the unions insisted on such extra staff as to make the development uneconomic. This is only one of a multitude of instances that can be quoted and that raise many moral issues.

The second problem is the avoiding of work. This refusal to do a fair day's work is far from uncommon. That does not mean that all the newspaper stories one reads are true and indeed a judgement can usually only be passed by someone close to the particular job who can understand all that is involved in it. But even with such reservations and caution one has to admit that there is a considerable amount of work-dodging in industry. This problem is bound up with the whole question of work and no solution will be found until the true Christian attitude to work is widely understood.

A contribution of this nature has to be mainly based on actual facts and the selection of examples to illustrate problems that exist does exclude the many examples that can be quoted of attention to work, of zeal in the employer's service, of care and thought above that which could be expected. Many employees are far better than some employers deserve. Unfortunately there are too many who leave a lot to be desired.

The problem is a personal one, but more than that it is a social one. It is the pagan atmosphere of our times that makes so many of these problems possible. I have tried to suggest that in addition to the sins we all may commit, knowing that they are sins, there will be found a bland ignorance of the moral law that prevents so many immoral acts being seen in that light.

Never mind how one attempts to produce a balanced picture of the concrete situation faced by employees of all types, the result is a fairly dismal picture and illustrates how Britain is falling into paganism, a paganism with little in the way of tribal taboos to preserve some form of moral order.

Of course it is clear that the picture is not all dismal. There are very many Christians in Britain, and while they may fall into temptations they do recognize moral standards and make at least some attempt to abide by God's law.

If that completed the positive side there would be little hope, for such a negative outlook would not survive the tempo of the recurring temptations and by gradually eating into the moral fibre would in time bring such Christians down to the level of the pagans. What is needed is a more deliberate attack on the problems that exist.

Such deliberate attacks are not unknown and indeed are growing so that it may well be possible to call a halt to the dechristianization of Britain, even in our lifetime. Whether this is a dream or a hope that can be realized depends to a large extent on the better formed Christians and their acceptance of their responsibilities to help and train their fellowmembers of the Mystical Body. An apostolic outlook on the part of all of us is the first requisite.

What is possible can be seen in such an organization as the Young Christian Workers. There an apostolic training is given to the members and this training is specifically directed to the concrete problems which the young people meet in work. It cannot be said that all the training is successful or that every member becomes a true apostle. But even in the unsuccessful cases, where, either through the individual's reluctance or through the failure of a section, real formation has not taken place, something has been given to the young person that appears to stick. In section reports sent to headquarters there is ample evidence that by tackling concrete problems that are within their scope the members of the Young Christian Workers can do much to remove obstacles to the Christian life, and on the positive side, do at least a little to bring an understanding of the Christian life to others.

There is in such reports evidence of how easy it sometimes is to stop an undesirable practice once two or three Catholics resolve that something must be done. Traditional initiation ceremonies have been ended in a few places, at least, by such a decision on the part of some Y.C.W. members. At least a temporary easing of the general attitude to sex has followed action at work by members of this movement.

There is enough evidence that it is possible to change conditions; that Britain is not yet sufficiently pagan to be given up as hopeless. There is sufficient evidence that apostolic-minded people can influence their fellow workers to such an extent as to change the atmosphere of the workshop.

This is not the place to argue as to the right method of producing apostles among the laity. Let it suffice to say that if we produce an apostolic outlook among the Christian laity we can do much to tackle the problems described above. Such an apostolic training must give an important place to the understanding of work, for if work was generally seen as being the co-operation with God in the working out of his plan of creation there would come about such a revolution that our present industrial and commercial society would be changed beyond recognition.

XIV

THE EMPLOYER'S PROBLEM

by

Anthony Howard

THE employer as a person is practically defunct in modern industry, and only survives in the small, one-man, businesses. Legally speaking, of course, the employer in the limited company is the body of shareholders, but, as we know too well, they are not able to exercise any personal influence upon the people that they employ, except through the elected directors. I shall therefore use the word 'employer' in its widest sense as being equivalent to what the text books term the *entrepreneur*, who of course has duties in a number of different directions. He has a duty to the customer which involves us in discussions about the 'Just Price', a duty to the owners of the business which is covered by the principle of the 'Fair Return', and a duty to the community. This last duty includes such activities as support of local charities, and, in general, efforts to be a good neighbour. On the national plane, his duty to the community prevents him from supplying immoral goods or services, e.g. horror comics. The *entrepreneur's* final duty is to his employees, and it is in this sense that we shall talk about the employer who, in a modern industrial firm, may be anybody from the managing director down to the charge hand—since they all have their duties towards their subordinates.

This particular aspect of the employer's job, i.e. his relations with the people he employs, is perhaps a greater challenge to the Christian employer than with the other people we have mentioned. With them, the employer is only dealing with a part of their personalities, but with his own employees he is dealing eight hours or more a day with the whole man—mind, body and soul—and surely it is here that the employer can prove whether or not he is the leaven in the lump or the salt of the earth. 'By their fruits ye shall know them,' and the challenge of this text to the Christian employer is to show if and how he can produce results this side of the grave, better by his own Christian moral standards than those of the non-Christian employer, who—for the sake of brevity—we shall refer to in future as the 'humanist' employer.

The employment of labour is not an end in itself, and there must be very few people today who have the money to employ people just for the sake of providing work. This function can only be assumed by the State in large-scale schemes for the relief of unemployment, and even here it is hoped that useful work will be done. The usual object of employing labour is to add value to raw materials or ideas so that they may be sold at a profit that will enable the employer to live and to carry on his business. If we accept this, there is no basic difference between the Christian and the humanist employers in their material purposes. The Christian employer, like any other employer, has a competitive outlook on life and must be forgiven if he puts his problem in the form of the question how he can do better than his humanist colleague. Before he can do this, however, he must study how the good humanist employer treats his people, because only when he has examined his rival's product can he decide what is lacking in it. The humanist employer recognizes that a man has a number of needs that require to be satisfied before he can be a fully efficient and contented personality.

First is the basic need to survive—perhaps the most primitive of all. Today, this need is recognized first by pay and material rewards which provide a man with food, shelter and clothing. These rewards will be added to according to the circumstances of the individual firm, by sick pay, pensions, paid convalescent leave, help towards house-ownership and help when asked for in dealing with private problems.

Secondly, it is recognized that it is insufficient to pay a man a good wage if his life is endangered by his job, and therefore the conscientious employer will take all possible steps to preserve the health and life of his employees, and protect them against the hazards of the job.

Lastly, the conditions of work must not be so arduous that they endanger, not necessarily the life, but the general state of health of the employee. Under this head, the employer makes reasonable regulations, unless they are already made by the State, regarding hours of work and holiday periods. Attention is paid to the heating and lighting of the place of work, and precautions are taken to ensure that no job exceeds the limits of human tolerance. Beyond this, the humanist employer endeavours to provide a security of tenure for his people, and to act fairly when it is necessary to dismiss people in times of slump.

There may be some people who think that an employer's duty is done when he has paid a just wage, but of course this is not so. In the first place the cynic will say, and rightly so, that forces outside the employer's control, e.g. the State and the Trades Unions, compel him to pay a just wage whether he wants to or not. But in any event this conception implies that the employee is no more than a unit of cost, on a level with raw materials, rent, rates, etc., and entitled to no more consideration and respect than a machine—indeed, to rather less. It implies that a man needs no more than economic satisfaction, but any employer who thinks like this today may well end up without any profits, or indeed any labour.

The humanist goes beyond this limited view and realizes that man is a combination of bodily and mental processes which must be taken into account, but nevertheless he still regards labour as a unit of cost, and this is a point to which we shall revert when considering what more the Christian should do.

Having dealt, therefore, with the basic need to survive, we go on to the need which everybody has—to do something well, to excel in some particular department of life. The humanist employer, recognizing this need, will do his best to meet it. At its simplest, this need may be satisfied if the worker can see the jobs he has done, piling up in front of him, or marked on a tally, as physical evidence of his performance. Going beyond this, however, it is customary to recognize the amount of work done, by some form of token—thus we get the money incentive paid for above average output; a special uniform in such spheres as the armed services, titles and decorations both in civil and military life; awards for merit; special privileges; and just the simple word of commendation. If work is not recognized in one or more of these forms, the performance will not be good. Again, by offering prospects of advancement, the need to excel is encouraged. We all know there is nothing more stultifying than being blocked from promotion by a man who is older than ourselves and whom only death will remove from our path. Some people will blossom if they are given a variety of work so that they can build up confidence in their ability to tackle well more than a single job. On the other hand it must be borne in mind that some people prefer to do the same job day in and day out, leaving them free to think about other things. There have been cases of employers who, appalled by the monotony of certain jobs, have thought to do their employees a good turn by changing them round at intervals, but the result has been quite contrary to their expectations, and the reaction of the people concerned has been that they are being 'pushed around'. No two people are exactly alike, and therefore no one approach is going to provide the answer universally. In the case of the young and new entrant to industry, we find apprentice schemes which have the object of training a young person in some trade or craft where he can do well. In the case of new entrants to a particular firm, the good employer provides training facilities to ensure, in his own interests of course, that not too much time is lost before the new employee becomes efficient, but at the same time this approach does make it easier for the new entrant to settle down quickly in his job, and not feel frustrated and unhappy because he cannot do it well.

The last form of recognition that need be mentioned here is the existence of professional bodies which admit to membership people who have attained certain standards in their particular profession. The ability to put some letters after one's name is a token of personal achievement in just the same way as the first example we took of the man's output piling up in front of him.

Man also has a basic sexual need to reproduce himself, and it may well be asked what, if anything, the employer should do about this. All that he can and should do is to recognize this urge, and to take care that it finds no improper outlet within his organization, and he will do what he can to remove the sources of temptation to prevent any immorality such as initiation ceremonies, and by choosing good leaders to set a good example in the way of personal behaviour and language. When it is necessary for members of opposite sexes to work near each other under difficult conditions, the employer will not blind himself to the dangers.

We come finally to what is perhaps the most important need of all. This is the need of everybody to feel that he belongs to a community which he respects and which respects him. Whatever paper systems we may devise for breaking divisions down into departments, and departments into sections, and sections into teams, men and women will form their own informal groups within industry. The individual's loyalty to his primary group if ignored will lead to unrest. Outside working hours, a man's basic loyalty is probably to his family, and while at work he will be loyal first to the little team for which he works, but he will not necessarily have the same ideas on the leadership of the group as do his superiors. We all know from our own experience that the recognized leader is not always the chairman of the board, the office manager, the school prefect or the foreman, and although it may not always be possible, or even wise, to promote to official leadership the unofficial leader, his presence must nevertheless be recognized, because it is from him that the rest of the group will take their lead when decisions are to be made.

What then is the employer to do in order both to recognize the existence of these little communities, and at the same time to run his business efficiently? We agree, I hope, that it is asking for trouble to ignore the groups and fight them, because although that may bring temporary success, it is storing up trouble for the future. We all know that the appalling conditions at the time of the Industrial Revolution are responsible for the bitterness that still exists today. Decisions may be taken quickly, but their results are forgotten slowly, if ever.

First, the employer will take care that from the moment a man or woman enters his employ, he or she is treated as an individual with this urge to 'belong'. The thoughtless employer will greet the new man with a casual word, point out to him the shop where he is to work, and say to him, 'If you go in the door there and ask for the supervisor, he will tell you what to do.' There is no need to go into great detail, but the reaction in the mind of the normal man to such a start may be imagined, particularly if, when he arrives in the shop, nobody was expecting him and the supervisor was unfortunate enough to have been nagged by his wife that morning. The new man will immediately sense, if not an unfriendly, at least an uninterested atmosphere, and feel that nobody cares very much whether he settles down or not. Who can be surprised if in such circumstances the man doesn't turn out a good performance while he is with the company?

The good employer, on the other hand, will make certain that the new man is personally greeted by a responsible official and taken by him to the supervisor of the particular shop where he is to work and introduced. The supervisor and the shop steward, aware that he is coming, will make him feel at home and introduce him to his new workmates, take trouble over explaining the job, and make sure that he sits with his new acquaintances in the canteen.

I hope this example will suffice to show the two different approaches which can be made, and the likelihood of better results coming from treating a man as a social being and not just as a self-propelled tool. One should, of course, go further than this initial reception and introduction, by explaining the job properly and showing how it fits in with the products or services provided by the firm as a whole. In this way the community spirit begins to get built up. When a man has settled into a job, he should be consulted from time to time about it, and it should be made clear to him that his ideas and suggestions are always welcome and will be used, and in certain cases rewarded when they are acceptable. One hears of cases where ideas are not forthcoming for the reason that they never get beyond the foreman, who then takes them to his manager as though they were his own brain-child. This is an excellent way of starting an unofficial and unhappy community on the shop floor.

This problem of catering for the community sense of the worker becomes more acute as the size of the industrial unit increases. In the case of the one-man firm, the small shop or the small office, it may be simple enough for the employer to build up a team spirit, because he knows all his people personally, and they know him and see him every day. Although from time to time we are urged to do this or that for the State, the Church, the Party or the local community, we cannot really be moved to love or hatred for those organizations because they are too remote. Similarly, if a man has a good foreman, he will tend to like the firm for which he is working. If he has, however, an inconsiderate and uncouth superior, he will have a very poor view of his company. Unless, therefore, this existence of primary loyalties is recognized, it is quite purposeless to attempt to appeal to larger loyalties and feel aggrieved when no response is forthcoming. Loyalties of the nature that were produced after Dunkirk or in times of national crisis will produce results over a limited period, but, taking the long view, the loyalty and efficiency will only come if the loyalty is already there, at the immediate personal level.

I have made no mention under this heading of schemes variously described as profit-sharing, co-partnership, co-ownership and co-management. These are all closely tied up with the financial and political considerations, but I would only say here that they must be tested by their success or failure in building up a better community spirit in an organization. In my view, if a company is owned entirely by the people who work for it, the moral standard may still be bad; the important things may still be overlooked.

So much for the needs the employer tries to satisfy. But to enable him to do this he must be able to lead his particular group. The following quotation from St Mark's gospel (10: 42–5) gives an excellent piece of advice to all employers, humanist and Christian alike.

But Jesus called them to him, and said to them, You know that, among the Gentiles, those who claim to bear rule lord it over them, and those who are great among them make the most of the power they have.

With you it must be otherwise; whoever has a mind to be great among you, must be your servant, and whoever has a mind to be first among you, must be your slave. So it is that the Son of Man did not come to have service done him; he came to serve others, and to give his life as a ransom for the lives of many.

This text shows the difference between authority and leadership. The good employer, if he is to be effective, will choose to be a leader rather than an authoritarian, and therefore he must make this text the basis of his conduct. Many of us who served in the Armed Forces have met people whose motto was 'Don't do as I do, do as I say.' One wonders what became of them when they were demobilized, because certainly no one of that calibre can, or should be allowed to, exercise leadership in industry today. True authority is vested in the leader by the group voluntarily, and this means that there is no such thing as a quality of natural leadership that will automatically be applicable in any and every group. Community spirit does not necessarily make a good foreman, and the good managing director may be hopeless as a general. Without the unspoken consent of his subordinates, a leader on paper will never be a leader in fact. There is a very good slogan in circulation in management circles which sums up this attitude very nicely: 'Follow from in front', unlike the Duke of Plaza-Toro who led his regiment from behind because he found it less exciting. It is in fact more exciting to follow from in front, and there is no place in industry today for the employer who is not prepared for an exciting life.

For Catholics the first example of this precept is the Pope, who is described as 'the servant of the servants of God'. The good employer must be an example in the round. He is necessarily in an exposed position in which he can be either commended or shot at. His virtues and his vices stand out for all to see, and so he must be not only good at his job, but good as a man. He must watch his step and his tongue. In this country, every employer has an example in the Royal Family, which is in just such a position as I have described. The word paternalism has been overworked, and is not generally approved of in industry since it has come to be associated with despotism, benevolent or otherwise. Nevertheless, I think that paternalism in the sense that I have described is what every employer should aim at, so that to his people he represents what I believe the psychologists call 'the father figure', but not—I would hasten to add—a 'heavy father figure'.

In this necessarily very brief review of the way in which the good humanist employer tackles his job, I hope I have shown enough to give an idea of the challenge that faces the Christian employer. What is lacking in the outlook I have described? The humanist has a duty to achieve maximum efficiency in all departments of his company, but the Christian employer goes further, because he recognizes the true end of man. The true end of redeemed man is sanctification. Whether he does his particular job voluntarily or not, he should, so far as the job will allow, contribute to it all that he has. I do not like as a rule taking liberties with Scripture and making unjustifiable assumptions, but I hope that in this instance it will be justified. It is quite possible that our Lord was not keen on carpentry, and that our Lady had other ideas of employing her time than cooking, but nevertheless we may be perfectly certain that both of them devoted all their efforts to doing a good job of work, however uncongenial it may have been. The Christian employer's attitude must be to do all he can to help his employees to develop themselves fully in their work, so far as the work will allow and they themselves are capable, and in so doing to achieve his own sanctification.

The Christian employer who, like any other employer, has to show results if he is to live, will, when tackling this particular problem, be tempted to search for a system that he can install which will produce and, if possible, show results in the spiritual sphere, but a little consideration will show that even if this were a desirable attitude, it is not possible. Employers today are agreed that it is quite improper to interfere uninvited in the private life of their employees. If this is so, surely it is far more improper to attempt to interfere in their spiritual lives. What then can the Christian employer do towards helping the sanctification of his people and himself?

As I see it, his objective must be the creation of a climate in which spiritual factors will flourish, and in which he can allow his own outlook to filter through the other levels of management to the shop floor. This is easy to say, but very difficult to do. The larger the firm the larger the number of levels, and the less assurance that all levels will be of the same moral calibre. He may console himself by the thought that if his humanist colleague is getting results from his employee, it is because he is treating him properly, or as Frank Sheed would say, according to 'Maker's Instructions'.

However, the Maker also has a part to play, and no Christian should be so conceited as to think that he can do it all himself. He must, therefore, take the long-term view, and first do his utmost to be saturated by Christ, and then go on to saturate the job.

NOTE ON CHAPTERS XIII AND XIV

DISCUSSIONS which followed these two papers provided the material on which this note is based.

The springs of morality rise from the waters of love. Love is essentially a relationship between two persons. It is impossible properly speaking to love an impersonal collective; a body of people can only be loved as a result of love relations between the persons who make up that body. Even love for the Church is based on a love relation with Christ. In this sense love and loyalty are possible towards a corporate body; and springing from this love, moral prescriptions are felt to be valid in relation to such a body. But the possibility of such a love and loyalty towards an unknown body of shareholders or any invisible collective or aggregate is diminished almost to nil; moral prescriptions in relation to such large bodies, commercial or otherwise, are not felt to be binding, they are not felt in fact to be moral. They become merely rules, penal laws. 'Stealing' is not felt to be stealing; and logically it would be difficult to predicate stealing of many of the actions described in Mr Walsh's paper; it could well be said that what is 'stolen' is in fact admitted to be the property of the person who takes it; the employer reckons on a disappearance, in this way, of a given quantity of material and makes little attempt to prevent it—he does not undertake the normal responsibilities of ownership towards it.

In this situation many of the problems which might be seen as moral problems become merely technical problems of efficiency. Mr Howard describes how the whole matter of treating an employee as a person becomes, to the efficient employer, a purely technical matter. In this sense it is perfectly true that the Christian employer can do no more, in the practical sphere, than the perfectly efficient non-Christian. But it may reasonably be asked whether he cannot act in this way with a greater assurance. Whilst the non-Christian treats men in a way which implicitly acknowledges that they are persons, the Christian does so with the certain knowledge that they are persons to whom he owes not only justice but the charity of Christ. The Christian employer does not need to claim that his immediate motives are other than ordinary business motives, but he can say that his attitude is consonant with what he is sure are absolute certainties and not merely changeable statistics. It should not really be so surprising that the good, the right and the efficient should sometimes, even most of the time, coincide. But the test comes in times of crisis; for instance when an employer has to rearrange and possibly dismiss men, the Christian employer should be sharply distinguished from the employer who has no real respect for men as men, but treats them as persons only when convenient from the point of view of efficiency. Some non-Christian employers will also be seen at such testing times to have a real respect for men. The Christian should be able to provide the philosophical and religious justification for this respect, a respect which should also extend in measure towards all created matter, to the raw material used in the work. Here a firm intellectual basis is essential; mere piety and good intention are not enough.

Eric Gill and others connected with him made the only substantial attempt in the last fifty years to work out a Christian philosophy and theology of work. But it was done more or less apart from the main stream of contemporary life, and failed to provide a solid basis for Christians in their existing situations. The two papers printed here provide a picture of those situations, and a measure of the problem.

In Chapter v of this book Dom Aelred Watkin writes: 'It is a different thing to buy and sell within the limits of the Ten Commandments and to buy and sell to support Christ incarnate in ourselves and our neighbours' (p.66). There is a great temptation today to limit our Christianity to the mere keeping of the law, thus turning morals into loveless penal rules and nothing more. The temptation arises because, as is clear from Mr Walsh's paper, it is precisely at the points in day-to-day conduct where Christian moral prescriptions are most clearly violated that the Christian is inevitably most clearly distinguished from his fellow. But the ultimate motive—support of Christ incarnate in self and neighbour —involves much more than avoiding abuses and doing all the other usual and legitimate things with the right intention. It is a matter of constant prayer—being saturated with Christ, as Mr Howard says—and it is a matter of long and hard study and planning. Mr Walsh ends his paper with the statement of his conviction that the present industrial and commercial system would be altered out of all recognition if a sense of the apostolic mission of the Church were present in those who take part in the system, and if an understanding of the ultimate nature of work was present. But this transformation will not happen automatically; it can only be achieved if those Christians with a sense of the apostolate engage in careful and detailed planning, research and experimentation. And for this a fully articulated philosophy and theology of work is indispensable. Rules of thumb about respect for persons and respect for material have a certain value; but in the end this respect, like the motive of supporting Christ incarnate, involves much more than righting immediate offences against the nature of man and of matter: it involves more than this mere attitude of censorship.

We have in fact to say that if men and matter have a particular sort of nature, then it follows that they should be organized in a way consonant with that nature, enabling it to be developed to the full. The

G

whole set of relationships between men and matter has to be organized in a way which positively discourages sinful attitudes, for instance avaricious attitudes as treated in Chapter IX of this book, and which positively encourages holiness. The purpose of this book is, in one sense, to indicate the conditions over many spheres of life which do just this.

The application of this principle to the problem of work is still exceedingly baffling. A radical judgement is required; yet when one is given, as by Eric Gill, it is impractical. An immediate practical programme is required; yet when one is given, it turns out to be little different from the existing set-up, rid of its abuses. Thought, research, experimentation are needed. The golden rule, it may be suggested, is that machines must always be looked on as tools for men; their design, manufacture and use must all be judged by their services or dis-services to the whole man. Chapter I refers to the need for an Institute of Theology. This subject of work would certainly be one of its principal preoccupations.—*Editor*.

XV

THE WRITER'S PROBLEM
by
Hugh Dinwiddy

IF we ask what literature is about, we have to answer that it is about the mystery of the human heart and its passage through time. And from this we conclude that the writer is a person bound in fidelity to interpret this mystery and its movement, to his own, and, perhaps, to all succeeding generations. His task is no less than this. In every age his first problem is to remain creatively alive on the substance that his generation provides. He is an individual reaching out to individuals, and, if he is not only to live but to grow, he must be gradually deepening his understanding of what he observes, so that in and through the individual he is confronted by some concept of universality in which his mind can ultimately rest. Yet, in the modern setting, he scarcely dare think in abstract terms, for immediately he does so, a cold barrier is projected between him and his subject. The writer, for the most part, knows what he knows through the intimate experience of observing and creating. Like all creative acts, and, indeed, like the moral law itself, his work is founded in the order of love which is as infinite in its operation as are the ways of Providence. There is, then, at the very centre of the activity of being a writer, no conflict between the genuine writer and Christian morality.

Yet, in ages when the order of love, the belief in the ultimate goodness of Providence, is questioned, conflict arises between the writer and the moralist. At such times, religion comes to be, increasingly, an external restraint, in itself tentative and uncreative. At such times the old disrupting arguments of whether art is useful or free or religious are heard again, and we know that we have to return to fundamentals, and to begin, amid the confusion of creeds, to work our way back to an acceptance of the state in which the order of love informs moral life. Indeed, it is upon the order of love that the writer lives, and he is concerned, not only with the act of creation, but with the sense of destiny that accompanies it. So deeply ingrained is this sense in the writer that every movement, motive and action in his writing is penetrated with it, sometimes to the point of absurdity. Thus the Russian literary critic Druzhínin wrote in a letter to Tolstoy on the publication of the first part of *Youth* in 1857:

> You have an inclination to super-refinement of analysis which may become a great defect. You are sometimes on the point of saying that so-and-so's thigh indicated that he wished to travel to India. You must restrain this tendency, but do not extinguish it on any account.[1]

We may, perhaps, speak loosely of a 'philosophy' of the thigh, of the hands or face, or back of the neck that seems to indicate a direction towards an end, and the writer, like the sculptor or painter, must begin with the body in his search for meaning, contrasting, like Portia, man's 'little body' with 'this great world'. Here Druzhínin is pointing to an element in Tolstoy's writing that is merely an attitude, but it is an attitude, though he makes it look absurd, which the writer must on no account extinguish, for, by it, he may reach the animating nerve of destiny in human affairs. It is this which brings significance to disparate observations, and which points the way to the writer's choice of subject. In many ways the writer is like a fisherman who envisages beforehand what his catch will be, and yet who patiently, and with fascination, goes in search of it. There is, in Kafka's recently published *Note Books*, a passage that exactly illustrates this point.

> I have—who else can speak so freely of his abilities?—the wrist of a lucky, untiring, old angler. For instance, I sit at home before I go out fishing, and, watching closely, turn my right hand first this way and then that. This is enough to reveal to me, by the look and the feeling of it, the result of the fishing expedition on which I am about to set out, and often down to the very details. A prophetic intuition of this pliant joint, which, when I am resting, I enclose in a gold bracelet in order to let it gather strength. I see the water of the place where I shall fish and the particular current at the particular hour; a cross-section of the river appears to me; distinct in number and species, at up to ten, twenty, or even a hundred different places, fish thrust towards the edge of this cross-section; now I know how to cast the line; some thrust their heads through the edge without coming to harm, then I let

[1] Quoted by Aylmer Maude in his *Life of Tolstoy*, Vol. I, p. 175 (World's Classics).

the hook dangle before them, and at once there they are hanging on it; the brevity of this moment of destiny delights me even at the table at home; other fish thrust forward up to the belly, now it is high time, some I still manage to overtake, others again slip through the dangerous edge right up to their tails and for the time being are lost to me, only for this time though, from a real angler no fish escapes.[1]

Though many writers would contend that this is too perfect a description of what happens, the aim here is to illustrate the attitude of godlike knowledge that a writer has to his creation. His way is to trace the nerve of destiny in the meetings and decisions in individual lives, to find justification for one being chosen and the other left. To do this is to follow the path of meaning, and, as is frequently said, and which was repeated in a broadcast talk by Joyce Carey printed in the *Listener*[2]: 'Meaning is form'—and meaning divorced from a moral purpose is formless.

Yet, in a period like the present, when, for one reason or another, the writer believes the religious moralist to be speaking negative, uncourageous, meaningless and unloving words, he must needs become his own moralist. We find him, therefore, preparing to follow his calling to be a writer in isolation, and, in the case of Rilke —in its extreme form—with the reverence and inward preparation of a hermit. In his advice to the young poet, he writes:

> You are looking outwards, and of all things that is what you must not do. Nobody can advise and help you, nobody. There is only one single means. Go inside yourself. Discover the motive that bids you write; examine whether it sends its roots down to the deepest places of your heart, confess to yourself whether you would have to die if writing were denied you. This before all: ask yourself in the quietest hour of your night: *must* I write? Dig down in to yourself for a deep answer. And if this should be in the affirmative, if you must meet this solemn question with a strong and simple '*I must*,' then build your life according to this necessity; your life must, right to its most unimportant and in-significant hour, become a token and a witness of this impulse.[3]

The inner necessity that is here so pressingly felt, followed by the plea to dedicate every 'unimportant and insignificant hour' towards its manifestation represents such an exclusive and total way of living

---

[1] Franz Kafka, *Wedding Preparations*, pp. 63, 64.

[2] *Listener*, September 30th, 1954.

[3] Rainer Maria Rilke, *Letters To a Young Poet*, p. 12.

that it can only be a law unto itself. The poetic integrity—the quiet, but intense centring of one's life round, and being true to, the poetic experience—that this entails is, in the case of more fiery individuals than Rilke, likely, in its unguided absolutism, to seek to overturn much of the moral teaching of society. That Shelley's verdict that 'Milton's Devil as a moral being' is far superior to his God should have been so widely approved is remarkable enough, but the concluding two sentences of his argument in *The Defence of Poetry* are even more striking, for they represent the complete and explicit turning away of the poet from accepted morality. In praising Milton, he praises him as a rebel poet and divorces his great work, the poem that was to be 'doctrinal to a nation', from its entire theological content.

> Milton has so far violated the popular creed (if this shall be judged to be a violation) as to have alleged no superiority of moral virtue to his God over his Devil. And this bold neglect of a direct moral purpose is the most decisive proof of the supremacy of Milton's genius.[1]

Nevertheless, as Shelley knew, better than almost anyone else, the poet needs a morality by which to live and to work. Yet there were born, subsequently, in puny boldness, a succession of 'geniuses', whose intent was to divide art from morals. The intention, though it must inevitably fail, is widely held today.

'Another thing they say to young novelists is,' writes Joyce Carey deprecatingly, 'If you want a public, do not moralize; because morals are a bore. . .' And he goes on to show how the greatest novelists of the world 'are just those who take the greatest interest in morals: it is because of that they are so exciting to read. Think of Dickens, Tolstoy, Hardy, Conrad.'[2]

These are men who, being, above all things, interested in human destiny, know the innate position of morals in a life spent in creation. It is not against this that the twentieth-century revolt took place in England, but against the mild clerical-tinged background of English middle class values with regard to the writer and his work that are represented, for instance, by Thackeray in the opening pages of his lecture on, of all people, Jonathan Swift.

> The humorous writer professes to awaken and direct your love, your pity, your kindness—your scorn for untruth, pretension,

[1] *Defence of Poetry*, English Critical Essays (XIX Century), p. 148.
[2] *Listener*, September 30th, 1954.

imposture—your tenderness for the weak, the poor, the oppressed, the unhappy. To the best of his means and ability he comments on all the ordinary actions and passions of life *almost* [my italics]. He takes upon himself to be the weekday preacher, so to speak. According as he finds, and speaks, and feels the truth best, we regard him, esteem him—sometimes love him. And, as his business is to mark other people's lives and peculiarities, we moralize upon *his* life when he is gone—and yesterday's preacher becomes the text for today's sermon.[1]

It is from this explicit, moralizing pietism that D. H. Lawrence and the twentieth century have revolted, and their revolt has broken the last fragile link between the writer and the accepted moral code of his age. Apart from the notion of the writer as 'the weekday preacher', it is the word 'almost' that sounds so naïve in our ears. And now, with the initial waves of that revolt over, we stand watching ourselves being carried forward by events, by 'the ordinary actions and passions of life,' so that there are 'moments of destiny', when, perhaps more than in any other age, we identify our life, and the newness of our experience, with our own time. The century of the 'mealy-mouthed lie' has bred its reaction in the arrival of the apparently honest, undermining fact. Unguided by tradition and alone, we reduce the huge powers of freedom and love to our own level. Like Stella Rodney, in Elizabeth Bowen's *The Heat of the Day*, contemplating an illicit love in war-time London, the writer may feel:

> The fateful course of her fatalistic century seemed more and more her own: together had she and it arrived at the testing extremities of their noonday. Neither had lived before.[2]

Here we find the theory of 'living in to the answer' in operation. The writer is too close to his subject for him to exercise the just and loving detachment which is his special gift of wisdom, and it requires wisdom, and not only fact and logic, to explain the testing extremities of human feeling.

'In all these things there is not any logical sequence,' writes M. Claudel to the readers of the English translation of *Soulier de Satin*, 'but please climb to the top of a tree with me, ladies and gentlemen.'[3]

Certainly the book written at close view, that does not deepen

---

[1] *The English Humorists of the Eighteenth Century*, a series of Lectures given by W. M. Thackeray in 1853, Grey Walls Press, pp. 13, 14.
[2] p. 127.   [3] p. vii.

towards wisdom, can, as it stands, be scarcely more than a docu-
mentary. Yet, if it is not its sensation, it is its 'seriousness' that draws
our attention. It is this which looks like an approach to morality,
and which, in Rilke's letters to a young Poet, is an attempt to deflect
morality from its centre, into a land of pure 'perhaps'.

> Do not search now for the answers which cannot be given you
> because you could not live them. It is a matter of living every-
> thing. Live the questions now. Perhaps you will then gradually,
> without noticing it, one day live right into the answer. Perhaps
> indeed you carry within yourself the possibility of shaping and
> forming, as a particularly pure and blessed kind of life; train
> yourself for it—but take what comes in complete trust, if only it
> comes from your will, from some inner need of yours, take it to
> yourself and do not hate anything. Sex is difficult; yes. [And,
> then, paraphrasing Spinoza] But it is the difficult that is enjoined
> upon us, almost everything serious is difficult, and everything is
> serious.[1]

His advice to the young poet to 'draw near to Nature' may preserve the creative spirit, but if the close view is applied to the small,
more or less sophisticated world of town life, we find that its poten-
tiality is quickly exhausted by the writer, and in endeavouring to
interpret it, he is faced with the problem of survival. The problem is
posed by Bernard Sands, the homosexual novelist, in *Hemlock and
After*, while speaking to his daughter about the difficult relations
with his wife.

'I remain a person,' he says, 'who is kept working, kept alive,
kept whatever you like, by emotional and physical contact.'[2] This
"feverish" living is explained as being an escape from boredom.

'It's the cardinal sin, I think, to let life bore you . . .'[3] he observes.

Now, if the writer really believes that every form of morality is a
bore, he rejects all that is personal in man and cannot write. What,
in fact, happens when writers and moralists are in conflict is, quite
simply, that, from the writer's side, an individual comes to believe
that his freedom to create is being threatened by an external, absolute authority, and his revolt against morals becomes a revolt
against authority; and this is to put the issue into a false perspective
from the start. For the revolt against morals is much more fundamental than that: it is a revolt against the nature of man as God
made him. Perhaps it should be said here that we are not moral
because the Church or some other authority tells us to be; we are

---

[1] p. 21.   [2] p. 60.   [3] p. 56.

moral because God made us free, loving, rational creatures. When
a writer revolts against the morality of his age, and then, like
Shelley, constructs his own system of morality, he is bearing witness
to his moral nature as a man.

> I must create a System, or be enslav'd by another Man's;
> I will not Reason and Compare: my business is to Create . . .

wrote William Blake in his 'Jerusalem'. The only world so far constructed without morals is the de-personalized, slave world of
George Orwell's *1984*, where there is no freedom, nor responsibility,
nor love, nor literature. Behind it lies the spectre of 'Arrogance'.

> I saw bleak Arrogance, with brows of brass,
> Clad nape to sole in shimmering foil of lead,
> Stark down his nose he stared; a crown of glass
> Aping the rainbow, on his tilted head.
>
> His very presence drained the vital air;
> He sate erect—stone-cold, self-crucified;
> On either side of him an empty chair;
> And sawdust trickled from his wounded side.[1]

This spectre that Walter de la Mare has here anatomized is not a
new one: it is the vision of death, whose 'very presence drained the
vital air', and it is this cold presence which lurks in the empty
shadows when the novelist uses the euphemistic word 'boredom'.
It is closely associated with King Lear's bleak and bitter question:
'Is there any cause in nature that makes these hard hearts?'

The subject of the writer, as we have observed, is the simple,
throbbing heart of man, but, if he is faced, in his contemporary
scene, with numbness of heart, or with hard-heartedness, he is up
against the problem of having to transform into his writing an
utterly unyielding substance. We have seen the awful figure of
pride, self-crucified, and between two empty chairs. We know its
opposite, the figure of suffering and of creative redemption which, in
spite of himself, the writer imitates every time he uses his transforming power. The writer knows what he knows by observing and
by creating; his way is not to reason and compare, and yet in the
modern setting he is compelled to do so, for the moral sense with
which he was born compels him to create a system, to give him substance to work upon and to protect what he writes from misinterpretation. And every new system that arises with every new approach

---

[1] *The Burning Glass and other Poems*, p. 57.

G*

to the art of writing is an attempt to return to fundamentals. It is touched in some part by a sense of destiny that reaches beyond the experience of the art itself. For, as Berdyaev has written, 'The experience of knowledge, moral experience, and in fact the experience of life in its fullest sense, is only possible if one shares in the destiny of man and of the world.'[1]

If the moral theories that accompany writers are now less frequently stated than the aesthetic theories, that is what one would expect to happen in an age when morals are a bore, yet we notice that aesthetics have the force of morality within their narrow sphere of influence. And, lest it should be thought that a system of morality, unlit by theological guidance, is, by itself, enough, we must remember the twice repeated 'Destiny waits in the hand of God' in the opening chorus of *Murder in the Cathedral*. Yet, for so long has the writer been separated from a live theological background that modern literary apologists, not knowing what it is, treat theology with disdain. Their attitude is expressed in the words of Middleton Murry in his book *Keats and Shakespeare*.

> Theology can only be interpreted by those who have no need of it; and so with all attempts, inevitable though they are, to translate soul-knowledge into terms of mind-knowledge.[2]

This may be sensitive writing, but it bespeaks, to use T. S. Gregory's phrase, a 'devout irrationality'.[3]

The inevitable attempt to make a supporting system is an attempt to find a way through to meaning and therefore to form. These are observations from the inside, from the writer's side of the curtain, and the problem of getting his meaning across (in other times it would be called his 'moral') to an audience, which is, for the most part, unreceptive to ideas, is a particularly nerve-testing problem to the writer. For 'meaning' in all art is more like a presence than an explicit moral code. The genuine writer, then, is now the victim of special circumstances. Unlike the painter or sculptor, he cannot for long seek refuge in the abstract, for the 'word' is closer to the heart than is 'paint' or 'stone'. He knows that his creative work lives by meaning and by form, and that it is struck into life by a sense of destiny. He knows too, especially if he is a poet, that his meaning is unlikely to be apparent to those who read him, yet he dare not, as could the nineteenth-century writer, pause and explain as he goes along—it is interesting to note the gradual disappearance of the

---

[1] *Freedom and the Spirit*, p. 340.   [2] p. 142.   [3] *The Tablet*, March 11th, 1950.

'explicit' from Eliot's drama. Yet, perhaps, never before has the writer felt the need so strongly to explain himself to his uncomprehending public—he has certainly never been so widely criticized for being obscure—but, without becoming a preacher, or, in modern terms, a propagandist, he is, within his creative work, unable to speak openly in explanation. 'We hate poetry that has a palpable design upon us,' wrote Keats to Reynolds, 'and, if we do not agree, seems to put its hand into its breeches pocket.'[1] He is writing in criticism of Wordsworth, and no man felt so deeply, nor for so long a time as Wordsworth, the burden of the poet having to bear the responsibility of being his own theologian and moralist. It is when the burden of this responsibility becomes too oppressive that the writer may today become a Communist or a Christian.

The writer, then, may still find his inner revelation in accord with some already established system of ideas, yet, to a greater or lesser extent, like 'the poet in the theatre today', in the words of Norman Nicholson, he 'must not merely adapt himself to his audience, he must create an audience to which to adapt himself. . .'[2] And then, should he gather an audience, a following, he has the added responsibility of guiding its thought. This makes the writer a leader of thought, and more conscious than ever of having, or of trying *not* to have, a moral purpose. Thus do we find the blend of creative writer and philosopher in the French Existentialists, which represents a further extension of the need to establish a system of aesthetic and moral values before one can write.

With this in mind, it is interesting to turn back to a world in which all art was seen as being a series of variations upon a theme, and in which the total dedication of the artist is not, as in the case of Rilke, to his separate art, but to an interpretation of a noble system which is innate within the artist. In *Il Libro dell' Arte* of Cennino Cennini, written perhaps in 1372, we find a paragraph on 'how you should regulate your life' in order to become a painter.

> Your life should always be arranged just as if you were studying theology, or philosophy, or other theories, that is to say, eating and drinking moderately, at least twice a day, electing digestible and wholesome dishes, and light wines. . .[3]

A similar sense of need to prepare the spirit in dedication is found

---

[1] February 3rd, 1818.

[2] 'Orpheus I', *A Symposium of the Arts*, edited by John Lehmann, p. 149.

[3] Vol. II, *The Craftsman's Handbook*, translated by Daniel V. Thompson, Jr., Yale University Press, p. 16.

in the opening treatise of Dante's *Il Convivio* which emphasizes the need for intellectual purity, for theological right thinking, before one may taste of the fruits of literature. If we, in turn, put *Il Convivio* beside François Mauriac's theory expounded in *God and Mammon* concerning the responsibility of a novelist and the purification of the source, we find, in the latter case, a man torn by the abysmal distinction between the saint and the common man, and by the necessity of the writer 'to hand himself over'. In all humility he acknowledges the elusiveness in human life of the finger of God, and yet it is just at this point that one feels his sincere and moving apologia to be intellectually inadequate. Purification of the source is not enough, and, as Donat O'Donnell points out in his book *Maria Cross*, 'we have seen no examples of a "purified" art that was not also a sterilized art'.[1] For the purification of the writer's intention is achieved, if it is achieved in this instance, by a stern effort of the will, which by itself, does not encourage creative growth. What we have again been looking at is a mode of feeling and not a mode of thinking. Those who taught us, Mauriac writes, 'formed not Catholic intelligences, but Catholic sensibilities', and the resulting situation whereby an extrinsic and authoritative morality becomes a bastion round these sensibilities is a familiar one. It may provide the dramatic tension that a writer requires, but it has the effect of being opposed to nature, and it compels him to write negatively. It comes as a reaction against the doctrine of acceptance which we have glimpsed in Rilke's *Letters To a Young Poet* and in a moment of destiny in *The Heat of the Day*. Mauriac writes the history of this briefly in *God and Mammon*.

> Our contemporaries, far more than the Romantics are the sons and heirs of Rousseau. The Romantics were corrupt children of Christ, and they held strongly to the old distinction between good and evil, even though they exalted evil and played the part of fallen angels. Today there are many who force themselves to accept themselves as they are, as Rousseau did.[2]

Nothing on earth can be created in nature nor in words without being given a body, and without an infusion of grace; nor can an act of creation be performed without love. 'The fruit of the spirit is love,' so that in the final analysis creation by words is a 'love-feast', Agape, which, in the Christian setting, entails, by way of preparation, an acceptance of our unworthiness before God, and the ac-

[1] p. 228.   [2] p. 9.

companying realization of God's mercy and justice. Perhaps the day has arrived 'when the charity of most men will grow cold, as they see wickedness about everywhere, but that man will be saved who endures to the end'.[1] Yet, to create a live, meaningful drama, poem or novel is a practical activity of love, and to do so strengthens the writer's faith in his vocation, in what St James calls the 'royal law' to love one's neighbour as oneself. The writer, of all people, is committed—dare we say 'condemned'—to love, and he knows that each genuine creation is in the nature of a discovery and a growth. It is a discovery of reality, of what indeed *is* the human heart, and of how it responds to the tensions of our age. We have seen that the writer's revolt from morality, if it occurs, is but the prelude to his return to what he believes is a more fundamental morality. From the outside, all moralities not one's own appear to be systems impenetrable and separate. The ultimate problem then that the writer has to solve with regard to morality is whether he, as a growing, creative being, can continue to live innately with the beliefs about morality that he, at this or that particular point in time, holds. And, if the creative spirit of the writer is drawn, as it must at times be drawn, towards evil, it comes to it as one who would heal a breach in nature.

<blockquote>
Horror is round me here
Because nothing is as it appears to be. . .[2]
</blockquote>

says Jennet, the girl thought to be a witch in Christopher Fry's *The Lady's Not For Burning*. And the underlying movement of every drama, its inner necessity, is towards the discovery of what is real in human nature. Though the writer plays delightedly with appearances, if he is to avoid being swallowed by time, or by the horror of evil, or write a tale told by an idiot, he must cleave to his knowledge of the proper destiny of man. To this, he perilously gives his assent, and each voyage of discovery is by way of, in Jennet's words, 'that inland sea, the heart'.[3] And every return of the writer to what he feels to be a more fundamental morality is a return to a law which can live in his heart.

If his work is to develop, and therefore to avoid the spiritually restricting bane of repetition, he has to find his way to a morality that is itself practical, alive and rooted in reality. The inner necessity to write breeds a threefold indivisible moral responsibility which we have tried, in this small measure, to examine. There is the re-

---

[1] Matt. 24: 12.   [2] p. 51.   [3] p. 69.

sponsibility to oneself, then to one's subject and then to one's reader, and all is enfolded within the order of love. It is this which prompts the writer to make an inner preparation before he sets out to create that he may meet reality faithfully. It is the sense of fidelity to the truth of reality that made Keats write in a letter to Bailey: 'I am convinced more and more every day that a fine writer is the most genuine being in the world.'[1] And neither Keats, nor Shakespeare and Wordsworth, about whom Keats was writing, are genuine poets because, in their search for experience, they turn their backs on morality. They are genuine beings because they seek, in reasoning fidelity, the correspondence between the totality of their experience and its meaning in words, and their discoveries are discoveries that reveal the moral nature of man, without which, in Macbeth's aside, 'nothing is but what is not.'

At this point in time, then, we may return to re-examine the picture of St Faith, whether presented by a medieval artist in Westminster Abbey, or carried in the mind's eye.

> I cannot fail to notice [writes Gabriel Marcel] that where Fidelity is at her most unmistakable, where her face shines with clearest light, she goes hand in hand with a character as opposed to Pride as anything we can imagine. Patience and Humility gaze from the depths of her eyes. Patience and Humility; virtues whose very names today are forgotten, and whose true nature is further darkened to our sight with every step forward in man's technical and impersonal equipment, his logical and dialectical equipment with the rest.[2]

Fidelity is indeed the very ground of love, and the writer's way, which is the way of love, is also the way of the Cross.

[1] August 5th, 1819.　　　[2] *Being and Having*, p. 56.

XVI

THE CONFESSOR'S PROBLEM
by
Gerald Vann, O.P.

PSYCHIATRISTS are sometimes poor psychologists: they may have science but lack art; and so they may make some elementary blunder because, though they know all that the textbooks can teach them, and can pin the appropriate type-labels on to their patients, they cannot see the personality and therefore the particular needs of this or that individual as such: they lack intuition. The parallel between psychiatrist and priest is not to be pressed too far; but there are similarities as obvious as the differences, and this danger is one of them. For the confessor too needs art as well as science: when he has assimilated all that his books of moral theology and canon law can teach him his preparation is not at an end but only beginning. If he is to do his work properly he must learn how general principles are to be brought down to particular individual circumstances, how general rules must be adapted to the conditions and needs of X and Y. *Sacramenta sunt propter homines*: the sacraments were made for men: but the old axiom means precisely 'made for this man and that man', and every human being is unique. All that is especially applicable to the task of the confessor, is indeed the core of the confessor's problem; and it applies to every aspect of his work: as father, as doctor, as teacher, as judge.

The aspect of fatherhood is primary, and must colour all the others. In the moment of absolution the priest, acting in the place and in the power of Christ, is the giver of life: he represents therefore the fatherhood of God the creator and re-creator of life; he must act then not merely with the authority of a father but with a father's understanding, patience, indulgence, love. In the Canon of the Mass we pray that God our Father may look upon our offerings *propitio ac sereno vultu*—as Mgr Knox puts it, 'with an indulgent smile'; Pope Leo XII reminds us that the priest, having 'put on the mercy of Christ Jesus, must know how to deal carefully, patiently and gently with sinners; for "charity is patient . . . charity suffers all things, endures all things." ' No doubt there are moments when it is proper for those who represent Christ to exhibit a just anger as he did; but the symbol of the sacrament of penance is not the driving out of the traffickers from the Temple but the episode of the woman taken in adultery. 'Go in peace': that is the end to which everything must lead; and so there can never be room for anger, disgust, astonishment, reprobation, pharisaism: only the loving warmth and welcome of the father in the story of the prodigal—but with this in addition, that the priest must always realize that as a private in-dividual he is a prodigal too.

This last point is capital. Just as you can never help anyone in any real sense if you minister *ex alto*, with the chilly condescension which kills all sympathy, so the priest can never help the sinner if the sinner is for him a stranger, as remote from his own experience as an intruder from Mars. Consequently, for priests so graced by God that they have no immediate acquaintance with grave sin in their own lives, the first duty is to use their imaginations, to see how easily they could stand where others stand, and to realize that if in fact they are different it is simply because he who is mighty has done great things in them; it is moreover to reflect on the ambiguity of the word 'sinner' and on how silly it is to think of the pharisee as sinless and the publican as sinner.

That is not to say, of course, that it can ever be right for the con-fessor to minimize the gravity of what is in itself grave; on the con-trary, it may at times be his duty to try to increase the penitent's sense of sin and sorrow for sin. Yet even so the end remains the same: to send him away in peace of soul: he must urge him and help him to sorrow, not remorse: to something creative, not sterile, to the sort of sorrow which is somehow simultaneously joy because the sense of sin is also at the same time a sense of God's love and mercy, and the darkness is that creative darkness in which the Light is found, adored, loved.

But this in its turn demands great understanding and gentleness. It will never be achieved if there is any element of anger or repulsion or condescension; it will not be achieved merely by some under-standing of human weakness in general. You cannot help John or Susan simply by having a general scientific knowledge of boy or girl, man or woman, you can help only by having also some sort of intuitive understanding of this boy, this girl, this man, this woman. It is not for nothing that we speak of holy *Mother* Church: just as our concept of God's fatherhood will be faulty if we exclude from it the qualities we associate in our human categories with the idea of motherhood, so we have to remember that, as Mgr Bougeaud put it, just as there is something priestly about the heart of a mother, so there must be something of motherhood in the vocation of the priest, something of a mother's tenderness and compassion, but also something of her deep intuition where her children are concerned. A good mother is never shocked, never loses patience, never abandons her son, precisely because she understands him and understanding can sympathize—can console and encourage. Go in peace: the test of whether the confessor is really fulfilling this aspect of his office lies there: does the penitent go away restored, re-created, encouraged, no matter how deep his degradation or how hopeless his situation has seemed? *Non veni vocare justos*: our Lord came to call sinners, not the just: but to call them to renewal, to hope, to the taking up of life again with fresh courage and strength and joy.

But there is something more which this aspect of fatherhood suggests. It is the vocation of parents to help their children to find and live their own vocations: to help them, in other words, to grow up, to grow to maturity. In the supernatural life as in the natural there are the stages of infancy, childhood, adolescence, maturity; there are the phenomena of arrested development, of life-refusal, of childhood or adolescence never transcended. The Church, not through her fault but through ours, *can* become a 'devouring mother': we *can*, if we are unwise or cowardly, use her as an escape from life, we can hide behind her skirts, we can try to throw back all our responsibilities upon her. If we do that we shall never live our own vocations as Christians in the world; we shall never bear witness to Christ; we shall never make use of the talents given us; we shall never help to save the world. The confessor, then, has two things to do. First he must try as best he can to sense the 'age' of his penitent; for he will have to act in one way towards the Catholic of long standing and mature mind and soul, and in quite another way towards the child in years, the recent convert, the timid soul incapable of making firm decisions for himself and acting decisively upon them. Secondly, he must decide whether for instance an infantile state of soul is right and proper, is 'natural', in the circumstances, or whether in fact it represents a state of arrested development, for again his treatment must differ accordingly: you do not treat a child in the way you treat a mental invalid. In both cases maturity is the aim; but in both cases also the aim remains peace;

and so the confessor must avoid trying to dragoon an ailing penitent, trying to make him go too fast; at all costs he must avoid
treating a real ailment of mind and soul as though it were a mere
fiction, something to be brushed aside with a single gesture... What
irreparable harm can be done by the brash use of such slogans as
'Just pull yourself together'!

It is here that the second aspect of the confessor's office is most
easily abused: that of judge. The confessional is indeed a tribunal:
the penitent is the self-accused, the priest represents Christ the
Judge, he administers the law and imposes sentence. Yes, but with
what qualifications, what un-juridical colourings of the situation!
For the judge remains first of all a father. To forget that is to drive
people away from the sacraments: if the confessor uses his authority
to browbeat his penitents, to harass them, to deny or belittle their
difficulties; if he has an exaggerated idea of his own preceptive
power; if he confuses objective wrongness with subjective guilt, and
shows only impatience and incomprehension for the penitent's subjective situation; if he makes impossible demands; if he can express
only blame, censure, disgust and horror; then he is failing in his
ministry: he is not leading men back to God but driving them away
from him.

It is surely a reflection on some of the representatives of the
ecclesia docens that the *ecclesia discens* should so often accuse itself in
confession of sins which are not sins at all—the Sunday Mass unavoidably missed, the harmless and indeed commendable love-
making, the temptations never given in to. It is still more sinister
to discover the extent to which Catholics attribute far more importance to a breach of ecclesiastical law, such as Friday abstinence,
than to breaches of divine law, the sins against justice and charity.
Furthermore there is the undeniable fact that so many Catholics
think that the really important sins are the sins of the flesh. And one
cannot help wondering to what extent a misguided technique in the
confessional is responsible, when indeed it is not simply a question
of a false scale of values in the mind of the confessor himself.

For instance, interrogation is sometimes part of the duty of the
confessor as judge: but how carefully it must be done! The difficulty
often is that for the integrity of the confession a question must be
asked about some sin which is not at all the most *important* thing
mentioned by the penitent: surely then it is wise in such cases to
offset the questioning by some animadversion about the more important matter, as a question for instance about the precise species

of a sexual sin might be offset by some remarks about the importance of being faithful to the duty of daily prayer. (And how essential it is to be prudent in any questionings about sexual sins: *melius in pluribus deficere quam in uno superabundare*: it is better to ask too little in many cases than to ask too much in one. For here again, and in the whole matter of questioning in general, the confessor has to try to estimate the spiritual age of the penitent, and to act accordingly. Indiscretion, where the young in age or in the spiritual life are concerned, can easily do great harm: can shock the penitent, can put ideas into his head, can confuse him, can set up a real and perhaps insuperable inhibition which will prevent him from going to confession again. Here if anywhere the winds of the theological textbooks need tempering by the virtues of prudence and gentleness and by a fatherly insight.)

The penitent's age is again relevant when it is the penitent himself who asks questions. 'Was it a mortal sin, Father?'—how is the confessor to answer? He must of course, where objective right and wrong are concerned, answer quite simply: 'Actions of the type X are (or are not) mortal sins.' But what of subjective degrees of guilt? Surely once again he must study the age of his penitent: the spiritually adult he must help to make up their own minds—'You know the conditions which must be fulfilled if a sin is to be mortal—full knowledge, awareness, consent—were they in fact fulfilled in this case or not?' At the other extreme there are the scrupulous, who by definition are incapable of making up their own minds: here is a case where the priest, if he is to be truly a father-judge, must shoulder all responsibility, must be categorical; his main concern here is therapeutic, to lead the penitent away from his ceaseless self-analysis, unreal and neurotic and sterile, to the love and mercy of God not as an abstract truth intellectually apprehended but as a lived experience. If he is wise he will restrict his penitent's confession to some simple, general formula from which there must be no departure: I accuse myself of all the sins I have committed since my last confession and all the sins of my past life; and for the rest he will go on reminding him again and again: God is your Father, not a policeman; think about God and his love, not about yourself. . .

But it is not only the scrupulous who have to be helped to guard against anxiety. A sense of sin and of guilt can be a creative thing, creatively used: can be the darkness, the dark waters—the parallel with baptism is obvious—out of which life comes. But if sin is allowed to breed anxiety, the anxiety itself will breed further sin, and the further sin may in the end produce despair, so that what is in fact just a moral difficulty like any other may become a crisis, a reason for turning away hopelessly from the sacraments and from the Church altogether. Anxiety is one thing; tension is quite another. Tension is the condition of life and of growth: the fact that you have this moral disability, this failing which you cannot seem to conquer, is no cause for despair; on the contrary, it is there to be used, to engage your energies, to provide the exercise without which you might become flabby and the 'divine discontent' without which you might become proud and complacent.

Here the judge becomes the doctor: the priest's office is now to diagnose, perhaps to warn, certainly to advise. He must try to discern the cause of the trouble in order to suggest a remedy. To suggest: the advice of a spiritual director is meant to be precisely directive, not preceptive. There is a danger here, on the penitent's part, of a sort of spiritual masochism: a surrendering of one's personality, one's mind and will, into the hands of another human being so as to escape from maturity and in the last resort from life itself; it is for the confessor, on the contrary, to try to lead the penitent towards an ever greater degree of maturity: towards a more and more adult attitude to religion, in prayer, in worship, in the moral life.[1] Religion can so easily become magic, superstition, a seeking for comfort, for irresponsible security, an escape; and the human mind can be a very tortuous instrument. If you try, by the adroit way you put things, to engineer the priest into saying that X is not a sin (though deep down you know that it is) so that then, regarding his dictum as oracular you feel you can sin with impunity; if you look to him to answer every question, to be a sort of continual source of private revelation, instead of using the mind that God gave you; if you look to him for a slick and immediate solution of all your moral difficulties; you are using him not as a minister of God but as a magician, you are misusing the sacrament.

It remains true that the confessor as doctor has often to try to suggest remedial measures: and again he meets the same difficulty as before; he is dealing with an individual. There are of course certain remedial measures for all moral difficulties: the sacraments,

---

[1] Examples of immaturity and the need of instruction or clarification readily suggest themselves from the sphere of sexual ethics but are of course far from being confined to it; they are equally to be found in the spheres of social justice, or prudence, or fortitude.

prayer, devotion to our Lady, to one's guardian angel, and so forth; there are particular types of remedy against particular vices; but what in the last resort is needed is *this* particular remedy for *this* man's particular failing. It is, alas, the fact that sometimes advice is given which falls into none of these three categories: a homosexual described recently in a letter how he had been told in confession to 'find a nice Irish girl and marry her' and how, when he remained silent, the priest asked him if he disliked the Irish.

As doctor the priest must advise; as teacher he must instruct; but again with the same reservations. In order to instruct adequately he must have a grasp of the science of moral theology; he must also have the art of discerning the needs and abilities and limitations of individual souls. Obviously he will fail in his duty if he withholds information which is necessary and which the penitent can assimilate; but equally he will fail if his instruction causes anxiety, scrupulosity or bad faith. *Conscientiae non sunt inquietandae:* there are certain traditional guiding principles which help us to see how and when information may and must be given without danger of disturbing peace of mind and conscience.

Ignorance is either vincible (culpable and curable) or not. If the former, information about this or that obligation must be given since the ignorance denotes bad faith; but what if it is, as the theologians say, invincible? Here you must distinguish: if you feel convinced that the penitent will be able to understand your instruction and to follow it, you must give it; otherwise you must not (for it would be useless and you would be simply turning good faith into bad faith and material sin into formal sin), unless the penitent himself asks, or your silence would be considered as an encouragement to evil, or the ignorance or doubt concerns the first principles of the natural law or their immediate consequences (for such ignorance could not be long invincible and therefore excusable), or finally if lack of instruction would leave the penitent in proximate occasion of sinning. But *conscientiae non inquietandae*: in doubt, we are told, it is better to abstain; and the doubt, it must once again be emphasized, means primarily a doubt about the subjective dispositions and capacities of this or that particular penitent.

Conscientiae non inquietandae is the negative aspect of the positive purpose of the sacrament contained in the phrase, Go in peace. If instruction is not given it is in order that the penitent may quite literally be left in peace; if it is given it must be given in such a way as to stress its positive and creative content. Not just, 'This is something you must not do'; but, 'This is to be avoided in order that that may be achieved'. Nothing is more discouraging than a tirade about the importance of a negation. Battling against vices and failings has to be set in the perspective of an attempt to achieve the good life; and virtue itself has to be set within the supreme aim, which is charity or holiness. It is a good thing to be a man of high moral character, but not if it means a lack of love. Better to love God out of weakness than to love oneself in one's strength. Great charity is compatible with many weaknesses; but the most perfect moral probity does not of itself imply humility and love. Hence the problem for the confessor here is one of great delicacy: Should he give instruction on this or that point or not? If so, in what way is it to be done? How can he put the emphasis on the positive without minimizing the negative? How can he stress adequately the importance of avoiding sin while at the same time giving a positive emphasis to all that he says? And finally, How can he urge the importance of moral effort while at the same time making it clear to the penitent that the one essential thing is not action but 'passion', that *patiens divina* which is the root of holiness?

These are questions to which there is no slick answer; but they do not as they stand represent the confessor's problem in its entirety: they have to be put into the context of the over-riding problem with which we have already been concerned—the problem of adapting *all* decisions, judgements, advice, exhortation to *this* particular individual. And this might well seem to make the difficulties insoluble. For how can the confessor adapt himself to the individual penitent unless he knows the penitent; and how can he know him if he is no more than a transient whisper through a grille?

It should perhaps be made clear that in this paper we have been concerned to keep within the terms of reference set by its title; no doubt in the great majority of cases there will be no particular 'confessor's problem': the confessions of ordinary, simple, uninhibited people usually call for nothing more complicated than the giving of penance and absolution with perhaps a little homily if time allows. But we are concerned here not with the usual confessions but with the unusual; we are concerned with a problem because we are concerned with the Church's problem-children—and if they are a minority they are certainly not a small minority. Even the best-informed and most balanced of mortals need advice sometimes, need, sometimes, the ministrations of the confessor as teacher or doctor. And then, inevitably, the problem makes itself felt. Compare the priest, faced with an invisible, anonymous penitent and conscious of the long queue waiting outside, with the psychiatrist who learns gradually, through a long series of lengthy interviews, something about the individual with whom he is called to deal. How *can* the priest hope to succeed?

No doubt the ultimate answer is that he must rely on and hope for the requisite supernatural help in the form of some infusion of discernment and wisdom: that, after all, apart from the main work of absolution, is his share in the sacrament. But it would be wrong to rely upon grace alone: he is bound to take such natural measures as are open to him to make his task more feasible: what are they?

The first is to acquire a real understanding of the task itself. The priest who tells himself that he is quite adequately equipped because he knows all the textbook answers, all the moral and canonical tags, is headed for disaster. As we have seen, his job is also to make sure that he understands human frailty and sinfulness, not from some remote eminence, but from being acquainted with it, really or imaginatively, himself. He will never advise aright, still less encourage and strengthen, unless first he can sympathize; and he will never sympathize unless first he understands. *Nil humani alienum* has its application here more forcibly perhaps than anywhere else.

Secondly, he must think himself gradually into the *totality* of his office: he may never be just the judge or the teacher; he must always be father and doctor as well. If he judges, it must be as a doctor looking to the health of his patient; if he instructs, it must be as a father striving to lead his son to maturity and to the achieving of his own vocation in the world.

Thirdly, he must learn gradually by experience. It might be supposed that a mere whisper must be entirely unrevealing of a personality: it is not so. Words are always revealing, whether whispered or not. A turn of phrase, an emphasis, an intonation, the whole way in which what has to be said is in fact tackled: all these can reveal the speaker: can reveal sorrow or cynicism or levity, self-complacence or humility, real trouble and anxiety or the lust for self-display, simplicity of heart or a hard-boiled over-sophistication, timidity or courage, maturity or infantilism. . . All these can reveal the speaker: but in very varying degrees. Sometimes it will be no more than a hint that is given, a probability suggested; and then with what care, what caution, the confessor has to proceed! That is why his two guiding principles must always be to say too little rather than too much, and to be above all things gentle. For if he says too much, or in saying even a little is brutal, he will do much harm; if he says too little but says it with true gentleness the chances are that his penitent will return, to increase his understanding of him and to give him an opportunity of offering further enlightenment, encouragement and help. At the very least he will have achieved the purpose of the sacrament: he will have allowed the penitent to go in peace.

To go in peace: two facts, sad but certain, have to be admitted and allowed for in all this discussion of the confessor's problem. First, there is the great and perhaps growing lack of peace in so many individuals in the world of today. Mention was made above of the simple, uncomplicated souls about whom there is no problem; but nowadays fewer and fewer penitents are likely to be wholly simple and uncomplicated, at least in countries such as ours. We live in an age of anxiety and fear; and these tensions once experienced are not likely to be confined to political or economic matters. True, religion *can* be the stabilizing factor which minimizes and perhaps dissipates altogether the natural fears which today oppress humanity; but the thing can also work the other way round, and a person suffering from a natural sense of insecurity may easily feel its repercussions in the sphere of religion. Again, the conditions of life as we know it are likely to produce moral tensions and difficulties: one has only to think for example of the appallingly high incidence of moral problems connected with marriage—real problems to which there is just no easy solution, and sometimes no solution at all short of heroic virtue. Finally, we live in a climate of opinion the tendency of which is to make faith difficult and religion unreal. It may be assumed then that many penitents if not most will lack peace, quite apart from the sense in which any sin-laden soul may be said to lack peace until it has received absolution. Hence the phrase, 'Go in peace', assumes today a special significance, and its fulfilment is attended by special difficulty. To restore a soul to grace does not necessarily mean, nowadays, to restore its peace: it may well have to be led gradually to the point at which grace will in fact mean peace because it will in fact overcome the fears and anxieties, natural and supernatural, to which modern life has given rise.

But the second fact shows that this goal is far from being achieved. On the contrary, the fact is that many Catholics—and again it is perhaps a growing number—leave the confessional with discouragement, depression, perhaps with resentment and rancour, in their hearts because of what they regard as a total lack of comprehension on the part of their priests. It just will not do—it is not enough—to tell the penitent that he must say his prayers and go to the sacraments and all will be well, when he knows already from bitter experience that all will not be well. It will not do to upbraid people for sins the avoidance of which would be tantamount to heroic virtue. And so we come back to one of the essential elements in the equipment of the confessor, one of the things without which he can never hope even to begin to solve his problem: the need of a sympathy based on a real and deep understanding of his penitents' difficulties. Without that, the already terrifying gulf which separates clergy and laity must simply go on widening: on the one hand a laity battling with real and often heart-breaking problems and often looking desperately for guidance and help; on the other, a clergy too often living in a quite different world, a closed world of their own, talking a language no longer understood of the people and quite unable to reconcile the academic formulas they have learnt from their textbooks with the real problems with which those formulas ought, if they are to have any value at all, to help them to deal. It will be recalled that Pope Pius XII recently called upon theological students precisely not to be satisfied with absorbing the contents of 'little manuals' but to do some real thinking: and his words might well form the text for all courses of pastoral theology.

Da mihi intellectum: give me understanding: that must surely be the prayer of the confessor. Give me understanding of principles as opposed to rule of thumb; give me understanding of the difficulties which beset people in the world of today; and finally: give me understanding of the individuals who come to me, *as* individuals, for otherwise I shall not be able to help them, and when they ask me for guidance I shall not give them peace, I shall send them empty away.

MORALITIES OUTSIDE THE CHURCH

XVII

THE MORALITY OF PRIMITIVE SOCIETIES
by
Nana Kobina Nketsia IV

BY primitive societies, anthropologists mean, in Professor Evans-Pritchard's words, 'Those societies which are small in scale with regards to numbers, territory and range of social contacts, and which have by comparison with more advanced societies a simple technology and economy and little specialization of function.' This is the sense in which I use this difficult word in this paper; for it is scarcely necessary for me to say that I am not attempting to compare a hypothetical primitive morality with some more evolved morality, as some old-fashioned students of the subject were wont to do, but simply to enquire into the sorts of conduct which are condoned, and those which are condemned, in some primitive societies.

It is impossible to attempt in such a short paper to generalize about all primitive societies; there are great differences between these small-scale societies no less than those to which we are accustomed in larger societies. The mores of my own society, the Akan of the Gold Coast, in which for many important reasons descent is reckoned in the female line, would doubtless in some respects appear in very unfavourable light to a strongly patrilineal people, setting great store by the counting of descent exclusively in the male line, such as the Nuer and many other African peoples.

I have decided therefore to speak of some features of the morality of the Akan people of the Gold Coast, and of the Nuer of the Southern Sudan, who are among the best documented peoples of Africa. There are advantages in confining our attention to the two, because I think in that way you will come to know them both fairly well; also the structures and modes of livelihood of these two societies are very different from each other, and in considering them together we will perhaps be able to see in what way the moral standards and practices of each society resemble each other, irrespective of the conditions in which they are found.

I give first a brief description of the form of the social organization of these two peoples, and of their most characteristic institutions. I shall then proceed to discuss in turn the morality of each people under the headings of:

(1) Sexual morality and marriage.
(2) Political morality.
(3) Some relations between morality and religion.

Nuerland lies roughly between latitudes 10°N and 7°N on both sides of the Nile. It is open savannah land. Nuer cultivate maize, millet and other crops, but are at heart pastoralists with a great love for cattle. Cattle feature in every aspect of their life; in ritual, in marriage, in food supply and in games and dances. In poetry cattle is the most precious theme. Each year during the dry season they move from their villages to special cattle camps (anthropologists use the term 'transhumant' to describe such people).

Nuer lineages are exogamous and patrilineal. Marriage is effected by the transfer of cattle as bridewealth. Kinship and age-sets influence relationships and behaviour a great deal. Nuer are tall, proud people and their society is marked by the absence of any rank or class. There are no chiefs or any body of people with power in any of their communities or settlements. The society is held together by a system in which equivalent segments of the tribe are opposed to each other, but join together if one of them is attacked. In the composition of feuds Leopard-skin chiefs—priests—take a leading part; they are respected for their ritual status and not because they possess any coercive power.

The Akan people of the Gold coast mainly occupy the central and southern part of the country. The vegetation here is tropical forest and is abundantly supplied with rains between the months of June and September. Farming is the main occupation and among the food crops produced for home consumption are maize, yams and plantain. Cocoa, the main cash crop, is very extensively cultivated and exported. Other resources are timber, gold, diamonds, bauxite and manganese.

Lineages are matrilineal and also exogamous. Akans have a centralized political system with chiefs, and administrative and judicial institutions by which law and order and defence are maintained. There is no age-set system. But there is in every Akan state a military organization whose function is both military and civil. Membership of a company is generally inherited from the father.

Among the Nuer marriage is a contract between two lineages.

Simple legal marriage is a union between a man and a woman characterized by the payment of bridewealth and the performance of certain social and ritual ceremonies. The payment of the bridewealth legalizes the marriage, makes children legitimate and ensures their inheritance. The children form a link between the two kinship groups to the marriage and there are consequently initiated between them certain patterns of behaviour and also some reciprocal obligations. Part of the bridewealth goes to the bride's family. It indemnifies them, in a sense, for the loss of her services as well as her children who go to swell her husband's group. Part of the bridewealth cattle is used to provide a wife for her brother, whose children would then extend her own group. Again some of this cattle is dedicated to the spirits of her lineage, a duty which earns for the latter the blessings and protection of the ancestors. Thus the bridewealth to a certain extent stabilizes the marriage, for if the wife, for instance, does not perform her duties to the man and his kin, the bridewealth would be recalled and the marriage dissolved; and if especially (as is the custom) her brother should have taken a wife with the cattle, her kin would find the situation most difficult and would consequently advise and encourage her to be dutiful and loyal.

Bridewealth is distributed in fixed proportions among the bride's own family, her father's family, and her mother's family; and this means that for every marriage that is contracted in the society two lineages are directly benefited, are given the means whereby further marriages are contracted and are linked up to a third, that of the bridegroom with which directly or indirectly they co-operate. Thus the zigzag paths traced by marriage cattle portray the lines of human relationships and fellowship in a transhumant society which must needs pull together from season to season.

Professor Evans-Pritchard says of the Nuer:

> Sexual activities are from their earliest manifestation given the stamp of cultural values. They are from the first associated with marriage, which is the final goal of sex life of men and women. Even the very poor and the disabled form domestic establishments of some kind, talk proudly of 'my father-in-law' and 'my mother-in-law'. It is the chief ambition of a youth to marry and have a home (*gol*) of his own, for when Nuer speak of marriage they speak of home. Even in childhood it is clear to Nuer that marriage and the birth of children are the ultimate purpose of the sexual functions to which all earlier activities of a sexual kind

—play, love-making, and courtship—are a prelude, a preparation and a means. . . In its earliest expression, sex is associated
with marriage, and the first sexual play occurs in imitation of one
of the routines in marital life. It occurs in response to a cultural
and not to an instinctive urge.

Girls are not expected to marry as virgins, but they, however,
expect their friendship with their boy friends to develop into marriage. Seduction of an unmarried girl is considered wrong, for she
may fall into the much despised category of an unmarried mother—
a category which often reflects instability and fetches fewer bridewealth cattle if she is married at all. Once they are married, however, girls are expected to be faithful to their husbands. Nuer are
polygamous—polygamous life being the ideal family life, though
comparatively rare.

Adultery is morally reprehensible and may lead to divorce; and
where this occurs the husband is entitled to compensation because
of his right in the wife. Again it is considered wrong for a woman to
desert her huband or nag him or willingly desist from fulfilling her
marital and domestic duties, for all of which she could be put
away. It is considered right for a man to take similar action if she is
barren. This, as we have already said, issues from the desire to per-
petuate the lineage. The wife of course could take a like action if
he is impotent or sterile but usually in cases of this nature the husband might not discourage her from having intercourse with lovers
whose children would legally be his. A wife has a right to divorce a
husband who ill-treats her, or is stingy or mean, or fails to support
her and her children. An interesting point to note here is that no
stigma attaches to a child born from concubinage or adulterous
relation. Nor for that matter does the mother suffer from any shame
or embarrassment as she surely will in certain more advanced
societies. (Nuer think however that divorce is bad and should not
be encouraged.)

And now to a consideration of marriage and morality among the
other people. As among the Nuer, marriage among the Akan is also
a contract between two lineages; a legal marriage is characterized
by the transfer of bridewealth (money in this case) and the performance of certain ceremonies. The payment is made by the man's
lineage head and is divided between the bride's father and her
lineage. Here also it is the bridewealth which legalizes the marriage
and the children resulting from it. It is returnable on certain conditions on the dissolution of the marriage. Marriage, when legal,

brings two lineages together who in certain situations would fulfil reciprocal obligations and behave to each other in certain customary ways.

An Akan girl is made to understand that it is wrong for her to indulge in sex relations before she marries; in fact she is expected to marry a virgin and it is wrong for any man to seduce her. When married, she is to remain faithful and loyal to her husband, and could be divorced for adultery, for stealing and also for being barren or a witch, or for her inability to keep house. She on her part can divorce her husband for maltreatment, sterility, partiality to other wives (if the union is polygamous) or if he is unable to support the household. I must say, however, that the vast majority of unions are monogamous, but in a society where polgamy is permissible a husband may take another wife if he so desire. The wife should of course be consulted in the matter and duly compensated; it would be definitely wrong for the man not to do this.

Let me put in here a word or two on witchcraft and barrenness as grounds for divorce. As Professor Evans-Pritchard points out in his famous work on the Azande, witch action is set in operation and maintained by ill feeling, jealousy and hatred, all of which are considered immoral. But is a man right in putting away his wife because of her inability to bear children? The Akan think so, for very great shame attaches to a man who has no issue and many have been known to take their own lives for that reason; it is therefore a man's desire to prove himself (especially where he cannot take another wife) able to produce children who will keep green his ancestral names and help him on the farm, which, for the Akan, justifies his behaviour. And often the woman's family, because of the urge to increase the lineage, after a period of her unfruitful union, would be sympathetic or even encourage her if she sought a divorce.

Among the Nuer kinship values guide and facilitate relationships, and in practice everybody is kin or potentially so. Behaviour patterns, though formally set by kinship, are adjusted in any specific case by genealogical distance, spatial distance, and the feelings of the persons concerned. Broadly speaking, however, kin relationships are conditioned by two types of values—the agnatic type and the type through women. The agnatic type who live together with common interests and rights in cattle, land, watering places, fishpools and so on, have opportunities for quarrelling and for the cultivation of petty jealousies, especially when duties and personal interests conflict. A kindly disposition and tenderness characterize

H

relatives of the latter type. Here there are no common rights to induce conflicts, and it is said that while your mother's sister would always welcome you and put all sorts of delicacies before you when you are hungry, your father's sister blesses you only with her mouth, not meaning it in her heart. A mother's brother is a kind of male mother on whom you can always count, and often he and his sister, though they are not obliged to do so, would happily contribute to a nephew's bridewealth. 'Of all Nuer relationships', says Professor Evans-Pritchard, 'it is the one of the most unadulterated benevolence.'

Nevertheless it is primarily to his agnatic kin that a man looks for help and support and to whom he owes duties. In quarrels he is expected to take sides with them irrespective of the moral issues involved, and in inter-community fights kinsmen finding themselves facing each other will quickly change places to avoid having to fight one another. For, as Nuer say, 'they are at peace.' When a man sacrifices in honour of his dead father all his kinsmen bring gifts of beer to his great joy and satisfaction.

Property, especially cattle, is distributed as and when needed by kin. The result is very little inequality. Nuer generally keep open house and frequently eat in one another's byres and windscreens with kin, neighbours and age-mates. They believe in giving and begging and readily lend milch cows and gifts of food to friends. Sacrificial meat, for instance, is supplied not only to kin but to neighbours as well. 'Nuer strut about like lords of the earth, which, indeed,' Professor Evans-Pritchard tells us, 'they consider themselves to be. There is no master and no servant in their society, but only equals who regard themselves as God's noblest creation. Their respect for one another contrasts with their contempt for all other peoples.' Yet a Nuer would be duty bound to grant your request if you addressed him in kinship terms as 'Son of my mother, do so and so.'

There are dispersed in all Akanland seven totemic clans and there are in every community lineages of all or some of these clans with known ancestresses. Each such lineage is a corporate group distinguishable from others by its name and totem; it owns lands, other property and an ancestral cult. It is a political unit which is represented on the chief's council by the lineage head; and citizenship, status and inheritance of property all are acquired in this society through the mother by whom descent is traced.

Members of the same lineage, or segments of it, usually live in the same locality and moving from this place does not discharge them from obligations to the group, or from the enjoyment of any rights. Members of the group come together from time to time, especially for the observance of funerals and ancestor worship. A man is expected to care not only for his wife and children but also to provide for his mother and to seek the welfare of his uterine sisters and their children. His greatest concern, however, is the happiness of his mother and his grandmother. Akan say, 'If your mother dies you have no lineage-kin left.' Professor Meyer Fortes speaking of the mother-child relationship among the Ashanti says: 'A man's first ambition is to gain enough money to be able to build a house for his mother if she does not own one. To be mistress of her own home, with her children and her daughter's children around her, is the highest dignity an ordinary woman aspires to.'

But a man owes a duty also to all members of the lineage. He is expected to visit them when they are sick and attend funerals personally whenever possible and pay his share of the cost of funerals; he is to stand by members who happen to be in some kind of misfortune or difficulties. It should be his concern that ancestral lands are not alienated and he must endeavour to participate in the worship of the ancestors. These are duties to the dead, the living, and as far as preservation of lineage land is concerned, a duty to the unborn as well. For failure to discharge them brings condemnation not only from the living and the dead, but succeeding generations would ponder with regret upon such misdeeds.

With reference to the attendance of funerals, Mr J. B. Christensen in his *Double Descent among the Fanti* reports a Fanti elder as saying this:

'My sister has not been to any of the family burials for thirty years. She was passing through town when my brother died, and did not stop to see my mother, which is a serious thing. She has contributed nothing to funerals during this time. Now it would be impossible for her to attend a funeral of a member of the family, because if she came to one the spirits of the dead would think, "So you came to this funeral but not mine. Do you think more of them than you do of me?" If she did this she would die immediately or at least within a month's time, for she would be summoned to go before the ancestors and explain her conduct. When she dies, she will get no help or assistance from our family.' And needless to say all members who fulfilled such obligations enjoyed all rights in and the protection and help of the family.

Yet just as among Nuer agnatic kinsmen the common holding and use of property and living together provide opportunities for friction and suspicion, so in the Akan matrilineage there come moments when quarrels break out. This is quite often characterized by accusations and counter-accusations of witchcraft among members of the lineage, especially among the various households. Any misfortune can in this society be attributed to witchcraft: illness, barrenness, indebtedness and death (especially of children). A victim of any such misfortune, searching in his mind for imagined or potential enemies, always finds them (and it is invariably confirmed by diviners) among members of his lineage—people with whom he is in daily contact and whom he is likely to offend and in dealing with whom there are likely to arise conflicts over common rights and privileges.

This as you can see is a rather serious situation, for it brings a great deal of mistrust, suspicion, confusion and division in many a home and shame upon many an upright character, for the suspicion might be unfounded.

In any Akan community kinship knits the society together and if the matrilineal descent pulls the child into the mother's lineage, the belief in the 'ntoro' (that the father's spirit in the child gives him his personality) also links the child to his fathers in an intimate, loyal and dutiful kind of way. Thus round the year there are reciprocal obligations among all lineages in the community as fathers name their new-born babies, as puberty rites are observed, as bride-wealths are given and taken, as relations meet at funerals and when, during ancestor worship, children, grateful for blessings received, bring sacrifices before their fathers' shrines.

In an Akan society, all old people are 'grandmothers' and 'grandfathers'; men and women of one's parents' generation are 'fathers' and 'mothers' and only persons of one's own generation are 'equals'. In this society an elder is constantly reminded to respect himself and to uphold fair play, and the young are urged to be respectful, loyal and dutiful to the old, whoever and wherever they are in the community. A stranger settling in that community, especially if Akan, will only have to approach the representatives of his clan there and is readily accepted as a brother. I remember as a boy a man in our family whom I called 'uncle' and who was very kind to us children and very much liked by all. I was very surprised, when he died and was taken to the part of the country where he belonged, to learn that he was not biologically one of us but just a fellow clansman sojourning among us.

We pass on now to consider the connexion between morality and law and government. Nuer are economically homogeneous, proud and egalitarian. These qualities and a transhumant mode of life deny them political leadership and a centralized administrative system. It is rather their lineage structure which provides the framework of their political organization.

Nuer in the past lacked any judicial institutions and the force of a politically organized society; and if law be conceived as the command of a sovereign, a general rule of conduct laid down by a political superior to an inferior with the threat of sanction in case of disobedience, then Nuer had no law. However they had a sense of right and wrong, with the terms *cuong* and *duer* respectively for them. *Duer* means the non-recognition or infringement of another's right. There were therefore rules in the society expressed in terms of right and wrong—the moral rules discussed above—which were enforced where possible by the sanction of self-help. Even now Nuer native courts consider their main function to be the simple statement of what is right.

Every aspect of Nuer life was regulated by these rules; homicide and harm to the body, rights in women and children, property and so on. And in any case of an infringement of a right there was some corresponding fairly well-known compensation. The kinship structure, collective liability, the natural tendency to obey and the fear of contamination and pollution, especially in cases of homicide, all played a part in the composition of wrongs. All anti-social acts like murder, adultery and theft brought disorder into the society and the application of these rules was calculated to restore harmony, and had nothing punitive about it, since not even homicide was considered a public crime. When a murder was committed Nuer considered it a very serious matter indeed. For a group was deprived of a member whose line in the lineage, it was feared, might be forever obliterated and the lineage thereby impaired. The compensation which was collected by the killer's kin was largely used to provide a wife to raise children to the name of the deceased. And the leopard-skin chief (the priest) who performed the ritual to remove the contamination and the state of feud between the two groups was obeyed just because his services were always welcome and appreciated. For he had no power to compel.

The Akan, as was mentioned earlier, had a centralized political system with administrative machinery and judicial institutions. The chiefdom or state of the paramount ruler was a territorially defined area made up of divisions each containing several villages. The divisional ruler was responsible to the paramount chief for the good government of his territory. The chiefship of a territory was supplied by a lineage with a constitutional right to do so, but the people have a say in the choice of the candidate, and also the right to destool him if they were dissatisfied with him.

The stool which the paramount ruler occupied symbolized the people's spirit, their strength, their exclusiveness and solidarity; it connected them to their ancestors and the past and ensured their future. It was sacred and made the ruler so, and so long as he occupied the stool the ruler was the chief exemplar, lawgiver and chief justice; he stood for whatever was valuable in his people's culture. He maintained law and order, performed rituals to ward off evil and prayed to the ancestors to grant his people health, peace, children and good harvests. He was at all times expected to be kind to all, especially strangers.

The village was concentrated and whatever happened in any part of it was very quickly known elsewhere and very soon discussed. Public opinion found its most effective expression in songs, and in cases of theft the culprit might be paraded all over the place with the stolen property on his head followed by a happy band of jeering children.

A body of customary laws was administered by a court of chief and elders, and from time to time new rules were adopted for the settlement of specific problems and were promulgated by gong-gong in the name of the chief. Offences were either public or private; the former were concerned with the central authority and certain taboos of the state, such as incest, suicide, treason, cowardice, murder, all regarded as offences against the chief and his ancestors. Penalty for any of these was death. Private offences concerned the living only. Public offences were tried by the state but private ones were submitted in the first instances to private arbitration. I need not labour the point that laws here also, however strongly sanctioned, are moral in origin and are obeyed chiefly for that reason. A man knows for instance that having sexual intercourse with a sister is legally forbidden because it is wrong, and not wrong because it is forbidden.

And finally I turn to the relation of morality to religion in the two societies. To Nuer, God, who created all things and is Lord of life and death, is a spirit, and as ubiquitous as the wind or air. He is essentially a sky God but he is not removed from the earth. He is close to man and at the same time separated from him. He falls in the rain, flashes in the lightning, rumbles in the thunder, and when he shines in the new moon, Nuer rub their foreheads with ashes (an act of dedication) and pray, 'Grandfather, let us be at peace.' He is grandfather and ancestor who gave them their food and culture and ritual powers, and in whom they find explanation for all things. He has no fixed earthly abode or shrine or prophets, and communication with him is through prayers and sacrifices. But although God (*Kwoth*) is, to borrow an Old Testament metaphor, the God of heaven, he is nevertheless connected with man and society in many ways. The spirits of the air, which are also known as *kwoth*, are connected to particular personalities and groups in the society, and are all manifestations or what Professor Evans-Pritchard calls 'refractions' of God. And during invocations, it is not only the God or Spirit in the sky who is invoked but also spirits of the air, spirits of persons killed by lightning, totemic spirits, nameless age-mate spirits and even 'spirit of my community'.

To Nuer these are all spirits for they are all like air. God, however, though partaking of the same nature as the others, is yet not a particular spirit of the air. Nuer know the difference very well; a spirit of the air for instance has prophets and votaries, exacts demands and visits men with misfortunes. Yet any sacrifice to any of these spirits is also a sacrifice to God. The difference to note here is that whereas the One is creator and father of all, and is transcendent over all social groups and invoked in all exceptional human misfortunes like earthquakes, the many in their various ways are associated separately with individuals and groups.

Consequently Nuer believe that if one fulfilled one's obligations to spiritual beings and kinsmen, that if all taboos were observed and relationships well maintained, then one would avoid the misfortunes which come to correct faults. Another Nuer belief is that God gives long life to the righteous and upright; right action is thought to be followed by good and wrong conduct by ill. But this order of cause and effect is not so mechanical; God in his justice takes into account deliberation and ignorance. Thus it is believed that if people ignorantly commit incest they suffer no punishment; or if a man apologizes to another he has offended and makes reparations and the offended man forgives him and removes a curse by blessing him, then God also forgives.

Nuer religion as such does not give moral rules to man, but it implies them. To quote Professor Evans-Pritchard again,

> Nuer ideas on the matter amount to this . . . that if a man wishes to be in the right with God he must be in the right with men, that is, he must subordinate his interest as an individual to the moral order of society. A man must honour his father's age-mates, a wife must obey her husband, a man must respect his wife's kin and so on. If an individual fails to observe these rules, he is, Nuer say, 'yong' crazy, because he not only loses the support of kith and kin but also the favour of God.

We may conclude that Nuer belief in God as the author of the moral order makes that order good and right for them, also that behaviour is influenced by the consciousness that God blesses the good and punishes the bad. Rites, especially sacrifices, show man's dependence upon God and the necessity of maintaining relationships with him by doing good and behaving properly to man. But perhaps to Nuer the greatest importance of religion is that when an offence like incest or murder has been committed, it affords the means of propitiating the spirits, of appeasing their anger and averting calamity. It affords, that is, a way of dealing with sin.

> Odomankoma
> He created the Thing
> 'Hewer-out' Creator
> He created the Thing.
> What did He create?
> He created Order,
> He created Knowledge,
> He created Death,
> As its quintessence.

So sings the Akan poet on the talking drums. For the Akan believe in a supreme, immortal God who created all things, and in whom again all things are explained. He gives to every man before he appears on earth a bit of Himself which goes back to Him on the death of its possessor. To the Akan God is known by his many attributes among which are 'The Everlasting', 'The Creator', 'The Dependable One', 'No one shows God to the child,' they say, for he is known instinctively to exist, though he has no priests and is not worshipped.

He created many gods and lesser spirits to whom he gave power, who have earthly abodes and priests and worshippers. The strongest link between the living and the land of the spirit is furnished by ancestor worship. Life exists beyond the grave in *samanadzi* where all the dead go and where life is very much the same as on earth. Thus chiefs, for instance, have their usual retinue and hold their courts and fulfil all functions with the usual pomp and pageantry; and lineages, their corporate nature still unimpaired, actively seek the interest of living relations.

The living, on their part, realize that the dead are as much a part of the lineage and the race as themselves, that they harbour and cherish the same values as on earth, and, what is more, steadfastly and zealously preserve and uphold these values and have the power to punish those on earth who depart from them. No wonder therefore that the dead are buried with gold and clothing and other necessities and are asked to convey messages concerning the welfare of the lineages to the ancestors.

Missionaries who went to the Gold Coast in the last century were, for instance, very much appalled by the practice of human sacrifice. The Reverend T. B. Freeman, in the first journal of his visits to Ashanti in 1839, mentions an instance when in two days forty people were killed in Kumasi because a member of the royal house had died. He says 'these poor victims were allowed to lie naked and exposed in the streets, until they began to decompose; and such is the callous state of mind in which the people live, that many were walking about among the putrefying bodies smoking their pipes with amazing indifference.'

Now can anybody, in view of such an apparently horrifying and revolting state of affairs, credit such people with any moral consciousness? But the point is that these people were not killed to satisfy the whim or caprice or tyranny of a king. The Akan king never dies; 'he merely goes to the village,' and in the natural order of things he is accompanied thither by a retinue. The state provides these attendants, but both those who elect to go and those who are 'conscripted' die in duty to king and country as though they had fallen in battle. And some conceived it a singular honour to go with their master. Rattary reports in *Religion and Art in Ashanti* that on the death of King Kwaku Dua I two of his wives and a minor chief volunteered to go with him and did. It should not be surprising therefore that Freeman, after preaching a sermon one day on the Ten Commandments in an Ashanti town was asked by the chief and the people if human sacrifice was murder.

H*

It is obvious that although morality among the Akan is related to their religious beliefs and practices, moral rules as such are not either God- or ancestor-given. They have their roots in the values of the society, but these values are upheld not only by the living, but also by the dead members of the society—dead members, who though dead, are none the less near at all times to bless the good or punish the sinful. But they are never felt to be so near as when on the great day set apart for their worship, like Thomas Hardy's 'Souls of the slain' they

> Bear homeward and hearthward
> To feed on our fame,

when their exploits and virtues are recounted and set up as examples to the living—especially the young. In this connexion may I end this paper by quoting the reply to the Augustinian priest who in the seventeenth century at Ouidah in Dahomey threatened hell fire to those natives who would not yield to some of his teachings:

> Our fathers and our grandfathers, to an endless number, lived as we do; and if they must burn then, patience, we are not better than our ancestors, and shall comfort ourselves with them.

It is in such a kind of loyalty and piety that the source of much of the behaviour of primitive peoples is to be found.

XVIII

CATHOLICISM AND PRIMITIVE MORALITY

by

Michael J. Walsh, S.M.A.

ONE of our greatest difficulties perhaps in studying pagan morality arises from a scarcity of written sources. While the principles governing Christian morality have through the ages been concisely codified and virtually every aspect of their application covered by libraries of learned volumes, the principles of pagan morality can generally be arrived at only by deduction from their still largely oral tradition. Not in libraries, therefore, but in the pagan's social institutions, in his juridical organizations, in his arts, in his customs, in his traditions, in his language, in his beliefs and even in his religious rites must we search for these principles which can be said to govern his way of life and thought.

The quest is made all the more difficult today since European influences of every description, good and bad, have been permeating pagan territories, but more particularly since the nineteenth century. The pagan stands puzzled and distressed to see his old landmarks being swept away in a flood of new ideas and new beliefs and to see the outlook of his children, if not his own, being transformed by the subtle influences of western education and western example. Consequently, one cannot judge with certainty what is purely primitive morality, or how much existing codes of behaviour have been influenced by early Moslem or Christian tradition. Some indication, however, of how closely primitive religions have guarded their fetish secrets from foreign influence can be adduced from the existence in some West African territories, for example, of relatively unaffected pockets of solid pagan resistance in spite of intermittent attempts at evangelization from the fourteenth to the nineteenth century, and more intensified efforts down to our own time.

To discover the possible points of contact between the message of the gospel and primitive religions, above all a sympathetic and objective approach is indispensable. A predisposition to measure the attainments of pagan peoples against a western cultural or theological background or to argue that because the Commandments forbid the worship of false gods, we should overthrow their idols, outlaw their priests and officially declare the pagan worship to be extinct, would only result in estranging the masses who devotedly cling to their tribal traditions. It is far easier to overthrow the more public manifestations of a creed than to destroy its inner vital force. The missionary should not forget that he too sprang from pagan stock, that the Spaniards, Franks, Gauls and even Britons were once barbarians; that the Greeks and Romans, whose literature was to become the model of classical writings, consulted augurs, exposed infants, examined the entrails of animals, and that the pagans of the British Isles practised druidic divinations, worshipped the sun and offered human sacrifices. It should also be remembered that it is yet another paradox of Christianity that the application of a universal code of beliefs and morals to differing races, far from destroying racial aptitudes, brings them to their fulfilment and at the same time creates an individual contribution that enriches the whole church. In the words of Cardinal Newman the missionary should:

> . . . seek some points in the existing superstitions as the basis of his own instructions, instead of indiscriminately condemning and discarding the whole assemblage of heathen opinions and practices; and he will address his hearers, not as men in a state of 'the wrath to come', because they are in bondage and ignorance. . . And while he strenuously opposes all that is idolatrous, immoral and profane in their creed, he will profess to be leading them on to perfection, and to be recovering and purifying, rather than reversing, the essential principles of their belief.[1]

Christ himself said that he did not come to destroy but to fulfil and we can read in the Gospel how understandingly he accommodated his heavenly doctrine to the mental capacity of his hearers. His parables and talks treated of subjects within the homely grasp of his audience: the lost groat, the army taking the city, the labourers in the vineyard, the house built on sand, the sheep and the goats, the prodigal son. Yet the same Master could speak in the synagogues and teach in the temples to the amazement of the doctors of the law. While the teaching of Christ was mainly accommodated to the Jewish way of life and thought, he gave his apostles a mission to

[1] J. H. Newman. *The Arians of the Fourth Century*, p. 84.

preach the Gospel to all nations. Consequently, without a shadow of compromise, St Paul refused to force upon the Gentiles the unbearable yoke of the Old Law, particularly the rite of circumcision.

The early Church in general followed St Paul in a sympathetic approach to existing pagan customs. Let us take for example the introduction of Christianity to the British Isles. In a celebrated letter to Melletus, a companion of St Augustine, Pope Gregory suggested a very practical method of evangelization in pagan England. He advised the missionaries not to destroy the pagan temples, but, rather, if they were well constructed, to purify them and to dedicate them to the true God. Further, since the people loved grand public feasts, he saw no reason why on those days they should not be allowed to run down, roast and eat beef before the very portals of the Church.[1] While St Boniface used the oak of Thor to build a church and Irish missionaries rededicated the sacred druidic groves to the new religion, little but condemnation has ever been heard of the pagan groves that abound in Africa.

The conversion of Ireland is an oft-quoted model of broad-minded missionary approach; and the methods employed by St Patrick are in the best traditions of modern anthropological research. He learned the Gaelic language so thoroughly, we are told, that he almost forgot the Latin of his school and cloister days and in moments of great stress and emotion his soul unburdened itself in Irish poetry. It was through his understanding approach and his respect for native institutions that within a lifetime 'the sacred wells, the sacred trees, the sacred shrines, while retaining the devotion of the people, were consecrated to new owners and acquired new associations.'[2] St Patrick did not disturb the tribal basis on which the social life of the people rested but rather worked through it. He left intact the Brehon system of oral jurisprudence except where it needed to be brought into harmony with the commandments of God.

The evolution of the Irish cross is a fair example of how a native art was pressed into the service of the new religion. With its 'cross and circle' pattern it most likely came from the solar representations of the Bronze Age rock carvings. The cross which represented the rays of the sun was of secondary importance to the outer circle which represented the sun's disc. When this combination of cross

---

[1] Ven. Bede, *Historica Ecclesiastica Gentis Anglorum*, I, 30.
[2] Christopher Dawson, *The Making of Europe*, pp. 91ff.

and circle was continued as a Christian emblem, the cross very naturally became of primary importance. Its arms were therefore extended beyond the circumference of the circle resulting in the well-known Irish cross, mistakenly called the Celtic cross.

One could not, however, expect pagans to become Christian overnight. On the contrary it was a long and painful process before even those who accepted Christianity and were baptized shook off their traditional associations. It is not surprising, therefore, to find examples of divided loyalties, as in the case of some ninth-century carvings which bore the symbols or names of pre-Christian gods in addition to the cross of the new faith. Even in Ireland today one can still find farmers who on May Eve, a traditional date in the pagan Celtic calendar, visit the springing crop fields and place a sprig of the rowan tree (the berries of which were the reputed ambrosial food of the gods) at the four corners of every field. Then they proceed to sprinkle the crops with water blessed at Easter-time. In Catholic countries where such relics of pagan ceremonial still survive and where even the symbolic ritual, as in the fires lighted for the feast of St John, are still observed, the customs no longer have any pagan associations. In the minds of the people the sole remaining purpose of such practices is to beg God's intercession through one of his saints or one of the sacramentals.[1]

The primitive Church provides many illustrations of that phrase which sums up the preaching and practice of St Paul: 'all things to all men'. Names for example which appear in our calendar of feasts today, such as Isidore, Dionysius, Ambrose, were adopted from the pagan mythology of Egypt or Greece or their meaning was linked up with some superstitious cult. Our days of the week and most of our months of the year were originally consecrated to pagan divinities or pagan Caesars. Our liturgical names, as bishop, priest, deacon, church, basilica, baptism, mystery, host, sacrifice, immolate, asceticism, soul, sin, redemption and the very word liturgy itself, were borrowed from the current vocabulary and signified pagan realities. The deliberate Christianizing of pagan feasts took place, the transference of worship from a pagan grove to a Christian church, Yuletide became Christmas, the sun feast of the summer solstice became a festival in honour of St John, and the original feast of Candlemas was a counter-attraction to a pagan feast with similar ceremonial.

[1] Rev. M. J. Walsh, S.M.A., 'Notes on Fire-lighting Ceremonies', in *Folk-lore*, Vol. LVIII, June and September 1947.

The Fathers of the early Church found themselves in a world as saturated with paganism as Africa was in the nineteenth century. They had the advantage, however, of not being far removed from the prevailing pagan culture which surrounded them. One of the reasons suggested for the rapid spread of Christianity among the peasants of the British Isles, who were outside the dominion of Rome, was the monastic organization of the Church and the fact that the monks, themselves of peasant origin, stood so near the peasant culture that they were able to fuse that culture with a spirit of religion. It is further suggested that it was through them also that the cult of the spirit of nature was transferred to the saints. The dictum of Origen as quoted by St Gregory sums up the attitude of the early Church towards the pagan world: 'that we should philosophize and collate with all our power every one of the writings of the ancients whether philosophers or poets, rejecting nothing (save the writings of the atheists) but giving a fair hearing to all'.[1] 'The faith you bring', to quote from an Instruction of the Sacred Congregation of Propaganda in the seventeenth century, 'neither rejects nor impairs the customs or usages of the people when they are not perverse, but on the contrary wishes to protect and preserve them.'

With the Renaissance, however, came a change of heart and a change of approach to the evangelization of pagan peoples. During the age of discovery there was a notion, often commonly shared by colonizers and missionaries, that all non-European culture was crude and barbarous and had to be uprooted. The superior pattern of their own western culture was to be superimposed on conquered peoples, with the implication, in theory at least, that to be a good Christian one had first to be a good European. The lives and conduct of many colonizers, however, belied the teaching of the Gospel, and served only to confuse the pagans all the more.

For economic or political reasons, colonizing forces from Europe, of which the missionaries formed an important part, regarded the pagan mode of life not merely as differing from their own, but as inferior; some went so far as to deny that members of pagan tribes were human beings endowed with conscience.

While it is true that many pagan beliefs and customs may have seemed primitive to the western way of thinking; that their social system may have been incomplete; their conception of law and equity entirely inadequate, yet there were undeniably present the

[1] Christopher Dawson, *op. cit.*

essential elements of human culture. General progress was often retarded by the colonizer's failure to respect the peoples' modes of thought, their tradition and environment. Few would claim that the old culture of the natives should be completely preserved, for it was adequate only under the old cultural conditions; but it was insufficiently realized in practice that a new culture could not be absorbed unless it had traditional roots. Even in the field of colonial education, it was not until the 1920's that an official directive was issued which suggested that education should be adapted to the mentality, aptitude, occupation and tradition of the various peoples, conserving as far as possible all sound and healthy elements in the fabric of their social life, and adapting it where necessary to changed conditions and progressive ideas.[1]

The Instruction from the Sacred Congregation of Propaganda already quoted asked what would be more absurd than to transport France or Spain or Italy or any other part of Europe to mission countries. It therefore urged the missionaries not to make the mistake of comparing the usages of the pagans with those of Europe but rather to accustom themselves to the ways of the people. Men of outstanding apostolic courage, like Père de Nobili in India or Matteo Ricci in China, had already tried to put into practice the principles enunciated in this Instruction. They may in their zeal have swung the pendulum too far the other way, and, as in the case of the Malabar Rites, their missionary methods were misrepresented and misunderstood; yet the more recent pronouncements of the Sacred Congregation of Propaganda on the development of the Church in the Far East, in the light of new investigations, have vindicated their approach.

In no pagan country has the missionary ever found an empty vessel into which he could pour the content of Christian truth, nor an empty void where he could plant the Church. He would find vague popular notions rather than a system of accurate intellectual beliefs, pagan doctrines bearing certain affinities to Christian truth, and pagan practices that could perhaps be chastened and brought into harmony with Christian moral thought.

Up to the end of the nineteenth century that much-abused word 'fetish' awakened in Europe only a vague notion of adoration of animal matter and profound pity for the unfortunate fetish worshippers. Europeans arriving on the coast of Guinea, for example, encountered at every step idols of wood or clay, as grotesque as they

[1] Advisory Committee on Education in British Tropical Africa, 1925.

were unclean, rudely made and daubed with blood and palm oil. A glance was sufficient to fill them with horror and contempt for such worship. When they learned that those shapeless divinities thirsted for human blood this contempt turned to indignation. On examination, however, it would be discovered that underneath the coarse and repellent exterior lay a chain of doctrine and a complex religious system of which spiritualism formed the greater part, and whose doctrines offered striking analogies to the pagan civilization of antiquity. However, while experts took infinite pains to study the ancient worship of Greece and Rome, they were slow to explore the mysteries of fetishism which constituted the religion of millions of living people.

Even to the modern missionary the beliefs and practices of an African tribe must present a seeming jumbled mass of truth and error, distortion and contradiction. One point stands clearly out: religion, taken in its widest sense, could be said to rule the lives of the people; and one or other of the many deities they worshipped was responsible for such important issues as life and death, sickness and health, war and peace, in fact all the vicissitudes of their daily life. It was the gods that gave them children; it was the gods that sometimes took them away. The gods sent them both plentiful harvests and desiccating droughts.

Those same gods were often terribly exacting. They were not always satisfied with the produce of the earth for sacrifice, as palm oil and cola nut, nor with the animal creation such as the goat and the cock. They sometimes demanded even more precious offerings, the lives of human beings. On the eve of a pagan feast the town crier might be heard announcing: 'If your fowl are not locked up tonight, you need not worry; if your sheep or goats are wandering on the roadside no harm will come to them; but if any son of man is found abroad this night, we shall not be responsible for his fate.' The king and priest, often one and the same person, ruled supreme according to the sanctions of a rigid law. Thousands of slaves were obliged to do their masters' bidding in this life and at his death accompanied him to another world which was just as real to them as this. It was indeed the age of the gods. The people were patient in times of suffering and when one of the tribe had reached a reasonably ripe old age, they rejoiced to see him go to the heaven where they believed he would be happy. They loved their children and at the same time exposed twins to die in the bush; they were hospitable to strangers but would sacrifice them if occasion demanded. They cared for the sick but would feel no guilt in abandoning to die those striken down with smallpox.

Ethnographic and missiological studies, especially within the last quarter of a century, have helped to make intelligible many conflicting beliefs and customs and have shown how one must distinguish between faith, fetish, religion, magic, totem and taboo. They have opened a door to the appreciation of intrinsic values of indigenous cultural traditions. It is not an unmerited criticism of missionary endeavour generally that considering the greater opportunities missionaries have had and used for knowing and understanding the inner life of pagan peoples, eminent names and eminent works in the field of ethnography are all too few. Missionaries may have erred at times in trying to implant a new doctrine without first knowing the old or in adjusting an existing moral code without having grasped its pagan signification. Yet, if in the past the collecting of data has been haphazard and the sifting insufficient, if the collating has been untrained or the application vague, it should be remembered that the missionary's life in the vineyard is a full one. Not for him the scholarly retirement of writing.

No missionary priest today and no thinking government official would doubt the existence of pagan codes of morality. If we take particular tribes, for example the Yorubas of Western Nigeria or the Akans of the Gold Coast, we find in their language words connoting good and evil, true and false, just and unjust. They readily distinguish between what is permitted and what is forbidden. Listen to one of the many palavers that take place in a native compound. It may be concerned with a theft, an unfaithful wife, a disobedient child, a calumny or a slander. Attend one of the pagan feasts from their crowded religious calendar and see if elements of morality can be discerned in the rites that compose it.

A concrete example is the scapegoat feast at Ile-Ife. This movable feast, known as the Edi, takes place during the month of November to commemorate the victory of the Ifes over their enemies the Igbos. During the seven days of the feast, no work is done and no markets are held. Violaters of this pagan sabbath risk having their market stalls upturned by passers-by who by custom are free to loot them. On the first day ceremonies of purification by fire take place, first in the palace of the king and then in every family compound all over the town. The people take up burning firebrands and waving them about their heads shout: 'May death, disease and every misfortune be carried away from us.' The lighted firebrands are then carried in procession to a pagan shrine in the bush. On this day also the king is said to engage in a mock wrestling bout with his personal attendant who falls to the ground in token of submission.

The third day is specially dedicated to Moremi, who gave her only son in sacrifice for the deliverance of the people. Hymns of praise are sung to the memory of her dead son. Litanies too are chanted imploring a blessing 'on the pots and the pans, on our father and mother, on you and on me'. It is customary also during the feast to attack and sometimes even to destroy houses of people convicted of stealing since the last Edi ceremony took place. Bands of people armed with sticks and stones and rubbish of all kinds can be seen rushing towards such houses, the tempo of their songs quickening as they near the site.

On the closing day, king and chiefs and people gather together on the green outside the palace. The chiefs pay public homage to the king in elaborate ceremonial. The head of the townswomen, on behalf of her sex, gives public token of submission. That evening the climax of the festivities is reached when a human scapegoat, who must not be a native, is driven out into the bush. The people throng the palace grounds and the open space outside. While the scapegoat makes his way through the mocking throng, as on the occasion of the ceremonial fire on the opening day, they throw their hands wildly above their heads calling on him to carry away all their miseries. The people accompany the scapegoat to the fringe of the town. Thence, alone save for two attendants, he proceeds to the grove of Moremi. But whereas in the past the scapegoat was sacrificed, nowadays a goat is substituted. The people then return home praying that they will live to celebrate the next Edi festival.[1]

To a casual observer this feast consists of a seemingly endless series of songs and dances, interspersed by meaningless ceremonies. But when one has analysed the ritual, translated the songs and litanies, and discussed the feast in objective detail with the pagan priests and worshippers, interesting features come to light. To dismiss as 'arbitrary puerilities' the ceremonies of these rites is to fail to recognize in them concepts found in our own Christian theology and liturgy, e.g. sacrifice, justice, prayer, purification, blessings, submission to authority, satisfaction as well as punishment for crime, litanies, carrying of lights, etc.

The pagan is not totally corrupt, and faith and baptism do not

[1] Rev. M. J. Walsh, S.M.A., 'The Edi Festival at Ile-Ife', in *African Affairs*, Journal of the Royal African Society, Vol. 47, No. 189.

suppress his nature to create another. It is ignorance rather than perversion which is responsible for the errors and distortions some-times noticeable in their moral judgements. The principle of the natural law, for example, which forbids the unlawful taking of human life is known in West African society, e.g. among the Yoru-bas or the Akans. It is in the application of the principle that diver-gencies begin. To kill a human being for sacrifice, thus giving the best in creation to the gods, was not considered murder. People knew it was good to relieve parents in time of suffering. Thus they did not regard it as unfilial to expose or kill their suffering parents in time of famine or distress. Theologians point out that the special aptitude or disposition by which men are inclined to apprehend general axioms may be corrupted or perverted by education, tradi-tion, evil passions, extreme intellectual and moral degradation due to climatic conditions or to the severity of the surroundings or the like.[1]

It may be asked if the pagan customs are purely social observ-ances agreed to for the smooth running of the affairs of the com-munity, or the outcome of a moral conviction, unconsciously based on religion. More than sufficient evidence has been collected to prove that in pagan territories all over Africa the Supreme Being is worshipped. Much of this evidence tends to show that the sanc-tion of their moral code, ultimately, if unknowingly, relates to the Supreme Being and not to any social convenience, but the collected data are not of sufficiently universal application to permit an authorative statement being made or a final conclusion drawn.

The Yorubas, for example, believe in Olorun, the all-knowing, all-wise, all-good Supreme Being, who sustains and directs in this life and who punishes and rewards after death. While the people regard Olorun as too important to be concerned with the trivialities of the humdrum daily round, they invoke him before ceremonies to the other gods, never blaspheme his name and honour him in frequent salutations such as: 'God save you,' 'May God bring you safely through the night.' Even if their concept of the Supreme Being differs from ours, as does their concept of Eshu, the devil, it should be remembered that the early Church incorporated the words Deus and Theos, purged them of their plural declensions, and then applied them to the worship of the one true God.

It is not suggested that there can be any reconciliation, any com-promise between the Christian truth and the pagan beliefs. The

[1] M. Maher, S.J., *Psychology*, p. 335.

Church has never condoned pagan rites or practices, or permitted any suggestion of syncretistic growth, or levelling down of Christian principles, for in virtue of its divine origin the Church of Christ is self-sufficient, absolute and unique. Even the good in paganism, guided by the principles of the natural law or containing the remnants of primitive revelation, cannot serve as a foundation for the teaching of Christ. Christianity can never be a synthesis of the best in pagan religions. But if paganism, according to theologians, should disappear entirely, they add that it need not be destroyed and replaced with something different: rather its imperfect content should be suppressed in the perfect which it is to become, as the child is suppressed in the adult without being killed.[1] Nothing provokes more hatred and aversion, states the seventeenth-century Instruction from the Sacred Congregation of Propaganda, than to upset the immemorial ancestral customs, or worse still to overturn and replace them by those of one's own country.

The Church in her wisdom realized that religion, taken in its widest sense, went to form part of the warp and woof of the texture of pagan racial and cultural traditions, and she prudently distinguished between essential and accidental elements in various cults. She recognized that 'every genuine value, everything that came from pure and uncorrupted nature, belongs to God and has citizen rights in his Kingdom.'[2] As missiologists put the case, the objective content of Christian dogma, universal in its application, is independent of race or clime or circumstances. The expression of that objective reality, that is to say the outward forms and signs of piety, is moulded in its accidental aspect by heredity and environment, and depends consequently on regional peculiarities and the varying conditions of changing times. It is clear, therefore, that, while the essence of Christianity which is of divine origin can admit of no accommodation, the human and consequently—under Divine Providence—accidental development is not of metaphysical or universal value, but admits of change and modification.[3]

Our present Holy Father sums up what should be the attitude of the Church and missionaries to foreign peoples and cultures:

The Church of Christ, the faithful depository of the teaching of divine wisdom, cannot and does not think of depreciating or disdaining the particular characteristics which each people, with

[1] Père Charles, S.J., *Manual of Missiology*, Art. 19.
[2] Karl Adams, *The Spirit of Catholicism*, p. 158.
[3] G. Voss, S.J., *Missionary Accommodation*, pp. 39ff.

jealous and intelligible pride, cherishes and retains as a precious heritage. Her aim is a supernatural union in all-embracing love, deeply felt and practised, and not the unity which is exclusively external and superficial and, by that very fact, weak. . .

She has repeatedly shown in her missionary enterprises that such a principle of action is the guiding star of her universal apostolate. Pioneer research and investigation, involving sacrifice, devotedness and love on the part of her missionaries of every age, have been undertaken in order to facilitate a more deeply appreciative insight into the most varied civilizations and to put their spiritual values to account for a living and vital preaching of the Gospel of Christ. All that in such usages and customs is not inseparably bound up with religious errors will always be subject to kindly consideration, and, when it is found possible, will be sponsored and developed.

Our immediate Predecessor of holy and venerated memory, applying such norms to a particularly delicate question, made some generous decisions which are a monument to his insight and to the intensity of his apostolic spirit. Nor need we tell you, Venerable Brethren, that We intend to proceed without hesitation along this way. Those who enter the Church, whatever be their origin or their speech, must know that they have equal rights as children in the house of the Lord, where the law of Christ and the peace of Christ prevail.[1]

----

[1] Pope Pius XII, *Summi Pontificatus*, published in *Acta Apostolicae Sedis*, 1939, p. 548.

XIX

BUDDHIST MORALITY

by
David Snellgrove

THERE is no framework which will bring Christianity and Buddhism into a relationship which is fair to both of them. It might of course be expected in a Christian symposium that an orthodox standpoint would be maintained and an interpretation given of the various doctrinal and moral tenets of Buddhism from this viewpoint alone. However this would only be possible if Buddhism were rooted in the same historical context and capable of definition within the same terms of reference. This is not so, and any attempt to fit it into western forms merely results in missing its significance altogether. Thus in terms of western concepts Buddhism may be definable as a form of pantheism. There are some who describe it so and think thereby to have relieved themselves of further interest in the subject. Others describe it as atheistic and hope thereby to have demonstrated its hopeless falsity. They have failed to realize that their use of those terms is but relative at best to their own western standpoint. Within Buddhist tradition itself, in its doctrine and practice, pantheism and atheism become almost meaningless terms. The religious experience, to which it bears witness, finally makes such definitions altogether empty.

Likewise falsification of another kind results when Christianity is regarded from the Hindu or Buddhist point of view. Thus a Mahāyāna Buddhist would have no difficulty in accepting the truth of a Christ crucified. To him it would be neither foolishness nor a stumbling-block. But he would fail entirely to conceive of it in the rigid historical sense expected of him by the missionary. It would seem perhaps a powerful means to salvation, but nevertheless one of several. It would be another *yana* ('Way'). Had Christianity been presented in this way, it would probably have succeeded in oriental countries, but it would have been a very different Christianity from that of the apostles. One may perhaps remember the gnostics in this respect.

On both sides there has been a failure to realize that we are looking at things from entirely different points of vantage. Therefore
our present consideration of the problem of the relationship of these
two religions dissociates itself from such fixed notions and moves
from one viewpoint to another. If Buddhism seems to be favoured,
this must be because it is the lesser known.

Now it may seem that in any case this whole subject is rather of
academic than of immediate interest. It is true that it is the missionaries, working far away in other lands, who are directly and
urgently concerned. But those of us who believe that the rather presumptuous western world has much of value to learn from the traditional teachings of the east find here considerations of vital import,
which should affect all who are perplexed by the sterile appearance
of religion in the west. That which is true should manifest itself undoubtedly as true to anyone who sincerely seeks the truth. It would
be cowardly to ignore the fact that Catholic Christianity (or of
course any other form of Christianity) does not present itself as true
to many who seek in all sincerity. It may seem presumptuous to
suggest that the reason is its apparent insistence on outward form
and expression and a corresponding dearth of spiritual attainment.
But those who seek for religious truth do not need a manual of instruction (of these there are far too many in the world) so much as
direct contact with a teacher who really knows as true the teaching
which he transmits. This of course is the common oriental concept
of a master, and it has been equally fundamental in Christianity
during past centuries. Perhaps in this century our contacts with the
east will remind us of this and other things which are essential to
the successful propagation of a religion that may claim to comprehend all truth.

Since as in all things we must begin with what is clearly within
reach, the problem of the missionary may seem to loom large in
this present article.

An admirable historical study of the meeting of Buddhism and
the west has recently been produced by Henri de Lubac,[1] and to
this those who are interested may be referred without more ado. In
referring to the slowness with which Europe became aware of
Buddhism in the sixteenth century, he writes:

> One must say above all that for a long time the greater part of
> the missionaries, in spite of contact which was often close with

---

[1] *La Rencontre du Bouddhisme et de l'Occident*, Aubier, Paris, 1952.

their converts, were loath to interest themselves very much in this religion, and did not always succeed in making the necessary effort to understand it [p. 68].

This of course is still the case to a large extent, but the blame now no longer attaches to the missionaries alone, who must often be sufficiently occupied with their regular daily labour. Until the middle of the last century the west relied entirely on the accounts of missionaries and other travellers for their knowledge of oriental religions, but since then a new and more authoritative source has been put at our disposal, namely the texts themselves, in Pāli and Sanskrit, Tibetan and Chinese, which are the four chief languages in which the Buddhist scriptures are extant. Moreover a fairly representative selection has appeared in translation in all the modern languages of Europe, and this stock of translations increases yearly. There are now available several serious works on the subject, of which a bibliography has been easily available for several years in the little pamphlet on Buddhism, published by the Catholic Truth Society. The author of this pamphlet, Louis de la Vallée Poussin, was one of the foremost of Buddhist scholars.

Apart from these serious works, popular accounts and anthologies continue to appear. Yet Buddhism and oriental religion generally seem to remain largely unknown, one might say almost incomprehensible, to the modern western mind. In reading through a recent journal of the Mahābodi Society, I found that the expression 'as ignorant as a Christian' appeared more than once. If we now add, that the Buddhist world is even more ignorant of the real nature of Christianity, we have defined in the simplest terms the present unhappy relationship of east and west in their spiritual and intellectual life. Considering the comparatively small number of scholars who have been engaged in research upon oriental studies, the amount of information now available is quite prodigious. Yet the ancient world is still largely conceived of in terms merely of Israel, Greece and Rome. In this respect I would like to quote a fairly long passage from a recent work of Jean Daniélou,[1] for it presents our present problem in its proper perspective.

Up till now we have identified our civilization with western civilization. It is this civilization that we have Christianized. But we are becoming conscious nowadays of the vitality of other civilizations, which are not Christian. One will say perhaps that

[1] *Essai sur le Mystère de l'Histoire*, Seuil, Paris, 1953.

Christianity extends over the whole world. But we must here guard against a dangerous illusion.

He then notes that in the third century Tertullian thought that the whole world was Christian, but although it was true that there were Christians throughout the whole known world, these were mainly Roman colonists, and when these colonists left the coasts of North Africa and the Black Sea, Christianity left with them. In the same way, he continues 'with the withdrawal of western influence, Christianity too withdraws from the former colonial territories. It continues to be considered there as a product of exportation.' I would add from personal experience how true this is of India, where to be a Christian of any sort is *ipso facto* to be unpatriotic. We now come to Jean Daniélou's answer to the problem.

In face of this situation, the necessity for Christianity to embody itself in the civilizations of the East, the Near East and Africa, appears in all urgency. . . This evangelization of whole civilizations appears necessary, but it is also absolutely normal. Christianity is not bound to any particular civilization. It is not a fact of civilization. It is breaking of God into history. The fact that it has expressed itself primarily through the western world does not mean that we must identify it with the west. Moreover one must not forget that the revelation was first made manifest in the Semitic race and language. The evangelization of the Greco-Roman world represented a first transfer of the Word of God from one cultural world to another. We are nowadays in the presence of the necessity of a new transfer [pp. 39–41].

We must not therefore be impatient with the existence of cultures other than our own, wanting to destroy them in order to impose our own. But on the contrary, we should think that we have need of these cultures in order to complete our own. Nothing is less intelligent than a linguistic exclusiveness. Humanity would be less noble, if there were no China, no Arabia and no world of dark-skinned people [p. 60].

The same idea is expressed in de Lubac's *Catholicism*. He lays down the twofold axiom of willingly to accept whatever can be assimilated and to prescribe nothing that is not of faith (p. 148 of the English edition).

Now it is clearly one thing to announce such a programme, and quite another to set it out in detail. Very many years, indeed centuries, must pass, before the programme can be complete, and it will seemingly proceed largely by trial and improvisation. The one immediate essential is that all concerned should constantly keep the goal in view and render themselves as knowledgeable as possible concerning the beliefs and traditions of the people amongst whom they are living. Nor is this the concern of the missionaries alone, but of all whose business it is to see Christianity in its full historical context. We should begin to extend our conception of the pre-Christian world out of the limited confines of the Mediterranean basin until it includes at least the great civilizations of the east. It is these that remain active to the present day, and they are therefore not only among the forerunners of Christianity, but should logically still be awaiting their consummation by means of it.

After speaking in terms of these grandiose generalities, one is conscious of an anticlimax, when one turns to some of the actual details involved. There can so easily be a certain pettiness, when one attempts to define for instance what may be assimilated and what may not, but it is often a pettiness behind which stand serious doctrinal considerations. It is not for me to commit myself in any of these matters, but I shall try to present you with some examples from my own experience. So far, of course, these problems remain mainly theoretical, just because up till now, converts in Asia and Africa tend to reject their whole cultural tradition with their acceptance of Christianity, the very thing they should not do. Clearly they require sympathetic encouragement from their priest, if they are to achieve a proper balance between the old ways and the new. Even when encouragement is given, they seem slow to understand. I think particularly of the little community of St Augustine's in Kalimpong, on the Bengal-Tibetan frontier, where I was living during the winter 1953-4. The church there has been recently built and is adorned with exquisite wood-carving in traditional Tibetan style. The twelve apostles, who flank the main altar, in appearance are almost Buddhist monks, for it is as such that the craftsmen have conceived them, and from their point of view they have conceived them well. The acolytes appear on feast-days in Tibetan dress, long gowns of dark red and sashes of yellow silk, which in Tibet is the sign of a religious profession. One regrets all the more the zeal with which the congregation has taken to European dress. One wonders rather why they should not have equipped themselves with prayer-wheels, replacing the *Oṃ Maṇipadme Hūṃ* formula with one of a new significance. But one learns that there is a tendency for things to be precisely the other way round—a tendency to be Buddhist in sentiment while adopting the externals of Christianity and western life, rather than Christian in conviction and practice, automatically finding expression for their new faith through the externals of a traditional culture. It seems for instance that a conception of sin consists all too often just in the taking of life of some small creature, which the westerner would brush aside without more ado as a pest. But this does raise an important matter.

Not to take life is the foremost of Buddhist moral precepts, and the importance given to it in Buddhist teaching should lead one at once to reflect to what extent it is warranted by Christian teaching. The readiness of the Christian to take animal life is something truly abhorrent to a practising Buddhist, and his horror is not to be lightly ignored. One may discount it on the grounds that there is no transmigrating principle, the presence of which in any animal would render its life as sacred as that of any man. This is the doctrinal basis of the Buddhist prohibition. But surely one could concede the same innate sacredness to animal life, which is due to all created things. A cultured man does not destroy for the mere delight of destroying; nor should he take life for the mere delight of killing. This is perhaps one of the lessons that the west may learn from the east, and it possibly illustrates in one matter the give-and-take basis on which we should be willing to proceed.

In general there is little difference between Christian and Buddhist moral precepts. The difference between the two religions emerges at a much deeper level of doctrine and faith, where few minds can penetrate and still preserve clarity of intellectual insight.[1] Before discussing this difficulty in more detail, it may be as well to resume the chief items of Buddhist morality. First we have the old conventional set of ten prohibitions:

> not to take life,
> not to steal,
> to avoid unchastity,
> not to lie,
> not to slander,
> not to insult,
> not to chatter,
> not to covet,
> not to give way to anger,
> not to doubt.

[1] An example of the kind of insight needed is provided by Hubert Olympius Mascarenhas, M.A., Ph.D., D.D. In a short work entitled *The Quintessence of Hinduism* (Gemini Printers, Bombay), he has produced a remarkable interpretation of Hinduism

We have already referred to the importance that the injunction not to take life has in Buddhism. The only other item liable to a different interpretation in Buddhist lands is that of chastity. It does not necessarily involve monogamous marriage. Both polygamy and polyandry are found in Tibet for instance, and any form of union sanctioned by convention in a Buddhist land clearly cannot count as unchastity from the Buddhist standpoint. Its counsel of perfection is of course complete abstinence, and this is fully binding on all properly constituted orders of monks. The monastic disciplines contain some two hundred and fifty (the number varies somewhat between the different schools) major and minor rules of conduct. It would be impossible to consider these on this occasion, but I draw your attention to them in passing. What are far more relevant to this present short study are the positive teachings of Buddhism. The ten rules listed above and indeed the whole monastic code represent little more than the basic preliminary.

Now the formation of these positive virtues is partly the result of a historical development within Buddhism itself. There is a change from a negative to a conditioned positive position in the presentation of the doctrine, as represented by the extremes of Theravādin teachings on the one hand and Mahāyāna Vajrayāna on the other. This is a mere generalization, and one must not think that positive teachings were not taught at all times. We have for example the opening verses of Chapter x of the *Udānavarga*, a compendium of verses of great age (at latest the third century, B.C.), which in varying recensions seems to have been possessed by all the early schools.

> Faith, morality and charity, these are the qualities that wise men praise. This is the divine path, they say, and by means of it, one reaches heaven.
>
> Avaricious men do not reach heaven, so they are fools, who give no regard to charity. Pious men rejoice in charity, and by means of it they find happiness in the other world.
>
> Thus faith is man's best treasure. By practising the doctrine aright, he will gain happiness. This happiness is indeed the best of flavours. The man who lives by wisdom, is the best of men, they say.

The word, which I have translated here as *charity*, refers properly to the act of giving (Pāli and Sanskrit: *dāna*), and although this

---

in terms of Christian revelation. It would be interesting to see an analogous interpretation of Buddhism.

virtue is referred to in the Buddhism of all periods, it is only when the career of the *bodhisattva* (i.e. would-be *buddha*) is presented as the ideal goal for all living beings, that the act of giving becomes a prime virtue. It is this aspiration to universal buddhahood which characterizes the Great Way (*Mahāyāna*), making any lesser goal (e.g. the *nirvāṇa* of the early disciples) seem mean (*hīna*) by comparison. Instead of seeking tranquillity by a gradual loosening of the physical and mental bonds that bind him to phenomenal existence, the aspirant to the religious life is counselled to seek his perfection by leading all other beings to perfection too, in short in universal buddhahood. Such a goal requires a positive scheme of action, and this scheme was formalized as the Six Perfections, viz.: charity, morality, patience, energy, meditation and wisdom. Now I referred to the Mahāyāna generally as a conditioned positive position, and I now resume this point. Buddhism, at least in its philosophical texts, has usually defined its goal in negative terms, as neither existence nor non-existence, as an ineffable condition of bliss. But one should perhaps mention at the same time that the desirable goal has often been conceived popularly as paradise, and since Buddhism conceives of itself as transcending all non-Buddhist doctrines, it became necessary to conceive of a Buddhist paradise, such as that of Amitābha, the Great Buddha of the West, which transcends the futile heavens of the ordinary Indian gods. From these last, one will fall again into some unhappy condition of rebirth, when one's stock of merit is exhausted, but from Amitābha's paradise, where the sweet sound of the doctrine never ceases, only buddhahood is possible. When therefore one draws attention to the negativity of Buddhism, it is only proper at the same time to remember its positive content. The negative definitions have never received the sign of authority of a recognized teaching church. To understand its noncommittal position one must attempt to resolve its apparent contradictions within oneself, and this only a practising Buddhist can achieve. It has developed an important school of logicians, but it has never attempted to take a final stand on reason. It is this that makes it so difficult, if not impossible, to speak fairly of Buddhist morality from an established Christian standpoint.

Consider for example the discussion of Buddhist charity in Henri de Lubac's *Aspects du Bouddhisme*. He makes out very well the case for Buddhist charity, and I only wish that I now had time to do likewise. In any case one should not fail to refer to this short work of his, for it represents the only serious attempt to date to contrast

Christian and Buddhist teachings. De Lubac emphasizes quite clearly the point of difference between the two moralities.

> Even if we consider it (Buddhism) in its highest and most admirable forms, it differs in its inspiration from the other [Christianity]. It refers to another idea. It occupies another place in another system of salvation. If one presses the comparison a little, one cannot fail to make quite clear the different genius of the two religions [p. 30].

Nevertheless this statement is not quite fair. One may become aware of the deep differences which separate the two religions, but not by contrasting Christian charity with Buddhist charity. If this has any effect, it tends rather to obscure the differences. The differences in theory and doctrine are truly profound, and we should rather regard it as both remarkable and satisfactory that in the sphere of positive moral action there should be such close unanimity. It is not our task to show that Buddhist charity is inferior to Christian charity, even if this could be done to general satisfaction, but rather to show how Buddhist morality is only finally fulfilled by Christian revelation. If we do wish to apply any test, it clearly cannot be fairly done by appeal to texts. It must be done in actual life, and this is therefore a test that most missionaries can make.

I myself spent some six weeks at Jiwong Monastery in east Nepal in 1954 in the capacity of a scholar. Apart from the general friendliness and hospitality with which I was treated during that time, the one monk who actively befriended me and furthered the success of my plans has served to convince me that the career of the *bodhisattva* is not a mere unrealizable ideal and that Buddhist charity is not just pity. There should be no reason to regard him as an isolated example. Nothing is of course proved by personal impressions, but I would like to put before you the views first of a great traveller-missionary and secondly of a great oriental historian. The first is Ippolito Desideri, who produced the first account of Tibetan religion, an account which has not yet been bettered. He was a pioneer, who has never received his just dues, as Henri de Lubac points out.[1] Desideri writes thus:

> If one considers what I have stated about the Tibetan religion, although I believe the articles of faith to be absolutely wrong and pestiferous, yet the rules and directions imposed on the will are not alien to the principles of sound reason; they seem to me worthy

---

[1] *Rencontre du Bouddhisme*, p. 137.

of admiration as they not only prescribe hatred of vice, inculcate battling against passions, but what is more remarkable, lead man towards sublime and heroic perfection.[1]

The second quotation is from the last work of René Grousset, his *Bilan de l'Histoire*. (The whole work represents a final confession of faith. His testimony is an important one.)

> It would give an imperfect and even unjust idea of Buddhism to consider it merely from the speculative point of view. Half of Asia would not have taken refuge in it, if it had been merely a matter of dialecticians playing with such dangerous intellectual positions. Let us repeat, the best of Buddhism is Buddhist sensibility, that deep tenderness, which in spite of all doctrinal negations, creates around itself an atmosphere of fervour, of religiosity, of active charity [pp. 127–8].

Nor are the examples given in Buddhist writings always legendary and fantastic, and to supplement a comment of Henri de Lubac,[2] I will give you a quotation from the *Mirror of Künzang La-ma*. This is a Tibetan work, a summary of Buddhist teaching, produced probably in the middle of the last century by a monk of the Nying-ma-pa Order, and it seems to have maintained unrivalled popularity in Tibet for a hundred years. It has not yet been translated into any other language, but it would repay the effort. The writer is discussing the four 'immeasurable virtues', friendliness, compassion, joy and equanimity, and sums up thus:

> So if we wish to compress these four immeasurable virtues into one concept so that we can make them easily understandable, then they would unite in kind-heartedness. Thus at all times and all circumstances we must learn kind-heartedness. It is recounted of Atiśa that on one occasion, when his hand was hurt, he placed it in Drom-tön's bosom, saying: 'Bless it, for you are kind-hearted.' So great a store did he set by kind-heartedness. When he greeted anyone, he used to say: 'Are you kind-hearted?' (instead of 'Are you in good health?'—in Tibetan the change of one letter produces this change of meaning) and in all his instruction he used to say: 'Just be kind.'[3]

This may suggest perhaps a certain passivity, but the kind-heartedness is real none the less, and I think you will find it quite generally in those who have received a traditional Buddhist up-

---

[1] Desideri, *An Account of Tibet*, Broadway Travellers, p. 300.
[2] *Aspects*, p. 31.   [3] *Kün-zang La-ma*, folio 157.

bringing. This is of course provided by the monks, for secularized schools are a purely western device. Again there is no occasion here for personal reminiscences, but the Buddhists-born, whom I have met, have made a profound impression upon me.[1] It is they, of course, who will tell you with most persuasiveness that all religions, properly practised, produce the same desired result, and they will indicate the virtues which their own religion is capable of inculcating, and most ordinary men of good-will will not hesitate to agree, for, as I said above, the difference between Christianity and Buddhism emerges at a much deeper level. Let us now attempt to investigate this.

The fundamental idea of all schools of Buddhism is not negativity, as some have suggested, for both negation and affirmation are finally rejected. It is the idea of impermanence that is pre-eminent. One short quotation from the *Mirror of Kün-zang La-ma* will make this more clear than would a long exposition on the theme.

They asked Ge-she Pu-to-pa for instruction concerning how to deal with evil, and he said: 'Reflect frequently on death and impermanence. If you are conscious of the certainty of death, it will not be difficult for you to avoid evil and it will not be difficult for you to practise virtue. Furthermore you should meditate frequently upon friendliness and compassion. If these qualities are thus produced in your character, it will not be difficult for you to be of service to living beings. Furthermore you should meditate frequently upon the Void, which is the true nature of things. If you produce this as an inner conviction, it will not be difficult to keep free of delusions.' Thus we should always be aware of impermanence, and then we shall reject our attachment to things of this generation like hot food given to a bilious man. Atīśa once said: 'Whatever I see of the high and the mighty of this world, of the wealthy and the sophisticated, the fact that I should find them in no wise desirable and that I should direct my attention to that excellent and supreme condition of release, comes about because I have realized a little the truth of impermanence. I have no better instruction to give than this.' He was always talking in such a way. So you should realize this truth of impermanence to the extent of being like the hermit, Ge-she Kha-rag. He was going to meditate in the solitude of Jo-mo Ka-rag in Tsang Province, and as he was entering the cave, some briars at the entrance caught up in his cloak. At first he thought: 'Shall I cut them?' and then he

---

[1] For a discussion of the nature of Buddhism especially its Tibetan form, see my *Buddhist Himālaya*, Bruno Cassirer, Oxford, 1956.

thought: 'Well, as I don't know whether I shall come out of this cave alive, it would be better if I concentrated on the practice of virtue,' and so he did not cut them. Whenever he went out, the same thing occurred, and he thought: 'Well, I don't know whether I shall come back again,' and so although he stayed there for many years and gained perfection, yet he never cut down those briars.

However absurd this little anecdote might seem to the active modern westerner, I think its intention would have been appreciated by the early Fathers of the desert. Indeed in practice it corresponds with the Christian doctrine of the transitoriness, one might even say the 'nothingness' of this world. This is a Christian view of things in which nowadays most of us are no longer practised. We tend to think in terms of firm realities, not because Christian teaching would have it so, but for the very opposite reason that as Christian tradition has weakened in the west, so a realistic and supposedly reasonable way of regarding things has come to take its place. The Christian, no more than the Buddhist, should properly regard things as real in themselves. Thus rather than point an accusing finger at the Buddhist monk for founding his religious practice on absurd philosophical notions of universal emptiness, one should be prepared to watch for the practical fruit, that is to say the morality, which issues from those conceptions.

> The fair tree of the Void abounds with flowers,
> Acts of compassion of many kinds,
> And fruit for others appearing spontaneously,
> For this joy has no actual thought of another.[1]

The Christian doctrine of transitoriness is related to that of contingent being, and contingency suggests to us absence of self-nature (and I deliberately use Buddhist terminology in order to assist the comparison) but, not only this, it also suggests the existence of Being which is its own self-nature, for otherwise how should contingent being have any apparent existence? This positive aspect of Being is reinforced and given meaning by Christian revelation, and the time-sequence is seen as possessing an end and a purpose, so that no moment is meaningless.

Consider now the Buddhist position. Everything is seen to be impermanent in essence and thus sorrowful. In the early schools this impermanence was explained in terms of momentariness. In the

---

[1] Saraha's Treasury of Songs, v. 108, *Buddhist Texts*, p. 239.

later schools it was explained in terms of illusion or of false imagination. At no time did it lead to the dogmatic assertion of the existence of the One who is absolutely stable and absolutely real. It is this finally non-committal position adopted by Buddhism which confirmed its unorthodoxy vis-à-vis Brahmanism and Hinduism. One is therefore left with a sequence of fleeting moments with no necessary beginning and no necessary end and with no inherent significance, except the inevitable conditioning of what will come after by what has gone before. The knowledge of this is Buddhist wisdom, but this wisdom alone does not represent Final Enlightenment. For realization of this the active practice of the Six Perfections is required. It is on this active side that morality plays its part. Many of the Mahāyāna texts seem to suggest a world of make-believe, which can appear exasperating to the normal western reader.

He hesitates to believe that any solid moral conduct can be based on such empty notions. In the west we normally conceive of a moral law in relationship to a divine Being, and many people indeed conceive of no moral law other than the Christian one. Its existence comes to be acknowledged grudgingly, as though one feared that to recognize the excellence of the morals of another amounted to a recognition of the final excellence of that religion itself. We know that morality is not religion. It is the basis of the religious life, whether Christian or Buddhist. It is the next question that is the essential one. Is the type of perfection which is the goal of Buddhist religious life the ideal of human perfection? Is it the perfection that God intends for man? The answer to this question marks one as a Christian or a Buddhist. 'Religions and philosophies are not so many paths, that climb from different sides the slopes of the one same mountain. One should compare them rather, in their respective ideals, to so many different summits, separated by precipices.'[1] A very different view is represented by Aldous Huxley in his *Perennial Philosophy*, who would envisage us all on the one same mountain, our climbing speed hindered only by the false views with which our particular religious tradition is defiled. Christianity, based as it is on historical reality, seems almost too heavy a burden to carry. Buddhism, particularly Tibetan Buddhism, would seem to be in the lead. But useful and indeed stimulating as we may find such an anthology (for the selections of oriental religions are well made), let there be no doubt concerning the artificiality of the main thesis. There is no grand universal tradition. It is an invention of a few

[1] Henri de Lubac, *Rencontre*, p. 282.

Europeans of the last two centuries, invented, as such man-made schemes often are, by the bare denial of all that would conflict with the scheme. Any religion forced into it, not only Christianity, is robbed of part of its essential being.

Those of us who consider this problem of the relationship of these two great religions must recognize that there is no easy solution. De Lubac's comparison of the separate mountains is apt so far as it goes, that is to say, so far as their separate historical development is concerned. But we have not turned our backs on the precipice. There are still grassy slopes that lead across, if one has but the will to follow them. Buddhists do not wilfully reject an obvious truth. Those who follow a religious life make use of all means that are at their disposal. When we help them, our help might be more welcome if it employed the means that they understand, namely the way of contemplation and the wisdom that will listen as well as teach. Mr Dawson has drawn attention to the importance of learning and of centres of learning for the spread and maintenance of Buddhism in Asia.[1] During the same centuries, Christianity was using similar methods in the west. The modern west has largely lost its respect for learning and doubts the value of the contemplative life. The east, except for some who have been beguiled by social and political ideas of western provenance, still retains its respect both for learning and for sanctity. This is the east with which it behoves us to make contact.

Nothing is gained by denying the strength of its morality, by calling its asceticism misguided, or by doubting its ability to reach its avowed goal of tranquil perfection. We should accept it at its highest value and proceed immediately with the task of making clear to those who are prepared to reason with us where the essential difference lies. When a thoughtful Buddhist will willingly concede that Christian love has a significance more profound and more universal than any corresponding concept in his own teachings, then the affirmation will have value. It serves no purpose other than that of vain disputation, if one man makes this claim, while the other still does not fully understand the main point at issue. We are not contrasting here just two ideas in the abstract, and yet this is the only way in which the Buddhist would conceive of the matter. We are contrasting an idea and an actuality, and it is the actuality which we must present as the fulfilment of the idea.

It is noteworthy to what extent one can express oneself through

[1] *Religion and Culture*, p. 99.

Buddhist terminology. I referred above to Buddhist Enlightenment as a combination of *wisdom* (Buddhist wisdom of course) and the active practice of the six perfections. Now these six are subsumed under the one heading of *compassion* (Sankrit: *karuṇā*) which is the end of them all, or under the heading of *means*, for they are the essential means to enlightenment. *Wisdom* and *Compassion* or *Wisdom* and *Means* are constantly named together in the later Indian Buddhism. The first is tranquillity and the second is activity, loving activity for the welfare of all. But except in so far as they are realized by human endeavour, they both remain for Buddhism in the sphere of pure idea.

Compassion is sometimes conceived as the mere means to enlightenment, which at the last resort remains alone in wisdom, the wisdom of the void. This is truly a lonely summit, cut off by sheer precipices, and woe to those who climb it. On the mountain which should be our goal, and theirs too, he who is Perfect Wisdom remains eternally active through the means which he has eternally ordained. In practice many Buddhists have accepted this interpretation, and it is then that their chosen divinity makes up the deficit of lonely wisdom. You must have heard mention of one of the most popular of these, Avalokiteshvara, Lord of Mercy, who, like all the other great beings of Buddhism, who are strong to save, is the embodiment of an attribute of divinity, in his case, the compassionate gaze. To understand the relationship of a devout Tibetan to Avalokiteshvara, one must try to understand it in Buddhist terms. Most European Buddhists, who in any case normally dislike this sort of Buddhism, which they call corrupt, would assure you that, in any case, it is a mere idea, a support to be used and cast aside, when one has outgrown it. They would conceive in fact of the man as transcending the idea. But a believing Tibetan, of whatever spiritual capacity, does not reason thus, for he himself is mortal and subject to rebirth, but Avalokiteshvara has reached the goal and turns back ready to assist those who invoke his aid. At the same time it is the Perfection of Wisdom literature with its insistence on universal voidness which forms the doctrinal basis of Tibetan religion. But no one says, 'Avalokiteshvara does not really exist, so it is a waste of time to supplicate him.' The only Tibetans I have known to say this are those (and they are very few indeed) who, under western influence, have rejected their religion altogether, and replaced it by nothing better.

It seems that Christianity has not been the only one to suffer at the hands of expositors, who base their views on texts of their choice, and ignore the living traditions. For Buddhism is treated likewise by many neo-Buddhists. Oddly enough, a Catholic could probably accept and reinterpret far more of Buddhist practice than any European Buddhist can. Buddhist faith, devotion, moral discipline and religious zeal are worth more to their cause and to ours than all the books they have ever written. The texts are as they have received them, whereas their practice is what they continue to make of it themselves. The texts do not initially explain the practice. They merely serve its purpose. No text for instance will explain the real origin of Avalokiteshvara or of any of the great beings, but a vast number of liturgical texts exist in praise of them. It has been left to oriental scholars to search out their origins, and as I said above, they are generally the embodiment of aspects of divinity and buddhahood. There are names such as All-Good (*Samantabhadra*) Brilliance (*Vairocana*), Imperturbable (*Akshobhya*), Sweet-Voice (*Mañjughosha*), Boundless Life (*Amitāyus*). So much is involved, that it would be unwise for any missionary, perhaps, to be as bold in his identification of the God they unknowingly worship as was St Paul with the Athenians; but at least he may be assured of the right aptitude and disposition among these people, and, in the fullness of time, if he will use vast sympathy and understanding, nothing that is worth preserving will be lost.

It might seem that by suggesting these equations, I am minimizing the doctrinal differences. The doctrine is a vast subject, and I have only broached it in so far as it has immediate bearing on the moral problem, and even then scarcely at all. I have referred to the doctrine of impermanence very briefly. I have made but one fleeting reference to the doctrine of rebirth, which is another conviction fundamental to historical Buddhism. It has been possible to ignore it in this brief study, for it has less effect on one's attitude to the present life than one who is ignorant of the doctrine might suppose. It is taught for example that human rebirth, whence alone progress on the way towards enlightenment is normally possible, is a rare achievement. The chance is as remote as that of a turtle, who dwells at the bottom of the ocean and only comes to the surface once in a hundred years, putting its neck through a yoke, which has been thrown on the water and is carried this way and that by the waves. This simile is often used to urge profitable use of the human life that the Buddhist now possesses.

It should be clear from this brief survey that, for the Buddhist as much as for the Christian, morality involves something far deeper than a code of ten precepts. The vitality of both religions is rooted in a metaphysical reality. In the case of Christianity this reality is the Body of Christ; in the case of Buddhism it is the realization of enlightenment. It is at this point that we come to their fundamental difference. Christianity is essentially a God-given revelation historically conditioned by the one incarnation of Christ. Buddhahood is a timeless actualization of essential reality, realizable by man through his own striving in time. It will be clear therefore that Buddhism as an active religion must depend upon the development and the practice of suitable techniques. If final truth has to be won by one's own efforts, it is essential that one should know the best course to pursue. In the course of its long history new ways and new methods have been propounded. In most of them virtuous moral conduct has been a necessary preliminary. In a few of them moral conduct, just because of its subsidiary value, has been entirely by-passed. These latter however represent a peculiar form of Indian religious practice, and for the most part the noble eight-fold path of right views, right intention, right speech, right action, right livelihood, right effort, right mindfulness and right concentration, this path has provided the basis of Buddhist practice. At the same time the mere fact that some schools thought to transcend normal moral conduct does draw attention to its relative value. A good action in itself brings one not one jot nearer to buddhahood. Unless it is permeated by knowledge and confirmed by concentration, it might just as well never have been performed.

It is because nowadays so many men conceive religion to be just a matter of doing right or wrong that they are unable to recognize genuine religious practice when they see it. A monk appears a useless member of society compared with the preacher or the welfare-worker. It must be confessed that Buddhism has excelled in its monks and produced few preachers and perhaps still fewer welfare-workers. Indeed without monks there can be no Buddhism, just because it depends for its very existence upon men who are concerned with realizing its truth for themselves. Now perhaps it has been possible for Christianity with its reliance upon God-given grace to become less aware of the need for effort in the same direction. This was certainly not so through the early centuries and the Middle Ages, when Christianity spread and established itself by means of religious communities, who represented or strove to represent in their lives the full consequences of Christian revelation. Indeed when one makes an historical appreciation of Christianity, one finds that even in the use of the type of religious discipline and practice which transcends mere morality there is much that may be parallelled in Buddhism: the vows of poverty, of chastity and obedience, the use of fasting, not as an occasional convention, but as directed towards the acquisition of clarity of intellect, the watchful control of all actions and thoughts, meditations upon conventional forms and the use of repetitive invocations for the achievement of singleness of mind. In theory the Christian ascetic could never claim to have gained for himself sublime realization, but he can try to remove all impediments to the inflowing of divine grace. But to an outside observer the means and the result might seem to be very similar. Practices of this kind must in no wise be confused with their occasional by-product, visions and hallucinations, which are common features of all religions and which have sometimes been a snare of western mysticism.

If Christianity appears to lack vitality in the west, it may well be because too few Christians are attempting to realize its implications to the full. It all too easily gets bogged down in the territory of what is socially desirable.

While it seems unlikely that Christianity has anything essentially new to learn from Buddhism, there is much of which it might be profitably reminded by a study of this other religion. It is in some ways easier to learn from Buddhism, just because one is able to start completely afresh in one's appreciation of it, free from preconceptions and prejudices.

This study of Buddhist morality inevitably raises the final question of philosophical and theological foundation. Is the Ultimate Reality as understood by the Mahāyānist schools, and as the Buddhist contemplative seeks to experience it, negative or ultra-positive? Is the void what, at first sight, it appears, sheer non-entity, or is it a Reality so real that all contingent and finite beings are by comparison unreal and it therefore *is not* in the sense that they are?

It may be urged that since the mystic's experience is, as he himself insists, incommunicable to those who do not share it, the question is unanswerable. Mystical experience however is not wholly incommunicable. Otherwise mystics the world over would not be, as they have been, so lavish in communicating accounts of it. And mystical writings would be *wholly* unintelligible to their readers which obviously is not the case. Nor would it be possible to compare the teaching of one mystic with the teaching of another. The conclusion surely emerges that, although the experience in its concrete reality is incommunicable, the mystic can and does give us information about it, speaks significantly of it.

The unanimous testimony of Christian mystics, to speak first of them, is that the Divine Reality with which they experience a vital contact is indeed ultra-positive. Fullness of Being, of Good, of Truth, of Bliss. Nevertheless, since no image or concept can express Reality so transcendent, the mystic is driven to use negative language, to pile up the negations of Denys's Mystical Theology—denying even existence to God, to speak with Baker of the mystical union as a union of nothing with Nothing, to say with St Gregory the Great that man's final knowledge of God is 'to know that he cannot know God,' or with Abbot Chapman 'What do I mean by God? . . . I have no idea.' Why, one may well ask, shall the same negative language in the mouth of a Buddhist philospher or contemplative have a totally different significance? Why shall Nāgājuna's 'Void' be less positive than Baker's 'Nothing'?

As this paper has shown, this Buddhist doctrine of Ultimate Reality is the formulation not only of a noble and in many respects Christian morality, but of monastic lives spent in austerity and contemplation. Is it likely, is it even humanly possible, that all this should in fact be founded on a pure nihilism? Can union with nonentity or the search for it produce such fruits and provide such satisfaction to the human spirit?

This is not to say that the Buddhist formulation or even conceptualization is wholly acceptable. For the Jesuit student of *Vedānta*, Fr Johanns, has argued that though the doctrine of Godhead Brahma, taught by Śankara's *Advaita*, agrees with Catholic and Thomist theology, he misconceived the relation to that Godhead of creatures and not least of the human soul. We may perhaps think much the same of Mahāyāna Buddhism. But here also Absolute Divine Reality, in a word God, is truly and genuinely experienced. And in both cases it is known and experienced not as negative but as ultra-positive, not as unreality but as the sole Perfect and Absolute Beauty.

XX

JUDAIC MORALITY

by

Irene Marinoff

THE Christian who treats Judaic morality must beware of the danger of considering Judaism merely as a precursor of Christianity, atrophied since its advent, and condemned to lead a life of sterility until such time as the 'remnant of Israel' is gathered into the one fold. This is an oversimplification which cannot serve as a starting point for serious investigation. Judaic morality is a coherent system which has proved capable of determining the conduct of the, religiously, most highly gifted of peoples throughout the vicissitudes of a history unparalleled both in range and depth of experience, and at this very moment put to the test of a new and provocative situation.

Any outline of Judaic morality must necessarily be based on the fullness of orthodox belief and practice to the exclusion of progressives, reforming as well as liberal, and of conservatives. Both these are heresies from orthodox Judaism. The former deny that the whole of the Jewish Law is binding upon modern man. Consequently they have eliminated ritual law, at least in the home, and have rejected such fundamental tenets as the divine nature of the Sinaitic revelation and the belief in a personal Messiah with all its national implications. On the other hand the conservatives, who are mainly found in U.S.A., have divorced belief from practice. They combine full freedom of enquiry relating to Israel's creed and Israel's past with an observance of Jewish law, which they regard as the product of the collective experience of the Jewish people.

In an article on 'Reform and Liberal Judaism' in the *Jewish Chronicle*, March 25th, 1955, Sir Basil Henriquez gave a definition of Jewish Orthodoxy which may serve as a convenient starting point.

The Orthodox maintain that Judaism is a revealed religion and that that revelation is contained in the Pentateuch and the interpretation of the laws of the Pentateuch by rabbis and sages of all ages. The interpretation is contained in the Shulchan Aruch. Both the written Law and the interpretation of it in the oral Law are the word of God and must be obeyed implicitly, joyfully and lovingly by every Orthodox Jew, who may ask for an explanation of its meaning, but must not question its Divine Authority.

In Judaism as in Christianity the ultimate sanction of morality rests in God, who gave his commandments to Moses on Mount Sinai. But while for the Catholic Christian the significance of the Sinaitic Revelation by itself is exhausted in the recognition of the natural law, for the Jewish people this revelation has a far more intimate sense, which is related to their special destiny, for it singles them out to be in a unique manner witnesses to the sanctity of God and collaborators in his moral purpose for mankind which is closely bound up with the Messianic hope. On Sinai the Covenant God made with Abraham: 'Walk before me and be perfect' (Gen. 17:1), is re-enacted with all the descendants of Abraham. Here the Chosen People accept 'the Yoke of the Law', which, as the rabbis explain, was refused by all other nations. In doing so they were separated from the rest of mankind as 'a priestly kingdom and a holy nation' (Ex. 19:6), with the mission of converting the pagans to the practice of a morality which will suffice for them to fulfil the purpose of their creation—to become agents in the divine enterprise: 'co-workers with God towards the fulfilment of the purpose that He has for the individual, the race and humanity'.[1] The moral precepts of 'this religion of humanity', which was communicated to Noah, are seven in number, six prohibitions and one positive command. They run: abstention from (1) idolatry; (2) blasphemy; (3) incest; (4) murder; (5) theft; (6) the eating of a limb torn from a living animal; and, finally, (7) the command for the administration of justice.

It seems remarkable that these precepts should not have included an express command to believe in the one and only God. However, provided there is no idolatry, which Judaism condemns not so much as a false religion as because it is a false morality, humanity as a whole is not charged to accept the pure and sublime conception of Hebrew monotheism.[2] Only in the Messianic Age, when the Jews would be the priests of the universe, would all men be charged to do so.

[1] I. Epstein, *Judaism*, p. 8.   [2] *Ibid.*, p. 8.

The moral code of the Chosen People is far more comprehensive than the Judaic code for non-Jews, and embraces the whole of life. The reason for this lies in the unique manner of its promulgation. The repetition of the commandments and other judgements which occurs in Leviticus is punctuated with the affirmation: 'I am the Lord your God,' and the central Chapter (XIX) is prefaced by the words: 'And the Lord spoke to Moses, saying: Speak to all the congregation of the children of Israel and say to them: Be ye holy, for I the Lord your God am holy.' This holiness of God is conceived primarily as transcendence—the word *Kadosh* (holy) itself is derived from a root signifying 'to set apart', 'independence of all besides himself', and 'mastery over the universe'. Only secondarily are all those positive qualities, such as goodness, awful purity, justice and mercy, generally associated with holiness, attributed to him. Yahweh, whose name is never pronounced, is the *mysterium tremendum* the *Numinosum par excellence*. This transcendent God nevertheless entered upon a covenant with his humble creatures. He is the example set before Israel; and all the manifold laws and precepts which cover every possible thought, action and experience of human life are only a means of achieving that perpetual 'walking in the presence of God' which is the ideal of Jewish sanctity. Hence it is evident that for Judaic thought there can be no division between the secular and the sacred. Every activity has a religious significance; and morality and piety, in the sense of religious sentiment and practice, are identical. Before discharging his religious duties, the Jew is commanded to say: 'Blessed art Thou, O Lord our God, King of the Universe, who has hallowed us by thy Commandments.'

Considering this close tie between morality and religion it is understandable that Jewish moralists have never been much concerned with the philosophical bases of their ethics. Such questions as that of man's free will, of the nature of transgression, of the character of virtue, which occupied Greek and Christian thinkers, have never presented a real problem to the Jew. Believing as he does in divine retribution, as evidenced in the fourth commandment, he can and does derive from this idea the necessity of complete free will for man. Akiba's saying: 'All is determined, but liberty is given,' is often quoted; likewise the still more significant sentence: 'All things are in the hand of God save the fear of God'; and 'At man's birth God determines whether he is to be strong or weak, wise or foolish, rich or poor, but not whether he will be good or wicked.'[1] It also follows from this identification of morality and religion that every transgression assumes the nature of sin, and every good action (a *Mitzvah*-commandment) is the fulfilment of a divine precept carrying merit with it.

Before entering on a closer study of the principles and precepts of Judaic morality, it is essential to mention two characteristics of the Sinaitic revelation which were bound to influence the subsequent development of Judaic morality most profoundly. It is a matter of common knowledge that the Pentateuch contains not only general laws which are independent of time and place, but also numerous precepts and judgements which were to fashion the life of the people of Israel down to its minutest details. As a written law, delivered at a definite point in history, only the *principles of morality* which it contained could remain unchanged within the course of millennia, while their applications to a definite age and state of society were bound to become obsolete sooner or later.

The provisions which Leviticus contains for the maintenance of priests and Levites, the establishment of cities of refuge for those who had committed manslaughter, and certain marriage regulations inevitably lost their meaning even before the beginning of the Christian era. The most striking example of this is offered in the sacrificial system (the Sacrifice was frequently called a *Korban* which means 'nearness' and expressed the desire of a man to return to God), to the elaboration of which numerous chapters in Leviticus and Deuteronomy are devoted. When the Second Temple was destroyed in 70 A.D. all sacrifices ceased, and it is not uninteresting to note that after the establishment of the State of Israel in 1948, thoughtful Jews began to ask themselves the question what they should do if the ancient site of the Temple were restored to them, since animal sacrifices as demanded by the Written Law are no longer consonant with modern ideas and practices.

In order to prevent the Written Law from becoming petrified and sterile, the concept of an Unwritten or Oral Law, contained within the Written Law and going back to the Sinaitic revelation, was developed. By this means the static law was endowed with a dynamic quality and flexibility which enabled it to encompass more than three thousand years of history, and be applied to the most diverse situations. One of the most famous instances of this adaptation is the case of Rabbi Hillel of the first century B.C., who invented a legal device called Prosbol, to evade the observance of

[1] J. Bonsirven, *On the Ruins of the Temple*, p. 111.

the sabbatical year, commanded in Deuteronomy: 'At the end of every seven years thou shalt make a release: every creditor shall release that which he hath lent unto his neighbour. Of a foreigner thou mayest exact it, but whatsoever of thine is with thy brother, thine hand shall release.'

In consequence no Jew could ask payment of a debt from a fellow Jew in a Sabbath year. . . Now the Prosbol transferred the collection of the private creditor to the public authorities, who by legal fiction became the agents for the private creditor. A special clause was inserted in the deed by mutual agreement between borrower and lender that the debt was repayable even during the sabbatical year, and then the deed was registered in the court of public trustees, and thus Deuteronomy was evaded.[1]

The justification of this reinterpretation of the Written Law by means of the Oral Law was found in the words of Deuteronomy: 'For the precept which I command thee is not in heaven . . . but it is very nigh unto thee, in thy mouth and in thy heart' (30: 11–14). And Epstein adds, 'Yet it is the Mosaic Revelation that invests the teaching of the Oral Law with authority, and it is only in so far as the teachers and expounders of the Oral Law took the Mosaic Law as their basis, that their teachings are accepted as genuine and authoritative.'[2]

An unbroken chain of tradition stretches from Sinai to the present day, contributed to by judges and prophets, sages and rabbis. The three principles which guided the activities of the Rabbis after the age of the prophets had passed are as follows: 'Be deliberate in judgement,' 'Raise up many disciples' and 'Make a fence round the Torah.' By Torah is signified the whole of the Written and Oral Tradition, covering all religious, legal, ethical and historical teaching. What is meant by 'making a fence round the Torah' can be illustrated by the following example. The whole elaborate practice of orthodox Jews to this day, of having separate dishes and cooking utensils for the preparation of 'milk' and 'meat' foods goes back to the Biblical provision 'Thou shalt not seethe the kid in its mother's milk' (Ex. 23: 19).

It was the prophet Ezra who, realizing that the salvation of the exiles who had returned from Babylon depended on their acknowledgement of the Torah as the revelation of God's will for them, summoned the people and caused their leaders to sign a covenant to ensure the acceptance of the Torah as the constitution of the

[1] J. P. Arendzen, *Prophets, Priests and Publicans*, p. 165.   [2] *Judaism*, p. 87.

new community in Judea, twelve years after his own return from Babylon in 444 B.C. Ezra's work was followed by the Men of the Great Synagogue who endeavoured to teach and interpret the Torah in synagogues and schools. These were the 'scribes', i.e. professional class of lay theologians, scholars and lawyers, of the New Testament.

Two main methods of expounding the tradition were developed: firstly the running commentary on Biblical texts (the *Midrash–Quest*) and secondly the teaching independent of the text in the form of *Halachah* (walking i.e. in the ways of the Lord). If the commentary yielded legal teaching, it was termed *Midrash Halachah*, and if it took the form of non-legal, ethical, moral or devotional teaching, it was styled *Midrash Haggadah*. The earliest codification of *Halachic* lore goes back at least as far as the first century of the current era. As the process of interpreting the law was continued throughout the centuries, the material amassed since the last codification became so vast that new codifications had to be made. Famous among the early codifications is the *Mishnah*, or Repetition, of Rabbi Judah the Prince (135–217 A.D.) embracing the whole of the legal system up to that date. This is divided into six main divisions, dealing respectively with:

(1) Seeds; the agrarian laws; tithes and donations to priests, Levites and the poor; the sabbatical year; prohibited mixture in plants, animals and garments.

(2) Feasts: sabbaths, festivals and fast days; the ceremonies ordained, and the sacrifices to be offered on them. Special chapters are given to the Passover, the New Year's Feast, the Day of Atonement, Succoth and Purim.

(3) Woman: betrothal, marriage and divorce. Vows and obligations.

(4) Damages: this section includes the major portion of the civil and criminal law; ordinary money transactions; idolatry: witnesses; legal punishments and 'sentences of the Fathers'.

(5) Sacred things: sacrifices; first-born children, measurements and details of the Temple and its utensils.

(6) Purification: Levitical and hygienic laws; impure persons and things, and the methods for their purification.

Teachings external and additional to the *Mishnah* were crystallized in the *Gemarah*, and together these two codifications constitute the *Talmud*, which contains material of legal as well as non-legal character. Its method of instruction is by means of story, saga, legend, fable, parable, homily, maxim, proverb, wise saying. Its aim is to edify, inspire and elevate. The time consumed in the completion of the entire Talmud is stated to have been three hundred and eleven years. In its present form it consists of twelve folio volumes, containing the precepts of the Pentateuch with extended commentaries on them. Throughout the Middle Ages the Talmud was studied and gave rise to a series of new commentators and hence the necessity for a reassembling of the entire mass of material. The *Mishne Torah* or Second Law of Maimonides (1135–1204) was followed in the sixteenth century by the *Shulchan Aruch* (The Prepared Table) of Joseph Caro (1488–1545), printed in Venice in 1565, which together with a later commentary by a Polish rabbi is the latest authoritative code of Jewish Law (1578). Nor is there any reason to believe that the experience of emancipation at the turn of the nineteenth century and the recent establishment of the State of Israel will not give rise to renewed interpretations of the Law and, at some future date, lead to a new codification.

The Torah, the entire body of Judaic teaching, is the pivot round which the life of the orthodox Jew revolves. And it is the prayer of every Jew that he may have a share in the Torah and lead others to it as well. Every individual Jew is charged with the task of studying the Torah, and, by his own investigation, adding to the store of interpretation and deeper understanding of it. In actual fact the primacy of place in the Jewish hierarchy of values is assigned to the study of the Torah as against prayer, and it is possible to convert a synagogue into a house of study while the reverse is not permissible.

Hence the great respect enjoyed by the teacher or rabbi. The very title 'Rabbi' is equivalent to 'My Lord'. The teacher takes precedence to the father, for, as the rabbis say, 'both son and father owe respect to the teacher.' The loss of the teacher has to be repaired before the loss of the father, unless he be a rabbi himself, and the teacher's burden carried before the father's.

But apart from this corporate duty to study the Torah and enrich the tradition by one's own contribution, if possible, there is also an individual obligation to do so, as a means of sanctification. It is of the essence of Jewish belief that he who occupies himself with the Torah in the spirit of humility and sincere searching for truth will enter into communion with the Most High, or as the rabbinical saying goes: 'Even if one man study the Torah alone, *Shechinah*— the Presence of God—is with him.'

It is comparatively rare to read in the accounts of Judaism any reference to the unique and individual relationship that, by virtue of the sacraments, is possible between the creature and his creator, a relationship, which, in the Christian dispensation, seems to be the true well-spring of moral action, of the life of grace as opposed to the life 'under the Law'. The reason for this lies in the second characteristic of the Sinaitic revelation referred to above. On Mount Sinai the Law was given to Moses as a way of life for a people rather than for a number of isolated individuals. The use of the plural throughout is remarkable. And it is by no means insignificant that the very heart and centre of Judaism, the *Shema*, should use the first person plural, while the *Credo* of Christianity is pronounced in the first personal singular. The *Shema*, so called from the Hebrew word with which it opens, begins: 'Hear, O Israel, the Lord Our God the Lord is One' (Deut. 6: 4).

It is as a people that Israel was singled out by God, and the value of the individual is only secondary. This is evidenced in various passages in the Pentateuch, where through the mouth of Moses God speaks to the Chosen People as a whole. 'As the nations which the Lord destroyed at thy entrance, so shall you also perish, if you be disobedient to the voice of the Lord your God' (Deut. 8: 20).— 'Know therefore that the Lord thy God giveth thee not this excellent land in possession for thy justices, for thou art a very stiff-necked people' (Deut. 9: 6). Charity in the sense of almsgiving is considered a contribution towards the fulfilment of a common obligation, and the right to property is strictly limited by social considerations. In the nineteenth chapter of Leviticus provision is made for the poor. 'When thou reapest the corn of thy land, thou shalt not cut down all that is on the face of the earth to the very ground; nor shalt thou gather the ears that remain. Neither shalt thou gather the bunches and grapes that fall down in thy vineyard, but shalt leave them to the poor and the strangers to take' (vv. 9–10). And in the laws relating to war in the twentieth chapter of Deuteronomy, it is written: 'What man is there that hath planted a vineyard, and hath not as yet made it to be common, whereof all men may eat? Let him go and return to his house: lest he die in the battle, and another man execute his office' (v. 6). In connexion with the Prosbol mention has already been made of the sabbatical year (Lev. 25: 1ff). In the same chapter the fiftieth year of jubilee is instituted, in which remission, that is a general release and discharge from debts and bondage and a reinstating of every man in his former possessions, to all the inhabitants of the land is proclaimed. Even a slave is not absolute possession; if he is injured his master is bound to set him free. To the present day in liturgical prayer the corporate aspect is stressed before the private.

It is therefore evident that the main stream of Judaism flowed in its corporate life—though the people of Israel never lacked outstanding individuals. They had their great leaders, men of marked personality such as Moses and Joshua, their judges, kings, and prophets whose relationship with their God did not exhaust itself with a spirituality which was the outgrowth of their observance of the Law. They were mystics in the fullest sense of the word, and brought a gradual deepening of the conception of holiness and sin, redemption and messianic hope. The idea of Israel as a Holy People by virtue of the covenant was developed into that of Israel— the Bride of Yahweh chosen by Love. Nor did this mystical trend die with the last of the prophets, though we can only catch glimpses of it in the course of the centuries.

In the New Testament we meet figures such as Joseph, Anna, Simeon, and John the Baptist, deeply religious men and women 'walking before God' in humility and love, and at the same time devoted to the Temple worship and the religion passed on to them by their fathers. They bear witness to the existence of that charismatic religion which lies at the centre of every living institutional religion. The very fact that Mary, Mother of God, pronounced a vow of virginity proves that there must have been a mystical tradition—as does the existence of an esoteric sect such as the Essenes.

Jewish tradition has very definite teaching as to the nature of saintliness. A curious distinction is made between 'holiness' and 'saintliness'. Holiness demands the exact fulfilment of all that is prescribed in the Law; saintliness goes further; it is essentially an individual thing, demanding, in addition to the Law, observances which are not definitely prescribed. During the long centuries of Jewish history from Rabbi Akiba ben Joseph who was martyred under Hadrian in 135 A.D. to the mystics of the German school of crusading times (1150–1250)—from the school of Isaac Luria of Safed in Galilee in the sixteenth century to the Polish Chassidim led by Besht (Baal Shem-Tob, 1700–60), the 'Saint', the 'Chassid', repeatedly makes his appearance. And he is still to be found in the orthodox *Yeshivoth* (academies) of Jerusalem, while close by in the Hebrew University a chair of Jewish mysticism has been established.

However the student of the two streams of Judaism, the charis-

matic and the institutional, will come to the conclusion that during
the long centuries of dispersion following on the final separation of
Church and Synagogue, it was the external discipline demanded
by the Law which was best suited to preserve the people of Israel
in its integrity in the face of the most terrible persecutions and
temptations to apostasy. Nor can he fail to be impressed and edified
by the vast numbers of men, women and children prepared,
through their living of the Torah, for martyrdom 'for the sanctification of the Name'! It would indeed seem high time to revise the
opinion still current among Catholics that with the rejection of the
Redeemer by the high priests and members of the Sanhedrin together with a rabble such as will assemble in any capital of the
world at festive times, the well-springs of Jewish piety dried up,
leaving nothing but mere formalism and casuistry. One does not
go to one's death for an empty formula.

Before endeavouring to extract the principles of Judaic morality
from the entirety of the Written and Oral tradition it must be borne
in mind that although according to Jewish thought mankind is
divided into Jew and non-Jew (son of Noah) this division has only
a religious significance. There is no question of there being two
moralities, one for the Jew and another for the non-Jew. In Numbers (15: 15) we read: 'There shall be one law and judgement both
for you and for them who are strangers in the land.' In Leviticus
(19: 33-4) the reason for this injunction is given: 'If a stranger
dwell in your land and abide among you, do not upbraid him: But
let him be among you as one of the same country; and you shall love
him as yourselves: for you were strangers in the land of Egypt. I
am the Lord your God.' As the Jew, when still in possession of the
Holy Land, acknowledged the same law for the stranger and himself, so he readily submitted to the law of the land of his domicile
during the ages of dispersion. The rabbinical dictum: 'The law of
the state is law', enabled him to live as a citizen of other countries,
while his private life and religious obligations continued to be regulated by the Torah. It is only recently since the establishment of the
State of Israel that a number of questions, which were of no immediate urgency for nearly two thousand years, have arisen and
demand settlement. I am referring to the central problem whether
Israel will be a theocracy or a secular, modern democratic state.

As we have seen, the highest moral value for the Jew is holiness
which is identified with complete observance of the Torah. However this is only a very summary way of stating the case. Judaic

teaching does not ignore the two facts: (*a*) that, as the rabbis put it, there are seventy aspects to the Torah, and (*b*) that of its six hundred and thirteen commandments only about a hundred affect the life of the ordinary Jew. Nor is mere external observance of the Torah intended. 'The Almighty requires the heart' is a frequent saying—similarly the other, 'Love is at the beginning and at the end of the Torah.' For an epitome of the Jewish ideal of morality we must turn to Micah. 'To do justice, shew mercy and walk humbly before thy God' (6: 8). Another rabbinical saying is 'The world stands on three things: Judgement, truth and peace.'

The Judaic conception of justice is closely bound up with the idea of divine justice. 'Each receives his measure according to his measure', is a saying that is often repeated, and though the reward is frequently conceived as due on earth, there is a strong tradition that the true and final retribution is reserved for the beyond. Moreover stress is laid on the necessity of pursuing the good for the love of God and in submission to the holy will. The following rabbinical saying, attributed to Antigonus of Socho, expresses this aspect of the question: 'Be not like slaves who serve their masters with a view to a reward: but be like slaves who serve their master without desire for reward: and let the fear of heaven be upon you.'

The God of Justice demands that those who worship him should seek to safeguard the legal claims and moral rights of their fellow men (*Mishpat*). In the course of time the Old Testament practice of justice (*Mishpat*): 'An eye for an eye and a tooth for a tooth', which was in itself an advance upon indiscriminate retribution, developed into something higher, into righteousness (*Zedakah*). In the words of Dr Epstein, 'Jewish ethical teaching holds up as the rule of conduct the principle whereby man is urged not to insist on his own rights but to act "within the margin of judgement". This principle stands at the border line between justice (*Mishpat*) and its higher synonym, righteousness, *Zedakah* (derived from a root meaning victorious) . . . which transforms the negative concept of justice into a positive moral virtue, overcoming all presumptuous self-seeking, and *victoriously* at work. Whilst justice is one of three things without which human society cannot exist, righteousness is fundamental in the idea of God's Holiness as well as the duties God requires of men'.[1]

This righteousness is fulfilled in that love of our neighbour which

[1] *Judaism*, p. 19.

finds its expression in 'the practice of goodly deeds' of which the following are instances:

(1) Dowering the bride;
(2) Visiting the sick;
(3) Paying the last respects to the dead;
(4) Advancing a loan free of interest.

Charity in the sense of almsgiving is above all the discharge of a common obligation. 'The poor in Jewish thought have a claim to support from the more fortunate as a *matter of right*, the "haves" being regarded as mere trustees appointed by Providence on behalf of the "have-nots".'[1] In the words of King David: 'Who am I and what is my people, that we should be able to promise thee all these things? All things are thine: and we have given thee what we received of thy hand' (1 Para. 29: 14).

Man's duty to himself is expressed in the words of Rabbi Hillel, 'If I am not for myself, who is for me; and if I am only for myself, what am I? If not now, when then?'

Above justice and truth it is 'peace' that ranks highest among the virtues. The idea of *Shalom* is suggestive of complete integration realized through the performance of the divine will as expressed in the various commandments and precepts. It is achieved by that self-control which, without falling into the excess of asceticism, enjoys the good things of this world without becoming subject to them. It may seem strange to Catholic ears that abstention from anything not proscribed by the Law is accounted a sin. 'A man is to give account in the hereafter for permissible pleasures from which he abstained.'[2]

At the present time the entire structure of Judaism is subjected to the most searching of tests through the impact of newly acquired statehood. It is not as though moral principles themselves could be changed. But the morality of the Jew is so closely connected with his entire *Weltanschauung*, which includes the belief in a Messianic Kingdom for this world, that the reality of the establishment of an independent state is bound to have a profound effect. The moral tradition which has so long operated in vacuo without nationhood to sustain it is now to be applied to an entirely new set of circumstances. Long cherished belief is faced with fulfilment, and implementation is demanded in the place of hope. In this situation it is understandable that the ultra-orthodox Jew will reject the modern State of Israel on the grounds that it is not founded by the Messiah

[1] *Ibid.*, p. 20. [2] *Ibid.*, p. 28.

and debases the sacred language of the Scriptures to the vile currency of secular traffic. On the other hand 'the Progressive' will tend to shed all remnants of belief and endeavour to anchor the unity of the people in realities such as a common land, a common history, a common language. It would be irresponsible to make any prognosis of future developments at this early stage. I should like to close this paper with a parable taken from the Talmud which is of especial interest to the Christian. It is called: 'The Bride and the Bridegroom.'

There was once a man who pledged his dearest faith to a maiden, beautiful and true. For a time all passed pleasantly, and the maiden lived in happiness. But then the man was called from her side; he left her; long she waited, but he did not return. Friends pitied her and rivals mocked her; tauntingly they pointed at her, and said, 'He has left thee; he will never come back.' The maiden sought her chamber, and read in secret the letters which her lover had written to her, the letters in which he promised to be ever faithful, ever true. Weeping she read them, but they brought comfort to her heart; she dried her eyes and doubted not. A joyous day dawned for her; the man she loved returned and when he learned that others had doubted and asked her how she had preserved her faith, she showed his letters to him, declaring her eternal trust.

If it is of the essence of love to do the will of the Beloved, wherein, then, has Israel failed?

XXI

A SCIENTIST'S APPROACH TO MORALITY

by

E. F. Caldin

SUMMARY

IT seems that a scientist who approaches the study of Christian morality has some important advantages derived from his experience of scientific method, though he may also have acquired some disabilities from the particular climate of thought in which western scientists are mostly brought up. From scientific method, if he treats it as a microcosm of rational method, he can learn the right approach to moral philosophy; he will expect an account of ethics based on rational interpretation of experience. If he appreciates the evidence for the rational nature of man, he will reject the view that a rational ethic is impossible. If he recognizes that moral concepts are *sui generis* and cannot be reduced to any other kind, he will not be impressed by attempts to base ethics on science. He will see that there are genuine questions about ends and means in human life, which need careful reflection; that the long tradition of moral philosophy, from Socrates onwards, has been grappling with real problems which are not of a scientific kind. Finally he may come to see that in Christian morality the new element of revelation introduces a unique kind of knowledge, and that through the grace of God this is a morality that we can live by.

I

LET us suppose that a scientist, a real scientist permeated by the spirit of science, is induced to leave his laboratory and consider the subject of ethics. We will suppose that he has not previously dabbled in philosophy or theology. He will approach his new study with the confidence of one who feels himself to be part of the great living tradition of scientific enquiry, whose results are daily verified in practice, and whose method is daily shown to be successful in solving scientific problems. He is not afraid of abstract questions, because he has been trained to think in abstract terms; he approaches them as one born to command their solution. Altogether he is intellectually a man of hope, not of scepticism. He realizes too that the mainspring of science is the unprejudiced desire for truth and understanding; he knows that he must uphold high standards of intellectual impartiality, and do his best to exclude wishful thinking, deceptive rhetoric and irrelevant emotion. His experience of research has bred in him the habit of working from direct evidence so far as possible, rejecting hearsay and unverified statements. He knows that a beautiful theory can be wrecked by a single ugly fact, so that he must respect the evidence, all the evidence, and only the evidence. He will therefore naturally approve an ethic that is based on fact, on the nature of the human situation. This will have a further advantage to him in that, in his scientific experience, facts can be agreed upon by all, so that he expects an ethic grounded on fact to have a clear, agreed and irrefragable basis. The belief that the facts of the human situation can be made as clear to all men as the facts of science is indeed too simple-minded, but at least it may lead to a hopeful and positive approach to the enquiry. Nor need it necessarily lead to an aggressive over-optimism. A scientist knows that science was not built in a day, that it is a cumulative affair, advancing from generation to generation; and his ideal of a branch of study, if he reflects, is probably that of a cumulative and co-operative enterprise in which new territory is continually conquered while the ground won in earlier advances is consolidated.

Our scientist will hope, then, to reach an ethic based on facts. He will, moreover, be predisposed by his scientific training to seek a *rational* ethic, constructed by reason working on experience; an ethic which has a clearly articulated structure and can be applied by reason to particular cases. By contrast, in our society many people base their conduct not on reasoned principles, but on sentiment. It seems fair to say that in modern England practical decisions are very commonly based on family sentiment, for example, or patriotic sentiment, or gentlemanly sentiment, or proletarian sentiment—much more often than on a reasoned view of the nature and destiny of man, or on contemplation of a divine model. No doubt these judgements of sentiment have an element of reason in them, but it is often so hidden and hedged about as not to be easily accessible to counter-arguments which might well be decisive in a truly reasonable consideration. This reliance on sentiment affects us all, to a greater or less extent. It is hardly surprising therefore that our practical maxims are sometimes inconsistent with each other and that our social relations, for instance, are governed in practice by an uneasy mixture of 'Love your neighbour' with 'Look after Number One.' As against this hotch-potch of maxims applied according to convenience, a scientist's instinct is for an ethic that is universal and self-consistent, applicable at all times and to everyone, without privilege or exception. Such an ethic must be a rational one; an orderly affair of principles and applications, the principles based ultimately on facts of experience.

Again, our scientist, just as he does not want action to be isolated from fact and reason, will not be satisfied if principles are divorced from action. He will insist that the two must be in harmony; action must be in accord with principles, and principles must be learned through action. At least, this is what he will say if he makes use of the example set by scientific life, in which experiments are undertaken in the light of previous knowledge, and knowledge is based on the results of previous experiments. In any rational practical activity, thought leads to action, and action enriches thought, so that the two must be kept in unison. This is the belief behind the scientist's view, and it is a belief fundamental to Christian ethics. In this respect, as in others, scientific work is a microcosm of rational life in general. Ethics, in the Christian tradition, is concerned ultimately with practice, with life; it gives us reasoned principles on which to base our practice. When Karl Marx said 'Hitherto philosophers have only interpreted the world; the point is to change it,' he was stating a temptation that always besets intellectuals: it is easier to analyse a situation than to try to improve it. But this criticism does not invalidate the great tradition of Christian morality, which has always insisted on the unity of thought and action.

II

So FAR the approach of our hypothetical scientist to ethics would be recognized by Catholic thinkers as perfectly sound in its general outline. Admittedly the scientist we have imagined is of a type not to be found everywhere. He is a genuine scientist, not a camp-follower of science. He has an open mind, prepared to admit that there are problems other than those of science. He is able, as few are in practice, to transfer to other fields the training in rational procedure with which science has equipped him. None the less, our scientist is not wholly a creature of the imagination; his good qualities are simply those of the honest scientist, and are possessed in greater or less degree by the great majority of scientists. Such men possess a large part of the preliminary equipment for the study of ethics.

A trained scientist, however, is seldom without tacit assumptions about questions other than those which are his professional concern. Here the difficulties begin, for often his assumptions have not been examined with the critical attention, based on sound training in the relevant methods, which they deserve. Let us first consider the scientist's approach to philosophical ethics, leaving questions concerned with revelation until later.

In the first place, the ordinary western scientist today lives in an intellectual milieu that may present him with certain strong temptations to abandon altogether the hope of a rational ethic. Some of these temptations come from philosophers, such as the fashionable school of linguistic analysts, who are often believed by scientists to have shown that ethical statements are meaningless. Others come from ideologies, of which the most obvious is Marxism. Although Marx himself was full of moral fervour and his works abound in moral judgements, the effect of Party membership seems to be to make a man less and less aware of morality, because an action is judged not on its own merits but in terms of its contribution to the Party's cause. These difficulties are discussed elsewhere in this volume,[1] and so I leave them aside, merely remarking that scientists seem to be particularly susceptible to them. I pass on to certain difficulties in the way of a rational ethic that appear to arise from the results of the sciences themselves.

Each of the great branches of science—physical, biological and psychological, dealing respectively with inanimate, animate and human beings—has in its time given rise to such difficulties. When the Newtonian physics first caught the imagination of Europe, in the eighteenth century, the materialistic thought of such men as Diderot, La Mettrie and Holbach appealed for support to the new mechanical picture of the world. If the heavens are a great machine, may not man too be nothing more than a machine? The appeal to the imagination is strong, so strong that it may overbear the intellect, but there is a fallacy. The argument from analogy in the simple form used is a weak one, and the analogy breaks down just where the weight is put on it; man has characteristics that a machine shows no signs of having, such as the inner experience of intellec-

[1] See 'Communist Morality', p. 298.

tual knowledge and of moral responsibility. Science itself illustrates at every turn rational activity, actions directed consciously towards distant goals for stated reasons; and such actions are necessarily done by men, not by their tools. Again, nineteenth-century biology recalled western thinkers to a realization of man's place in nature and his kinship with the animals, and it was easy for materialists to claim that he was no more than an animal. Twentieth-century psychology threw up a similar notion in the behaviourism of the twenties and thirties. The argument rests again on pure analogy, and biological and psychological materialisms fail in the same way as physical materialism because they omit the unique attributes of man.

In recent years, the development of mechanical and electronic devices for computation and for the control of machines has given a new imaginative power to the notion that man is a machine. The new devices can handle mathematical computations and also logical problems such as chess-playing very much more quickly than men can; and striking analogies have been found between the modes of operation of such machines and of the human brain. The Christian naturally accepts these scientific advances, and agrees that when a man is reasoning his brain may very well work in a way more or less analogous to that of a calculating machine. But, as so often happens, he has also to point out that the materialistic interpretation placed on this conclusion is not really justified. The brain is a bodily organ, a material system, and it is not altogether surprising (though it is scientifically very intriguing) that its operations when its owner is reasoning are analogous to those of other material systems designed to help him with the same job. In this respect the brain is a tool of its owner just as a machine is, and if we are to ascribe to the tool what is due to its owner, then, as Sir Thomas Browne remarked, 'let our hammers rise up and boast they have built our houses, and our pens receive the honour of our writings.' It is the owner's awareness of what he is doing that makes him different from his tool.[1] Reasoning is not, moreover, the main or most characteristic element in human knowledge. Recognizing the universal in the particular thing, and becoming aware of the meaning of a sign, are two obvious elements in our conscious experience which are by their nature beyond the reach of any non-conscious entity (though machines can be devised that will simu-

[1] The relation of machines to brains and mind is a subject much canvassed at present. See e.g. *British Journal for the Philosophy of Science.*

late them fairly well as far as behaviour goes); these are far more important in human knowledge than the semi-mechanical operations of logical ratiocination.[1] We have space only to glance at these problems. The point here is simply that while it is in accord with the evidence of the physical and biological sciences to speak of the *analogy* of a man to a machine, to postulate their *identity* is to go beyond that evidence and come in conflict with other evidence (from reflection on our own and others' operations) that man is an intellectual and responsible being, as well as an animal and a physical object.

The psychological sciences also have contributed influences that have made scientists less ready to recognize the ideal of a rational ethic. By the 'psychological sciences' I mean here all those that deal primarily with man, including anthropology and comparative religion as well as psychology in the normal usage of the term. These sciences, as C. H. Waddington noted in a discussion of science and ethics,[2] have seemed to destroy the *universality* of moral principles and so to make a rational ethic impossible. Anthropology 'tended to show that ethical beliefs differ extremely from culture to culture and can therefore have no general validity'. Psycho-analysis 'seemed to imply that man's ethical system is a mere product of his early sexual reactions to family life, and has no more generality than that has'. As a physical scientist I have no real competence to judge whether these generalizations are good science; but certain methodological criticisms are fairly obvious. First, with regard to the objection from anthropology, it must be noted that ethical principles are very difficult to state correctly, even with the help of a highly-developed intellectual tradition, and that no apologist for universally applicable moral principles need claim that they have been universally discovered. As to the second objection, it is important to realize that the question of the psychological *origin* of beliefs is not the same as the question of their *validity*. For instance, true beliefs may be inculcated in childhood by authority, but recognized as rational only much later in life. Children believe the multiplication table on authority, and their belief is correct, though

[1] On universals and particulars see e.g. M. Pontifex, *The Existence of God* (Longmans, 1953). On the interpretation of signs in human knowledge, see M. C. D'Arcy, *The Nature of Belief* (Sheed and Ward, 1934).

[2] *Science and Ethics*, by C. H. Waddington and others (George Allen and Unwin, 1942), p. 1. Dr Waddington argues in favour of a rational ethic, but thinks that it can be based on science. See below, page 279.

its origin is not due to rational interpretation of evidence. So a non-rational origin of moral beliefs—whether those beliefs arise from the child's own reactions or are inculcated authoritatively by parents—does not necessarily imply that they have no rational basis.

The objections, then, seem to be valid not against ethics in general, but against a too facile ethic. From this point of view, we can learn something from them. The anthropological evidence certainly shows that it is very difficult for man to reach explicitly the fundamental moral principles. Western thinkers, steeped in the tradition of Greek thought, have often forgotten the immense difficulty and effort of reaching the principles by which they have lived. Anthropology recalls us to a realization of the intellectual indigence of primitive man, of the uncertainty and inaccuracy of his moral beliefs, and of the need to treasure the hard-won tradition that we have inherited. The psychological evidence, for its part, suggests that rational moral behaviour may be more difficult and more rare than some had suspected. Fully free and human actions (that is, actions directed deliberately towards a clearly envisaged purpose) may possibly be a smaller proportion of our doings than we supposed; we should perhaps see them as strenuous victories over habit, laziness or self-love. Motives are usually more mixed than we care to think, and the motive of pure love can only be achieved by arduous self-discipline. Catholic ascetical writers have always recognized the great power of self-love and the ineradicable root of pride in all men,[1] and to them the impact of psychological discovery is much less than to those who believed in the perfectibility of man by his own rational efforts. None the less, it is salutary to recall the weakness of man's will, as manifested in psychology, as well as the darkness of his intellect as suggested by anthropology. These psychological sciences thus illustrate vividly the mental situation of fallen man, just as evolutionary biology called attention to his place in the world of organisms. Interpreted in this way, they illustrate our need of redemption. But this is to touch on questions belonging to revelation, whereas we have still not finished with moral philosophy.

III

LET us suppose now that our scientist has rejected the attempts to persuade him that there cannot be a rational ethic. It does not follow that he will at once turn to philosophy and theology for his ethic; instead, he may hope to extract it from science itself. This is indeed

[1] Cf. e.g. Walter Hilton, *The Scale of Perfection.*

the position of certain influential scientists who are aware of the need for moral ideals and seek to fill the contemporary vacuum by an 'evolutionary ethics' claiming support from science. They wish to say that the good for man is the goal of his evolution, and that the right is whatever brings him nearer to it. The direction of evolution is taken as a natural fact, which is to be discovered by the scientific method. Thus Dr Julian Huxley in *Evolution and Ethics*[1] appears to claim that the theory of evolution gives new grounds for the view that the development of the individual, in and through society, is the great principle of ethics. And Professor Waddington[2] regards ethical principles as derived from experience of the nature of society; his view is that society develops naturally in a certain direction, and the ethical principles which it adopts are those which help along development in that direction.

A difficulty at once arises if by 'evolution' we understand simply biological evolution, for that would exclude the special characteristics of man, of which morality is one, and it is hard to see how anything relevant to the development of man's moral nature could emerge. But let us consider the argument in its stronger form, and take 'evolution' to mean the evolution of human societies, their laws, customs, rituals, beliefs and means of livelihood. We will leave aside the difficulty that the intensive study of primitive societies has shown that different peoples have not passed through the same stages of development in the same order, and that the different elements in the way of life of a given people are seldom at the same stage of development. The great question is, such difficulties aside, whether the scientific study of the direction of change of human societies could in principle yield a firm basis for ethics. Supposing that we can see a clear direction of change—from social to individual responsibility, for example, or from conventional uniformity to adventurous diversity—can we claim that it is necessarily the direction of ethical improvement, simply because it is the actual direction? When we recognize as morally better a society in which there is realized a greater degree of personal liberty, security and opportunity, is it because we compare it with the direction of change as noted by sociologists, or on independent grounds? And when we ask a moral question—for instance, whether we may legiti-

---

[1] *Evolution and Ethics*, by T. H. Huxley and Julian Huxley (London, Pilot Press Ltd, 1947), pp. 124, 131 seq.

[2] *Science and Ethics*, by C. H. Waddington and others (London, George Allen and Unwin, 1942), Chapter 1.

mately kill the old or the incurably sick—do we deduce the answer from the trend of social change? In other words, is the historical process (in the broadest sense) always in the right direction?

It seems to me that the problem has only to be put in such terms for the answer to be clear. We do not believe that the historical process must, simply because it is the historical process, be in the right direction. Just as we stigmatize as immoral certain particular developments, such as the re-emergence of slavery in modern totalitarian states, so we make universal ethical judgements about social change. On slavery, for instance, we should have to make the same judgement even if the whole human race accepted it both in theory and in practice. The grounds for our judgement would not be altered at all. Our consideration is not based on the ground that slavery is out of step with evolution, but on the ground that it is in conflict with the obligations of man to man, implicit in the nature of man; or (in other language) that it violates essential rights of man. Now these are moral concepts, and we have made a moral judgement. Such a judgement is a statement of a different kind from a scientific statement. You cannot deduce the statement 'No man ought to be enslaved' from any descriptive statements, such as 'All men are enslaved' or 'No man is enslaved' or 'Fewer men are enslaved than formerly.' The statements are of different kinds. Similarly you cannot deduce a statement about what *ought* to be happening in human evolution from a bare statement about what *is* happening.[1] Here I am simply recalling a distinction that has been clearly stated many times by moral philosophers. Moral concepts are *sui generis*; the truth of moral principles cannot rest on grounds that are not moral. Scientific statements, then, cannot by themselves form a basis for ethics; they are not statements of the right kind.[2] If we try to substitute scientific statements for ethical ones, we shall find we have simply omitted the ethical element.[3]

It may seem queer at first sight to say that anthropology cannot be a source of ethical principles, since all agree that it is concerned

[1] You would need an additional premiss such as that the historical process in its general lines is divinely guided. The secular belief in evolution as a guide may thus be a disguised form of belief in divine providence.

[2] The kind of fact that can be used as a basis for morality is discussed in the chapter on 'The Philosophical Concept of Morality', pp. 8 ff.

[3] For instance, Professor Waddington in his effort to find a scientific basis for ethics (*Science and Ethics*, p. 18), substitutes psychological *compulsion* for moral obligation. The two are not equivalent; a man may neglect his moral obligations, while psychological compulsions put his actions under constraint.

with human acts, just as much as is ethics. How can there be two independent branches of study with the same subject-matter? The answer is that the subject-matter is regarded from two different points of view. The anthropologist as such is interested in human actions from the point of view of correlation; from particular actions which he observes, he proceeds to generalize about acts that are typical of the society he is describing, and he tries to see how these types of behaviour fit into the pattern of the working society. This is typical of the point of view of science, which is that of description and correlation. The moral philosopher, on the other hand, is not as such concerned with these problems; he will treat the anthropologists' data on human behaviour as he treats his observations of his own and others' behaviour, as material for reflection upon the moral life and the correct analysis of it. His point of view is different, and his method also, because he is trying to answer different questions from those of the scientist. A single subject-matter is being examined from two different angles.[1]

We conclude, then, that there is no scientific short cut to solutions of the problems of ethics, no by-pass round the intricacies of moral philosophy. The method of ethics is not that of science. None the less, the scientist should not feel that he can give no help with ethical problems. The anthropological scientist has a special rôle, not indeed that of discovering moral principles by scientific methods, but that of providing material for moral philosophers to reflect upon; the analysis of moral concepts is a complex and arduous task, and to contemplate a wide variety of data may be helpful to those engaged upon it.[2] But all scientific work contributes to the knowledge we need for the right *application* of moral principles. For science tells us what the results of certain actions will be; and this is important in practical decisions, for an action cannot be right if its foreseen consequences are on balance bad. For instance, physicists can tell us what the radio-active products from ten thousand hydrogen bombs would be, and biologists can tell us that these would make the survival of man on the earth at least problematical; this is a factor to be considered in judging whether a war in which these weapons were used could be a just war. Similarly if we have decided that a certain end is desirable, we may have to turn to

[1] For a distinction and comparison of methods, see my *Science and Christian Apologetic* (Blackfriars Publications, 1951) and *The Power and Limits of Science* (Chapman and Hall, 1949), Chapter IX.

[2] Cf. A. Macbeath, *Experiments in Living* (Macmillan, 1952).

science to tell us the best means; obvious examples are the reduction of disease by the new antibiotics and insecticides. Science by its prediction of consequences may thus be very important in practical moral action. To play this useful and necessary rôle, rather than to posture as the source of ethical principles, is the true part of science.[1]

IV

CHRISTIAN morality is not just moral philosophy; it goes beyond, intellectually in virtue of Revelation, practically in virtue of divine grace. These new features, revelation and grace, introduce new elements foreign to scientific work, and our enquiring scientist will demand explanations of them.

Assent is given to the divine revelation, conveyed through the Scriptures and the Church, on grounds quite different from those for scientific beliefs. When we believe a revealed truth, we may not have evidence that directly supports it; we believe it on the authority of a witness who is reliable because divine. When for instance we believe that the death of the body is the beginning of a new life of a particular kind, we do so not because we have any evidence bearing directly on the question, but because God tells us so, through Christ and the Church. Such an appeal to the authority of a witness has some analogy with the method of the historian, who necessarily relies on the testimony of witnesses (of varying reliability); but it is not a procedure characteristic of science. It is true that a scientist will appeal to experimental results obtained by others, but this is to save time, not because any one scientist has insight of a kind denied to his fellows. Thus a scientist's work predisposes him to be suspicious of appeals to authority. In the natural sciences this is very proper, because there is no competent authority available.[2] But this attitude cannot be assumed to be the right one towards all kinds of knowledge. For knowledge by revelation, it is claimed that the authority is divine, therefore to be believed.

---

[1] Professor Dingle, in his essay on the subject in *The Scientific Adventure* (Pitman, 1952), sees clearly that ethical questions cannot be solved by the methods of science; but he jumps to the conclusion that they cannot be solved rationally at all, only by appeal to some authority. This is often true of practical problems, but it is not true that there can be no philosophical ethics. The role of authority is considered briefly below, in section iv.

[2] Although the contrary has occasionally been supposed, notably by those who condemned Galileo's Copernican views and those who supposed biological evolution to be in conflict with Genesis.

K

Nor is this asserted without evidence. Faith is not blind trust, it is properly an act which is intellectual and certain. The authority of Christ and the Church is seen to be divine by recognition of the meaning of signs. Such signs are miracles, prophecies, the life and character of Christ as portrayed in the Gospels, and the essential characteristics of the life of the Church. By interpreting these signs we recognize their divine origin. The theme cannot here be treated adequately;[1] but the point at present is simply a methodological one, to show that there is an appeal to evidence, not a mere exhortation to fall back on our emotions or imagination. The argument consists in pointing to certain data, with an invitation to regard them as signs and interpret them. This may seem at first sight to be a form of argument foreign to science, but reflection will show that interpretation is in fact very familiar to scientists; we speak of 'interpreting' experimental results in terms of theories, and the expression is correct, for we treat the observations as signs of objects—atoms, waves and so on—which we could not otherwise be aware of. Thus the argument offered in revealed truth is not only intellectually respectable but has analogies with scientific argument; and there is nothing incompatible between rejecting authority in science and accepting it in fields where human enquiry alone cannot give us certainty. Acceptance of the teaching of a competent authority is here the rational approach. With this goes acceptance of the grace of God, which alone enables us to live up to the ethical ideals that revelation puts before us.

The submission to God of the intellect and the will in Christian life calls for different modes of thought from those which are used in science, and different practical attitudes from those which science by itself might encourage. It is not incompatible with science, because science is a different kind of knowledge, concerned to answer different questions, and cannot support the whole framework of life. A Christian who is a scientist need have no reservations about scientific knowledge, and has even greater incentives than the non-believer to maintain scientific integrity. None the less, the different climates of thought may well produce tensions in the life of a Catholic scientist, and these may be painfully felt by a scientist seeking faith. But tensions are to be expected, indeed welcomed; tensions between action and contemplation, thought and sensation,

---

[1] Cf. Masure, *La Grand' route Apologetique* (Paris, Beauchesne, 1937); M. C. D'Arcy, *The Nature of Belief* (Sheed and Ward, 1934); J. Coventry, *Faith seeks Understanding* (Sheed and Ward, 1951).

rule and spontaneity, are essential if the mind is alive. Such tensions do not necessarily impose an undue strain, any more than does the tension of a muscle in a healthy body. Ideally they imply a poised equilibrium of forces, a balance of interests, though the ideal may be hard for us to attain. To use the right method for a given problem, to put on the right thinking-cap—this is the aim, rather than to try to reduce every kind of problem to the scientific kind. If one line of thought masters the others and shuts them out, the whole personality suffers.

The scientist's danger, like the danger of other learned professions, is obsession with one mode of thought; this is what lies behind the antagonism shown by some scientists to moral philosophy and more particularly to Christianity. There is a solution, which lies outside science altogether. It is to interest one's self in all sorts of problems; to keep in touch with the great human realities of birth, growing up, love and death; and to study so far as one can the best that has been thought about the relations of nature, man and God, whether in imaginative literature or in philosophy and theology.

XXII

SECULAR MORALITY

by

John Coulson

ALTHOUGH secular morality is a difficult term to define at all precisely, most of us have a rough idea of what we mean by it. The dictionary says that to be secular is to be 'concerned with the affairs of this world, to be worldly ... sceptical of religious truth or opposed to religious education', and this is the sense in which the word is used when we say that secular morality is that of those who can find no satisfactory connexion between human behaviour and the purpose of human existence. At the same time it must be distinguished from more positive moralities such as Communism, for it is fundamentally agnostic. Baffled by its vagueness, the Christian frequently underestimates its prevalence; especially as there is still much lip-service paid to the opinion—even by unbelievers—that a man must believe in something before he will accept the inevitable restrictions of a moral code. If this opinion is true, how does our secular society stand, composed as it is of an increasing number of unbelievers and, what is worse, of a majority who seem indifferent to any values which conflict with material success? Perhaps it is unlikely to last much longer, for if a society is to remain in being at all, it must rest on a generally accepted code of behaviour, since, without it, government—even in a police state—would be impossible. But, obstinately, our secular society goes on surviving. No longer particularly Christian, it has survived two great wars, so it is not unreasonable to suggest that it possesses some code of behaviour which works, however illogical or imperfect it may appear to be when it is examined.

Does this mean that morality without religion is possible after all, or is the real reason that our society only remains in being because it is living off a capital which is slowly diminishing and cannot be renewed except by the means which formed it? Is the present-day Englishman who is not a Christian regulating his life by standards which have been uncritically derived from the Christian values passed on to him by his forefathers? This is a point of view which Christians are only too ready to accept, for at first the differences between secular and Christian moral practice appear to be slight. Directly, however, we examine particular cases, difficulties arise.

Take social betterment for instance. Christians and secularists agree that we have an obligation to make the world a better place to live in. Old age pensions, slum clearance, prison reform—all these have found Christian leadership; but it is when such reforms are achieved that differences begin to appear. They appear when the question is asked: 'Why did we fight?' and the vague answer 'In order to progress' satisfies very few of us. Expanded and clarified, the answer given by the non-Christian would be something like this: 'Since virtue is the child of knowledge, and vice is the child of ignorance, all barriers to the betterment of a community must be removed. In a country without slums, classes or other impediments to social development, people at present vicious will become virtuous. Man is born in chains; free him and he will be able to live a finer and nobler life than ever before; this is progress.' To this there are many familiar objections: Can man attain such a life by his own unaided efforts and what sort of life would it be? Are the connexions between poverty and vice, betterment and virtue quite so clear? Are well-educated people necessarily virtuous and illiterates necessarily vicious? Perhaps there is as much suffering and frustration in a welfare state as in one in which the poor are less well cared for. Under these new conditions suffering and frustration may indeed be of a different kind but they may be harder to bear and, finding ourselves

> Light half-believers of our casual creeds,
> Who never deeply felt, nor clearly willed,

our last state may be worse than our first.

These well-worn arguments show us how an apparent agreement between Christians and secularists upon an immediate social duty obscures what is more fundamental: a conflict about the purpose which the task is to fulfil—its end.

Another question on which there is apparent agreement upon 'means' but not on 'ends' is that of 'toleration'. In theory our society —if it is liberal—is committed to infinite toleration but in practice it must discriminate. Both Christian and secularist are committed to toleration; the secularist (if he is a liberal) absolutely, the Christian only in a relative sense. For him toleration is a derivative virtue, starting from our duty to love our neighbour and to turn the other cheek. For the person who is not a Christian, his belief in toleration is probably derived from a thorough-going scepticism. He is likely to believe that we can know nothing for certain and that, therefore, the convictions of today may seem, tomorrow, to have been mere prejudices. This is how he may reason: 'Never commit yourself, the other man may be right. The only thing we can be sure about is what everyone agrees to accept: *Vox populi, vox dei*. Accept the majority verdict, but never cease questioning even after a rule has been accepted, because all questions are open questions and remain so.' Here is the point of difference. To the Christian some questions are not open questions and, on a certain number of limited issues, he must consider his opponent wrong absolutely and permanently. There is therefore a limit to the Christian's toleration. In particular cases he still has the difficulty of deciding whether he is confronted, for example, by a case of murder, or by one of manslaughter; but once the decision can be made, his duty is clear. He is not committed to the principle of uncertainty and is therefore not committed to absolute toleration.

The liberal's dilemma becomes even clearer when we examine a very topical problem: that of horror comics and their suppression.

For the secularist the argument that horror comics are just plainly obscene is hardly relevant. He tolerates pornography in advertisements and daily newspapers, so why then does he decide to clamp down on a particular class of pornography? He does so purely for reasons of social expedience; opportunities for debauchery may be tolerated for adults as long as they are not extended to children. We do know that a thoroughly debauched society will not survive, but we are not so pessimistic about the fate of a society in which the opportunities for debauchery are kept relatively in check. Hence papers which attempt to do to the young what is already done to the adult must be suppressed.

If the liberal wants to justify the suppression of horror comics as activities which debauch morals and taste, he has to do so on irrational and subjective grounds; at the most, he can appeal to nothing more objectively certain than the voice of the majority and, in the century of the semi-educated, the majority is only intermittently on the side of the angels. He remains perilously poised between alternatives, always uncertain about the means he should adopt to achieve his purpose, never clearly certain about the ends which his means are to achieve. And nowhere is this failure more dangerously displayed than in education; for even at the simplest and earliest stage, conflicts arise.

When and for what purpose should children be curbed? Is their education to be a means of self-expression, by allowing them to develop their capacities as they please, or is it to be seen as an introduction to a discipline and a tradition to which they must be encouraged to conform? Is it a means of developing what is innate, irrespective of its value, in order that it may flower? Of course it is both, but if a conflict of precedence arises, which aspect must predominate: indulgence to the child or making him do what is good? How do we know what is good for him better than he knows it for himself? By what authority do we teach?

From the person who does not hold a religious belief, there can only be this answer: 'Because it is the done thing, because it is the custom of a particular school and social class, or because it is the will—or whim—of a man I respect.' Here is the Christian answer: I have taken it from the Preface to Newman's *Idea of a University*.

> It is a matter of deep solicitude to Catholic Prelates that their people should be taught a wisdom, safe from the excesses and vagaries of individuals, embodied in institutions which have stood the trial and received the sanction of ages and administered by men who [are] supported by their consistency with their predecessors and with each other.

People who are not Christians do not deny the need for such a wisdom, but they fail to explain how it can be derived from principles which are arbitrary, subjective and ultimately irrational. Although isolated actions may appear wise, they are not wisdom; for apparent agreement about 'means' is usually little more than coincidental and it hides what is inevitable: the prospect of a collision about 'ends'. It is certainly true that many people owe certain habits of mind to what they remember of traditional Christian morality; but it is also true that their means will be derived from their attitude to ends.

For example, the surest way to material success is to appear honest and yet be prepared to be dishonest when it is to one's advantage; to face one way and to row another, as Bunyan put it. It pays to appear kind and to have a reputation for fair dealing. But if your end is material success, you will have to drop such means when to persevere in them would be to your material disadvantage. Consistency must be sacrificed and this points to the most dangerous characteristic of all secular morality: the willingness to accept a confused and inconsistent relationship between 'means' and 'ends'.

This inconsistency is especially striking when we try to find out what answer the secularist has to the most important moral question of all: 'Why shouldn't I be selfish, if I am not going to be found out?' Here, Mrs Margaret Knight—a self-confessed secularist—obliges us with an answer:

> Because we are naturally social beings; we live in communities; and life in any community, from the family outwards, is much happier, and fuller, and richer if the members are friendly and co-operative than if they are hostile and resentful. [1]

This is the old enlightened self-interest argument in a rather more biological form. How do we know that we have a moral obligation to live in communities? Would we choose to live in them, if we could avoid them? The modern drift from the towns as places to live in seems to suggest that we are not at all anxious to live in communities when it is possible to do otherwise. Anyway, are some communities better to live in than others? If we can say that there are right and wrong communities then we are begging the question. To say that, because something has happened, it would be to our advantage if it went on happening is not to say it ought to happen. Indeed, community structures are changing so rapidly in our modern society that we may ask in what sense it is any longer possible to talk of a 'community' in the local and stable sense that Mrs Knight refers to; for, unlike earlier traditional communities, modern society—far from developing moral awareness—seems to be having the reverse effect. Its material comforts and distractions continually protect or divert us from making choices of any kind. Advertisers regularly save us from having to choose household goods and there are even book clubs to save us from choosing books.

This argument applies with even greater force to the modern factory, that large and impersonal working unit, which is frequently too large for any but the most sensitive to feel a direct moral responsibility for its welfare. But in the older communities which those factories have superseded, moral awareness was developed by means of the work and its obligations, normally and without excessive self-consciousness.

[1] *The Listener*, January 20th, 1955.

This change is particularly clearly realized by George Bourne in his book *Change in the Village*. Of the wheelwrights he says:

> They knew each customer and his needs; understood his carters and his horses and the nature of his land; and finally took a pride in providing exactly what was wanted in every case. So, unawares, they lived as integral parts in the rural community of the English.

Feelings of loyalty and duty for such impersonal concerns as the great factory or the housing estate are highly intellectual activities, requiring thought from those who can think and propaganda for those that cannot. What is thieving in a small unit becomes scrounging in a large one; and a subtle but definite change in moral values has taken place. Similarly the simple appeal to patriotism has changed under modern conditions into the complex approach of 'psychological warfare'. Direct relationships between employers and employee, landlord and tenant, producer and customer, give way to perpetual committees and to all the techniques of persuasion. All the finer and sharper aspects of personal relationships melt away and, with them, goes moral awareness. It is so much more difficult to feel responsibility for someone you never see, or meet merely at an annual works' party. This may help to explain some of today's apparent social and moral irresponsibility: 'unofficial' strikes, wage demands which are not related to resources, excessive National Health prescribing by doctors.

I do not wish to develop such illustrations and comments to their full extent, merely to provide sufficient evidence for my point, viz.: that the peculiar conditions of our mechanized society are failing to provide the traditional opportunities in which moral responsibility may be developed naturally, during the course of everyday contact in work. It is, thereby, encouraging a loss of interest in moral questions; and a degree of self-consciousness, almost of ability to conduct an analysis of motives, is being required from many who do not possess these qualities.

The question still remains unanswered: What has the secularist to say to the person who wants to know why he should not be selfish? Mrs Knight gives a further and final reply:

> Most people are prepared to accept as a completely self-evident moral axiom that we must not be completely selfish, and if we base our moral training on that we shall . . . be building on firm enough foundations.

K*

But there is—although Mrs Knight says she has not met him—the obstinate child who will not repress his immediate desires to be selfish and hostile until he is told why he should. If this is the best that those who believe in morals without religion can offer, they are unable to provide adequate reasons for behaving as they do and this is because they lack a clear picture of what their end should be.

Their reply could be that the Christian is frequently in the same predicament. He knows that he has to do God's will but what is his will in a particular situation? All of us find it hard to make right moral choices, since none of us, Christian or secularist, knows for certain whether an action which seems right will produce good or evil. Is the point of my criticism merely that the secularist does not bother to ask why he makes moral judgements, that he takes over his moral attitudes ready made and is insufficiently conscious of 'ends'? But this has been the eternal criticism of every thinker from Socrates to Matthew Arnold; we must allow the free play of mind upon our cherished opinions, as they may be prejudices; we must examine our assumptions. 'And what is more,' the secularist goes on to say, 'these Christian ends you recommend are too vague. They are so vague that many Christians in trying to bring about the best have brought about the worst. Look at the Puritans, the Wars of Religion, the Spanish Inquisition: the road to hell is paved with good intentions. My morality may seem to you to be arbitrary and illogical but that is because it is empirical. I select the best means to achieve my ends but because those ends are not so ultimate and are more practical, limited and mundane than yours, I can often see more clearly what I want to do and this makes it easier for me to do it. I do, in practice, frequently have a much clearer picture of ends than the Christian.'

This is partly true. Although, to the Christian, such a programme may seem very short term and to be concerned only with material ends, it is a purpose and as long as the secularist is content to accept it, his behaviour is dominated by it and acquires consistency and discipline. The ends he proposes to himself may not satisfy the scrutiny of Christian or even of his own moral philosophers but, as long as they work and he is satisfied with them, then he has a code by which he can live.

The fundamental moral difference between Christian and secular morality is one about ends; but in practice, the Christian, unlike the secularist, is committed not only to certain ends but to certain means; a whole code of means in fact. He may not achieve ends by any other than the permitted means, and whatever he considers God's will is for him, he can only accomplish it in certain ways. He moves in the light of absolutely binding commandments which he claims to obey upon the authority of divine revelation. At present, the effects of those commandments and of the conflicts between secular and Christian moral practice which they imply are most keenly felt in sexual and political relationships.

Irrespective of circumstances, the Christian knows that marriage is a permanent union and that sexual intercourse outside marriage is wrong, that social reforms can only be achieved by merciful means and that, when such means are tried and fail, then all he can do is to be patient. He must certainly not adopt other, less legitimate means to bring about his purpose, although the illusion that good can be produced by evil is one of the most fashionable of our time. The Christian is expressly forbidden thus to dominate his means that his ends shall be more easily gained; instead, he must rest content to pray for his ends when he is unable, legitimately, to accomplish them; he must remain dominated by his means.

On the other hand, the secularist is often very certain that he knows what should be done in a given situation; what, in other words, his end should be. He thinks that it is easier to find the good for oneself and for one's society than it really is, for he is less aware than the Christian that his vision may be impaired by a well-buried bad intention or other defects of insight produced by our fallen nature. Impatient to reach his goal, he adopts means without a thorough scrutiny of their consequences. He is inclined to place too much reliance upon short-term ends and unexamined assumptions; e.g., that to nationalize the means of production and distribution is to promote social health; that each nation is a law to itself and has a sacred right to determine its own destiny; that man would be freer in a world state than in the present world of independent states.

It is here that some meaning can be given to the phrase 'the secular worship of power'. Nations and individuals seem moved by a desire for power for its own sake and the struggle to retain diminishing power is—both for individuals and societies—even more bitterly waged than that to gain it. Why is this so? Does it not spring from a belief that by controlling means we can dictate ends and that moreover those ends can be achieved during our own lifetime? If you believe, on the other hand, that we cannot be certain of this happy possibility, you become less concerned with power and more with purity of means. Your efforts, individual or political, are then likely to do more permanent good. This touches upon a major political problem. In politics, morality works fitfully, for moral values are frequently invoked as matters of expedience and for their propaganda value. Afterwards they are as frequently brushed aside without protest when a higher value called 'national interests' is involved. Too many international problems are tackled in this frame of mind, as though all the results must be enjoyable within the lifetime of the politicians who are planning the programme.

Moral judgements which are expedient in time of war—that our enemies are naturally aggressive, that their leaders are war criminals—are abandoned and reversed if it is expedient to make allies of our former enemies. In this manner the real disquiet in honest minds about the rapid rearmament of former enemies and the repudiation of treaties with former allies is dismissed as inexpedient. Inevitably the moral coinage is debased. In his Encyclical *Darkness over the Earth*, Pius XII wrote:

> One leading mistake we may single out as the fountain head, deeply hidden, from which the evils of the modern state derive their origin. Both in private life and in the state itself, and, moreover, in the mutual relations of state with state and country with country, the one universal standard of morality is set aside, by which we mean the Natural Law, now buried away under a mass of destructive criticism and neglect.

The secularist emphasizes the ends rather than the means; for the Christian, in practice, the reverse is true. His emphasis falls upon self-purification. He must not fail to be sufficiently aware of the right means in case he should impair God's purpose by his failure. I think this is what St Paul has in mind when he says: 'My conscience does not, in fact, reproach me; but that is not where my justification lies; it is the Lord's scrutiny I must undergo.'

The extreme case of this opposition between secular and Christian morality is given by Newman when he contrasts the model citizen with

> a mere beggar-woman, lazy, ragged, filthy, and not over scrupulous of truth . . . but if she is chaste, and sober and cheerful, and goes to her religious duties . . . she will, in the eyes of the Church, have a prospect of Heaven, quite closed and refused to the State's pattern-man, the just, the upright, the generous, the honourable, the conscientious, if he be all this, not from a supernatural power . . . but from mere natural virtue.[1]

[1] *Difficulties of Anglicans*, p. 207.

This remark can be misinterpreted. It is unfortunately true that many Christians live in this world as though their whole duty were merely to avoid sin; a species of quietism which effectively transfers the political initiative to liberals, Socialists and Communists. We have a positive duty to make the world a better place for people to live in and for Christians to be saved in, however hard it may be for us to achieve this and however difficult it may be for us to find out what, precisely, God wills to be done.

It is harder but no less necessary for the Christian to do this than for the secularist whose scrutiny falls not upon the purity of his intention but upon the end. The secularist is, indeed, 'end-dominated' and his judgement of a wrong action is frequently that it is anti-social rather than immoral; for the very idiom of valuation changes under this influence. His attitude to himself and to others also changes into one of impersonality. The self acquires value only in so far as it is ready to become lost in the desired end; the outer world acquires significance only in so far as it is willing to become totally organized for such a purpose.

Under such 'totalitarian' influence the man changes. He becomes insensitive to human relations, for they are necessary only in so far as they assist his purpose which may be the pursuit of commercial prosperity, social betterment, political power or popular fame. He may even go so far as the Communist and deny the validity of such relationships and their claims. Even the facts of history may no longer be sacrosanct. Acting on the assumption that any stick is good enough to beat a dog with, he may attempt to discredit his opponents by 'smearing' them, believing that he will have attained his ends (and thereby public approval) before his misrepresentations have been pinned down and exposed. What starts as a device by an ends-dominated enthusiast may culminate in the corruption of the entire personality. The witch-hunting of alleged Communists and subversives in America is very much in my mind when I say this.

When a government is established by such means how is it to be maintained and adapted to new situations? Who is to decide what is the party line, who are deviationists and what is justice and injustice? Without common agreement on such matters a society will not survive the first flush of that enthusiasm for short-term ends which brought it into being. Man should be free in those periods when the law is silent, but he can only remain so if he can be relied upon to maintain a reasonable personal freedom and not give way to licence. Without moral standards held in common and freely accepted, without some agreement upon what are legitimate and illegitimate means, society either breaks down or has to increase the size and scope of its police force.

A society which has rejected the guidance of traditional wisdom, of the gods of the copy-book headings, has got to find some means of smuggling them back. The present fashion is to speak of international order, to advocate the setting up of Leagues of Nations, and Organizations of United Nations, which are expected to have sufficient authority to promulgate and enforce a code of morality. The difficulties of setting up yet another co-ordinating committee should be obvious. Will its decisions be right because they are true or right only because a majority has agreed to recommend them? Such a body can claim no greater moral certainty than the bodies that constitute it. You cannot have common moral standards just for the asking because they are politically convenient. Can a common moral law come only through religious belief—as in the past— or is a new method possible? Secular moralists believe that it is. The liberals place their hopes in international authorities, the Communists in world conquest.

What has led to the secular rejection of traditional moral teaching? In discussing the grounds for toleration, I suggested that the secular case is that all questions are open questions because we can know nothing for certain. For those who think this to be so, each moral situation is a fresh situation; they are unable to agree that any general rule can be deduced from such situations and applied to them, since this would imply some characteristic common to each situation which, by continually reappearing, might claim some permanent status. The most they would admit would be that such observations were hypotheses which appeared to apply to other situations, when the circumstances were approximately similar. But as circumstances are never, *ex hypothesi*, similar, general moral rules can only exist theoretically; and, if they existed, could never be clearly enough distinguished for any practical purpose.

But in practice we do invoke such general rules and try to conform to them. Even when we claim to be justified by circumstances in telling lies, we feel uneasy and are not satisfied to be told that our dissatisfaction is merely the operation of conditioned reflexes. If on each occasion that we have to make a moral choice an ethical philosopher has to be standing by, our society is not going to last very long. It needs rules, but can it say why they shall be applied? Given its assumptions about all questions being open questions and each situation a fresh situation, I believe that it cannot. It is committed to a thorough-going relativism and its conduct is fundamentally irrational. Hence it will always have a growing crime problem as, with the spread of semi-literacy, more individuals awaken to the discrepancy between theory and practice, between what is taught and what is respectable.

As Christians we are committed to moral rules and in particular to those which are contained in the moral teachings of the Church; but, as philosophers, can we show that rules which we accept unconditionally upon the authority of Revelation, far from conflicting with human experience are a convincing answer to its demands. The secularist may admit their expedience, but he may say that they are derived from nothing more than custom or enlightened self-interest, and how then can they be binding?

Before considering this, we must see what grounds we have for saying that moral laws are necessary because of their practical value. They keep us sensitive to moral issues and give us authority for rejecting principles—however tempting—that have as their consequences practices that have been universally condemned as harmful to any society. For example, a man who accepts the law 'Thou shalt not kill' should not tolerate thoughts that have as their consequence the liquidation of social undesirables, euthanasia, political assassinations or war as a means of social development. The man who regards marriage as a permanent institution will be opposed to theories which imply the spread of free-love and frequent divorce which can reduce marriage to legalized prostitution. In a country whose individuals hold to this rule absolutely, the family will remain what it has been and the tendency of parents to shelve the responsibility for bringing up their children upon the state will be reversed.

The practical grounds which confirm our acceptance of moral laws lead us to the philosophical ones. The classical vision of the human situation (temporarily obscured in the nineteenth century by a sort of revolutionary optimism) is not one of a growing progress from strength to strength but rather of a continual battle with evil under many changing guises; and there arise from this view permanent problems and, in a sense, recurring situations. Who was it said that there are only five original plots in the world and that all human situations are variations of these set themes? Permanent problems and recurring situations imply permanent solutions. The difficulty of recognizing what is permanent in a problem, situation and, therefore, solution remains, for this is the eternal difficulty of classification. We have still to decide, for example, whether we are confronted by a case of fraud or by a piece of skilful but shady book-keeping; but such difficulties do not invalidate the principles and to abandon moral rules for certain short-term advantages might well produce long-term consequences of an appalling kind.

Marriage to many unbelievers is no longer regarded as a permanent union, although the full effect of this rejection of a moral law upon the relationship between men and women and upon a parent's sense of responsibility has yet to be felt.

I want in conclusion to touch on the most difficult problem of all, that of moral responsibility. Few deny absolutely that we are responsible for our actions, but it is rightly suggested that our free moral choice applies to far fewer situations then we like to believe. This is, however, not the same as saying that we never recognize a choice when it is offered to us and that we are not really responsible for our actions. To accept such a view uncritically is to take us straight to those extraordinary defences which we read in the police court reports. Cases of assault and shoplifting are frequently explained in terms of mental and moral black-outs: 'I did not know what I was doing. I acted automatically.' It is becoming almost customary to find persons committed for trial on a capital charge pleading insanity, as though crime were a form of lunacy and sin a mental aberration for which one's Creator were solely to blame.

A discussion of the grounds for accepting the existence of free will would be outside the scope of this paper, and I have merely wished to point out the social consequences of allowing the issue to become blurred.

But to consider this topic is to return to an earlier one: those voices in contemporary society which far from encouraging us—as was once the custom—to make choices, exhort us to a diabolical political, commercial and moral inertia: 'Let us choose for you', they say, 'in any case you never choose for yourself. Your conduct is merely the result of the interplay of your glandular structure and environmental influences.'

It is this tendency to deny moral responsibility on the one hand and to require it for political purposes on the other, that is the particular moral predicament of secular society on both sides of the Iron Curtain. It is a tendency which has its origins in the character of secular morality: its domination by short-term ends. Not only is it less discriminating in its choice of means than Christian morality; but, in practice, it must continually face a dangerous breach between ends and means, for both are in a permanent state of flux.

But after two great wars and a social revolution we are reaching the state where the only people who will accept—with continuing complacence—this persistent failure to answer fundamental moral questions will be those who are—at present—the most highly regarded of our secular moral philosophers.

XXIII

COMMUNIST MORALITY

by

Joseph G. Dawson

'RIGHT and wrong in human acts should be discussed in the same temper as good and bad in things.'[1] This advice, coming from a great theologian, but at once sober and down-to-earth, is particularly appropriate to our enquiry, though it also serves to emphasize two important respects in which the project of this present discussion is less than complete. In the first place any adequate treatment of an atheistic system of morality requires that it be taken up into the context of theology to receive its final assessment there. This I am not in a position to do. On the other hand, Communism is a scientific creed and a satisfactory discussion of its ethics would call for a far-reaching study, of a positive nature and based on accurate scientific data, into the whole range of the ethical habits of the many peoples that live under communist rule—a task clearly beyond the limited scope of this paper.

There remains, however, a restricted but, nevertheless, a legitimate and important task which I propose to set myself—a peculiarly philosophical task, if that term be accepted in the dialectical rather than the metaphysical sense. What we have to examine and bring into relief are the main principles which guide the relationship between the dialectic of Communism and the ethics of its behaviour. In this way it should be possible to state the true nature of the disagreement which lies between the communist and other systems of morality. I propose, furthermore, to restrict the analysis to the special case of bolshevist morality, disregarding other vast ramifications, both to the left and to the right, which still might legitimately be regarded as communistically inspired. I do this, not only out of necessary considerations of economy, but also because in Bolshevism, it seems to me, there continues to be found the authentic

[1] St Thomas, *Summa Theologica*, Ia, IIae, xviii, 1.

298

element of integral experiment which makes Communism both interesting and important.

It is frequently objected that dialectical materialism does not, and could not, contain any genuine elaboration of a moral philosophy: and force is lent to these objections by the fact that a specific theory of ethics as a separate treatise hardly ever appears within the classical expositions of dialectical materialism. Thus encouraged, many critics dismiss all ethical pretensions of Communism out of hand and are disposed to reject it as no more than one further and blatant example of ethical relativity. There are, of course, arguable grounds for such a view; but it seems to me that the objection is, nevertheless, misguided. Too often it derives from a failure to appreciate the warning given long ago by Aristotle,[1] that there is always a certain relativity involved in genuine discussions of the practical; and that the more detailed these become, the further one has to depart from general principles. Moreover, whatever may be his relativism in respect of practical decisions, the Communist, when challenged, appeals to the 'honesty' or 'rightness' or 'justice' of the course he adopts; and he is prepared to argue that his use of such terms is neither empty nor arbitrary.

This only serves to emphasize what I believe to be a more serious defect from which such objections suffer, namely a failure to appreciate the full measure of the gravity of the challenge offered. Frequently this arises from an attitude of mind which cannot or will not understand that the inner dialectic, the theory of Communism, was born of a deliberate attempt to eliminate the empty and abstract conceptions which had become indigenous to western idealism.[2] Thus the communist ethic must be discussed and appreciated within the general framework of a total rejection of these conceptions. It would, therefore, be trivial and misleading to put forward objections to it which depend for their force upon an idealistic interpretation of morality, since this is precisely what is being refused. The Communist believes—not without some appearance of justification—that what he has to offer, despite its shortcomings, is a better solution than those which have, for so long, been marked by failure.

[1] *Nicomachean Ethics*, I, 3.

[2] The term 'idealist' is commonly used by Marxists in a much wider way than by other western philosophers. Here it is used strictly to refer to the main stream of idealism connected with Hegel. But at various times I have not hesitated to use it quite loosely. The context should prove a sufficient guide.

Communism originated in a vast attempt to put an end to this long and painful history of failures. It came from a whole-hearted effort to avoid an apparent collapse of values in western civilization brought on by continuing theological and philosophical disagreement. It is not surprising that in this effort it turned to the one genuine value that still seemed to remain, that of the practical, earthy field of matter; or that it attempted to utilize the one method that still seemed to offer hope for the future, that of the positive sciences. If then our present enquiry is to achieve an understanding of the true character of bolshevist materialism it must be conducted within a context of the positive rejection of idealism and at the same time it must take note of the *prima facie* claim of the Marxist that he is able to begin with two authentic values; that of the material universe which provides the content of his investigations, and that of the method to be adopted, namely a method of practical, scientific, experiment.

Communism then is an experiment, and is most adequately characterized as an experiment in scientific atheism. It is the most recent and most crucial example of that series of portrayals of atheistic humanism which marked in particular the history of the nineteenth century.[1] It is a last desperate attempt to put an end to a long history of failure, generated first by the theological disputes that marked the rise of the Reformation and later carried on more generally into the realm of metaphysics. A similar experimental and scientific attempt has been made more recently by logical positivism within the theoretical field of language to put an end to man's lack of success in his search for an adequate metaphysic. By adopting a suitable practical criterion for meaningful talk it was hoped to eliminate the problem of metaphysics.[2] In like manner the Communist attempts to put an end to man's failure in his search for God by an ultimate denial of God. But this new atheism, precisely because it is designed to end the unsuccessful search in a practical manner, differs profoundly in scope and method from its predecessors.

Bolshevism has recognized and accepted the fact that merely to deny the existence of God is a pointless and self-stultifying procedure and in this the communist finds himself strangely at one with St

---

[1] Cf. Père de Lubac's brilliant study of the subject, *The Drama of Atheistic Humanism*.

[2] The importance of the logical positivist movement lies in its practical approach to the problem rather than in any theoretical expertise. A fact which is frequently ignored by would-be opponents.

Anselm. Such a denial can never be more than a paradoxical attempt to state the unstateable. The only effective way of dealing with the situation is to resort to practice and with this realization we are brought to the full formulation of what is the essential proposal of dialectical materialism—the living of the dialectic. This proposal does not consist in the theoretical vindication of the superiority of one way of life over another: it consists in the practical establishment of the superiority of one way of life, including and by means of its dialectical theory, over all others.

Such a proposal is, of course, by no means unique in the history of human experience. In acting as he does the Communist follows closely the practical course adopted by many religious and ethical ways of life. He would claim, however, that what is new in the situation is the birth of a new ideological superstructure consequent upon the establishment of a truly socialist society. This is the arrival of a new ethos marked by a rigid adherence to the principles of historical materialism and by the practical and experimental application of the dialectical method.

The emergence and the conscious grasp and practice of this new ideology which is at once a theory of reality and a method of life was itself a long process with its own history of difficulty, of success and failure, and its own *rationale* of inner development. This development, the *dialectical* characteristic of dialectical materialism, is a matter which has received all too little attention from those who have commented upon the nature of Communism. In part this is due to the understandable difficulty which is always experienced when attempting to give a satisfactory account of any process of growth and development: a difficulty which is made plain by every great system of philosophy. At the same time there are other factors, peculiar to the communist dialectic, which make the explanation much more complex.

Three different levels of explanation are in fact involved. First there is the purely temporal sequence of events relevant to the establishment of Communism. Secondly there is the explanation of these events in terms of historical materialism. Lastly there is the growth and change of the dialectical method itself, instanced by the passage from its descriptive and explanatory phase to the deliberative and technological intervention into the life of society. Not a few of the confusions or inconsistencies which are so often attributed to Communism come in fact from a failure on the part of the critics to distinguish adequately between these different levels of explana-

tion.[1] On the other hand some non-communist writers, not themselves believing in the dialectic, refuse also to believe that others are
prepared to fashion their lives in accordance with it. Thus they often
fail to realize that, for instance, the later developments in the history
of Bolshevism do in fact exhibit the play of the dialectic, if only for
the reason that this is brought about by the members of the party
themselves.

As a matter of history the opening period of this development is
marked by the contributions of Marx and Engels. These consist in
the acceptance of the materialist transposition of the Hegelian
dialectic made by Feuerbach[2] and its generalization in terms of
historical materialism into a universal explanation of the nature of
man and of society. In terms of the new dialectic this is the first
moment of inner contradiction and revolt evoked by past failures.
It is the rejection of idealism which at the same time means the
establishment of objective materialism. It is also the first moment of
the new atheism established by the self-sufficiency of the material
universe and consequent redundancy of the first mover.[3] Matter
alone is the procrustean deposit of all possibility, itself continually
in movement in virtue of its inner contradiction.

This first moment, the development of the theory of historical
materialism in its antithetic and descriptive aspect, is the common
heritage of all the various sects of Communism. It is marked
characteristically by rejection of the past and revolutionary antici-
pation of the future. It rings with eschatological overtones in ex-
pectation of release from the ever-recurring story of mistakes. But
the full realization of the nature and the scope of the experiment
was to come but slowly. And, as with all genuine experiments,
many mistakes and failures were to be experienced. It was by no
means immediately realized that a purely historical, past tense and

---

[1] Not the least of the virtues of Fr Wetter's admirable study *Il materialismo dialettico
sovietico* lies in the care with which he has segregated historical exposition from philosophical analysis. I am heavily indebted to it in this article.

[2] In place of the thesis, antithesis and synthesis of the Hegelian logic we are offered
a dialectical explanation of matter which involves three principles: the unity of
opposites; the passage from quantitative to qualitative change; the negation of negation. Feuerbach's main contribution consisted in the suggestion that the mental dialectic was no more than a pale reflection of the pattern of change in the material
universe, which is the primary and sole reality.

[3] This is Feuerbach's main contribution towards exploding the illusion of religion.
Cf. Engels' frequently quoted remark about the enthusiasm roused by Feuerbach's
The Essence of Christianity.

passive interpretation of the emergence of communist man was inadequate. In the case of Marx himself and throughout the early period of the systematic construction of historical materialism, there is a note of pessimism,[1] a quality almost of fatalism and of passive acceptance of the inevitable process of the dialectic which does not match either the success or the progressive and aggressive policy of Communism in its later bolshevist guise.

Communist methodology, being thus born, now begins to exhibit its own characteristics of movement and inner contradiction. First the mechanistic interpretation of Marxism given by Bucharin, then the idealistic versions of Deborin and Trotsky, struggle for mastery but neither of these is adequate to the situation. They do no more than prepare the way. The final solution marks the achievement of the second phase of the dialectic, the emergence of a qualitatively different type of interpretation; the establishment of a new communist ideology made possible by the coming of Socialism and the rise of a new and far-reaching scientific sociology in the U.S.S.R. With it we pass from the theoretical explanation of past practice to the practical and experimental construction of a new theory of man.

Lastly, there comes the full development of the third stage of the dialectic, the negation of negation. This is the moment of synthesis which retains all that is good and profitable in the old stage of development and takes it up, universalizes it through the creative ideology of the bolshevist party to ensure the continuance of the process.[2] It is at this point that the practical genius of Lenin and later of Stalin, acting as his able disciple, is fully to be seen.

Since the full reality of matter lies not in inert extension as Descartes held, but in the movement of inner contradiction; and since the present stage of evolution of the material cosmos has reached to the human agent acting within the system of the community, there remains the final question of how to guarantee the effective continuance of this movement. The analysis of movement that is usually given by other systems of philosophy is useless. It is always static and idealist. The concrete analysis provided by the

---

[1] Pessimism to the extent of his opposition to the optimistic philosophies of the enlightenment which he was concerned to reject.

[2] This is the meaning of the principle of 'partyness' which plays such a predominant role in bolshevist thought and practice. This is the dynamic, fruitful rule of action which guarantees the unity of thought and of practice and thus ensures its scientific correctness.

materialist dialectic is alone dynamic. The only genuine instances of concrete thinking are those that go to successful performance. They lie in deliberation rather than in speculation.[1] But deliberation is about means rather than ends, so there still remains a problem of action. For even though the maxim that all activity takes place for the sake of some end be rejected as a piece of the ultimate metaphysical furniture of the universe, it remains true that few would deny the concept of intention and of purpose in the analysis of effective human action. And anyone who did would soon find out his mistake to his cost.

Thus Bolshevism is brought by the inescapable requirements of its own dialectic to admit that there are always two aspects to the problem of God's existence, the aspects of First Cause and of Final End. Merely to deny the existence of God, or to argue against the idea of a Creator, which is characteristic of all other atheisms, is bound to result in practical sterility. Once atheism is coupled to action the question of God the Final End is inevitably raised. An atheism that answers the question, 'Does God exist?' with the reply, 'You do not need to have a God to run the world' is bound to fail. It will fail because it has not appreciated that the existence of the Final End is an inescapable requirement for all successful *doing*: because conventional atheism, even of the sophisticated sort, is what Anselm said it was, empty, a failure, a falling short: because to explain away the idea of God as did Feuerbach, and to substitute humanity, is worse than useless. Feuerbach's 'homo' is even more impotent than the idealist god he rejected.

The importance of Lenin's contribution in establishing this third stage of the dialectic lies in the fact that he does not merely transpose the problem from the field of theory to the field of practice, but that he attempts to do this within the framework of a genuine analysis of practice which still remains integrally atheistic. This requires the admission of the necessity of God, the eternal source of opposition, without whom there would be no movement, without whom the dialectic would cease, without whom there would be no reality. This is the authentic anti-God movement.[2]

Thus the exact and remorseless claims of the dialectic manifest

---

[1] Hence, not merely the subordination of the theoretical to the practical, but the virtual elimination of any sort of theorizing for its own sake.

[2] It is strange how seldom full account is taken of the distinction between simple atheism and the positive anti-God ethos of Bolshevism. Yet in this lies all the difference between Feuerbach and Lenin.

an ancient truth of religion and of history. God may be blasphemed. He will not be denied. Thus also is established what had already been said so ably in his own way by Dostoievsky, that without God man cannot organize the world for himself. Without God he cannot effectively organize anything, for the simple reason that there is a principle—deny it if you will—that every agent must act for an end, and that the eventual success of action will be conditioned as much by the nature of the end as by skill in the choice of means thereto.

To refuse the essential condition that makes this principle possible—the existence of God—is to be static. It is death both for the individual and for the group. The inevitable culmination of the autonomous, agnostic, bourgeois ethic of Europe was, as Lenin very well saw, the negative atheistic ethic. This was the sign of its ultimate sterility and collapse, and it thus provided a further striking example of the general anthopological principle that societies die when their gods die.

Whatever may be the views of other deviationary versions of Communism, the ultimate aim of Bolshevism is not, as so many critics mistakenly seem to think, the achievement of utopia this side of the grave.[1] It aims at a society, yes, and at a universal society; but this is a practical, earthy, society; one which will continually exact its toll of blood and sweat. But the true price that must be paid for it is the unending rejection of God, because only God—if he did exist—could be greater than, and more important than, the group, the state, or the physical universe. To sink at any stage into atheism of the negative sort would be to confess that your god was not great enough; that he was not the right one. It is to fall inevitably into idealism, into not-being. It is to die.

If the preceding analysis is in the main correct it should help to throw light upon one of the major problems in the interpretation of Communism. How are we to understand the Communist's claim to be free, in particular when it is put in the paradoxical form of the freedom of necessity? With the earlier, mechanistic, interpretations of Marxism I am not here concerned. Nor should certain denials of freedom by the Communist mislead us. Frequently these are no more than protests against the empty and unreal concept of freedom proffered by idealist libertarians or else they are a dialectical refusal to confuse desire and freedom by bringing down desire to the level

[1] Frequently this derives from a failure to distinguish between the authentic line of bolshevist development and, in particular, the right-wing deviations of menshevism.

of the practically realizable by means of deliberation and choice; a refusal which already implies a certain dimension of freedom and of responsibility.

But it is in his insistence upon the possibility, indeed the necessity, of his ultimate rejection of God that the Bolshevist will be found to claim, and to claim truly, that he is free in a most important sense of freedom. This is at one with Lenin's continued insistence upon the voluntaristic character of the true dialectic of materialism, and with his repeated claim that only in purposive action is there a full and adequate dimension of freedom and of objective thinking. Thus the Bolshevist is able to safeguard the full range of choice. He remains free just so long as his rejection of God retains the authentic element of blasphemy. He is free because he is able to sin; because he does in fact sin. In this moment the range of his choice is oriented upon an Infinite Object. In denying this Object, in rejecting God, he deploys to the full the complete resources of human willing— short of a successful act of love of God. Only a true act of charity, conceived in the Christian sense, is greater and more powerful than this total rejection.

Thus in one step we are taken back to the most ancient dialectic of love and hate. In this ultimate and most terrible denial lies the rejection of all friendship and with it the impossibility of all society. For there can be no true society where there is no friendship; only the collective life of the mass held together by the force of opposition. True friendship is to be found only between persons and it is a regular characteristic of all secularist ethics that sooner or later they end in a denial of value to persons. Why indeed should there be persons? The only reason which will stand eventual scrutiny and make the concept a genuine one is precisely that which would make a secularist view of the universe untenable and impossible. Communism is no exception in this respect. Nevertheless its denial is more paradoxical and subtle than would appear at first sight.

In his Mercier lectures upon the *City of God*,[1] Gilson has made much of this point when rejecting Marxism as a serious candidate among the protagonists of the city of man. For him the atheistic humanism of Comte is 'incomparably richer' in content. 'The universal society of Marx adds nothing to the atheism of Comte.'[2] This judgement becomes well understandable if one bears in mind the reflexion made by Gilson that the Marxist dialectic is completely opposed, both in fact and in principle, to the traditional conception

[1] E. Gilson, *Les Métamorphoses de la Cité de Dieu*.   [2] Gilson, *op. cit.*, p. 286.

of a society founded upon an appreciation of a common aim and bound together by a common love.[1] In many respects it is true to say that the Marxist stands much closer to the stoic predecessors of Augustine than he does to any of his more proximate ancestors. À propos of this stoic acceptance of a cosmic order, Gilson penetratingly remarks:

> This enlarging of the political horizon, this becoming a cosmopolitan, a citizen of the world, contains within it a radical equivocation; the cosmos is not a society. To find one's place within the order of the physical universe whose laws one accepts and with which one unites oneself can well be an act of wisdom. It can never be an act of citizenship.[2]

The Stoic in his ethic, an ethic of humanism, purports to set out certain laws which are proper to human acts; in this respect it must be regarded as an ethic of obligation. Stoicism becomes a possible theory of morality only within the context of a juridical system which guarantees the order within which it operates. Thus its concept of personality is primarily a legal concept. Yet Stoicism must always be in disagreement with this order; it must always be seeking escape from it. For Stoicism is a solitary ethic, an ethic of withdrawal and of rejection of that very state of affairs which makes it possible. The only way such an ethic can be universalized and thus escape identification with the positive order of politics is by equating itself with the cosmic order, in which case it ceases to be descriptive of specifically human actions and in this sense destroys the distinction between moral and physical principles.

The traditional pagan morality avoided this dilemma by coupling the stoic ethic with a neoplatonic universe of values and thus guaranteed the authenticity and rightful subordination of the physical to the moral order.[3] But for the importation of this neoplatonic element—fortuitously introduced for this very purpose— the stoic explanation of rightness is not capable *of itself* of explaining wrongness.

Only with such a broader context is it possible to talk of 'bad', of 'good and better'. In this respect the Stoic cannot explain generosity and friendship because he cannot explain persons;

[1] St Augustine, *De Civitate Dei, XIX*, 24. This definition provides the theme of Gilson's lectures, *op. cit.*

[2] Gilson, *op. cit.*, p. 6.

[3] Cf. the very interesting remarks upon this point made by N. Abercrombie, *St Augustine and Classical French Thought*, Chapter 1: 'The Principles of Augustinian Ethics'.

Stoicism takes for granted, it cannot explain, the human agent. Thus it is incapable of presenting a genuine view of human society, a society marked by friendship and concord. It can speak only in terms of the mass, the collective, the cosmos. . .

At the same time it is well to remind ourselves that the rationalist ethic of Comte is no better off in this respect.[1] The 'incomparably richer' city of positivism remains so only on paper. It is a conceptual richness condemned to remain sterile because it must draw its reality from that very order of western religious values that is denied and subverted by the atheistic pretensions of the system. The historical evidence of its impotence is a tribute to the perspicacity of the Marxist in rejecting it as empty and impracticable. So we return to the bolshevist conception of 'society' as a collective, bound together by force. For the Bolshevist this forcible bringing together and keeping in being is what he means by 'society'. Only thus does he see any prospect of escape from the eventual fatalism of the Stoic and the unreal utopianism of the rationalist.

But in this society there can be no room for love, or for friendship; for this would be static, it would mean accepting the opiate, it would be the end of dynamic contradiction—the end of process, which is death. This denial of friendship remains true at every level of human relationship, including that of the family; but it becomes most terribly real within man himself. If he is to live in the fullness of life, he must at all times reject the authentic 'I–Thou' relationship between creature and Creator.[2] This, for the Bolshevist, is 'the end'. All that promotes this perfect society is good and all that fails to do so is bad. Communism thus becomes compatible alike with the conception of failure and the conception of sin. It is available to a full range of values. To the construction of this new order all effort must be directed, and it is from this that the individual derives a new value. So to be a Communist is to have, in a genuine sense, suffered a re-birth, to be regenerated, to be a new man.

The epitaph of this communist 'city of man' was written long ago—by Aristotle.[3] At the end of the sixth book of the ethics, when

[1] Strangely, though he has assembled all the evidence required, Gilson does not seem to have taken account of this capital point that the *City* is the product, not of *theoria* but of *praxis*. This seems to explain his rather hasty dismissal of the candidature of Marxism.

[2] The kindred contemporary atheism of Sartre results in a similar solitary existence. The 'Other', the Creator, must be rejected by the existentialist.

[3] *Nicomachean Ethics*, VI, 13. 'To suggest that prudence exercises authority over wisdom would be like saying that political science commands the gods, because

faced with the problem of the relationship between the theoretical and the practical, he indicates a solution which does justice to the practical and social aspects of man's nature but at the same time leaves the way free for the practice of the contemplative 'life' which marks the completion and crown of all virtue. True there are many difficulties in his solution and it lends itself all too readily to an interpretation marked by an impossible dichotomy between theory and practice.[1] On the one hand the monastic, contemplative, solitary life of the intellect: aristocratic and privileged. On the other the earthy, egalitarian, common and productive life of the *polis*. Neither view, however, does justice to Aristotle's deep insight into the truly social character of man. Man's practical life is not exhausted by economic activity, nor even by the pursuit of virtue, for, as we saw in the case of the Stoic, if virtue is not open to generosity and to friendship it relapses into solitary sterility.

At the same time the 'activity of mind in its best part', successful knowing, is a matter of real effort involving a social dimension both at its beginning and at its end. Knowing is but the term to learning, which, for success, requires teachers and an adequate background of society. As to the term, the proper object of contemplation is One alone. To fail to reach this object is to practise, not contemplation, but self-delusion. The activity is correctly fulfilled when it takes man to God. Nor is there anything very aristocratic about this. All that is involved is the recognition of the finiteness and dependence of the universe, including man himself, upon God. The recognition of man in the universe, not as a solitary apex to an otherwise grim world, but as the sharer of the joy of creation with the One who created it. A recognition which brings with it an immediate response of love. Thus to know God the creator—even mediately, as all such knowledge must be—the creator of oneself, the giver of life and of all good things is at once to go out to him, to make the proper response, to love him.[2] Thus there is a place for the social dimension of friendship even in Aristotle's activity of contemplation.

---

it issues regulations about everything in the state, including what is due to them'.

[1] It would be idle to suggest that the *Ethics* offers a complete and consistent theory of the practical life. But it is to Aristotle's eternal credit that he does not baulk the issue by trying to oversimplify it. In particular the abiding Greek sense of *hubris* guarded him from many temptations to error.

[2] Cf. St Thomas, *De Caritate*, where he argues that a thing can be immediately loved, though mediately known, hence our will can reach higher than our intelligence when confronted by things that are above us. Quoted by Fr Gilby, *Aquinas*, Philosophical Texts, Nn. 785, 913.

So far from its being a privilege, not to achieve at least some measure of contemplation is a failure and a privation for the human agent. To be completely without it is to be without the measure and norm both of responsibility and of virtue. This is why the rejection of all substitute gods, of all failures in contemplation, is so necessary. If, however, man is prepared to go the hard road, to tread the path of the contemplative, if, loving his neighbour, he is ready to move into life and not away from it, if he maintains constant integrity of mind and will in face of the inevitable difficulties of the search, he will find the truth and an object supremely worthy of love. To give oneself thus is to find oneself completely in the universe. It is also the condition of all society.[1]

The attempted analysis of the moral content of Bolshevism which we have just concluded may be found sombre and disturbing, particularly when we contrast the new paganism with the old. It is necessarily over-brief and, as I have already had reason to point out, is inadequate on many counts. Because of this, and because of the inherent difficulties of the question it may well be challenged by Communists and by non-Communists alike. I believe, however, that a fuller and more careful investigation would only confirm that it is in general agreement, not only with the principles of Bolshevism, but also with its actual historical practice.

It must, however, be remembered that this has been an abstract analysis which has essayed the portrayal of the inner logic of the dialectical theory, while connecting it historically with certain persons and situations which played a part in its development. The conclusion, then, takes us no further than the statement that if there are any genuine Communists, this is what they are committed to in the field of practice, no matter what else they may compromise with or discard. In other words, Bolshevism can only remain true to itself, can only be realized, within an ultimate context of atheism, the like of which I have attempted to describe. The extent to which Communists themselves practise their dialectic, and the important and interesting issues of abnormal psychology raised by the peculiar motive to action involved, are questions which must remain undiscussed here. The latter point would indeed require an entire treatise to deal with it adequately. For the Christian it should be sufficient to realize that this reversal of the Christian praxis, this

[1] The critical temper of the Greek mind in matters of theology, always open, but guarded in its optimism, compares very favourably with the speciously optimistic closure and rejection practised by neo-paganism.

perversion of the great commandment that all we do should be done from a motive of pure love of God, derives in great measure from our own failure to live our lives from such a motive. We have entered a post-Christian world because Christians have not responded in kind to the love which was offered them by God. To the integral challenge which is offered by Bolshevism only one answer will prove sufficient, the life of perfect charity, however much we may fall short in our effort to live it. A morality of limited liability will not do.

XXIV

CHRISTIAN MORALITY

by

Dom Sebastian Moore

THIS paper falls naturally into two sections. In the first Christian morality is considered in relation to morality in general. In the second the picture of Christian morality that has emerged from this contrast is filled out, showing the substance of Christian morality to be the Body of Christ.

I

THE sum of Christian morality is the love of God. To say this is to pose, at the start, the whole problem of Christian morality. For morality regulates our relations with people and our use of things in this world, whereas charity belongs to the new eon which Christ has inaugurated. And when that eon has been finally established, charity alone will survive: the deepest perceptions of the human spirit, the highest prophetic inspirations, will have no more place. How, then, can it be translated into a moral code? It is customary, especially among those who know only the loose modern definition of a Christian, to regard 'the new law' simply as a higher, nobler morality, a sublime simplification of moral precepts. And even Catholics may be surprised when confronted with St Thomas's statement that the new law is the grace of the Holy Ghost (Ia, IIae, 106, 1, Resp). Though called a law, it does not appear to admit of definition in the language of law.

It should not, then, surprise us to learn that this tension implicit in Christian morality has been frequently dissolved. The ecstasy of the gnostics carried them beyond all moral concern—and gnosticism was the earliest, and has been the most persistent, of the Christian heresies. St Paul's biggest problem with his gentile converts was that of curbing their excesses without attenuating the transcendence of 'our new liberty in Christ Jesus'. We have a most interesting example of this dissolving tendency in Hugh Ross

Williamson's book, *The Great Prayer*. For him, the Sermon on the Mount is 'the epitome of pre-christian morality'—he even describes this statement as a truism. The only commands of Christ that are specifically and uniquely his are that to ' "Do this" and the other two commands which are inextricably related to it—the command to be baptized and the command to love to the death fellow-sharers of the Meal' (p. 12). It cannot be denied that the author catches here the exciting, even esoteric atmosphere of the first Christian generation. And it is true that the Great Sermon is not so much a morality as a description, in moral terms, of a new pact between God and man, sealed in the flesh of Christ. The description is secondary to the fact, but description is possible. What we have to do is to show the description *as* description, to relate the behaviour which Christ prescribes to that divine simplification of life which defies description.

The love of God lies beyond the purview of the moralist. But to avoid cutting the painter between God's world and his, it is necessary to ascertain, as it were, the point at which the love of God disappears from his view. To do this we must start with the idea of love, which, we shall find, takes us a little further than the extreme anti-liberal view of Hugh Ross Williamson will allow. For love takes us to the frontier of human experience. It starts *as* an experience, but in the final act of consent or willing surrender it appears more as 'that which is', a totality which pre-exists and encloses us. It is the very life of man, that in which he is one, in which all his experience has a single meaning:

> I wonder by my troth, what thou, and I
> Did, till we loved? Were we not wean'd till then?

Christianity reveals to us a totality of love in which the love which man has already experienced as somehow pre-existent is identified with the eternal ground of being, God himself. The Christian revelation cannot be fully apprehended unless we appreciate the significance of the human apotheosis of love. Eros is the creation of the human spirit, and so is not God. But the initial impulse to this creation is an essential factor in man's response to divine love. The mystic, in loving God, knows love *as* God. By him, God is recognized *in* love.

For the moralist, the ultimate principle of the Great Sermon is altruism. Hugh Ross Williamson is right when he rejects the common notion that that, and simply that, is Christianity. But the altruism which the Sermon describes is a totality of love that coalesces, as it were, in God and finds God in love. The burden of the sermon is altruism, while the heart of Christianity is the mysterious historical love-pact made by God with man. These two are distinct but not discontinuous: the love-pact is clothed by Christ in the language of altruism: he shows it to us as the human heart in a windless clarity of detachment, 'a condition of complete simplicity costing not less than everything'. To say that everything in the sermon can be paralleled from Jewish or non-Christian authors is about as relevant as to say that everything in the Sonnets can be paralleled from other poets. One does not read a text to make parallels but to receive its own unique communication. And the Sermon read in this way belongs wholly to the new law which, however, cannot be written down.

It might still be insisted that the Sermon, dealing as it does with man's love for God, must stop short of the Christian fact which is God's love for man. We touch here the supposed corruption of agape by eros which Anders Nygren finds in the Christian mystics. In reality, however, the idea of man loving God has only two possibilities open to it. It is either self-contradictory or it implies a divine initiative in this love. For love transforms its object, and God cannot be transformed. The creature can be transformed by love without losing his identity, and in so transforming him I do not love a creature of my own imagination. That is the working of love, in which the operation of a power beyond ourselves is already perceived. But a God who could be so transformed would not be God. A love of God based on man's decision involves an intolerable attenuation of that ineffable *is-ness* of God which is described with such astonishing unanimity by all those who have tasted him and which is 'the food of grown men, transforming into itself him who tastes it'. The finest fruit of human experience, the nearest it has got to affirming the substantial *is-ness* of love, is the statement 'love is God'. The converse, regarded as the fruit of human experience, is decadent. It is no such cheerful optimism that Christ offers in the Sermon, but a love for God that is real, and so is God's love in operation, making man his own.

We are now in a better position to map out Christian morality: to show that in it which comes under the scrutiny of the moralist and that which disappears into the mystery of God. To the moralist it can be described as 'love become total in man', a simplification of life that is mysterious in its source but manifest in its effects. The simplification points to the source which is God tasted, apprehended directly, that is in his simplicity. This is beyond the moralist, yet Christian morality is one. Its exploration in moral terms yields the idea of a total love rather than the source of that love. Yet this idea is essential to a full understanding of the source. The objectless quality which the total love has for the moralist is itself a precious pointer to the source. It has the strong savour of negative theology in which the final negation communicates an idea ineffably positive. In the severe detachment of the beatitudes can be sensed the passion 'comparée à laquelle la rose est grossière, et le parfum des violettes un tonnerre', something analogous to the tenderness which, quite incomprehensibly, comes through the description of the wreck in Hopkins's great poem. No poet, it seems to me, has come near Hopkins in the presentation of 'the unchilding, unfathering deeps', yet it is in these stanzas that the tenderness of God is felt, a tenderness beyond our understanding (and which, in terms of our understanding, must appear indifference, a blank, such as Hardy felt) yet nearer than our most intimate love.

We must not be in too much of a hurry to relate the more easily understandable part of Christian morality—that which, for many of our modern Christians *is* Christian morality—to God; to correct the ethical Christian by showing him that what the gospel prescribes is to be done 'for God's sake'. There may be already inherent in his conception a mystery which, for all its vagueness in his mind, has more of God in it than the idea 'for God's sake' prematurely introduced would have. There is a danger of leading him back when we think we are leading him on. What we have to lead him to, and what a serious concern with his conception of Christian morality may lead us to, is the point where the identification of 'God' and 'love' may precipitate a new understanding of both terms, a blessed vision in which the term 'God' will be enlarged by 'love' and, conversely—but this is much harder to describe—the word 'love' be weighted in a new way, given a precision, a density that is recognized from the depths of our being as final. In this vision God is not so much the object of love as its substance, yet not in such a way as to be subsumed under love but so as to draw love about himself. The full revelation of Christian morality, in its source and in its effect, is like the Plotinian image in which the sun appears above the horizon as the source of the ineffable, trembling beauty of the expectant sea. Revelation, in the end, must reveal itself. 'That which is' lingers diffidently in the background of a moral situation, and it can be shown there, as when Vaughan Williams associates for us Oates going out into the snow with a haunting melody and the lines of Donne:

> Love, all alike, no season knows, nor clime,
> Nor hours, days, months, which are the rags of time.

At the heart of Christian life is the utter simplicity of God, bringing the whole man to one. Failure to touch this centre makes us spiritually sterile, and this sterility is compatible with prodigies of mystical vision and, on the other hand, prodigies of moral energy, as St Paul says in the great hymn to charity. The fact that both the gnostic and the philanthropist come under the judgement of this hymn indicates its astonishing universality. Here is a test of human life that penetrates to the very roots of thought and action before these have been differentiated into that prodigious variety of conscious aims which we encounter in the world of men and which makes us despair of describing man as a single nature at all. The hymn may be paraphrased: 'As opposed to all other principles of human living, *charity gets there*.' We saw at the beginning of this essay that 'Christian morality' presents a problem in that its end is in that simple world that will succeed this world. That is true. But we can now see that charity, the eschatological virtue, searches out and judges life in this world as no other moral principle can. For every human moral principle can make but a limited demand on us. The practice of any virtue can be carried to excess, can upset the complex balance of the human being. Charity alone touches the heart of that balance, and so cannot be carried to excess. The transcendence of Christian morality over all human morality appears most clearly in this fact: that it cannot be carried to excess, that its demands on us will always increase yet will never lead us into the misery of scrupulosity. And as the Christian advances on this way it is the baffling simplicity of God that confronts him ever more closely and exactingly, dissolving one by one the aims which he has set himself. For the single-mindedness of the moralist the Christian substitutes the simplicity of God. This tension between human moral endeavour and God is expressed so finely by Thomas Merton, in *The Sign of Jonas*, in a way that conveys so well what 'God' should mean to the Christian, that I shall conclude this section by quoting him at some length. Here is the very opposite of that summary way of advocating the practice of virtue 'for God's sake' which so often passes for Christian morality. God really apprehended as our motive is a motive that always evades us yet leads us on—*fugis quaerentes te*.

God, my God, God whom I meet in darkness, with you it is always the same thing! Always the same question that nobody knows how to answer!

I have prayed to you in the day-time with thoughts and reasons, and in the night time you have confronted me, scattering thought and reason. I have come to you in the morning with light and with desire, and you have descended on me, with great gentleness, with most forbearing silence, in this inexplicable night, defeating all desire. I have explained to you a hundred times my motives for entering the monastery and you have listened and said nothing, and I have turned away and wept with shame.

Is it true that all my motives have meant nothing? Is it true that all my desires were an illusion?

While I am asking questions which you do not answer, you ask me a question that is so simple that I cannot answer. I do not even understand the question.

This night, and every night, it is the same question (p. 344).

II

THE conclusion of our first section is this: for the Christian, God is not an ideal, the highest image the human mind can form: for the Christian, God is Himself. To this presence of God which is charity, the whole of human life, every fibre of our being is exposed as it will be in the Day of Judgement. The cause of this presence is the Incarnation, and we have now to fill out our picture of Christian morality in the light of the Word made flesh. This order may seem curious. Surely we should have started with the Incarnation. In doing this, however, we should risk missing altogether the meaning of the Incarnation. For we might think of it as the mediation of God to us, and of the whole Pauline morality of the Body of Christ, which we have now to examine, as consequent upon this mediation. In reality, the point of the Incarnation is that God is immediately present to human life. As Irenaeus insists, it is the bringing of man into God's sphere rather than God into man's. It is fashionable nowadays to find fault with the order of the *Summa* which shows the creation and the creature's return to its source before describing, in the *Tertia pars*, the manner of this return: as it is fashionable to refuse St Thomas's opinion that the formal object of theology is God not Christ. But does not this order and this opinion reflect the fuller grasp of the Incarnation which appears in the formula on which he bases his formal treatment of the latter: *non conversio Dei in hominem sed assumptio hominis in Deum*? The Incarnation doesn't complicate religion, but simplifies it. It is understood best when we start with the experienced simplicity of God in Christian religion and show it as the source. Thus God is himself for us beyond the images we form of him: and this can only be because the whole of human life has been opened to him, simplified and brought to one in him: he no longer satisfies a specific, spiritual need: he is the simple object alike of our contemplation and our action. And as he no longer corresponds to a part of ourselves, he is no longer on a level with and in competition with the objects of our experience: he cannot be preferred to 'other people'. Hence the tension in Christian love is not between the love of God and the love of others, but between love and something less than love. And the ground of all this simplification, of man himself and of his relationships, in God, is the Incarnation.

We start then with the fact of God, as nothing less than God, in Christian experience, and then find the Word made flesh as the ground of this fact. The Word made flesh will appear now more and more as the substance of what we have been talking about.

What is so striking in the Hymn to Charity is at once the transcendence of its view-point and the universality of its scope. These two facts are interdependent. We cannot bring to the touch-stone of God himself anything less than the whole of ourselves. If there is anything of the flesh that is not formally relevant to our relation to God, 'God' becomes a self-chosen image of the spirit: and at the heart of this paradox is the Incarnation. The immediacy of God for the Christian involves what we may call an immediacy of the flesh, a care for humanity that is not motivated by anything external. We are set to a building up of man, every stone of which is *Dei aedificatio*. Here is the genius, the charisma of Christian morality, that in it which answers every genuine concern with man's life, and can genuinely condemn all erroneous moralities as inhuman.

This double quality in Christian experience, of being naked to God and to the world of man, finds its classical expression in St Paul's doctrine of the Body of Christ—if the word 'doctrine' can do justice to a whole way of thinking. It will be necessary to study this conception with some care.

Everyone has noticed the versatility, sometimes bewildering, of this expression in Christian writings. The thought of St Paul moves without warning from the physical body of Christ to his body which is the Church. Having explained that in one body the members have different functions, he concludes not: so is this organism of the Church which we have called the body of Christ, but: so it is with Christ.

There must be some principle, some way of thinking of the body, which makes this rapid movement of thought possible. We can see what this is if we contrast the hebraic way of thinking with our own, largely greek-influenced way.

What do we point to when we go out of our way to refer to a person's body? Our intention is to indicate a *part* of him, the co-principle with soul of his totality. The hebrew mind uses this expression with the opposite intention. To refer to a person's body is to refer, emphatically, to the whole of him. If I say 'John' I imply the whole John, but if I say 'the body of John' I state emphatically that what I have in mind is John in that full expression of himself which is the body. I do not isolate a part of him for separate consideration, I demand a synthetic consideration of him, I point to that mysterious full existence, that irreducible whole which John is.

Now if there is one thing that emerges clearly from the study of Christology, it is that Christ cannot be understood apart from his special redemptive relation to the human race. That which transforms for us this divine-human existence from a mere prodigy into the most meaningful terrestrial reality that the human mind can contemplate is the knowledge that here is the beginning of a new human existence. What is this humanity which does not serve an individual human person if not a humanity that serves the whole human race?

This consideration is precisely as necessary to a full understanding of Christ as a synthetic consideration, an emphasis on wholeness, is necessary for a full understanding of, say, John. Now if I am thinking in a terminology which gets this emphasis by using the term 'body', I shall refer to the whole Christ as 'the body of Christ'. There is one precious phrase in which we can catch St Paul's thought-process on the wing. Referring to the Old Testament types, he says, *haec sunt umbra futurorum: corpus autem Christi* (Col. 2: 17). If he had said *corpus autum Christus*, we should have paraphrased: 'the substance that threw these shadows along the past, the body, was Christ'—where Christ would be called a body with reference to the imagery here used. But the body is Christ's! It is what the soldiers fixed to the cross. Within the terms of the imagery, 'body' will mean substance, full reality. But for St Paul, body, a person's body, means all this in *absolute* terms. The imagery is suddenly and surprisingly outstripped by an all-controlling reality—and now we are beyond St Paul's and anybody else's thought, confronted with an original datum which he simply found and was inspired to expound, as was John when he understood the blood and water flowing from Christ's side. Like all divine revelation, it is disarmingly simple. As the gospel narratives approach their climax, the *excessus* (significant word, Lk. 9: 31) of Christ, the emphasis falls naturally on his body. He pointed this in the supper-room with the words 'this is my body', and the events of the next day made it tragically clear. It is because of its crucifixion that the body of Christ forms the current coin of Christian thought: so that the focus of history coincides with the focus of jewish thought, and we have revelation: a new medium of thought in which we apprehend singly Christ's body or fulness on the cross and the body of redeemed humanity that is born there. Singly, yet with no blurring of outlines. Paradoxically, the blurred conception of the mystical body that we find in some writers does not overdo, but falls short of, the real extension of Christ in his members. It operates with a phantasmal body, formed on the *analogy* of a human body, instead of the physical body of Christ.

This brings us to the point. When St Paul uses the analogy of a body to teach the *oikonomia* of the Church, he is not *comparing* the church to a body, he is drawing out the implications of the fact that it *is* the body or fulness of Christ. In other words, the mental image that one must, I suppose, form, on hearing that Christ is the head and we the members is not the fundamental thing that Paul is talking about. What he is talking about is Christ nailed to the cross, and us 'dead to the law through the body of Christ' (Rom. 7: 4).

Thus 'the doctrine of the mystical body' can be a misleading phrase. As applied to morality (our concern—I hope we have not forgotten it!) it implies merely a new way of looking at human relations, an image for making concrete our solidarity in Christ. But the reality is more concrete, not less so, than the image. *Corpus autem Christi*. It is only when we understand this original givenness of the body of Christ that we can begin to 'see life as one and see it whole'. Charity, open to God and to the most intimate, inconceivable needs of ourselves and of each other, is the response to a divine fact in the flesh. 'The Word-flesh is a fact,' as Vincent McNabb translated.

If we are to understand St Paul's doctrine of charity in its original three dimensions, we must get clear on this priority of the fact of the body over the image with which he clarifies it. Then we begin to realize that the force shaping his ideas is not his idea or anyone else's, but a fact by which he is controlled. The urgency of his charity (*caritas Christi urget nos*) is beyond any conceivable religious or human enthusiasm, it has a preciseness of objective that no enthusiasm can have. It is the failure to get this full perspective that has resulted in a style of writing about the mystical body that Père de Lubac has characterized as a maladroit mixture of excessive concreteness and deadening abstraction. The weight of concrete 'realization' has been placed on the *image* of head and members instead of on the *fact* of the Body of Christ. Open up the perspective again, and the force of charity reappears in all its original power: the words of Paul become reattached to men and facts, and we read the epistles with the feeling that we are at the origin of everything real and enduring that Christian men have built. *Ecce tabernaculum Dei cum hominibus, Dei structura, Dei aedificatio est.*

In those passages where he is considering the life of the body in its source, it is the body on the cross that he presents to us. 'Wherefore, my brethren, ye also were made dead to the law through the body of Christ; that ye should be joined to another, even to him that was raised from the dead, that we might bring forth fruit unto God' (Rom. 7: 4).

'That he might create of the twain one new man, so making peace; and might reconcile them both in one body unto God through the cross' (Eph. 2: 15–16).

And in one of the classic accounts of the one body and many members, he shows, with a carelessness for which we thank him, the deep spring of his thought, by leaving the word 'body' out of his conclusion. 'So', he says, 'is Christ'. Simply that.

The body of Christ, then, is not a figure on tracing paper to be stretched over the pattern of our relationships. It is the heart of those relationships, something more intimate even than the well known and loved curve of lip or eyelid. From this standpoint we can judge the criticism of Christian charity which says that it is too general to satisfy our modern demands for communication (e.g. Jaspers). We can judge it—yes. The spiritual man judges all and is judged of none. But have we not lent colour to it by our inadequate witness to the body of Christ?

'Christian morality'—an arid phrase pointing to a reality baffling in its simplicity, inexhaustible in its richness. When we read St Paul and contemplate the sacramental *koinonia* of the Church, we seem to be looking at everything solid that ever was. Belloc comes to mind, Belloc who saw Christendom not as the incarnation of the Christian idea but as the fulness of the Christian fact which is the Incarnation. The mark of the Church, of charity, in human life must be precise if it is to be the true mark. Do we begin to realize this? Do we realize that *caritas numquam excidit* refers to the resurrection of the flesh, that it is the full expression of Pound's immortal phrase, 'what thou lovest well remaineth'? Do we understand more feelingly than Ruskin himself the significance which that great prophet saw in the shoddy buildings of an usurious society? It is a sobering thought that Communism is the first real attempt since the feudal system to construct a complete human polity—and it should be a danger signal to us that we find such an attempt so easy to condemn on theological principles. We should remember that the moment Christian charity becomes for us essentially an idea, albeit a sublime idea and one which we intend to put into practice, God, too, becomes an idea.

Ezra Pound says of St Ambrose: 'St Ambrose didn't rise suddenly and without forebears. A transition from self-centred lust after eternal salvation into a sense of public order occurred somewhere and sometime' (*Guide to Kulcher*, p. 43). 'A travesty of the Christian notion of salvation,' we readily reply, and miss the fact that Pound, just there, is probably seeing more in St Ambrose than we do, that wonderfully precise care for human polity that flows from real charity. It is characteristic of our attenuated sense of the charity that builds that we no longer experience the abhorrence at usury that the medieval church felt and that Pound has expressed in searing images in one of the cantos. The introduction of this subject in a paper whose professed scope is so general will invite the suspicion that the writer's latent fanaticism has insisted on surfacing before he lays down his pen. Yet usury does represent the apostasy of our modern world, its descent into the shadows, in its most practical form. And it is a symbol of what might be called an 'imprecision in life' that is the denial of the care and precision of charity whose symbol is Christendom. We have given life to that which has no life and whose growth must be at the expense of life. We cannot see the wounds and the robberies inflicted by this form of uncharity, and this makes it bearable to us, yet all the more damnable for that. It makes everything vague, charity makes

everything precise. Charity has an edge, a body, the body of Christ.
Charity builds, not only in the heart but in good stone. And every
valid criticism of a Christian writer to the effect that his thought
does not 'hit' (to use Arnold's expression) points to an incomplete-
ness in his charity. I make no apology for quoting Pound's canto
as pointing up the Hymn to Charity *cum vi oppositi*.

> With usura hath no man a house of good stone
> each block cut smooth and well fitting
> that design might cover their face,
> with usura
> hath no man a painted paradise on his church wall
> *harpes et luthes*
> or where virgin receiveth message
> and halo projects from incision,
> with usura
> seeth no man Gonzaga his heirs and his concubines
> no picture is made to endure nor to live with
> but it is made to sell and sell quickly
> with usura, sin against nature,
> is thy bread ever more of stale rags
> is thy bread dry as paper,
> with no mountain wheat, no strong flour
> with usura the line grows thick
> with usura is no clear demarcation
> and no man can find site for his dwelling.
> Stone cutter is kept from his stone
> weaver is kept from his loom
>
> WITH USURA
> wool comes not to market
> sheep bringeth no gain with usura
> Usura is a murrain, usura
> blunteth the needle in the maid's hand
> and stoppeth the spinner's cunning. Pietro Lombardo
> came not by usura
> Duccio came not by usura
> nor Pier della Francesca; Zuan Bellin' not by usura
> nor was 'La Calunnia' painted.
> Came not by usura Angelico; came not Ambrogio Praedis,
> Came no church of cut stone signed: *Adamo me fecit.*
> Not by usura St Trophime
> Not by usura Saint Hilaire,
> Usura rusteth the chisel
> It rusteth the craft and the craftsman

It gnaweth the thread in the loom
None learneth to weave gold in her pattern;
Azure hath a canker by usura; cramoisi is unbroidered
Emerald findeth no Memling
Usura slayeth the child in the womb
It stayeth the young man's courting
It hath brought palsy to bed, lyeth
between the young bride and her bridegroom
                    CONTRA NATURAM
They have brought whores for Eleusis
Corpses are set to banquet
at behest of usura.[1]

Looking clearly at the shadow, we get a fresh appreciation of the substance. But we must return always to the substance. The energy of hate is a difficult thing to use creatively. The substance is charity: *corpus est Christi*, the body is Christ's.

We started with the statement that Christian morality is summed up in the love of God. I hope that what I have said has clarified rather than obscured that statement, has pointed up the salient fact: that the love of God is a fact, before it is a practice: and that the practice is only the implementing of the fact. The fact is simple, the world complex: yet to be controlled by the fact in our thinking and doing and making is the reverse of being irresponsible. The Church at Pentecost was sent into the world with the commission of making her own our Lord's words: *non perdidi ex eis quemquam.* The fact is our touchstone, and the Hymn to Charity a lyrical discipline of the spirit whereby we are schooled to it. All our thought and action must be an expansion of that great *poema*, marked with its divine suppleness of spirit. Our Christian thinking has the building power of charity when, confronted with contemporary signs of the desire for life, we feel impelled to lead people *on* to something they have not the courage and the vision for: lead them on without losing life, the simplicity of life, and getting lost in the dreary paths of 'service'. The same far reach of the Spirit embraces the world in all its complexity on the one hand and the single thirst of the mystic on the other. Always we return to this immediacy of God which is immediacy of the flesh.

Morality is a description of human life that is compelled, of its nature, to remain abstract—principles fitted on to but never closing

---

[1] Canto XLV: 'With Usura', printed in *The Penguin Book of Modern American Verse*, London, 1954.

with flesh and blood. It is to flesh and blood that the Church draws our thought and action, thus giving them final significance: as the flesh and blood of Christ in crucifixion carried human life beyond the light which the moralist can throw on it, and transfigured it in the light of God. A Christian is, above all, one who eats the flesh of Christ and drinks his blood, and whose whole way of thinking about human life is dominated by this intimacy. He knows what he is doing. The world for him is not a world of shadows, something half understood and claiming only half his interest, a world in which all action is provisional. His understanding of and care for the world is that of the craftsman in relation to his material, and as Ruskin says, the true builder builds for ever. It is in the body of Christ that we have that final precision in human life whereby morality is transfigured to become art.

Before we conclude, an important objection must be considered. Is not this emphasis on flesh and blood rather than on moral principles a sort of 'situational ethic'? Surely it is just the latter type of ethic that lays this stress on 'the body'. Yet at the heart of the situational ethic, this would-be concrete approach to ethical problems, there is a fatal imprecision. 'The body' as conceived by the pure existentialist is ephemeral, a 'situation' and nothing more. For the Christian it is otherwise. It is at the heart of the concrete situation that he meets what is eternal. The moment the last vestige of abstraction disappears from this or that relationship of his, when 'the penitent' becomes this individual cry for help, 'the needy' this single inescapable demand on him and therefore a demand for love and not merely for provisions, is the moment when Christ is met— the *body*, the final *reality* of Christ. For the pure existentialist the thing finally met is a dark compulsion dictating a course of action having no relation to principles. The Christian action is in accordance with principles though far beyond them. There are times when a Christian must act on those principles in seeming contradiction to the warm reality of the 'situation'. But these are times when he must remember that Christian action is done in grace, and that grace is more than a strengthening of the will to carry the painful business through. It is practical *lumen* as well as *vigor*. Given free rein, hoped and prayed for and relaxed into, it will bring the agonizing course dictated to the point of life, life of the body, where it will have the ease and generosity of life. It is a revealing paradox that the existentialist, in canonizing the situation, makes it too an abstraction. It is the same paradox that the most vigorous defence of 'the body' as against ideas, if it has not ultimately in view the body of Christ, takes on an abstract flavour. Even non-Christian literary critics have found this in D. H. Lawrence—the tedious reiteration which is always a sign of the abstract, the fanatical. Lawrence was a prophet. He saw that it is only in the body that we have life. But we cannot throw on that life any light of our own. The light is God's, in Christ.

It is through this consciousness of the body in which we are configured, its individual historical reality in no wise attentuated by its embracing of us but rather, mysteriously, the reverse: a consciousness of a precision in the flesh, to which the flesh cannot attain but towards which any real thinking always draws us, a precision in which eternity is felt and which strives to translate this eternity into the wood and stone and polity of Christendom: it is in this consciousness that we confess immediately the Word made flesh. It is in the body, in the final definitive meaning that 'the body' has in Christian life and worship, that we know the Son of God; the body precisely known, the body meaning precision; a way of thinking about man and his life compared with which all human thinking is abstract and ephemeral. 'Our little systems have their day,' only God remains; but his is not the eternity of an idea. It is faithfulness, the eternal covenant sealed in blood which is drunk, the consecrated place of Christendom. *Esto perpetua.*